The MCAT Biology Book

Nancy Morvillo
Matthew Schmidt

Additional Educational Products from Nova Press:

The MCAT Physics Book (444 pages)

The MCAT Chemistry Book (480 pages)

GRE Prep Course (624 pages, includes software)

GMAT PrepCourse (608 pages, includes software)

Master The LSAT (560 pages, includes an official LSAT exam)

LSAT Prep Course Software (Includes three official LSAT exams)

SAT Prep Course (608 pages, includes software)

Law School Basics: A Preview of Law School and Legal Reasoning (256 pages)

Vocabulary 4000: The 4000 Words Essential for an Educated Vocabulary (160 pages)

ISBN 1–889057–08–8

MCAT is a registered service mark of the Association of American Medical Colleges.

11659 Mayfield Ave., Suite 1
Los Angeles, CA 90049

Phone: 1-800-949-6175
E-mail: novapress@aol.com
Website: www.novapress.net

Acknowledgements

Many thanks to Michael J. Maddalena for his help with illustrations. We also wish to thank our students for their insight and critical reading of this manuscript, and for being the ultimate teachers. And to Mike Morvillo and Donna Parent, for all their love, support, and, especially, patience.

TABLE OF CONTENTS

Chapter 1
Introduction

A. Philosophy of this book

The MCAT Biology Book is designed to help you understand major concepts in biology and to use this knowledge to solve problems. Each chapter contains MCAT-style questions with answers and full explanations at the end of the book.

The MCAT questions are written to test your knowledge of basic concepts in biology and problem solving abilities; they do not stress rote memorization of facts. Most questions are based on short (approximately 250 word) passages. Four to eight questions will be asked for each passage. These questions may require you to interpret data from graphs, tables or figures. There are 10 to 11 problem sets of this type on the exam, as well as 15 questions that are independent of any passages and of each other.

Topics and concepts in biology are very extensive. The MCAT does not test your comprehension of all areas of basic biology, but instead focuses on vertebrates and microbes, with an emphasis on life processes. Although the MCAT includes organic chemistry in its biology section, we have chosen not to discuss this area and instead to concentrate solely on biology in this review book.

This introductory chapter will familiarize you with the concepts that form the foundations of biology. These key ideas are implicit in every topic of biology, and we recommend that you keep them in the back of your mind at all times.

B. Biology

We'll start with a simple definition of biology: *biology is the study of life*. This includes examination of the processes that govern how life is maintained and reproduced, and observation of how living things interact with each other and with the environment. Although this sounds rather simple, it involves studying many different and diverse areas, from the molecular level to the global scale.

There are two distinct perspectives from which one can study biological processes: *in vivo* or *in vitro*. *In vivo* means research is done in the body itself. *In vitro* means literally "in glass," as an experiment that is done in a test tube, or outside of the body. *In vivo* experiments, naturally, include all the factors that can influence a process; therefore the reactions being studied represent a "real life" situation. However, all these factors and reactions can make for a very complex system that is not easily understood. *In vitro* studies, on the other hand, allow researchers to manipulate the system to study only one or two isolated factors. This helps to determine exactly what these factors do.

Although each approach has its merits and drawbacks, both perspectives are needed and work synergistically. For example, the study of AIDS has benefited from both *in vivo* and *in vitro* studies. The course of the illness, from infection with HIV to full blown AIDS, has been well characterized in humans through the use of *in vivo* studies. But the exact mechanism of how the virus invades a cell is known through *in vitro* studies. Drugs designed to fight the virus are first tested in vitro using HIV infected cells grown in the laboratory. Drugs that prove effective *in vitro* are then tested *in vivo*.

C. The Scientific Method

As with all sciences, biological research involves methodically searching for information. The procedure associated with this search is called the *scientific method*. It involves

1. asking questions, which are then followed by one or more *hypotheses* (educated guesses or hunches that answer or explain the question).
2. making predictions from the hypothesis, usually in the form of "if....then" statements (*if* the influenza virus causes the flu, *then* those exposed to it will become ill).
3. testing the predictions through experimentation, observation, model building, etc., including appropriate controls with which to compare the results.
4. repeating the investigations and devising new ways to further test the hypothesis (this may include modification of the hypothesis based on the results of the tests).
5. reporting the results and drawing conclusions from them.

A *theory* is similar to a hypothesis in that it is subjected to the scientific method, but a theory usually explains a broad range of related phenomena, not a single one. Theories are well supported hypotheses, shown to be valid under many different circumstances.

In science, there is no real beginning or end. All hypotheses are based on previous work, and all results and conclusions can be expanded in the future. Often experiments raise more questions than they answer.

D.   Characteristics of Life

If biology is the study of life, then it is natural to ask: What is life? There is no one definition of life that can encompass all living things. However, there are certain characteristics that all living things share:

- ◆ *order and organization*: The basic unit of life is the cell. It is capable of performing all activities of life. For single-celled organisms, this is the limit of their organization. For multicellular organisms, cells may be arranged in tissues, tissues arranged in organs, and organs arranged in systems. Living things are further organized into populations, communities, ecosystems and, ultimately, the biosphere (the combined regions of the earth in which organisms can live). A corollary to this topic is the organization and structure of the genetic material: all living things have nucleic acids as the storage mechanism for genetic information.

- ◆ *growth and development*: All living things grow and develop during their life. This may be as simple as a bacterium that increases in size or as complex as a fertilized egg that develops into a elaborate, multicellular organism.

- ◆ *reproduction*: Organisms must reproduce in order for the species to survive. The exact mode of reproduction may be different (for example, *asexual* verses *sexual* reproduction), but the outcome is the same: an increase in the number of organisms.

- ◆ *energy metabolism*: All living things require energy to survive. Various processes are necessary in order to supply this energy. First of all, organisms must gain nutrition: those that can make their own food are called *autotrophs*, all others are called *heterotrophs*. The nutrients must be converted into energy, which includes the process of *respiration*. Finally, waste products must be eliminated.

- ◆ *stimuli response and homeostasis*: The ability to respond to the environment, whether it be the external or the internal environment, is a vital function in all living things. Organisms must regulate their life processes based on what is happening in the environment.

♦ *evolution*: The ability to change, to mutate, is an important characteristic of life. Were it not for this ability, the vast diversity of life would not exist on this planet. For that matter, no life would exist at all.

E. Structure and function

Another topic which underlies all aspects of biology is the correlation between structure and function. If the structure is known, often the function can be determined, and vice versa. For example, knowing the amino acid sequence of a protein (the structure) can help predict how that protein functions in a cell. Or, as another example, if an animal has the ability to see (the function), then it must have the structures necessary to support that function (eyes, optic nerves, a region of the brain to interpret nerve impulses, etc.).

F. Using this book

Remember: the MCAT stresses your problem solving skills and your knowledge of basic biological concepts. Therefore, you will be better prepared for the test by understanding these concepts rather than by just memorizing various facts and terms. The MCAT Biology Book will help you in this endeavor through a thorough treatment of the major topics included in the MCAT. Study to understand these topics, not just to memorize them.

Chapter 1 Problems

Passage 1.1 (Questions 1-4)

Karposi's sarcoma (KS) is a cancer marked by purple tumors on the skin. Although extremely rare in the population, it is found in approximately 25% of gay men infected with HIV, the virus that causes AIDS. It has been suggested that KS itself is caused by a virus, the human herpesvirus 8 (HHV8). To help confirm this hypothesis, the following observations were made:

Observation 1:

At regular intervals over a two year period, samples of blood were taken from gay men who tested positive for HIV at the beginning of the study. In 38 of the subjects, no KS developed, although 18% had antibodies against HHV8 in their blood samples. However, in 40 subjects who developed KS, 80% had HHV8 antibodies. In 11 of these men, HHV8 antibodies were detected from the beginning of the study, but 21 of the men developed HHV8 antibodies during the study. In these subjects, the antibodies appeared several months before the onset of KS.

Observation 2:

Individuals not known to have been infected with HIV were tested for antibodies against HHV8. In 141 blood donors, only 1% were found to test positive for the antibodies. In addition, 300 hemophiliacs who had regular blood transfusions were also examined. Three percent had HHV8 antibodies.

Observation 3:

In 176 patients who had syphilis, a sexually transmitted disease, 36 (or 20%) had antibodies to HHV8.

1. What conclusion can be drawn from these observations?
   A. Although HHV8 is associated with KS, it has yet to be proven that it causes KS.
   B. In observation 1, the fact that some individuals tested positive for HHV8 but did not develop KS proves this virus does not cause the disease.
   C. Individuals with syphilis will also develop KS.
   D. Hemophiliacs are at no risk of developing KS.

2. Which is the best hypothesis for the mode of transmission of HHV8?
   A. blood transfusions
   B. casual contact
   C. sexual transmission
   D. airborne particles

3. In another study, it was found that KS is prevalent in transplant patients taking drugs which suppress their immune system to prevent rejection of the new organ. This, along with the above evidence, indicates:

   A. a virus other than HHV8 causes KS.
   B. a weakened immune system is probably necessary for KS to develop.
   C. both A and B
   D. neither A nor B

4. Many researchers argue that viruses are not alive. Which of the following supports this hypothesis?

   I. Some viruses carry their genetic information in the form of RNA, not DNA.
   II. Viruses cannot reproduce by themselves.
   III. Viruses do not evolve; that is, they do not mutate or change.

   A. I only
   B. II only
   C. I and II only
   D. II and III only

SECTION 1
MOLECULAR BIOLOGY

Molecular biology, as the term is often used today, refers specifically to the study of the molecules involved in the transmission and usage of information, that is, molecular genetics. Modern molecular biology is a relatively new field, and its importance cannot be understated. Understanding the structure and function of DNA, how it enables information to be passed on from parent to offspring, and how it controls the cellular activities of an organism have ushered in the most exciting period in the history of biology. This knowledge has made possible potential advances in medicine and technology that are only now being realized. This section will explore the structure and function of DNA and RNA, their roles in protein synthesis, and the central position these molecules occupy in directing cellular activities.

The molecular biology portion of the MCAT, while including this information, has a broader scope, and thus uses the term in a wider sense. Also included in this section are topics that might traditionally be considered the province of biochemistry. These topics include the structure and function of enzymes and the various processes by which cells transform and utilize energy. This field is sometimes referred to as *bioenergetics*, or the study of cellular metabolism. All living things need energy in order to survive. Animals employ a complex series of interconnected chemical reactions in order to extract usable energy from the food they eat, and the pathways involved have been elucidated rather thoroughly.

What all of these topics have in common explains their inclusion in this "molecular biology" section. Whether we are discussing genetics, metabolism, or related topics, this section is looking at the processes of life viewed from the perspective of the molecules involved. It was recognized by early biochemists that the chemicals they extracted from living things were similar in all organisms, and could be grouped into four major categories. Initially referred to as "organic" molecules because they were associated with life, we now recognize that the proteins, nucleic acids, lipids, and carbohydrates we will explore in Chapter 2 comprise a small portion of all the carbon-based molecules that exist. However, they are all vital to the survival of every organism. In this section, we will thus also survey the structures and functions of the major biomolecules, and examine their roles in essential life processes. Although this survey of biological molecules is placed in the Chemistry portion of the MCAT, it is necessary to include it here as a foundation for understanding their behaviors and properties in a biological context.

Chapter 2
Biological Molecules

A. Introduction

The study of *biochemistry* specifically explores the structure and function of important molecules found in living organisms. All important biomolecules are *organic*, that is, based on the carbon atom. Such molecules are often called *macromolecules*, because they are relatively large in comparison with the molecules studied by traditional, *inorganic* chemistry. Biological macromolecules are often *polymers* -- molecules formed by the stepwise addition of smaller subunits (*monomers*). Four major classes of biological molecules have been identified, each with unique structural properties and different roles.

B. Carbohydrates

Carbohydrates get their name from the fact that they are composed of only three types of atoms in particular combinations. The term literally means "carbon and water", belying their atomic composition: $[C(H_2O)]_n$. This means that only carbon, hydrogen, and oxygen are present, and there is usually twice as much hydrogen as oxygen or carbon. In animals, the major function of carbohydrates is to provide energy for the organism. The fundamental carbohydrate subunit is the *monosaccharide* (see Figure 2.1). Monosaccharides can exist alone, or can be polymerized into larger *disaccharides* (see Figure 2.2) and *polysaccharides*.

- ◆ *Monosaccharides:* These are the simplest carbohydrate subunits found in nature. Along with disaccharides, they have a sweet taste and have thus been referred to historically and nutritionally as *sugars* or *simple carbohydrates*. Many nutritional monosaccharides are six-carbon compounds, such as *glucose* (the body's favorite fuel molecule), *fructose* ("fruit sugar"), and *galactose*. Other important monosaccharides are the five-carbon sugars *ribose* and *deoxyribose*, part of the

9

nucleotides that compose DNA and RNA.

♦ *Disaccharides*: Composed of two monosaccharide units joined by a *glycosidic* bond, these are also recognized as sugars or simple carbohydrates nutritionally. *Sucrose*, or common table sugar, consists of one glucose and one fructose subunit. *Lactose* ("milk sugar") is made up of one glucose and one galactose subunit. *Maltose* ("malt sugar") is composed of two glucose subunits. All of these molecules must be broken down into their constituent monosaccharides before they can be utilized by the body.

♦ *Polysaccharides*: Polysaccharides are made up of many, often hundreds, of monosaccharide subunits. In nature, all of the important polysaccharides are glucose polymers, differing only in their physical arrangement and the type of bonds that join the subunits. Because they do not taste sweet, they are referred to nutritionally as complex carbohydrates, and include such compounds as starch and fiber. *Starch* is an energy storage molecule found in plants, and often makes up a large part of the human diet in the form of grains and vegetables. Because it is a polymer of glucose, starch is broken down into glucose subunits to be used as fuel in our bodies. Fiber, or *cellulose*, is a structural polysaccharide, composing the cell walls of plants. Due to the nature of the glycosidic bonds joining the glucose subunits, however, most animals (including humans) are unable to digest it. *Glycogen* is very similar to starch, and is sometimes referred to as "animal starch". Animals often store excess glucose in this form in their livers and muscles as an energy reserve.

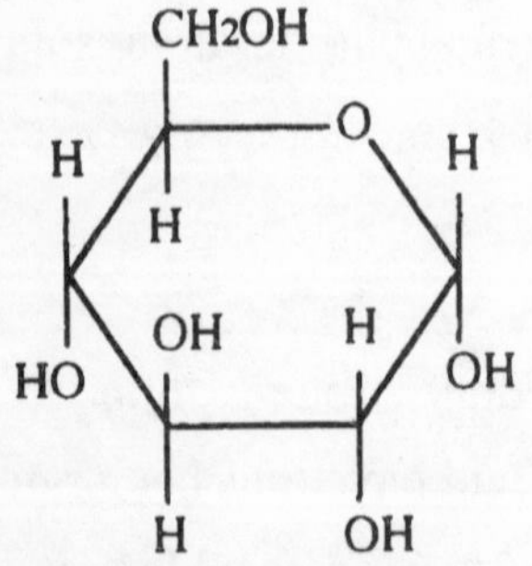

Figure 2.1: Glucose, a monosaccharide

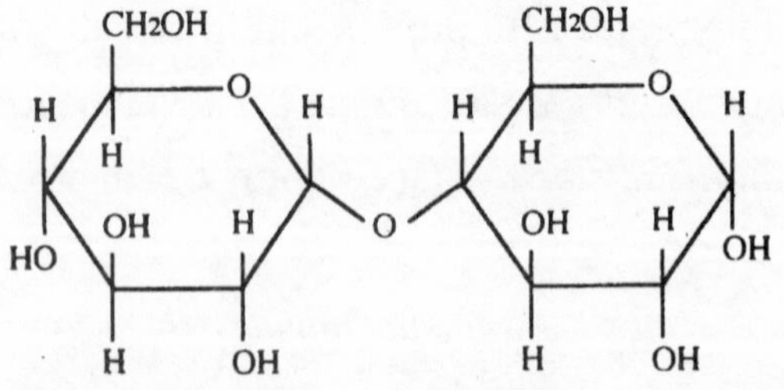

Figure 2.2: Maltose, a disaccharide

C. Lipids

Lipids are macromolecules grouped together for different reasons than are carbohydrates. They do not share any particularly constant chemical structure, but they do share an important physical property brought about by their basic chemical composition: lipids are biological molecules that do not dissolve appreciably in water. This is because they contain nonpolar covalent bonds, and are largely composed of hydrocarbon chains or rings. Since the body is a very watery place, lipids face a challenge, as they are not able to dissolve, and must be handled similarly with regard to their transportation and usage. Several types of lipids exist.

- ♦ *Triglycerides:* Triglycerides are composed of one molecule of the trialcohol *glycerol* covalently attached to three *fatty acid* molecules, hydrocarbon chains of varying lengths bonded through a terminal carboxylic acid group (see Figure 2.3). Traditionally called *fats* and *oils*, the major role of triglycerides in the body is long-term energy storage. Fats tend to be solid at room temperature because the fatty acid chains are *saturated*, which means they do not contain carbon-carbon double bonds. Chains containing double bonds are called *unsaturated*. The more unsaturated a fatty acid chain, the more liquid the triglyceride. Thus oils are often *polyunsaturated* triglycerides.

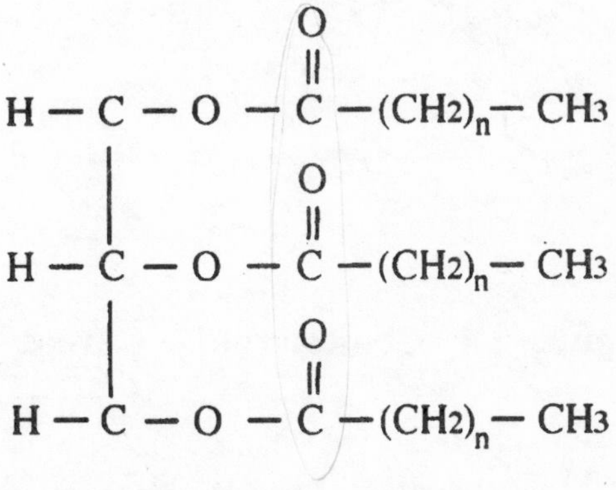

$$
\begin{array}{c}
\qquad\qquad\qquad\qquad O \\
\qquad\qquad\qquad\qquad \| \\
H - C - O - C - (CH_2)_n - CH_3 \\
\quad | \qquad\qquad O \\
\qquad\qquad\qquad\qquad \| \\
H - C - O - C - (CH_2)_n - CH_3 \\
\quad | \qquad\qquad O \\
\qquad\qquad\qquad\qquad \| \\
H - C - O - C - (CH_2)_n - CH_3
\end{array}
$$

Figure 2.3: A saturated triglyceride

- ♦ *Phospholipids:* Phospholipids are a class of related compounds that structurally resemble triglycerides. In place of one of the fatty acids bonded to glycerol, however, is a hydrophilic molecule containing a phosphate group. This gives phospholipids a chemical "split personality". A portion of the molecule is *hydrophobic*, and unable to dissolve in water, while another portion is strongly charged and *hydrophilic*. This interesting combination of properties allows phospholipids to form the structures of plasma membranes and lipoproteins. They also act as emulsifying agents, allowing other lipids to dissolve more easily in the body.

♦ *Steroids:* Steroids are lipids that do not structurally resemble triglycerides, but are composed of a series of nonpolar rings (see Figure 2.4). *Cholesterol* is the most well known and prevalent steroid compound in the body. Cholesterol plays a role in the structure of cell membranes, as well as serving as the starting compound from which many others are synthesized. Other important steroids include the sex hormones and vitamin D.

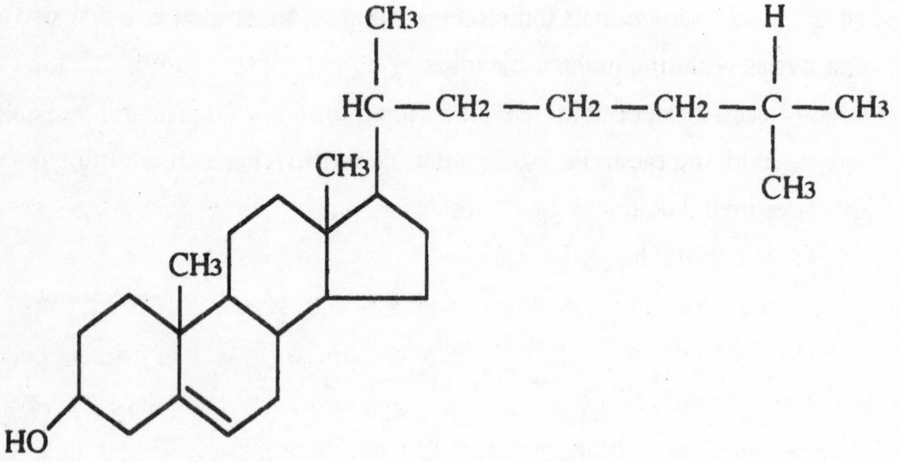

Figure 2.4: Cholesterol, a steroid lipid

D. Proteins

Proteins are polymeric macromolecules made up of subunits of *amino acids* (see Figure 2.5). As you might expect, amino acids all contain an amino group and a carboxylic acid group; what differentiates them is a variable portion referred to as the *R group*. In a sense, proteins are structurally simple, since every one consists of a number of amino acids linked by *peptide bonds*. There are twenty different amino acids, however, which can be linked together in any order, and a

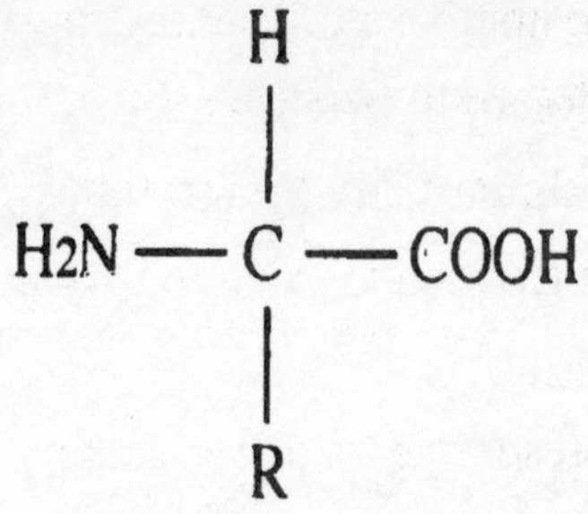

$$H_2N - C - COOH$$

Figure 2.5: An amino acid

typical protein contains anywhere from 30 to 1,000 amino acids. Thus, a remarkably vast diversity of different proteins is possible, and this is exactly what we find. There are probably close to 100,000 different proteins in the human body, each with a different function. The remarkable diversity of protein function is made possible by the fact that once a chain of amino acids is linked together (also called a *polypeptide*), it undergoes additional folding so that the final protein molecule exists in a particular three-dimensional conformation. It is this shape that allows it to function in a unique way. We can identify four levels of protein structure (see Figure 2.6).

- *Primary structure:* A protein's primary structure simply refers to the linear order of amino acids it contains.
- *Secondary structure:* The secondary structure of a protein comes about due to local interactions, usually hydrogen bonds between atoms of adjacent amino and acid groups. Common secondary structures include the *alpha-helix* and the *beta-pleated sheet*.
- *Tertiary structure:* A protein's tertiary structure refers to its ultimate three dimensional shape. It folds uniquely due to long range interactions between the R groups of the amino acids. Such interactions include hydrogen bonding, electrostatic interactions, and hydrophobic interactions. It is the tertiary structure that is responsible for the protein's function.
- *Quaternary structure:* Not all proteins have a quaternary structure; only those that consist of multiple polypeptide chains. Quaternary folding refers to the interactions between multiple chains of amino acids to achieve a protein that can only function in this complex state.

Proteins perform a vast array of functions, acting as enzymes, antibodies, structural components, hormones, and a wide variety of other functional entities. Well-known proteins include:

- *Hemoglobin*, which helps carry oxygen in the blood;
- *Collagen and Keratin*, major components of skin, hair, and connective

tissues;

♦ *Insulin*, a hormone that regulates blood glucose levels;

♦ *Pepsin*, an enzyme that digests other proteins in the stomach;

♦ and others too numerous to list!

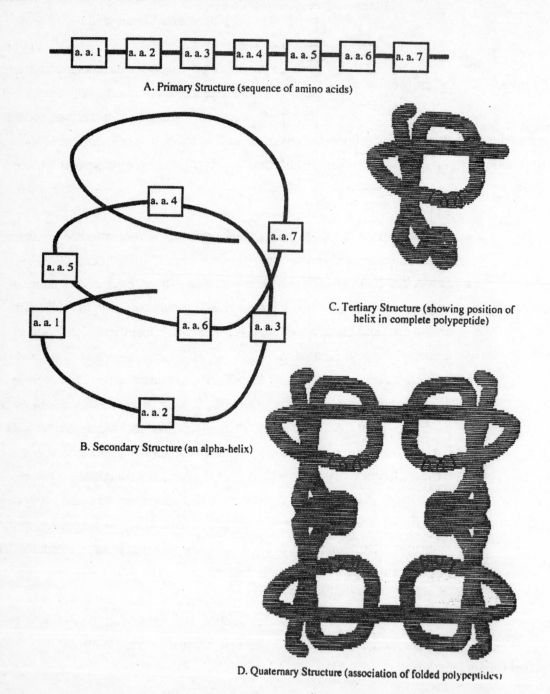

A. Primary Structure (sequence of amino acids)

B. Secondary Structure (an alpha-helix)

C. Tertiary Structure (showing position of helix in complete polypeptide)

D. Quaternary Structure (association of folded polypeptides)

Figure 2.6: Hierarchical folding of a hypothetical protein. aa: amino acid.

E. Nucleic Acids

Nucleic acids are also macromolecular polymers made up of a particular type of subunit, in this case, the *nucleotide* (see Figure 2.7). Nucleotides are more complex than the other subunits we have considered. Each one is made up of:

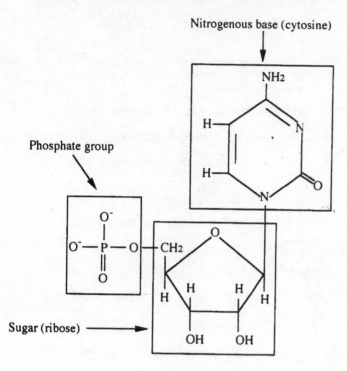

Nitrogenous base (cytosine)

Phosphate group

Sugar (ribose)

Figure 5.7: Cytidine monophosphate (CMP), a ribonucleotide

♦ a five-carbon sugar
♦ a nitrogenous base
♦ a phosphate group

Two general types of nucleotides are recognized, depending upon which sugar they contain. Therefore, two major types of nucleic acids can be constructed, depending upon which kind of nucleotide is used.

♦ *DNA (deoxyribonucleic acid)* is made of nucleotides that contain the sugar *deoxyribose*.
♦ *RNA (ribonucleic acid)* is made of nucleotides that contain the sugar *ribose*.

Deoxyribonucleotides are of four types, depending upon which of four possible nitrogenous bases they contain. The four bases are:

D GAC I

♦ *Adenine*
♦ *Guanine*   Nitr. bases
♦ *Cytosine*
♦ *Thymine*

15

Ribonucleotides are of four types, depending upon which of four possible nitrogenous bases they contain. The four bases are:

- *Adenine*
- *Guanine*
- *Cytosine*
- *Uracil*

As you can see, the bases are similar in DNA and RNA, with only one exception: the thymine of DNA is replaced by uracil in RNA. Due to their chemical structures, adenine and guanine are referred to as *purines*, while cytosine, thymine, and uracil are called *pyrimidines*.

Nucleotides are joined to one another by *phosphodiester bonds*, creating long chains. As with proteins, what makes one DNA molecule different from another is the sequence of bases that makes up the primary structure. This sequence carries encoded information, and is the basis for the "genetic code" (see Chapters 5 and 6). In fact, the major functions of DNA and RNA all deal with the storage, transmission, and usage of genetic information.

It turns out that DNA normally exists in the form of a double helix in nature. Two antiparallel strands of nucleotides are held together by interactions between the bases to form a structure that resembles a twisted ladder (this structure and its consequences are examined in detail in Chapter 5). On the other hand, RNA is usually single-stranded.

Chapter 2 Problems

Passage 2.1 (Questions 1-5)

Often, bacteria are grown on a medium that contains all of the components they need to survive. This includes an energy source, a carbon source, and sources of all the mineral salts the bacteria require to carry out their metabolic reactions. Sometimes, a mutant bacterium is isolated that needs more than the usual minimum requirements, because it cannot carry out the reactions necessary to produce a needed substance. These mutants are referred to as *auxotrophs*; if they are to grow, they must be supplemented with the substance they need but cannot manufacture.

Experiment 1

Bacteria were grown on media containing different radioactively labeled atoms to determine which types of biological molecules would be radioactively labeled. Molecules become labeled as they are synthesized by the bacteria using the raw materials provided by the medium. The bacteria were grown for a period of time that was sufficient to label all molecules that could be labeled, and the major types of biomolecules were isolated and tested for the presence of radioactivity. The following table shows the various strains of bacteria and the radioactive element present in the media in which they were grown.

Bacterial strain	Radioactive element
strain 1	carbon
strain 2	phosphorous
strain 3	nitrogen
strain 4	oxygen

Experiment 2

Auxotrophic bacteria were grown on media supplemented with the substance that they need but cannot manufacture. If they were not supplemented in this way, no growth would be observed. The following table shows two auxotrophic strains and the substance with which they were supplemented.

Auxotrophic strain	Supplement
strain A	arginine, an amino acid
strain B	decanoic acid, a fatty acid

Experiment 3

Auxotrophic strain A (from Experiment 2) was grown on a medium that contained supplemental arginine *and* radioactive phosphorus, and the major types of biomolecules were again isolated and tested for radioactivity.

1. Which of the following biomolecules isolated from Strain 2 would we expect to be radioactively labeled according to the table from experiment 1?
   A. RNA
   B. Proteins
   C. Glucose
   D. Amino acids

2. Which of the following biomolecules isolated from Strain 3 would we expect to be radioactively labeled according to the table from experiment 1?
   A. DNA, but not RNA
   B. DNA and RNA, but not proteins
   C. RNA and proteins
   D. DNA and fatty acids

3. Which of the following biomolecules isolated from Strain 1 would we expect to be radioactively labeled according to the table from experiment 1?
   A. Cholesterol
   B. Phospholipids
   C. Both A and B
   D. Neither A nor B

4. In experiment 2, the arginine requiring auxotrophic strain A was supplemented with arginine to allow growth. If the cells were not supplemented with arginine, the cells could not grow because arginine is directly required for the synthesis of:
   A. DNA.
   B. Proteins.
   C. Fatty acids.
   D. RNA.

5. In experiment 3, which of the following biomolecules would we expect to become labeled?
   A. All proteins, DNA, and RNA
   B. Only proteins containing arginine, but not DNA or RNA
   C. DNA, RNA, and only those proteins that contain arginine
   D. RNA and phospholipids

Questions 6-10 are independent of any passage and independent of each other.

6. Which of the following sugars does not need to undergo any enzymatic processing before it can be absorbed by the human digestive system?
   A. Lactose
   B. Maltose
   C. Galactose
   D. Sucrose

7. Which of the following is true of the differences between DNA and RNA?
   A. DNA contains a five-carbon sugar, while RNA contains a six-carbon sugar.
   B. DNA contains phosphate groups, while RNA does not.
   C. RNA contains the purine base adenine in place of the purine base guanine contained in DNA.
   D. RNA contains a different five-carbon sugar than DNA.

8. Which of the following statements is true regarding proteins?
   A. All proteins exhibit quaternary folding.
   B. The primary structure of a protein refers simply to the linear order of amino acids it contains.
   C. Not all proteins contain amino acids, only the ones that have extensive three-dimensional folding.
   D. All proteins are composed of one polypeptide chain.

9. Which of the following compounds would one expect to be liquid (with the lowest density) at room temperature?
   A. A saturated triglyceride
   B. A monounsaturated triglyceride
   C. A polyunsaturated triglyceride
   D. None of the above, as all would be solids at room temperature.

10. Which of the following carbohydrates is a polymer of the monosaccharide glucose?
    A. Cellulose
    B. Lactose
    C. Ribose
    D. None of the above

Chapter 3
Enzymes and Energy

A. Introduction

The study of energy transformations, or *thermodynamics*, is covered in the chemistry portion of the MCAT. However, it is useful to remind ourselves that the laws of thermodynamics apply as much to living organisms and cells as they do to inanimate objects. Cells therefore had to evolve methods of obtaining and processing energy that are in accordance with the general principles of energy transformations. It is a general chemical principle that in order for a chemical reaction to proceed, a certain amount of energy, the *activation energy*, must be absorbed by the reactants to break the bonds already in place. One way of providing activation energy is simply to add heat to the reactants. This is what we do when we light a match to start a fire, which allows a combustion reaction to proceed. Living systems, however, cannot withstand the high temperatures necessary to overcome the activation energy barriers for biochemical reactions. Another method must exist to allow cells to facilitate and control chemical reactions. *Enzymes* are biological catalysts that facilitate reactions by lowering the necessary activation energy (see Figure 3.1).

B. Structure and Function of Enzymes

What types of molecules are enzymes and how do they work? Enzymes are almost always large protein molecules, folded into a particular three-dimensional configuration (see Chapter 2). Recently, some RNA molecules have been found to have enzymatic functions, but the vast majority of enzymes are proteins. The protein is folded so that a particular portion of the molecule, the *active site*, is accessible and forms a surface that attracts and aligns the reactant(s) in a favorable configuration. The reactant(s) are referred to as the enzyme's *substrate*, and when they associate with the enzyme, the intended reaction is able to proceed efficiently at the relatively low temperature of the cell. The amino acids that comprise the active site are close together in space, but

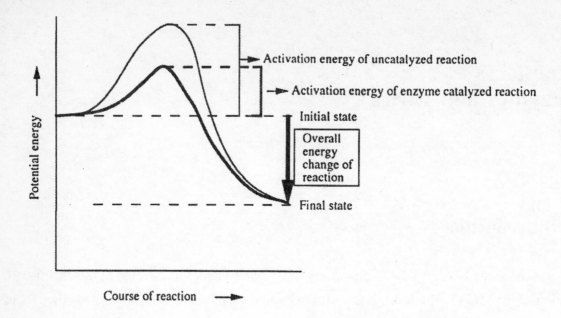

Figure 3.1: Activation energies of catalyzed and uncatalyzed reactions

may be far apart in the primary structure of the protein. Thus factors that disturb the overall folding of the protein may decrease or totally destroy the enzyme's ability to function.

The way the enzyme interacts with the substrate is only now becoming completely clear. Initially, the association was envisioned as a "lock and key" model, in which the shape of the active site matched the shape of the substrate exactly. This would account for their ability to come together easily. A more modern idea is the "induced fit" model, in which the active site and substrate have an affinity for each other, but the binding of the substrate may change the conformation of the active site, inducing a better fit and perhaps straining the bonds that will be broken in the substrate (see Figure 3.2).

Enzymes have great *specificity*, which means that one enzyme can catalyze only one reaction or a set of related reactions. This is of great benefit because it allows the cell to control different reactions independently, by regulating the activity or quantity of the enzyme involved. Furthermore, the enzyme is not permanently altered in any way by participating in the reaction, and so is "recyclable", being used over and over again. Therefore, enzymes typically do not need to be manufactured in large quantities.

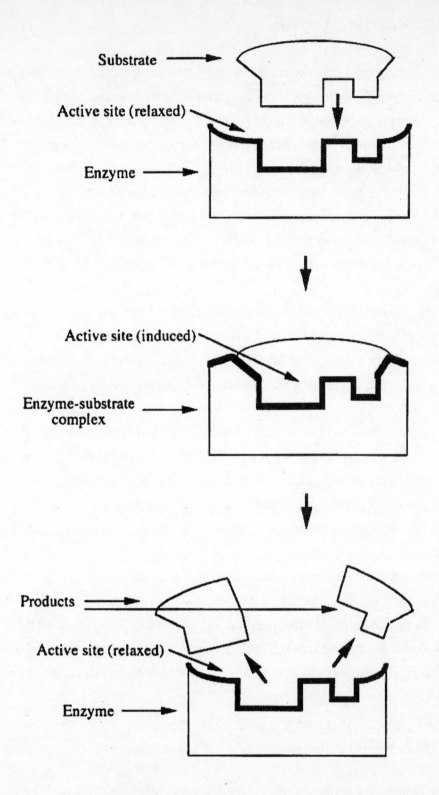

Figure 3.2: A model of enzyme action (induced fit)

C. Factors Affecting Enzyme Activity

Sometimes it takes more than just the presence of the substrate and the enzyme to allow a reaction to take place. Many enzymes require the presence of a *cofactor* to function. Simple cofactors are usually ionic minerals. For example, many enzymes require magnesium or zinc ions, for which they have binding sites, in order to act as catalysts. If the cofactor is not present, the enzyme will not work or will have reduced activity.

Sometimes the cofactor is a nonprotein organic molecule, called a *coenzyme*. The coenzyme plays a central role in the catalyzed reaction, often by accepting or providing electrons, and becoming *reduced* or *oxidized*, respectively, in the process. The vitamins of the B-complex group or their derivatives serve as coenzymes in the catabolic reactions that oxidize food molecules to release energy (see Chapter 4).

Environmental conditions also play a major role in determining an enzyme's effectiveness. In particular, temperature and pH influence enzyme activity enormously, and this is the major reason these parameters are so tightly controlled in humans. The temperature and pH of our bodies cannot vary considerably without dire consequences. Why are enzymes affected so profoundly by these environmental conditions?

Enzyme activity, in general, is reduced as the temperature drops and is increased as the temperature rises. If our body temperature becomes colder than normal, enzymes will function, but at slower and slower rates as the temperature falls. Ultimately, these rates will be too slow to sustain life. Raising the temperature will increase enzyme activity, to a certain point. If the temperature is too high, the interactions that maintain the shape of the enzyme will be disrupted, changing the overall shape of the protein and destroying, often irreversibly, the functionality of the active site. When an enzyme loses its activity due to disruption of its three-dimensional configuration, that enzyme has become *denatured*. Both low and high pH values can also denature enzymes by disrupting the interactions that hold them in their proper orientation, in this case by affecting the charges of various R groups and subsequently changing their affinities for each other. Every enzyme has an optimum pH and temperature at which it functions best; any deviation from these values will reduce its ability to catalyze reactions.

D. Control of Enzyme Activity

While ultimately the control of enzymes is accomplished genetically (see Chapters 5 and 6), several other processes affect when and how efficiently an enzyme works, so the cell carries out the desired reactions at the right times and rates. A classic example of an enzyme control mechanism is called *feedback inhibition*. Many enzymes, in addition to their active sites, contain binding sites for other molecules. These are referred to as *allosteric sites*, and enzymes that contain them are *allosteric enzymes*. If the allosteric site has an affinity for the product of the enzyme-catalyzed reaction, a feedback loop will automatically control how much of the product is produced. If product concentrations are low, the cell requires the reaction to proceed; little of the product exists to bind to the allosteric site, and the enzyme functions normally. As the reaction progresses, and enough of the product is made, it binds to the allosteric site. When this happens, the overall shape of the enzyme changes so that the active site is either hidden or disrupted, and the reaction will take place at a reduced rate or not at all. When product levels drop again, the product dissociates from the allosteric site, exposing the active site and allowing the reaction to resume. This process acts like a "thermostat", and is a common cellular strategy for regulating enzyme activity.

Sometimes molecules are present that act to inhibit an enzyme's function, and these are appropriately called *enzyme inhibitors*. *Competitive* inhibitors resemble the substrate, and thus compete with it for binding to the active site. *Non-competitive* inhibitors bind to an allosteric site, causing the enzyme's shape to change and affecting its function. Therefore, competitive inhibitors are less effective as the substrate concentration rises, while non-competitive inhibitors work regardless of the substrate concentration.

E. ATP as the Energy Currency of the Cell

Reactions that are *endergonic* require the input of energy. Cells must perform many endergonic reactions in order to remain alive; protein synthesis and DNA replication are just two examples. While enzymes are required to catalyze these reactions, they cannot provide the energy to drive them. Therefore, all endergonic reactions must be coupled to energy-releasing, or *exergonic*, reactions in order to proceed. While cells can ingest energy containing molecules in many forms (monosaccharides, fatty acids, amino acids, etc.), the energy contained in these molecules must be harvested and stored in a usable form by the cell. In almost all cases, this usable form of energy is the molecule *ATP (adenosine triphosphate)*, the triphosphate form of the DNA nucleotide adenosine (see Figure 3.3). When the bond linking the terminal phosphate to the rest of the molecule is *hydrolyzed* (broken), *ADP (adenosine diphosphate)* and free phosphate are the products, and energy is released. Thus, this is an exergonic reaction. Many enzymes that catalyze endergonic reactions associate with ATP, and often contain *ATPase* (ATP hydrolyzing) activity in addition to their other catalytic capabilities. Thus, it is ATP that directly provides the energy required by enzymes to catalyze endergonic reactions. This intimate association of exergonic ATP hydrolysis with endergonic reactions is referred to as *coupling* of reactions. The next chapter addresses the process by which cells transform the chemical energy of food molecules into energy stored as ATP.

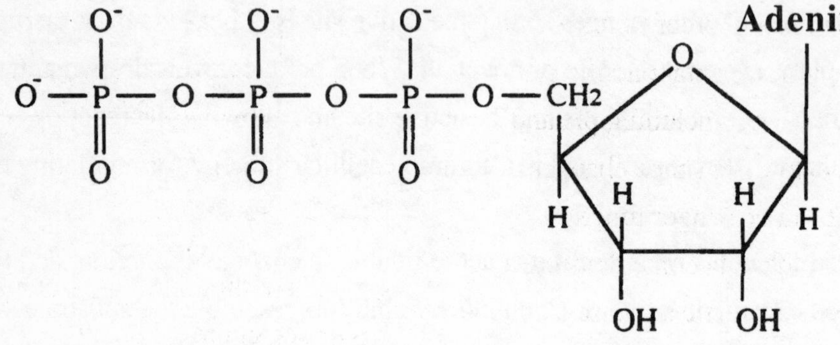

Figure 3.3: Adenosine triphosphate (ATP)

Chapter 3 Problems

Passage 3.1 (Questions 1-5)

In general, enzymes are protein molecules which must be folded in a specific three-dimensional shape in order to function properly. Certain environmental parameters can affect enzyme activity, including pH and temperature. If an enzyme's shape changes significantly and it can no longer function, the enzyme is said to have become denatured.

The enzyme pancreatic amylase is manufactured and secreted by the pancreas into the duodenum (the large, beginning portion of the small intestine). Pancreatic amylase breaks down starch into maltose, a disaccharide. Pepsin is an enzyme that is released by the epithelium of the stomach, and functions in the stomach to break down proteins into smaller polypeptide units.

The following graphs show the activities of various enzymes under various environmental conditions.

Graph 1:

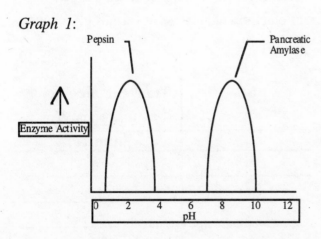

Graph 2:

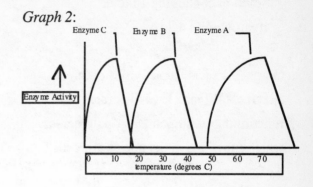

1. Which of the following statements is true with respect to graph 1?
   A. Pepsin and pancreatic amylase could never function together in the same part of the body at the same time.
   B. Pancreatic amylase could function in the stomach, but its activity would be low.
   C. The optimal pH for the functioning of pepsin is approximately 8.5.
   D. Normally, the small intestine must be slightly acidic.

2. Trypsin is a protein digesting enzyme that functions in the small intestine. Which of the following statements should be true about trypsin?
   A. The optimum pH for the functioning of trypsin is approximately 2.
   B. Both trypsin and pepsin would be expected to be found working together in the same part of the body.
   C. The optimum pH for the functioning of trypsin is approximately 8.5.

D. Trypsin could function well in a solution containing 1 molar hydrochloric acid.

3. Graph 2 depicts the activities of three enzymes. Which curve illustrates the functioning of human DNA polymerase, which functions in the nucleus of cells?
   A. Enzyme A
   B. Enzyme B
   C. Enzyme C
   D. None of the above could represent the activity of human DNA polymerase.

4. Which curve illustrates the functioning of DNA polymerase from a shark?
   A. Enzyme A
   B. Enzyme B
   C. Enzyme C
   D. None of the above, since sharks, like all fish, do not contain DNA polymerase.

5. At what temperature would enzyme B be completely denatured?
   A. $37^0 C$
   B. $15^0 C$
   C. $5^0 C$
   D. $50^0 C$

Passage 3.2 (Questions 6-10)

The reagent iodine potassium iodide (IKI) can be used to detect the presence of starch in a solution. IKI is normally light yellow in color; in the presence of starch it turns a deep blue. IKI can therefore be used to test for the presence and activity of the enzyme amylase, which breaks starch into maltose disaccharide units. (Maltose does not affect the color of IKI). Thus, if starch is initially present and mixed with IKI, the deep blue color created will begin to lighten and disappear if amylase is present as it begins to break down the starch to maltose. Using the same concentration of enzyme, the longer it takes for the blue color to disappear, the lower the amylase activity.

Amylase is usually present in vertebrates in two forms that work in different parts of the digestive tract. Salivary amylase, secreted in the saliva by the salivary glands, begins to break down starch in the mouth, which has a slightly acidic pH. Pancreatic amylase is manufactured by the pancreas and released into the small intestine, where it similarly breaks down remaining starch molecules to maltose.

The following tables show the results of an experiment designed to test the activities of one form of amylase at various pH's and temperatures.

pH	Time for blue color to disappear (in minutes)
3	10
6	1
9	5
12	30

Temperature (^{0}C)	Time for blue color to disappear (minutes)
15	10
30	5
37	1
60	blue color never disappears

6. Which of the following is the enzyme being tested?
   A. Human salivary amylase
   B. Shark salivary amylase
   C. Human pancreatic amylase
   D. Shark pancreatic amylase

7. What is the most likely explanation for the observation that the blue color never disappears at 60^0 C?
   A. The chemical bonds in starch are stabilized by the heat so that it cannot break down even though the enzyme is highly active.
   B. Heat causes the IKI to become unable to stain the starch.
   C. The amylase has become denatured at this temperature.
   D. All of the above are reasonable explanations.

8. What is the optimal temperature and pH for the enzyme being tested?
   A. 15^0 C, pH 12
   B. 37^0 C, pH 6
   C. 37^0 C, pH 12
   D. 15^0 C, pH 6

9. The breakdown of starch is an exergonic reaction, which would occur spontaneously at temperatures of about 200^0 C. Amylase allows the reaction to proceed at physiological temperatures by:
   A. Increasing the activation energy for the reaction.
   B. Increasing the potential energy of the reactants.
   C. Changing the amount of energy released by the reaction.
   D. Lowering the activation energy of the reaction.

10. Which of the following statements is true of the action of amylase at its optimum pH and temperature?
    A. The enzyme is irreversibly changed, so that one enzyme molecule can only catalyze the reaction once.
    B. It is denatured, and the enzyme's activity is the highest possible.
    C. The active site of amylase consists of every amino acid in the protein.
    D. This pH and temperature represents the physiological conditions under which it functions in nature.

Chapter 4
Cellular Metabolism

A. Introduction

All living organisms, as we have already discussed, require energy in order to survive. Animals obtain this energy by ingesting compounds that contain potential chemical energy (carbohydrates, fats, and proteins), and metabolizing them so that energy is released and stored in the form of ATP (see Chapter 3). Energy is almost always used directly in the form of ATP. What processes occur at the cellular level to accomplish these energy transformations and create ATP? The net sum of all reactions that take place in a cell or organism is called *metabolism*, but often the term metabolism is used to refer to the *catabolic* (breaking down) reactions that make energy available to the cell. These are the reactions on which we will focus in this chapter.

B. Types of Metabolism

While in theory there are many pathways cells could utilize to metabolize their food, in nature, especially in animals, only a few pathways are used. While rather complex, these pathways vary little from organism to organism. Two major pathways are generally available to heterotrophic animal cells during metabolism: *aerobic respiration* and *fermentation*. Aerobic respiration is an oxygen requiring series of reactions, and is necessary in all vertebrates. Fermentation does not require oxygen, and while most vertebrates can perform fermentation reactions, it serves them mainly in emergencies when extra energy is needed. Only organisms such as yeast and some bacteria can live entirely by engaging in fermentation.

While many molecules may be metabolized (monosaccharides, amino acids, fatty acids, etc.), most cells prefer glucose as their source of fuel. It is therefore convenient to examine glucose metabolism as a model for the overall process, while keeping in mind that other molecules may also be used. Whichever pathways are ultimately utilized to harvest energy from glucose, they always involve the oxidation of glucose and always begin with a series of reactions called *glycolysis.* If the aerobic pathway is used, glycolysis is followed by two processes: the *Krebs cycle*, a cyclic series of reactions, and the *electron transport chain (ETC),* where much ATP is synthesized. Let's look at each of these processes in more detail.

C. Understanding Glycolysis

Glycolysis, which literally means "splitting sugar", is a series of nine reactions that partially oxidize glucose and harvest two molecules of ATP. Figure 4.1 shows all nine of the reactions, but it is not necessary to attempt to memorize them all in this context. We are most interested in understanding the major events and the ultimate products of glycolysis.

Glycolysis occurs in the cytoplasm of animal cells, and it is important to remember three major aspects of the process:

- ◆ Glucose, a six-carbon compound, is ultimately broken down into 2 molecules of pyruvic acid, a three-carbon compound.
- ◆ Two molecules of ATP are produced when glycolysis is complete.
- ◆ Two molecules of the coenzyme NAD^+ *(nicotinamide adenine dinucleotide)* are reduced to *NADH* when glycolysis is complete.

A few comments may be helpful at this point.
- ◆ Glycolysis is the first step in glucose metabolism in all vertebrates and almost all living cells.
- ◆ The ATP made during the process is generated by *substrate level phosphorylation,* which simply means a phosphate group attaches to ADP directly from one of the reactants in the pathway to make ATP.
- ◆ NAD^+ is a common coenzyme (see Chapter 3) that acts as an electron shuttle. It contains more potential energy when it is reduced to NADH than in its oxidized form, so the generation of NADH represents the temporary storage of energy.

D. The Anaerobic Option: Fermentation

Glycolysis occurs as the first step in glucose metabolism regardless of whether the cell is performing fermentation or aerobic respiration. It is important to note that glycolysis can never occur alone. It must be coupled to other reactions to be useful. Since fermentation is a comparatively simple process, we will examine it first. If a cell performs fermentation, no oxygen is required, but the pyruvic acid generated in glycolysis must be further processed. While countless

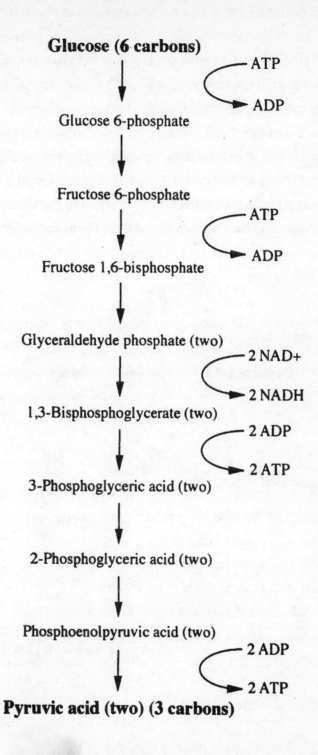

Figure 4.1: A summary of glycolysis

variations exist, two major types of fermentation are common (see Figure 4.2):

◆ In *ethanol fermentation*, pyruvic acid is broken down into ethanol (a two-carbon compound) and carbon dioxide (CO_2). This type of fermentation is especially prevalent in yeast, and is utilized in many commercial processes, including the baking of bread and the making of alcoholic beverages.

◆ In *lactic acid* fermentation, the atoms of pyruvic acid are rearranged to form lactic acid (another three-carbon compound). This type of fermentation is carried out by vertebrates, usually in their muscle tissues. During heavy exertion, not enough oxygen may be available to supply ATP needs via the aerobic pathway.

A. Ethanol fermentation

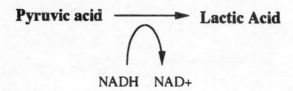

Pyruvic acid ⟶ Acetaldehyde ⟶ **Ethanol**

CO_2

NADH   NAD+

B. Lactic Acid fermentation

Pyruvic acid ⟶ **Lactic Acid**

NADH   NAD+

Figure 4.2: a summary of fermentation reactions

It is important to note in examining Figure 4.2 that no additional ATP is produced by either of the fermentation reactions. Why, therefore, must they occur? The answer is simple: the two molecules of NADH formed during glycolysis are oxidized back to NAD^+ during the fermentation reactions. If this did not occur, all of the NAD^+ in a cell would quickly be used up, and glycolysis could no longer continue. This explains why glycolysis can never "stand alone".

E. The Aerobic Option: Cellular Respiration

Vertebrates must perform *aerobic cellular respiration* in order to obtain enough ATP to live. This means that they need a constant supply of oxygen (a major participant in the reactions), and produce carbon dioxide as a waste. This explains the need for breathing, or *physiological* respiration. The reactions of aerobic respiration take place in the *mitochondria*, so, after glycolysis, the pyruvic acid to be processed must be transported to this organelle. We should note here that the mitochondrion (singular) is surrounded by two membranes; this creates an *intermembrane space* (see Figure 10.2). In addition, the inner membrane is folded to increase its surface area, and the folds are referred to as *cristae*. The inner, liquid portion of the mitochondria is called the *matrix*.

F. The Krebs Cycle

Pyruvic acid must now enter a cyclic series of reaction, the *Krebs cycle*, also known as the *citric acid cycle* or the *TCA (tricarboxylic acid) cycle*. The reactions of the Krebs cycle take place in the mitochondrial matrix, and are summarized in Figure 4.3. Again, it is inadvisable to attempt to memorize all of these reactions. Before pyruvic acid can enter the cycle, it must undergo some initial preparatory steps:

- ♦ Pyruvic acid is oxidized, releasing one molecule of CO_2 and a two-carbon acetyl group.
- ♦ The acetyl group is attached to a molecule called *Coenzyme A*, to form *acetyl CoA*.
- ♦ In the process, a molecule of NAD^+ is reduced to NADH.

It is important to note that carbon atoms from pyruvic acid can enter the Krebs cycle only in the form of acetyl CoA.

Next, the acetyl group is donated to the four-carbon molecule *oxaloacetic acid* to form *citric acid*, a six-carbon compound. The citric acid is subsequently broken down, in a series of steps, back to oxaloacetic acid. As with glycolysis, there are three main points to keep in mind regarding the Krebs cycle. Specifically, for each turn of the cycle:

- ♦ Two carbons enter the cycle as an acetyl group, and two carbons are released as carbon dioxide.
- ♦ One molecule of ATP is harvested.
- ♦ Three molecules of NAD^+ are reduced to NADH, and one molecule of another coenzyme, *FAD*, is reduced to *$FADH_2$*.

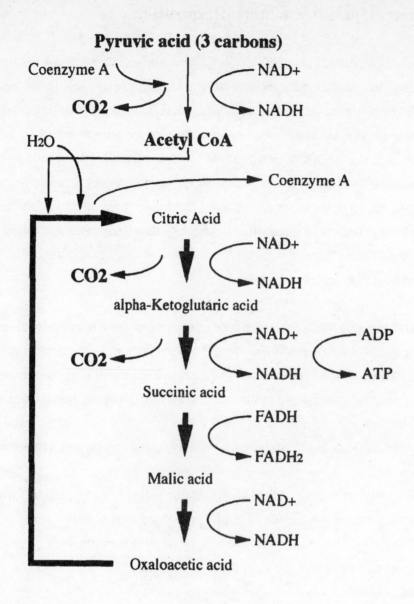

Figure 4.3: Highlights of the Krebs cycle

It is important to remember that for every glucose molecule we started with, two molecules of pyruvic acid were created. Since we have only been keeping track of one pyruvic acid molecule as it travels through the Krebs cycle, we must multiply our totals by two if wish to know the yield per molecule of glucose. If we consider the preparatory events with those of the Krebs cycle itself, we can summarize as follows:

♦ For each three carbon molecule of pyruvic acid that enter the mitochondria, three molecules of carbon dioxide are released, for a total of six carbon dioxides. This is the source of the CO_2 we exhale.

♦ A total of two molecules of ATP are harvested.

♦ Overall, eight molecules of NAD^+ are reduced to NADH, and two FAD molecules are reduced to $FADH_2$.

G. The Electron Transport Chain: ATP Harvesting

After the Krebs cycle, the original glucose molecule has been completely oxidized, which means that its potential energy has been released. One glucose molecule theoretically contains enough potential energy to manufacture close to one hundred molecules of ATP. It is clear that we have not stored a significant amount of the released energy in this form yet. Where is the energy?

The energy is temporarily residing in the reduced coenzyme molecules NADH and $FADH_2$. During the final stages of respiration, *the electron transport chain*, these coenzymes will donate electrons to a series, or chain, of carriers, and will become oxidized in the process, back to NAD^+ and FAD (the coenzymes can then go back and participate in glycolysis and the Krebs cycle). The carriers are physically located in the inner mitochondrial membrane, and include *cytochrome* proteins, among other molecules. As electrons are passed down the chain, energy is released; the final electron acceptor is molecular oxygen (O2), which is reduced and converted to water as it accepts electrons (this is where the oxygen we inhale is actually used). The energy released is temporarily stored and ultimately used to make ATP by *oxidative phosphorylation*. The *chemiosmotic model* explains how ATP is produced this way (see Figure 4.4). The model highlights three major points:

♦ The reduced coenzymes NADH and $FADH_2$ ultimately react with oxygen by donating electrons through a series of intermediaries. This reaction causes oxidation of the coenzymes to NAD^+ and FAD, and reduction of oxygen to water. A large amount of energy is released in the process. If the intermediate carriers did not exist, all of the energy would be released at once, which would be difficult for the cell to control and manage.

♦ As energy is slowly released, it is used to pump *protons* (H^+ ions) from the matrix into the intermembrane space by active transport (see Chapter 11). This establishes an *electrochemical proton gradient* which stores the energy that has been released. This gradient can be used to do work.

♦ The enzyme *ATP synthase* is embedded in the inner membrane, and protons diffuse through a channel in this protein back into the matrix. As the protons "fall" through the enzyme, the energy they release is used to do work: the *phosphorylation* (addition of a phosphate group) of ADP to make ATP.

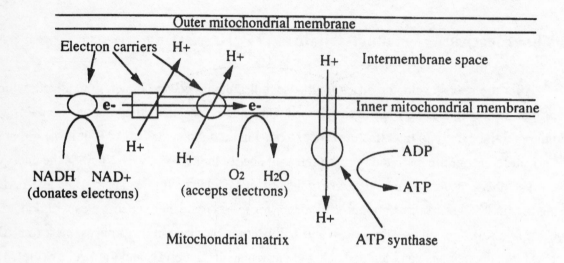

Figure 4.4: The electron transport chain and oxidative phosphorylation

When all is said and done, 32 ATP molecules are harvested by the electron transport chain from all of the reduced cofactors generated through glycolysis and the Krebs cycle. If we add this to the 2 ATP molecules obtained from glycolysis and the 2 produced in the Krebs cycle, we come up with a grand total of 38 molecules of ATP harvested. However, the net amount is 36 ATP molecules because some energy is used to transport pyruvic acid into the mitochondria.

H. Overall Energy Harvest

Given that glucose, if burned in a calorimeter, releases 686 kilocalories/mole, and ATP hydrolysis usually yields approximately 7 kilocalories/mole, we can calculate the efficiency of aerobic respiration. If we harvest 36 ATP molecules and multiply by 7 kilocalories/mole, we have obtained 252 kilocalories/mole of glucose burned. This represents an efficiency of 252/686, or approximately 37%. While far from perfect, it is certainly preferable to the efficiency of fermentation, which by the same logic is approximately 2%. Where does the rest of the energy go? The first law of thermodynamics tells us that energy can never be created or destroyed, so it must have been transformed into another type of energy. In fact, it was converted to heat, and is in effect "wasted" energy. Birds and mammals, however, have figured out another use for this energy so that it is not completely wasted: it is the major source of internal heat used to maintain a relatively high body temperatures (see Chapter 17).

I. Summary of Aerobic Respiration

After looking at all of the details of respiration, we can formulate a net equation that takes them all into account. That equation is:

$$\text{glucose} + \text{oxygen} + \text{ADP} + \text{P} \longrightarrow \text{carbon dioxide} + \text{water} + \text{ATP}$$

We can make this a proper, balanced chemical equation:

$$C_6H_{12}O_6 + 6O_2 + 36ADP + 36P \longrightarrow 6CO_2 + 6H_2O + 36\ ATP$$

Chapter 4 Problems

Passage 4.1 (Questions 1-5)

Yeast are unicellular fungi that are considered to be facultatively anaerobic. This means that in the presence of oxygen they can and will undergo aerobic respiration, but at the same time they will likely be fermenting glucose. Furthermore, when no oxygen is present they can survive, potentially forever, by fermentation. Yeast use ethanol fermentation, and this produces carbon dioxide as one of its final products.

One way of quantifying the rate of fermentation in yeast is to measure the rate at which the volume of gas changes in a test tube connected to a solution of yeast being fed with glucose. Since carbon dioxide is the only gas involved in fermentation, the rate of gas production should mirror the rate of fermentation.

The following table shows the amount of gas evolved in such an experiment under different environmental conditions.

pH	Gas evolved (in ml)
5	5
6	10
7	20
8	30
9	25
10	10

1. At which pH is the most ethanol produced?
   A. 5
   B. 7
   C. 8
   D. 9

2. It is likely that oxygen is present in this system, so that aerobic respiration is going on at the same time as fermentation. Taking this into account, which of the following statements is true?
   A. Since oxygen will be used up, using the net change in overall gas production as an indicator of the fermentation rate will be inaccurate.
   B. It is irrelevant to our experiment whether or not aerobic respiration is taking place or not; using the net change in overall gas production as an indicator of the fermentation rate will be accurate.
   C. Under these conditions, no fermentation will occur, since according to the passage yeast only undergo fermentation when no oxygen is available.
   D. The experiment is further complicated by the fact that the yeast will use up some of the carbon dioxide during glycolysis, so using the net change in overall gas production as an indicator of the fermentation rate will be inaccurate.

3. Which of the following statements is true of the yeast in this experiment?
   A. Fermentation reactions will occur in the mitochondria.
   B. Yeast have no mitochondria, and both fermentation and respiration take place in the cytoplasm.
   C. The Krebs cycle, to the extent it occurs, will take place in the mitochondria.
   D. The Krebs cycle clearly does not take place in yeast.

4. Assuming that respiration and fermentation occur at the same time, which of the following statements is true about this experiment?
   A. Since respiration yields more ATP per glucose molecule than fermentation does, the net amount of ATP produced by respiration must be greater than that produced by fermentation.
   B. Even though respiration yields more ATP per glucose molecule than fermentation does, the net amount of ATP produced by fermentation may be greater than that produced by respiration, as long as many more glucose molecules are processed by fermentation than respiration.
   C. Fermentation cannot take place in the presence of oxygen, because it is so inefficient.
   D. The question is impossible to answer, because respiration and fermentation can never take place at the same time.

5. Which of the following statements is true about the electron transport chain in yeast in this experiment?
   A. Yeast do not contain an electron transport chain.
   B. While yeast contain mitochondria and contain an electron transport chain, the energy released during transport is not used to make ATP, it is used to generate carbon dioxide.
   C. The electron transport chain plays no role in ethanol fermentation.
   D. The electron transport chain in yeast functions similarly to that of a human; since yeast do not have mitochondria, however, the chain is located in the yeast cell's plasma membrane.

Passage 4.2 (Questions 6-10)

Many chemicals that are poisons exert their toxic effects by interfering with some aspect of aerobic respiration, usually involving the electron transport chain of the mitochondria. Three such poisons are cyanide, 2,4-dinitrophenol, and the antibiotic oligomycin.

Cyanide is a potent and deadly human poison. It causes its effects by binding to one of the electron carriers and inhibiting the passage of electrons to oxygen, so that electron transport, proton-pumping, and ATP synthesis stop virtually instantaneously.

2,4-dinitrophenol is also a deadly poison to humans. It is an example of the general class of poisons known as "uncouplers", which allow protons to pass back from the intermembrane space to the matrix without passing through the ATP synthase enzyme. Electron transport and proton pumping continue, but ATP is not made. Such uncouplers are also called ionophores.

Oligomycin, an antibiotic, is not deadly to humans, but does interfere with respiration, which is how it kills bacteria, and accounts for its side effects in humans. It is representative of a group of poisons that directly inhibit ATP synthase by blocking the passageway for protons. As with the uncouplers, electron transport and proton pumping continue, but ATP is not made (although for a different reason).

Use the information above, the following observations, and your knowledge of respiration when answering the questions.

Observation 1

When a person breathes a particular deadly poison (compound A), the following effects are observed. Clinically, body temperature quickly increases, causing profuse sweating, and ultimate death. At the biochemical level it is noted that normal to greater than normal amounts of oxygen are used, and normal to greater amounts of carbon dioxide are produced. The pH of the mitochondrial intermembrane space does not change

appreciably; if it does, it may increase slightly.

Observation 2

When a person ingests a particular toxin (compound B), the following effects are observed. At the biochemical level, it is noted that the Krebs cycle continues to function, producing NADH, and that the NADH is oxidized back to NAD+ as it donates electrons to the electron transport chain. Strikingly, the pH of the mitochondrial intermembrane space is noted to drop significantly.

6. The toxin ingested that is referred to as compound A in observation 1 is likely to be:
    A. Cyanide.
    B. 2,4-dinitrophenol.
    C. Oligomycin.
    D. The information presented does not allow differentiation of the three.

7. The toxin ingested that is referred to as compound B in observation 2 is likely to be:
    A. Cyanide.
    B. 2,4-dinitrophenol.
    C. Oligomycin.
    D. The information presented does not allow differentiation of the three.

8. During cyanide poisoning, which of the following molecules would increase its concentration dramatically?
   A. NAD+
   B. NADH
   C. Carbon dioxide
   D. FAD

9. In the 1950s, certain weak uncoupling agents were used to promote weight loss. They worked very well; in fact, they worked so well at "burning calories" that many people died from using them and they were pulled from the market. Which of the following statements explains how uncouplers could cause weight loss?
   A. Uncouplers allow ATP to be made but prevent its transport out of the mitochondria, thus uncoupling its manufacture from its use.
   B. Uncouplers increase the metabolic rate, and allow caloric energy temporarily stored in reduced coenzymes to remain "unharvested" as ATP; it is simply released as heat.
   C. Uncouplers prevent oxygen from accepting electrons, so that ATP is not made, and energy is not available to digest and absorb food.
   D. Uncouplers, due to their toxic effects, cause appetite suppression, and lower the overall metabolic rate.

10. Glycolysis could continue to operate in all of the following poisoning situations except:
   A. Cyanide poisoning.
   B. Poisoning from a fatal uncoupler.
   C. Oligomycin intoxication.
   D. None of the above; glycolysis is not affected by the events of the electron transport chain.

Chapter 5
DNA Structure and Function

A. Introduction

Perhaps the most important molecule in all of biology is *DNA, deoxyribonucleic acid*. We will devote two chapters to this molecule. In addition, the chapters on mitosis (Chapter 12), genetics (Chapter 19) and evolution (Chapter 20) rely on a thorough understanding of DNA.

All living things contain DNA as the storage unit of genetic information. The DNA molecule in every organism has the exact same structure and function. How it is copied by the cell (*replication*) and how it is interpreted (*transcription* and *translation*) may differ in some details; however, the basics are the same in every living entity. We will concentrate on eukaryotic cells in this and the next chapter.

B. The Function of DNA

Earlier, in Chapter 1, we considered the relationship between structure and function. We will now see how the structure of DNA directly relates to its function. In brief, the functions of DNA are

- to carry the genetic information of the organism;
- to control the development of the cell and the organism;
- to direct the function of the cell, including its reproduction and metabolism.

Since DNA has the same structure in all organisms, and it dictates the function of the cell, it is natural to wonder what makes species different. It is not the basic structure of the DNA, but rather the exact arrangement of the components of DNA that determines this difference. In fact, this arrangement not only accounts for the difference among species, but also for the uniqueness of individuals in the same species.

C. The Chemical Structure of DNA

By the early 1950s, it was well known that DNA was a polymer made up of monomers called *nucleotides*. Each nucleotide consists of three chemical groups (see Figure 5.1, see also Chapter 2):

- a 5 carbon sugar, *deoxyribose*;

- a nitrogen rich *base* attached to the first carbon of the sugar;

- a *phosphate group* attached to the fifth carbon of the sugar.

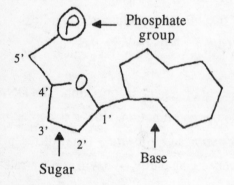

Figure 5.1: General structure of a nucleotide

Four types of nucleotides exist, and each differ only at the nitrogenous base:

- *adenine* (*A*),

- *cytosine* (*C*),

- *guanine* (*G*) and

- *thymine* (*T*).

In 1953, James Watson and Francis Crick proposed a model for the structure of DNA by considering a wide variety of data from other researchers. In particular, two observations became crucial to their model:

- Erwin Chargaff had discovered that, in every molecule of DNA, the amount of *A* was always equal to the amount of *T*, and the amount of *C* was always equal to the amount of *G*.

- Rosiland Franklin had obtained X ray diffraction data that showed DNA exists in a *double helix*, similar in structure to a winding staircase.

From this information, Watson and Crick were able to correctly determine the structure of the polymer (see Figure 5.2).

The monomers of DNA are linked together via the sugar and the phosphate groups in the nucleotides. This is often called the *sugar-phosphate backbone*, and the bond that forms between the monomeric nucleotides is called *a phosphodiester bond*. Remember how the phosphate group is attached to the fifth carbon on the deoxyribose? The phosphate from one nucleotide attaches to the sugar of another nucleotide at the third carbon. This actually gives DNA a direction, like north and south, except we call it 5' and 3' (pronounced "5 prime" and "3 prime," see Figure 5.2). We'll talk more about this attachment a little later.

One strand (polymer) of DNA is usually found attached to another strand of DNA, forming a double stranded molecule. The bases on each strand bond to form a pair. This pairing follows a strict rule: *A* always pairs with *T*, and *C* always pairs with *G* (this is what Chargaff saw). We call this *complementary base pairing*. When the strands of DNA come together to form a double strand, the structure twists around itself, creating a double helix (see Figure 5.2). By knowing the *sequence* (arrangements of nucleotides) of one strand, the sequence of the second strand can be determined. It is this sequence that determines the structure and function of the cell and the organism.

The base pairs are held together by *hydrogen bonds*, weak bonds that form between hydrogens and oxygens or hydrogens and nitrogens. The G-C base pairs form 3

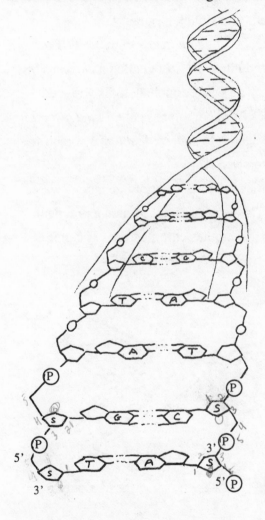

Figure 5.2: The structure of DNA. S: sugar; P: phosphate; A, C, G and T: nitrogenous bases

hydrogen bonds while the A-T base pairs form only 2. This makes the G-C pairs inherently stronger and more stable.

Another interesting feature of the double helix is that, in order for the bases to pair correctly, the two strands of DNA must run in opposite directions, or in an antiparallel fashion. This means that the 5' end of one strand pairs with the 3' end of the other strand (see Figure 5.2).

D. Chromosome Structure

Before going any further, let's look at the structure of the DNA as it exists in a cell. If you could remove the DNA from one of your cells and stretch it out, it would be approximately one meter long. How can so much DNA fit into a microscopic cell? The answer is in the packaging. DNA is highly organized into a structure called a *chromosome*. The chromosome is made up of DNA and proteins. The DNA double helix is wrapped around proteins known as *histones*, and the histones form complexes called *nucleosomes* (see Figure 5.3). The nucleosomes are further packaged into *supercoiled loops* sometimes called *solinoids*. These are packaged into chromosomes.

Human cells contain 23 pairs of chromosomes (46 total). Certain genetic diseases can be diagnosed by examining the chromosome. This is what is done when a pregnant woman has an amniocentesis. The field of biology that studies chromosomes is called *cytogenetics*.

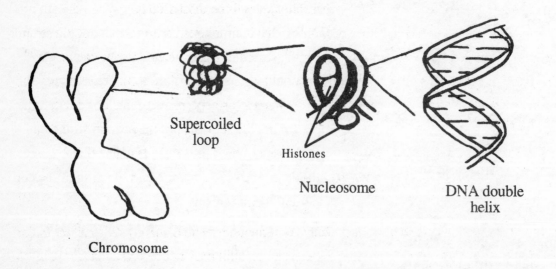

Supercoiled
loop

Histones

Nucleosome

DNA double
helix

Chromosome

Figure 5.3: Levels of DNA packaging

E. RNA Structure

Although we will discuss its function in the next chapter, this is an opportune time to examine the structure of *RNA (ribonucleic acid),* a molecule closely related to DNA. RNA is also a polymer of nucleotides, but differs from DNA in three major respects:

- RNA is usually single stranded, meaning it is not usually found base paired with another RNA molecule;

- the sugar in an RNA nucleotide is *ribose*, not deoxyribose. The difference is found on the 2' carbon of the sugar: ribose has an OH group attached while deoxyribose has only an H;

- a nitrogenous base called *uracil (U)* substitutes for thymine (T) in RNA. Uracil is similar in structure to thymine, and will base pair with adenine (this will become important when we discuss transcription and translation).

F. Replication

When a cell divides, the new cell (or *daughter* cell) must receive the same genetic information as the original cell, or the daughter cell will not function correctly. Therefore, before a cell divides, the DNA must be copied, or *replicated*, faithfully. It must also be transferred to the new cell. This entire process is known as *mitosis* and will be addressed in Chapter 12. The details of how DNA is replicated will be discussed here.

The beauty of the structure of DNA is that it simplifies its own replication. Due to the base pairing rules, each strand of the helix serves as a template to make a new strand. The copy is the complement of the template, and is identical to the strand originally bound to the template. This type of replication is referred to as *semiconservative*. Let's consider the details.

G. The Replication Machinery

One of the most important concepts to remember, which will come up again in the next chapter, is that polymers of nucleotides can be built only in one direction, in the 5' to 3' direction. The phosphate from one nucleotide binds to the 3' carbon of the sugar in the preceding nucleotide (refer to Figure 5.2). The process can never occur in reverse.

Before the DNA can be replicated, the two strands must dissociate (this is sometimes referred to as unzipping, as the DNA double helix resembles a zipper). The physical point at which the DNA is unzipped is referred to as the *replication fork* (see Figure 5.4).

The main enzyme involved in replication is called *DNA polymerase*. It binds to each single stranded DNA chain and builds a complementary strand by reading the template strand. We will now examine some of the details of this process.

H. Leading and Lagging Strand Synthesis

Since DNA is synthesized from 5' to 3', the template DNA must be read from 3' to 5' (remember the antiparallel structure of the double helix). This causes a problem at the replication fork: one strand can be copied *continuously* as the fork extends, but the other strand must be copied *discontinuously*. This discontinuous replication occurs in the following manner (see Figure 5.4):

1. An RNA *primer* (a short stretch of nucleotides) attaches to one strand via complementary base pairing. The primer is synthesized by a *primase* enzyme.

2. The DNA polymerase begins synthesizing a new, complementary strand in the 5' to 3' direction. The strands made between RNA primers are known as *Okazaki fragments*.

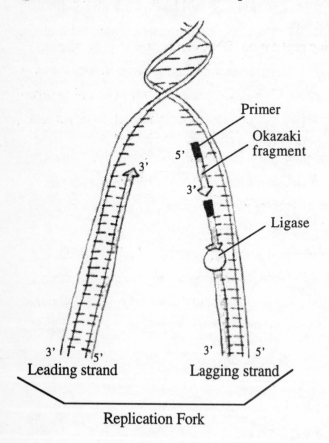

Figure 5.4: DNA replication

3. The primers are degraded and the Okazaki fragments are linked together by the enzyme *DNA ligase*.

The strand that is synthesized continuously is called the *leading strand*. The other strand, synthesized discontinuously, is referred to as the *lagging strand*.

I.   Proofreading and Repair

Everyone makes mistakes, and so does DNA polymerase. When this enzyme puts the wrong nucleotide into the growing chain, the result is a *mutation* which changes the genetic make up of an organism. Therefore, mistakes cannot be tolerated.

Fortunately, DNA polymerase has another ability besides synthesizing DNA strands: it also proofreads its work. If an error is detected, the enzyme cuts out the incorrect nucleotide and replaces it with the correct one.

In addition to random errors during replication, DNA can be mutated by other factors, such as UV light and cancer causing agents (*carcinogens*). If these mutations are not fixed, the function of the cell will be altered. This may cause the cell to die, or to grow in an unregulated fashion (cancer). Many repair mechanisms exist in the cell to detect and correct mutations, and more often than not they work just fine.

Chapter 5 Problems

Passage 5.1 (Questions 1-4)

Since only four types of nucleotides (adenine, guanine, cytosine and thymine) make up DNA, many scientists were skeptical that this was the hereditary molecule of life. Most believed proteins, with their building blocks of 20 amino acids, provided the complexity necessary to carry the genetic information.

In 1952, Alfred Hershey and Martha Chase designed an experiment to determine whether DNA or protein was the genetic material. They used a *bacteriophage* (a virus that infects bacteria) called T2. This bacteriophage was only composed of proteins and DNA. A short time after infecting a bacterial cell, the cell would *lyse* (break open) and release new T2 particles. T2 reprogrammed the cell to make more phage, but did it use DNA or proteins?

Hershey and Chase infected bacteria with T2 phage in growth medium containing radioactive sulfur (which labels proteins) and radioactive phosphate (which labels DNA). The resulting radioactive phages were then incubated with nonradioactive bacteria and allowed to infect these cells. After a short time, the mixture was placed in a blender to shake loose any phage particles remaining outside of or attached to the bacteria. The mixture was then centrifuged: bacterial cells would form a *pellet* at the bottom of the tube while any phage outside the cell would remain in the liquid portion (the *supernatant*). The radioactivity in each sample was measured.

1. Radioactive sulfur was found almost exclusively in the supernatant fraction, while the radioactive phosphate was found in the pellet fraction. This indicated:
   A. phage protein entered the cell, but the DNA did not.
   B. phage DNA entered the cell, but protein did not.
   C. both protein and DNA entered the cell.
   D. the phage did not infect the bacterial cell.

2. If the bacterial pellet were incubated in an appropriate growth medium, what would most likely occur?
   A. No phage would be produced as the protein coat was removed.
   B. Bacteria would survive as there is no proof they were infected with phage.
   C. Phage should be produced and kill the cells.
   D. The radioactive phosphate would kill the cells immediately.

3. A possible alternative to the blender technique used in this experiment would be:

   A. add a competitive inhibitor to the bacteria before adding phage.

   B. break apart the cell membranes with a strong detergent.

   C. incubate bacteria with a mutant phage that could not bind to the cells.

   D. shake the cell/phage mixture vigorously.

4. A modern experiment that confirms this experiment would be:

   A. injecting DNA into a cell which causes the cell to produce and enzyme it never had before.

   B. fertilizing an egg with a sperm in vitro.

   C. prescribing enzyme pills to help cystic fibrosis patients with digestion.

   D. consuming radioactive barium to view internal organs with X-rays.

Passage 5.2 (Questions 5-8)

The Watson and Crick model of the structure of DNA eloquently suggested the method of DNA replication. The double helical nature, and the complementary base pairing, implied that one strand of DNA provided the information for making the other strand.

Once the strands of DNA separated, each would be used as a template to make a new, complementary strand. Therefore, the two resulting strands of DNA would contain both an old strand and a new strand. This is known as the *semiconservative* theory of replication. The *conservative* theory stated that one double helix would contain only the newly synthesized DNA while the other would contain only the original strands.

In 1958, Matthew Meselson and Franklin Stahl confirmed the semiconcervative model. They grew the bacterium *E. coli* for many generations in a heavy isotope of nitrogen, ^{15}N. The isotope was incorporated into the DNA.

The bacteria were then placed in medium that contained only the light isotope of nitrogen, ^{14}N. The bacteria were sampled over a period of time. Their DNA was extracted and subjected to centrifugation techniques, which would separate the DNA based on density.

DNA containing solely ^{15}N was "heavy" whereas DNA containing solely ^{14}N was "light". After one round of division in the medium containing ^{14}N, all the DNA was found to be intermediate insize, between the light and heavy types.

This "intermediate" DNA was further analyzed. The hydrogen bonds between the base pairs were broken so the DNA was single stranded. These strands were then centrifuged. Half of the single stranded DNA was in the heavy form, and half was in the light form.

5. If the replication theory suggested by Watson and Crick's model was correct, then the density of the double stranded DNA after 2 rounds of replication in ^{14}N medium would be:
   A. half heavy, half light
   B. half heavy, half intermediate
   C. half intermediate, half light
   D. all intermediate

6. ^{14}N and ^{15}N were good choices as isotopes because they would be incorporated into the DNA via:
   I. the deoxyribose sugar
   II. the phosphate group
   III. the bases

   A. I only
   B. II only
   C. III only
   D. I and III

7. If DNA replication was conservative, after 1 round of replication in ^{14}N, the density of the double stranded DNA would be:
   A. all intermediate
   B. all heavy
   C. half intermediate, half heavy
   D. half heavy, half light

8. In this experiment, the Okazaki fragments would contain:
   A. only ^{14}N
   B. only ^{15}N
   C. neither ^{14}N nor ^{15}N
   D. both ^{14}N and ^{15}N

Questions 9 - 11 are independent of any passage and independent of each other.

---

9. Heat is often used to separate or denature double stranded DNA into single stranded DNA by breaking the hydrogen bonds between base pairs. Which of the following statements is true?
   A. G-C base pairs would require higher temperatures to break than A-T base pairs.
   B. A-T base pairs would require higher temperatures to break than G-C base pairs.
   C. All long DNA chains should denature at the same temperature.
   D. DNA-DNA double strands would require higher temperatures to denature that DNA-RNA double strands containing the same sequence.

10. Part of the process of purifying DNA from isolated chromosomes must involve:
    A. adding DNase, an enzyme that breaks apart DNA.
    B. adding proteases, enzymes that break apart proteins.
    C. adding RNase, an enzyme that breaks apart RNA.
    D. adding detergents, chemicals that break apart lipids.

11. An RNA molecule was synthesized to complementary base pair with a DNA molecule. The sequence of the DNA was: 5' ATCCGCTAAG 3'. The RNA sequence should be:
    A. 5' CUUAGCGGAU 3'
    B. 5' UAGGCGAUUC 3'
    C. 5' CTTAGCGGAT 3'
    D. 5' TAGGCGATTC 3'

Chapter 6
Transcription and Translation

A. Introduction

Every cell in an organism contains the same DNA. In multicellular organisms, cells often have different structures and perform different functions. Think about humans: we have heart cells and liver cells, skin cells and bone cells, nerve cells and muscle cells. But how can cells be so different when they contain the same genetic information?

The answer lies in how each cell uses the information. Although they contain the same blueprint, each cell in your body only uses part of the DNA. It's like two people who have access to the Internet. They both have the same information at hand, but they will probably use it differently.

This chapter addresses how genetic information can be transmitted from a stored source (the DNA) into a functional entity (protein). This procedure is traditionally known as the *Central Dogma* (see Figure 6.1) and details the transmission of the message from DNA into RNA into proteins via the processes of *transcription* and *translation*. The process of translation is also known as *protein synthesis*.

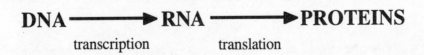

Figure 6.1: The Central Dogma

B. Transcription

Imagine you own a car factory, and there is only one set of blueprints on how to make cars. Many need to see the blueprints- the engineers, the designers, the assembly line foremen. You can't entrust the blueprints, the only set, to everyone who needs them. So what do you do? You make copies of the instructions. This way, everyone has their own set and can complete whatever task they need to.

This is analogous to how a cell works. Instead of directly using its only set of information (the DNA), the cell makes copies of it, in the form of RNA. This is known as *transcription*.

C. The Classes of RNA

RNA molecules fall into one of three classes: *ribosomal RNA (rRNA)*, *transfer RNA (tRNA)* and *messenger RNA (mRNA)*. rRNA and tRNA are involved in the process of translation, and we will discuss them in more detail later. In transcription, mRNA is made and carries the instructions for building proteins.

Within the DNA are discrete regions, called *genes*, which instruct the cell how to make proteins. It is the expression of these regions, which begins with the process of transcription, that determines the functions of cells. When genes are turned on or off they regulate the function of the cell, and, ultimately, the organism.

D. The Synthesis of RNA

The synthesis of RNA is similar to DNA replication (see Chapter 5). The template DNA strand is denatured and an RNA copy complementary to the template is synthesized. The same base pairing rules apply (except that *U* substitutes for *T* in the RNA molecule). Transcription is similar to replication in that it must proceed (the RNA must be built) in the 5' to 3' direction. Three major differences distinguish transcription from replication:

- ◆ only one stretch of DNA (the gene) is copied in transcription, unlike the entire DNA molecule in replication. Also, only one strand of the DNA is copied, not both;

- ◆ the resulting copy of RNA is single stranded, not double stranded as in replication;

♦ the enzyme responsible for making RNA is called *RNA polymerase*.

The transcription of mRNA begins when RNA polymerase binds to a specific sequence of nucleotides just in front of the gene, called the *promoter* . The enzyme then begins making an RNA copy of the DNA template, and continues until it reaches a stop sequence at the end of the gene. The RNA polymerase then releases the transcript (see Figure 6.2).

At this point, the RNA is technically known as *pre-mRNA*. All transcripts go through further processing before being translated.

E. Processing the RNA Transcript

Before the pre-mRNA leaves the nucleus to be translated, three additional events occur (see Figure 6.2):

1. A *5' cap* is added. This is a special nucleotide which is added to the 5' end of the message. It contains a methyl group and a phosphate group. The function of the cap is to help regulate translation.

2. A *poly A tail* is attached to the 3' end. This long string of 100-200 adenine nucleotides helps to regulate the degradation of the transcript after it leaves the nucleus.

3. The transcript is *spliced*. In eukaryotic genes, the coding regions of the DNA (*exons*) are interspersed with noncoding regions (*introns*). After the gene is transcribed, the introns are cut, or *spliced*, from the pre-mRNA so they never are translated. Why does the DNA contain these sequences if they ultimately do not code for the final protein product? It turns out that the presence of introns in the pre-mRNA is necessary for transport of the message out of the nucleus (the splicing machinery appears to be coupled with transport). In addition, *alternative splicing* can occur, which results in some exons being removed from the message. Thus, different messages can be made and, ultimately, different proteins can be coded for by the same gene. It is also believed introns play a role in evolution, allowing different regions of genes (i.e. the exons) to be rearranged, leading to new proteins.

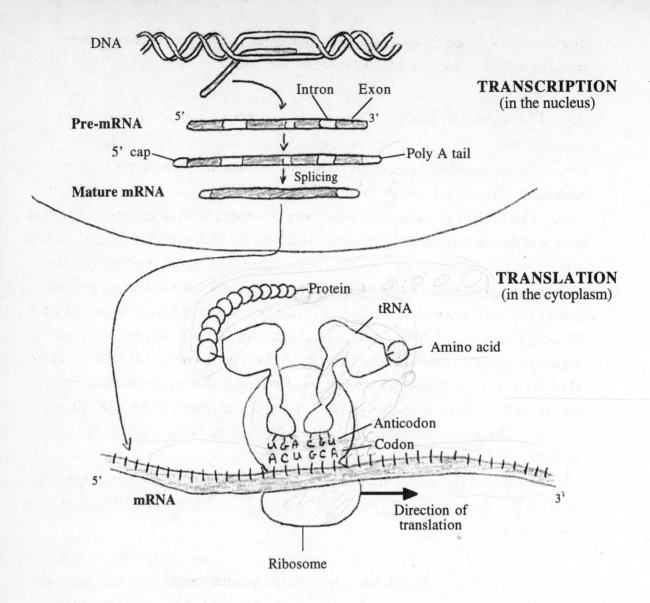

Figure 6.2: Transcription and translation

Once the fully processed mRNA (now called the *mature mRNA*) has been transported out of the nucleus and into the cytoplasm, it can be translated into a protein.

F. Translation

Once the mRNA has been transcribed and processed, the message can now be read and interpreted by the cell. *Translation* is the process of making a polypeptide chain based on the instructions in the mRNA. We use the term polypeptide here to denote that not all functional proteins are encoded by a single gene (see Chapter 2). Many proteins have subunits, each encoded by a different gene.

G. The Genetic Code

To communicate the message, the "words" of the mRNA must be read and understood. These words specify the amino acid that must be placed into the polypeptide chain. If we think of the nucleotides as the "letters" in the alphabet of the genetic code, then groups of those letters make up the words. As it turns out, each word in the mRNA is three letters, or nucleotides, long and is called a *codon*. Since there are only four letters in the alphabet, and each word contains three letters, there are only 4 X 4 X 4, or 64, possible words. The deciphering of the words is called the *genetic code* and is shown in Figure 6.3. By using this chart, an mRNA sequence can be translated. To use this chart, you must begin with the first nucleotide in the codon and find it's symbol on the left hand side of the chart (the first, or 5', position). Then find the second position from the top of the chart, and the third nucleotide from the right hand side (or 3' end). Now find where all three intersect in the interior of the chart. This is the amino acid the codon specifies. For example, the codon UUG encodes the amino acid leucine.

Only 20 amino acids are specified by the genetic code, yet 64 different codons are possible. How, exactly, is this code used by the cell? There are three interesting answers to this question:

♦ Three codons, UAA, UAG, and UGA do not specify any amino acids, but rather signal the end of the message. These are often referred to as *stop* or *termination* codons.

♦ Many amino acids are specified by more than one codon. We call this *redundancy*. For example, ACA, ACG, ACU, and ACC all code for the amino acid threonine. You should also note that, in each of these codons, the first two nucleotides are A and C. It doesn't matter what the nucleotide in the third position is. We call this the *wobble* effect.

♦ One codon, AUG, specifies the amino acid methionine. However, it also signals the start of translation for all mRNA molecules. Therefore, all polypeptide chains begin with methionine.

SECOND POSITION

		U	C	A	G	
F I R S T P O S I T I O N (5')	**U**	phenylalanine phenylalanine leucine leucine	serine serine serine serine	tyrosine tyrosine stop stop	cysteine cysteine stop tryptophan	**U** **C** **A** **G**
	C	leucine leucine leucine leucine	proline proline proline proline	histidine histidine glutamine glutamine	arginine arginine arginine arginine	**U** **C** **A** **G**
	A	isoleucine isoleucine isoleucine methionine (start)	threonine threonine threonine threonine	asparagine asparagine lysine lysine	serine serine arginine arginine	**U** **C** **A** **G**
	G	valine valine valine valine	alanine alanine alanine alanine	aspartate aspartate glutamate glutamate	glycine glycine glycine glycine	**U** **C** **A** **G**

T H I R D P O S I T I O N (3')

Figure 6.3: The Genetic Code.

H. Translating the Message

The process of translation involves three distinct steps, all of which occur in the cytoplasm (see Figure 6.2).

1. *initiation*: The mRNA binds to the *ribosome*, a molecular machine made up of rRNA and proteins. The ribosome binds at the beginning of the message.
2. *elongation*: The ribosome helps tRNA molecules bind to the mRNA. Each tRNA has two different regions. One region, called the *anticodon*, contains three nucleotides that bind to the codon in the mRNA transcript via complementary base pairing. The other region has a specific amino acid

attached to it. Once the correct tRNA binds with the mRNA, the amino acid on the tRNA is linked to the other amino acids in the growing chain by the ribosome. This results in the formation of a *peptide bond*. Then the tRNA is released and the ribosome moves down the mRNA chain to the next codon. The tRNA is "recharged" with another amino acid by the enzyme *peptidyl transferase*, so it can be used again and again.

3. *termination*: When the ribosome encounters a stop codon, it detaches from the mRNA chain and the polypeptide is released.

Most proteins are further processed before they can function in the cell. This processing may occur in the *endoplasmic reticulum* or in the *Golgi* (see Chapter 10). Proteins are often *phosophorylated* by specific enzymes in the cytoplasm. In addition, most proteins are *cleaved*, or cut, at the beginning of the polypeptide, which removes the initial methionine and other amino acids. So, although every mRNA codes for methionine as the first amino acid, few mature proteins retain this feature.

I. Mutations

Mutations, or changes in the DNA sequence, will often lead to changes in the amino acid sequence of the resulting polypeptide. If the structure of the protein changes, then the function will also change.

Mutations can come from several sources, including environmental mutagens and replication errors. In colloquial terms, mutations are not considered good. However, not all changes are harmful. Some may be neutral, while others may be beneficial. It is these beneficial mutations that can lead to evolution of species (see Chapter 20).

Mutations fall into three main categories (see Figure 6.4):

♦ *base pair substitutions*: When a gene is altered in one nucleotide in the sequence, then only one amino acid in the protein may be altered (but remember the degeneracy of the code and the wobble rules: a nucleotide change may not result in a change in the amino acid). This single amino acid difference may result in a fatal disease, alter the function of the protein (thus creating a new variation or trait: see Chapter 19), or it may not affect the function of the protein at all. However, if a codon specifying an amino acid is changed to a termination codon, the polypeptide will not be translated beyond that point. This truncated transcript will, in all likelihood, not function properly.

♦ *frame shift mutations*: If one or two nucleotides are either added to or deleted from the DNA sequence, the rest of the transcript will be affected as the codons will be shifted. The resulting polypeptide will have the incorrect amino acid sequence from the point of the mutation, and hence it will have a different function.

♦ *transposable element:* Often referred to as "jumping genes," these pieces of DNA can insert themselves into genes and thereby disrupt the sequence and expression of the gene.

Original sequence:

DNA: 5' A T C C C C A G G C C T A T A ....3'
Protein: isoleucine---proline-----arginine----proline----isoleucine..........

Base pair substitution:

DNA: 5' A T C C C C T G G C C T A T A ....3'
Protein: isoleucine---proline--*tryptophan*----proline----isoleucine..........

**Frame shift
(by addition of a nucleotide):**

DNA: 5' A T C T C C C A G G C C T A T A .....3'
Protein: isoleucine---*serine------leucine-----alanine-----tyrosine*---.............

Transposable Element:

DNA: 5' A T C C C C A G ████████ G C C T A T A...3'
Protein: isoleucine---proline------*translation disrupted*----------------------------

Figure 6.4: Examples of mutations

Chapter 6 Problems

Passage 6.1 (Questions 1-4)

A newly discovered genetic disease has been observed in several large families. Characteristics of the disease include mental retardation and coronary defects. Researchers studying this disease have isolated the responsible gene. The functional protein encoded by this gene consists of a single polypeptide chain. Experiments were done to determine the exact sequence of the gene with the following results:

Sequencing result 1: In a family with no history of the disease, the gene was found to be 849 nucleotides long, encoding a protein containing 283 amino acids. The mRNA sequence coding for the 22-26th amino acids is shown below:

5' AUUCCUAGUUGCACG 3'

Sequencing result 2: The genetic disease runs in family A. However, in this family, the disease is not severe and most affected individuals lead a fairly normal life. The mRNA transcribed form this gene is shown below (corresponding to the same region of the normal gene in result 1):

5' AUUCCUAGAUGCACG 3'

Sequencing result 3: The disease is also present in family B, but affected individuals are much worse off than those in family A. The gene was sequenced, and the corresponding mRNA is shown below (same region as sequence results 1 and 2):

5' AUUCCUAGUUGAACG 3'

1. What is the predicted amino acid sequence of the normal protein?
    A. isoleucine-proline-serine-cysteine-threonine
    B. phenylalanine-leucine-valine-alanine
    C. serine-stop-leucine-histidine
    D. serine-stop

2. The mutation in family A (sequencing result 2) will cause which of the following results?
    A. A protein will not be made.
    B. There will be a single amino acid change in the protein.
    C. The heart in an individual with the mutation will not develop correctly.
    D. There will be a change in the quaternary structure of the protein.

3. The disease in family B (sequencing result 3) is probably more severe than in family A because:
   A. there is a slight but significant change in the amino acid sequence.
   B. a frame shift mutation caused the amino acid sequence of the protein to be incorrect from the point of mutation on.
   C. a termination codon caused the truncation of the protein, preventing it from functioning.
   D. a point mutation altered a critical amino acid.

4. An *in vitro* transcription/translation system was set up to express the isolated genes. Which alteration in the system would allow the gene from family A to be translated into a fully functional protein?
   A. Include a ribosome that would not recognize the codon AGA.
   B. Use a tRNA with the anticodon UCU that carries the amino acid serine.
   C. Replace the normal splicing machinery with one that will remove the incorrect codon.
   D. Substitute the normal RNA polymerase with one that randomly makes mistakes to correct the mutation.

Questions 5-7 are independent of any passage and independent of each other.

5. Which of the following mRNA sequences encode the same protein?

   I.   5' UUAAGAUCC 3'
   II. 5' UUGCGUUCU 3'
   III. 5' CUGCGGAGU 3'

   A. I and II
   B. II and III
   C. I and III
   D. I, II and III

6. Due to a problem in the transcription machinery of a cell, an mRNA transcript does not have a poly A tail attached. This would probably result in:
   A. slower degradation of the transcript.
   B. unregulated translation of the protein.
   C. translation of a different polypeptide.
   D. deletion of the 5' cap.

7. The mRNA sequence of a particular gene is 5' AUGCCUAUCGUAACA 3'. What is the sequence of the template DNA from which this mRNA was copied?
   A. 5' ATGCCTATCGTAACA 3'

B. 5' TACGGATAGCATTGT 3'
C. 5' ACAATGCTATCCGTA 3'
D. 5' TCTTACGATAGGCAT 3'

should be G

4 4x4

SECTION 2
MICROBIOLOGY

Organisms are classified according to the structure and function of their cells and how those cells may be arranged into tissues, organs and systems. Most scientists use the following classification scheme, known as the *Five-Kingdom system:*

- *Monera* (bacteria)- *prokaryotes* (cells have no nucleus), single-celled;

- *Protists*- eukaryotes (cells have a nucleus), usually single-celled;

- *Fungi*- eukaryotes, mostly multicellular, *heterotrophs* (feed off of other organisms), digest food outside the cell;

- *Plantae*- eukaryotes, mostly multicellular, *autotrophs* (rely on photosynthesis for food production);

- *Animalia*- eukaryotes, multicellular, heterotrophs, ingest food.

Not included in this system are the viruses. Although they are not considered to be alive, viruses have much in common with living cells and depend on them to exist.

The next three sections of this book will explore the structure and function of different cells in detail. This section focuses on microscopic organisms (viruses, bacteria and fungi), often the cause of devastating diseases.

Humans and microbes have evolved together and now coexist in a variety of ways. This coexistence is known as *symbiosis* and can be classified based on the exact nature of the relationship:

- *mutualism:* the relationship is beneficial to both species

- *commensualism:* one species benefits but the other is unharmed

- *parasitism:* one species benefits and the other is harmed

Not all relationships are easy to classify into one particular category. In addition, changes in the environment will often alter the relationship. However, these labels help us to think about the nature and consequences of species interactions.

The transmission of microorganisms to humans (infection), and hence the mode of transmission of diseases, is classified into the following categories:

- *direct contact*: Sexually transmitted diseases, such as gonorrhea and syphilis, can only be transmitted through direct contact.

- *indirect contact*: Many microorganisms can be deposited on surfaces, including food, which can then be touched or consumed by other individuals. Two examples are typhoid and athlete's foot.

- *inhalation of airborne organisms*: Some organisms are spread through the air by coughing and sneezing, or can be inhaled from other sources and infect an individual via the respiratory tract. One example of this is the hanta virus.

- *transmission by biological vectors*: Some microorganisms can be carried by other organisms and, when a human is bitten, the microorganism will be transmitted to the individual. Lyme disease and rocky mountain spotted fever are bacterial diseases spread by ticks, and malaria is a parasite carried by mosquitoes.

Chapter 7
Viruses

A. Introduction

As we have already discussed, viruses are not considered to be alive. They cannot, on their own, perform many of the processes that are characteristic of life, including reproduction. Viruses absolutely require a host cell to propagate.

All viruses have the same basic structure. They are comprised of a protein coat surrounding the genetic material (which can be either DNA or RNA). In some viruses, an outer envelope is present, comprised of lipids and proteins derived from the cell membrane of their host.

Viruses come in a wide variety of shapes and sizes and have great capacity to mutate, especially in their protein coat and outer envelope. This often makes it difficult for the host organism to mount an immune response.

B. Life Cycle

Although viruses are not alive, they do have a "life cycle," a series of events that results in their reproduction. In general, viral replication involves five steps:

1. The virus attaches to a specific type of cell.
2. The genetic material enters the host cell.
3. The viral genetic material forces the host cell to produce copies of viral proteins and genetic material.
4. New viruses are released from the cell.

C. Bacteriophages

Bacteriophages (*phages* for short) are viruses that infect only bacteria. The most widely studied bacteriophages are *lambda* (λ) and the "T even" phages, *T2* and *T4*. The viruses contain DNA as their genetic material. The basic structure consists of the *head* and *tail* regions (see Figure 7.1). The head contains the protein coat (called a *capsid*) and the DNA. The tail is made up of a tube called a *sheath*, and, in the T even phages, several long *tail fibers* connected to the base of the sheath. The tail region attaches to a bacterial cell, and the DNA is injected into the cell through the sheath.

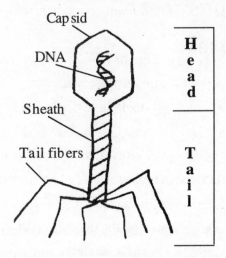

Figure 7.1: Structure of a bacteriophage

Once the DNA is inside the cell, two pathways are possible (λ can follow either pathway; the T even phages only follow the lytic cycle):

♦ *The lytic cycle*: The phage DNA instructs the cell to produce more viral particles. The cell *lyses*, or breaks, resulting in cell death. New bacteriophages are released and can infect other cells.

♦ *The lysogenic cycle*: Once infected, the virus enters a latent period, and the host cell is neither damaged nor destroyed. The phage DNA incorporates into the host cell chromosome and is replicated along with the host DNA. At this stage, the virus is technically called a *prophage*. The viral DNA, therefore, is passed on during cell division. Under appropriate conditions, the phage DNA will excise itself from the chromosome and enter the lytic cycle, thus destroying the host cell.

D. Animal Viruses

Animal viruses are very diverse in their size and structure, and the exact nature of their genetic material, which can be double or single stranded RNA or DNA. We will consider the *Human Immunodeficiency Virus* (*HIV*) as an example of an animal virus (see Figure 7.2).

The first stage of HIV infection involves attachment of the virus to the host cell. HIV has proteins on its outer membrane that recognize a specific protein (the *receptor*) on the host cell. After docking to the receptor, the virus enters the cell via endocytosis (see Chapter 11).

Some RNA viruses, such as HIV, must have their RNA copied into DNA for the cell to use it (these viruses are called *retroviruses*). This is accomplished by the viral enzyme *reverse transcriptase*. The DNA copy is made in the cytoplasm of the host cell and is then transported into the nucleus, where it can incorporate with the host DNA (the virus is now called a *provirus*, analogous to a prophage). Newly synthesized viral particles can be released via exocitosis. Therefore, the virus does not always kill the host cell.

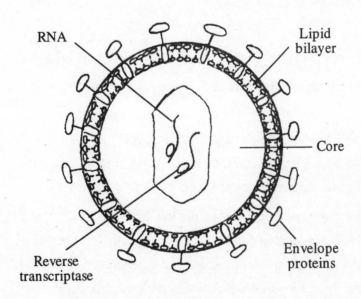

Figure 7.2: Structure of HIV

E. The Effect of HIV on Humans

HIV is such a deadly virus, and is so difficult to fight off, because it specifically targets cells in the immune system. The receptor for HIV is a protein called CD4, mostly found on helper T cells (see Chapter 15). In the progression of AIDS, the CD4 bearing cells are killed and the ability of the immune system to fight off other diseases and opportunistic infections is drastically reduced. Individuals do not die from AIDS, but rather from infections that can normally be fought off by a healthy immune system.

Chapter 7 Problems

Passage 7.1 (Questions 1-4)

The activity of bacteriophages is easily assayed. Bacteria are spread on a solid nutrient agar plate. Under appropriate growth conditions, the bacteria will form a cloudy layer completely covering the dish. In microbiology, this is called a *lawn*, as opposed to isolated spots, or *colonies*, of bacteria. If bacteriophages are introduced to the lawn of bacteria, the phages will infect single cells. Once the phages have reproduced, they will lyse the cells and the progeny phage will infect the surrounding bacterial cells. In a relatively short period of time, the phages will have lysed all the bacteria within a radius of the initial infection, causing a clear, circular spot to form in the lawn of bacteria. This is called a *plaque*.

A researcher working with bacteriophages set up the following experiment:

Condition 1:

Bacteria were spread on agar plates and incubated at 37^{0}C for 24 hours. A lawn was clearly visible and no plaques formed.

Condition 2:

The same strain of bacteria was mixed with a preparation of lambda bacteriophage. The mixture was spread on agar plates and incubated for 24 hours at 37^{0}C. An average of twenty plaques formed on the bacterial lawn on each plate.

Condition 3:

The same strain of bacteria was spread on agar plates and then exposed to UV light. After incubation at 37^{0}C for 24 hours, lawns grew and approximately fifty plaques formed on each plate.

1. After incubating the plates from condition 2 for an additional 5 days, the plates became totally clear. What is the most likely explanation for this result?
   A. Newly produced phages infected all bacteria on the dish, thus killing everything.
   B. The bacteria died off due to lack of nutrients.
   C. The bacteria protected themselves from the phages by slowing their growth.
   D. The phage forced all the bacteria to go into the lysogenic cycle and stop growing.

2. What happened in condition 3?
   A. Phage contaminated the dishes causing infection and lysis of the bacteria.
   B. The nutrients in the agar were insufficient to support bacterial growth.
   C. The bacteria were probably a lysogenic strain induced by UV light.
   D. The bacteria were not healthy and died off when exposed to UV light.

3. If a fourth experiment was done, where bacteria were mixed with lambda and exposed to UV light, what would you predict?
   A. The results would be similar to condition 2, with approximately 20 plaques per plate.
   B. The results would be similar to condition 3, with approximately 50 plaques per plate.
   C. There would be approximately 35 plaques per plate.
   D. There would be approximately 70 plaques per plate.

4. Before the phage life cycle was understood, researchers called the results from condition 3 *autolysis*. They thought an enzyme in the bacteria caused its own destruction and the destruction of surrounding cells. Which of the following would

lend support to the viral theory and help to disprove autolysis?
   A. Within a week, all the bacterial cells in condition 3 die.
   B. Viral particles can be purified from the plates in condition 3.
   C. Exposure of bacteria to X rays also causes plaques to form.
   D. With or without exposure to UV light, no bacteria grow at 4^0C.

Questions 5-6 are independent of any passage and independent of each other.

---

5. Strategies to fight the AIDS virus include drugs that mimic nucleotides, called *nucleotide analogs*. Reverse transcriptase incorporates these analogs into the newly formed viral DNA strand. The host cell cannot interpret the DNA correctly, so the virus does not propagate. Unfortunately, this therapy only works for a short time in infected individuals, probably because:
   A. the outer protein coat of the virus mutates so it is no longer recognized by the immune system.
   B. the patient's immune system starts to fight off the analog.
   C. the reverse transcriptase mutates to prevent incorporation of the analog.
   D. the viral DNA no longer incorporates into the host DNA.

6. Immunizations for viruses such as influenza and polio rely on the body's ability to recognize the virus and make antibodies against it. All of the following would allow for antibody production to prevent a virus from entering a cell except:

A. injection of a small amount of "live" virus.

B. injection of "heat killed" virus.

C. injection of part of the outer coat of the virus.

D. injection of viral reverse transcriptase.

Chapter 8
Bacteria

A. Introduction

The kingdom Monera is comprised of an amazingly diverse group of organisms, impossible to characterize using a few simple terms. In general, bacteria have the following features:

- all are *prokaryotes*, meaning they do not contain a nucleus;
- all have a single, circular chromosome, and some have *plasmids* (small circular pieces of extrachromosomal DNA);
- most have a cell wall made of *peptidoglycan*;
- most reproduce by *binary fission*.

We will highlight the major characteristics of this kingdom, but keep in mind how diverse it is. As researchers discover new species and find out more about the nature of the bacteria, we may soon see the kingdom Monera split into several different kingdoms.

B. Energy and Nutrition

Bacteria are classified into four groups according to their means of obtaining nutrients:

- The *photoautotrophs* make food via the process of *photosynthesis*, using sunlight and carbon dioxide. These include cyanobacteria.

♦ The *photoheterotrophs* use photosynthesis but cannot use carbon dioxide. These bacteria need to obtain carbon from another source.

♦ The *chemoautotrophs* gain energy from inorganic substances and get their carbon from carbon dioxide.

♦ The *chemoheterotrophs* obtain energy from inorganic substances but cannot use carbon dioxide as their carbon source. Most pathogens are chemoheterotrophs. This group is further broken down based on how carbon is obtained:

   • *parasites* obtain nutrients from a host.

   • *saprobes* obtain nutrients from wastes or the remains of other organisms.

C. Shapes

Bacteria usually take on one of three shapes (see Figure 8.1):

♦ *coccus* (plural: *cocci*): spheres.

   • *diplococci:* pairs of cocci

   • *streptococci*: chains of cocci

   • *staphylococci*: sheets or clusters of cocci

♦ *bacillus* (plural: *bacilli*): rod shaped

♦ *spiral*: twisted, or corkscrew shaped

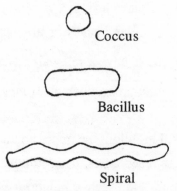

Coccus

Bacillus

Spiral

Figure 8.1: General shapes of bacteria

D. Structure

The generalized structure of a bacterial cell is illustrated in Figure 8.2. The main features include:

- ◆ *prokaryotic cell structure*: Although we have stressed that prokaryotes do not contain a nucleus, they also lack other internal structural compartments found in eukaryotic cells (see Chapter 10)

- ◆ *cell wall*: This surrounds the plasma membrane of the cell and helps to retain its shape. The cell wall consists of *peptidoglycan*, a substance composed of polysaccharides linked together via peptides. The exact structure of the cell wall can be determined via the *Gram staining test*. If the bacteria bind the dye used in the staining process, they are said to be *gram positive*, and contain one layer of peptidoglycans (*Staphylococcus* is one example). If cells exclude the dye, they are *gram negative* and the cell wall contains two layers: inner layer is made up of peptidoglycan, and the outer contains lipoproteins and lipopolysaccharides. *E. coli* is a gram negative bacterium.

- ◆ *glycocalyx*: The glycocalyx, which surrounds the cell wall, consists of a sticky mesh of polysaccharides, polypeptides, or both. If this structure is tightly organized, it forms a protective *capsule*. If it is loosely organized, it forms a *slime layer* that helps the bacterium attach to surfaces.

- ◆ *flagellum* (plural: *flagella*): Flagella are long, winding protein chains extruding from the bacterial cell. Flagella rotate to move the cell.

- ◆ *pilus* (plural: *pili*): Pili are short, filamentous proteins extending from the cell. They typically are present in large numbers. Pili play an important role in helping bacteria attach to surfaces or to other cells.

E. Reproduction

Most bacteria have the ability to reproduce very rapidly. For example, given the right nutrients and ambient temperature, *E. coli* can reproduce every 20 minutes. The method used to reproduce is called *binary fission* and begins with the replication of DNA. Once completed, the two DNA molecules move toward opposite ends of the cell. The cytoplasm then divides to produce two equivalent daughter cells.

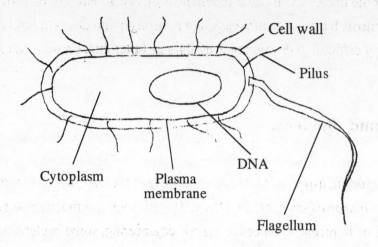

Figure 8.2: General structure of a bacterium

Another process that is often associated with reproduction is *conjugation*. Although this is not a form of reproduction *per se*, it can change the genetic make up of the bacterial cell. In conjugation, plasmid DNA is replicated and transferred from one bacterial cell to another via a special pilus, called a *conjugation tube* which connects the two cells. The plasmid carries bacterial genes that may alter the function of the recipient cell.

When the environmental conditions are not favorable for reproduction, some bacteria have the ability to form *spores*, which can preserve the cells. Once conditions improve, the bacterium begin to divide and multiply.

F. Antibiotics

Antibiotics are drugs that kill or prevent the growth of bacteria. These substances are produced naturally in many microorganisms and are used to fight off bacterial infections in humans. Keep in mind, however, that not all bacteria are harmful. Many species are beneficial and, if antibiotics are used to destroy pathogens, beneficial bacteria may also be killed.

The discovery and use of antibiotics has saved millions of lives, and the benefits of these drugs cannot be overstated. However, due to overperscription and misuse, many bacterial strains have become resistant to antibiotics. One example is the emergence of resistant strains for the bacteria that cause tuberculosis. Once all but purged form the human population, tuberculosis has mad a comeback and is stronger and deadlier than ever. It has become increasingly difficult to develop new antibiotics faster than bacteria can adapt to them.

G.   Ecology and Bacteria

Another important aspect of bacteria is their role in ecology. Bacteria account for a large portion of the *bioremediation* on the planet. They decompose much organic and inorganic matter. Due to recent advances in genetic engineering, some bacteria are being developed that can help clean up toxic substances. Most notably, many companies are designing bacteria that can "eat" oil, which can be used to clean up oil spills.

Chapter 8 Problems

Passage 8.1 (Questions 1-5)

Interestingly, many, if not most, bacterial cells can communicate with other cells in the same species. The bacteria secrete proteins, and, once enough bacteria are present, the concentration of the proteins increases. A high concentration often triggers the bacteria to turn on other proteins so the colony can perform a function. For example, individuals who have impaired immune systems or who have the genetic disease *cystic fibrosis* (*CF*) are often infected by the respiratory bacterium, *Pseudomonas aeruginosa*. Only when enough bacteria have accumulated, *P. aeruginosa* will produce an enzyme that degrades lung tissue which allows the bacteria to invade the blood stream.

Although many examples of this intraspecies communication exist, scientists wondered if different species can communicate with each other. To answer this question, researchers examined the relationship between *P. aeruginosa* and *Burkholderia cepacia*. *B. cepacia* causes fatal lung infections in CF patients, but only after these individuals have also been infected by *P. aeruginosa*.

Experiment 1:
P. aeruginosa were grown in an appropriate liquid medium the laboratory. The culture was centrifuged to remove the bacterial cells. A culture of *B. cepacia* was then grown in the medium. These bacteria increased production of molecules necessary for survival.

Experiment 2:
Mutant *P. aeruginosa* were grown in the laboratory in liquid medium. After centrifugation, the medium was used to incubate cultures of *B. cepacia*. Very few "survival molecules" were produced in the *B. cepacia*.

1. The experiments indicate:
   A. the two bacterial strains can communicate with each other.
   B. the *P. aeruginosa* bacteria help turn on production of survival molecules in *B. cepacia*.
   C. *B. cepacia* bacteria help turn on production of survival molecules in *P. aeruginosa*.
   D. no communication exists between the two bacterial strains.

2. The key to communication between these two bacteria is probably due to:

   A. a soluble protein secreted by *P. aeruginosa*.

   B. direct interaction between the two bacteria, possibly via cells of each species binding to each other.

   C. a soluble protein secreted by *B. cepacia*.

   D. unable to determine based on the available data.

3. A similar communication system exists between:

   I. nerve cells

   II. hormones and receptors

   III. photoreceptors in the eye

   A. I only

   B. II only

   C. I and II only

   D. III only

4. One important control that should be included in this experiment is:

   A. grow *P. aeruginosa* in medium used to grow *B. cepacia* first.

   B. infect mice with both species of bacteria.

   C. grow *B. cepacia* in medium that had not been used to grow *P. aeruginosa*

   D. no other control is necessary for this experiment.

5. The mutant *P. aeruginosa* used in Experiment 2 were most likely deficient in:

   A. replication

   B. transcription

   C. translation

   D. secretion

Questions 6-7 are independent any passage and independent of each other.

---

6. If the doubling time of a strain of bacteria is 30 minutes, how many cells would there be after 5 hours if the original culture had 1×10^5 cells?

   A. 5×10^5

   B. 3.2×10^6

   C. 1×10^8

   D. 1×10^{25}

7. Certain antibiotics work by inhibiting protein synthesis. However, proteins made before exposure to these drugs will continue to function until degraded by the cell. Which of the following would probably be true after adding these antibiotics to a culture of bacteria?

   A. DNA replication would not continue.

   B. Severely damaged flagella could not be repaired.

   C. New pili could be added to the bacteria.

   D. Damage to the glycocalyx would kill the bacterial cell.

Chapter 9
Fungi

A. Introduction

From the mushrooms growing on rotting logs to the yeast used in making bread and wine, fungi have a variety of morphologies and functions. Over 100,000 different species have been identified! As with other microorganisms, the fungi are diverse and we will only touch on a few common threads in this chapter.

B. Nutrition

Organisms are classified as fungi based largely on their mode of obtaining nutrition. Fungi are *heterotrophs* and need to obtain organic compounds from other organisms. Many fungi are classified as *saprobes*, feeding on dead organisms, thus facilitating their decay. Others obtain nutrition as *parasites*, feeding off of living tissue.

As fungi grow on organic material, they secrete digestive enzymes which break down proteins and other components outside the fungal cell. The fungi then absorb these digested products. This process is known as *extracellular digestion.*

C. Structure

Most fungi are multicellular and live on land. They have a special mesh called a *mycelium* that aids in food absorption (see Figure 9.1). The mycelium grows either on or in the food source. Inside the mycelium are special filaments, called *hyphae*, which contain nuclei. The walls of the hyphae are made of *chitin*, a hard, protective polysaccharide. The hyphae are sometimes divided into cells via structures called *septa*, although pores still allow movement of ribosomes, mitochondria and even nuclei through the hyphae. If no walls separate the hyphae, the organisms is classified as a *coenocytic* fungi.

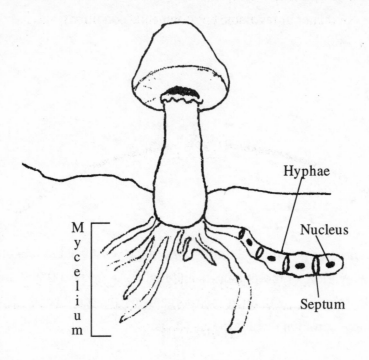

Figure 9.1: General structure of a fungus

D. Reproduction

Fungi have two stages of reproduction, as illustrated in Figure 9.2. Fungi reproduce either by asexual or sexual reproduction.

♦ *asexual reproduction:* Asexual reproduction is usually accomplished through the production of spores. In multicellular fungi, spores form on or in specialized hyphae called *sporangia*. In single-celled species, the spore can form directly in the parental cell. In other cases, no spores are produced at all. Instead, *budding*, or fragmentation, of the parent body occurs to form two cells.

- *sexual reproduction*: This type of reproduction is achieved thorough the production of gametes and spores. The gamete producing parts of the fungus, the *gametangia*, fuse to produce a diploid cell which then goes through meiosis to produce haploid spores. In general, sexual reproduction is less frequent than asexual reproduction and usually occurs only when fungi encounter unfavorable environmental conditions, such as starvation conditions.

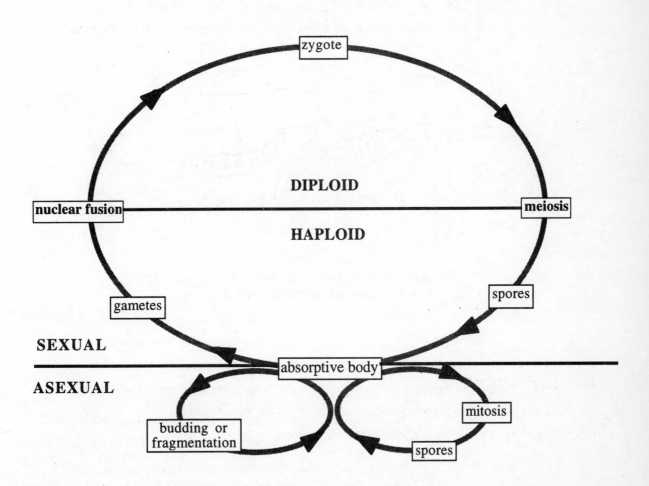

Figure 9.2: Life cycle of fungi

E. Classification

Fungi are classified based on their mode of reproduction:

♦ *Zygomycota*: The zygomycetes are coenocytic fungi that form thick walls around the diploid zygote. When hyphae from two different mating types come in contact with each other, they form gametes which then fuse to form a zygospore (see Figure 9.3). When nuclear fusion occurs, the diploid zygote goes through meiosis and produces haploid spores, which are then dispersed and can germinate to form new mycelium under appropriate conditions. The black bread mold *Rhizopus stolonifer* is an example of this group.

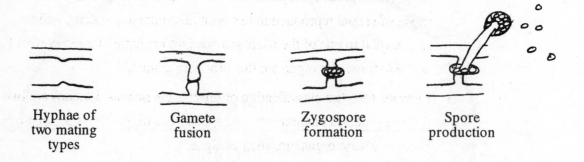

Hyphae of two mating types   Gamete fusion   Zygospore formation   Spore production

Figure 9.3: Zygomycota sexual reproduction

♦ *Ascomycota:* Also known as the sac fungi, ascomycota form saclike structures called *asci* (singular *ascus*) during sexual reproduction (see

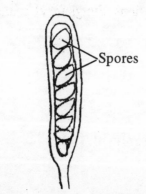

Spores

Figure 9.4). The asci produce haploid spores that are eventually dispersed. During asexual reproduction, spores, called *conidiospores*, are produced at the end of hyphae. Truffles, fermenting yeast (*Saccharomyces cerevisiae*) and the bread mold *Neurospora crassa* are examples of this group.

Figure 9.4: An ascus

- *Basidiomycota*: The fungi in this group form *basidia*, club shaped, spore producing structures (i.e. mushrooms). For this reason, the Basidiomycota are also called club fungi. This is the largest and most diverse group of the fungi. There is no asexual reproduction in these fungi. The hyphae of different mating types will conjugate to form mycelium containing two different nuclei. The mycelia produce basidia. Nuclear fusion occurs in the mushroom bodies to produce diploid cells that go through meiosis to produce haploid spores. These spores can then be dispersed to produce new mycelium.

- *Deuteromycota*: These fungi are classified as imperfect fungi, as they have no sexual reproduction phase that can be identified. In many cases, once a mode of sexual reproduction has been determined, a species will be reclassified to one of the other groups. One example of an imperfect fungus is *Penicillium*, the organism that produces penicillin.

- *Lichens*: One last classification of fungi is the lichens. Lichens are two different species that interact: one species is a fungus and the other a photosynthetic organism, such as algae.

F. Fungal diseases

Among diseases in humans caused by fungi are athlete's foot, ringworm, histoplasmosis (a respiratory disease), ergotism (from a fungus that infects rye: once the infected plant is consumed by humans, hysteria, hallucinations, convulsions, vomiting, diarrhea and dehydration can occur), and vaginal infections. Some fungi are beneficial to humans, producing antibiotics and other medications. Fungi are also important in many types of food production.

Chapter 9 Problems

Passage 9.1 (Questions 1-4)

Lichens are difficult to classify. They are an interaction between a fungus and a photosynthetic species, usually green or blue green algae. The species form a symbiosis, but there is a debate as to what the association between the two species really is. To answer this question, researchers designed a series of experiments. They took advantage of the photosynthetic abilities of an algae to examine the role of association with fungi in the production of sugar, a product of photosynthesis. The carbon in the sugar molecules comes from carbon dioxide (CO_2) in the air. Researchers exposed the algae to CO_2 molecules containing radioactive carbon. The following experiments were done and the data is graphed (note: all graphs use the same scale).

Experiment 1:

Algae were grown in culture in the lab and exposed to radioactive CO_2. The growth rates and production of sugar containing radioactive carbon are shown in the graphs below.

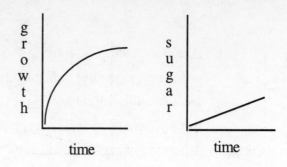

Experiment 2:

Algae were grown in the presence of fungi (therefore, this is lichen grown in the laboratory). The lichen was exposed to radioactive CO_2. The growth rate of the algae species and the production of sugar containing radioactive carbon are shown in the graphs below.

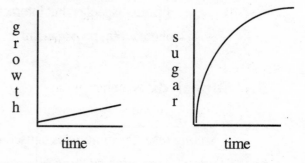

Experiment 3:

Lichen were grown under dehydration conditions while exposed to radioactive CO_2. The growth rate of the algae and the production of sugar containing radioactive carbon are shown in the graphs below.

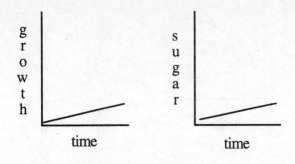

1. The conclusion that can be drawn
   from experiments 1 and 2 is
   A. the fungal species causes a
      decrease in sugar production in
      the algae.
   B. the fungal species causes an
      increase in sugar production in the
      algae.
   C. the algae cannot use the
      radioactive CO_2 efficiently to
      produce sugar.
   D. the algae grows better in the
      presence of the fungus.

2. The symbiotic relationship between
   the fungus and the algae is most likely
   a form of:

A. mutualism
B. parasitism
C. commensualism
D. cannot be determined

3. Sugar production in the lichen in
   dehydration conditions (experiment 3)
   indicates that
   A. there is reduced photosynthesis in
      the algae.
   B. there is reduced photosynthesis in
      the fungus.
   C. the fungi have been killed.
   D. there is a decomposition of the
      algae by the fungus.

4. This lichen would probably not be
   found in
   A. the tropics
   B. old growth forests
   C. suburban settings
   D. deserts

SECTION 3
EUKARYOTIC CELL BIOLOGY

Our discussion of cell biology must begin with two principles stated in *The Cell Theory*:

- ♦ The cell is the basic unit of life.
- ♦ New cells can only arise from preexisting cells.

In this section, we will explore the structure and function of eukaryotic cells, specifically animal cells, and how they reproduce. In many instances, cells will develop over time to change their structure and function. This will be addressed in Section IV.

It is important to understand that cells come in many different shapes and sizes. For example, sperm cells are basically DNA with a tail, muscle cells are filled with mitochondria (to supply energy for movement) and neurons have enormously long axons. The typical animal cell is 10-30 micrometers in diameter, whereas an egg cell is 100 micrometers, and the yolk of a chicken egg (which is one single cell!) is 3 cm. Although all these cells have different shapes, sizes and functions, they all have the same basic structure. In addition, with the exception of sperm and eggs, all cells reproduce in the same manner, via replication of the DNA and cytoplasmic division to produce two equal cells.

The next few chapters will discuss the structure and function of organelles and the cell membrane, and examine the process of mitosis.

Chapter 10
Cellular Organelles

A. Introduction

Organelles form separate compartments within the cell so various enzymatic reactions can occur in suitable environments. The barriers also prevent reactions within the cell from interfering with other cellular activities. Most organelles are membrane-bound sacs. Depending on the function of the cell, various organelles may be more or less prevalent. However, most animal cells contain all the organelles discussed in this chapter. Figure 10.1 is a schematic representation of a typical eukaryotic cell with the various organelles highlighted.

Although not necessarily considered an organelle, it should be noted that the cell is bounded by a lipid bilayer known as the *cell* or *plasma membrane*. It maintains an intricate relationship with organelles, and will be referred to in this chapter. It will be discussed in detail in Chapter 11.

B. The Nucleus

The most apparent function of the *nucleus* is to sequester the DNA from the enzymatic reactions occurring in the cytoplasm. However, many activities take place in the nucleus. It contains three separate structures:

- ◆ *nucleolus*: The nucleolus is a dense mass inside the nucleus. Ribosomal proteins and RNAs are assembled here.

- ◆ *nuclear envelope*: As stated above, organelles are bounded by membranes. The membrane surrounding the nucleus has been well studied. It consists of

99

two lipid bilayers, each similar to the cell membrane (see Chapter 11). This double membrane creates a barrier to water-soluble substances. *Pores* span both membranes and allow ions and small molecules to pass through. Large molecules are selectively transported across the membrane. The pores are responsible for transport both into and out of the nucleus. Ribosomes, the site of protein synthesis, are often found along the outer membrane, while chromosomes are attached to the inner membrane.

♦ *chromosomes*: Inside the nucleus is the DNA arranged in the structures called chromosomes (see Chapter 5). Chromosomes are made up of the DNA as well as proteins associated with organization, transcription, replication and repair.

C. The Endoplasmic Reticulum

The *endoplasmic reticulum* (*ER*) is a network of interconnecting tubes that begins at the nuclear envelope and runs out into the cytoplasm. Two types exist in the cell:

• *rough ER*: Ribosomes are attached to the cytoplasmic side of the ER. The rough ER often looks as though it is "stacked" in the cell. Polypeptides assembling on the ribosomes will be threaded into the ER if they contain a specific sequence of amino acids called a *signal sequence*. Once inside the ER, proteins become modified through the addition of oligosaccharides. Rough ER is very abundant in cells that secrete large amounts of proteins.

• *smooth ER*: Unlike the rough ER, the smooth ER is not studded with ribosomes. This organelle plays a role in lipid synthesis.

D.   Peroxisomes

Peroxisomes are sacs of enzymes. Fatty acids and amino acids are broken down here. Hydrogen peroxide (H_2O_2), produced as a byproduct from these reactions, is converted into H_2O and O_2 or various alcohols.

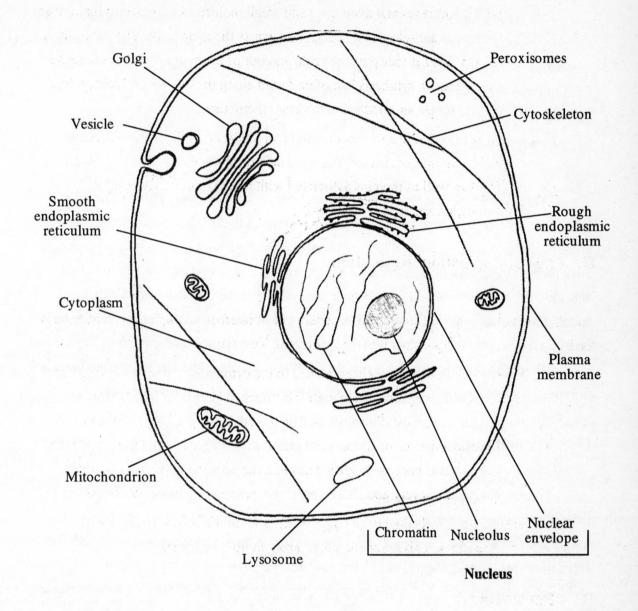

Figure 11.1: Typical eukaryotic animal cell

E.   The Golgi

The *Golgi* (or *Golgi bodies,* or *Golgi apparatus*) appear as "stacks of pancakes" in the cytoplasm. These organelles function in modifying lipids and proteins that are packaged into membrane bound *vesicles* for transport to specific locations in the cell. The vesicles form through the budding of the Golgi membrane.

F.   Lysosomes

One type of vesicle that buds from the Golgi is the *lysosome*. These organelles function in intracellular digestion. They contain enzymes that break down polysaccharides, proteins, nucleic acids and some lipids. Lysosomes can fuse with endocytotic vesicles that have formed from the cell membrane (see Chapter 11). These vesicles contain molecules, and sometimes cells, obtained from outside the cell. Once the lysosome fuses with an endocytotic vesicle, the digestive enzymes will break down the substances taken into the cell.

Sometimes the lysosomes digest the cell itself. For example, the tail on a tadpole is digested by lysosomes as part of the normal programmed development of a frog.

G.   Mitochondria

As we discussed in Chapter 4, ATP is the unit of energy in biological systems. This molecule is generated via the process of *respiration* in the *mitochondria*. Like the nucleus, mitochondria have two membranes (see Figure 10.2). The outer membrane is smooth and faces the cytoplasm. However, unlike the nucleus, the inner membrane is highly convoluted and forms "folds" in the interior of the organelle. These folds are called *cristae*. Two distinct compartments are bounded by the membranes: an outer compartment is formed between the two membranes, and an inner compartment (called the *matrix*) is bounded by the inner membrane. Most of the processes of respiration critical for the synthesis of ATP occur across the inner membrane, and therefore take place between the matrix and the outer compartment.

The structure of mitochondria is very similar to some bacteria. They contain their own circular DNA and divide on their own. It has been theorized that these organelles evolved from bacteria that were engulfed, but not digested, by other cells. This is known as the *endosymbionic hypothesis*.

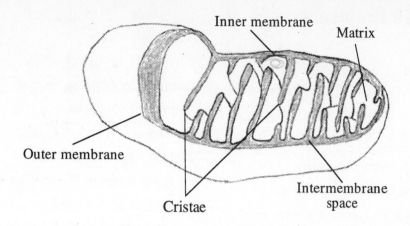

Figure 10.2: A mitochondrion

H. The Cytoskeleton

The cytoskeleton is not a membrane bound organelle, but instead consists of a meshwork of various filaments that extends from the cell membrane and provides the cell with organization, stability, shape and, in some cases, movement. Three main types of filaments make up the cytoskeleton, and each is composed of highly ordered protein subunits:

♦ *microtubules* : These structures are made up of *tubulin* subunits, arranged in parallel rows that form hollow tubes. Microtubules are critical in vesicle and organelle movement and in cell division.

♦ *microfilaments* : These structures differ in their subunits, but always contain the proteins *actin* and *myosin*. They are involved in cell movement.

♦ *intermediate filaments:* These cytoskeletal components differ in their proteins make up, depending on the type of filament, and most are cell specific. All intermediate filaments form structural meshworks in the cytoplasm or in the nuclear envelope. Researchers can usually determine the type of cell they are working with by identifying which types of intermediate filaments are present.

Chapter 10 Problems

Passage 10.1 (Questions 1-4)

Cells grown in culture are often used to investigate the role of organelles. As culture conditions can be easily manipulated, cells can be subjected to different chemicals and their responses studied and analyzed. In one such experiment, mouse cells were incubated in the presence of high concentrations of sucrose. The cells were examined under the microscope. Crystals of sucrose were found in the lysosomes of all the cells. When sucrose was depleted from the culture medium, the sucrose crystals in the lysosomes persisted for many days, but did not affect the growth of the cells. Eventually, the sucrose crystals disappeared. The rate of disappearance is shown in the graph below (note: all graphs are the same scale).

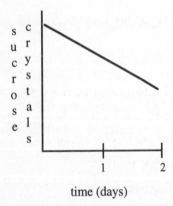

time (days)

Researchers performed two additional experiments:

Experiment 1:

Immediately after sucrose was removed from the culture medium, the enzyme *invertase* was added. Invertase catalyzes the cleavage of sucrose into monosaccharides. The cells were then examined for the presence of sucrose crystals. The results are shown below.

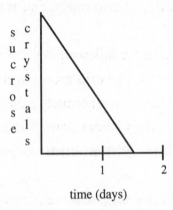

time (days)

Experiment 2:

Mouse cells grown in the presence of invertase (cell type A) were mixed with cells grown in the presence of sucrose (cell type B). A reagent that fuses cells was also added to the culture. After fusion, the cells (cell type AB) were grown in the absence of sucrose. The cells were then examined for the presence of sucrose crystals. The results are shown below.

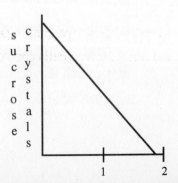

1. From the results in Experiment 1, what can you conclude about invertase?
   A. It irreversibly inhibits sucrose production.
   B. It catalyzed the break down of sucrose in the medium.
   C. It was internalized by the lysosomes.
   D. It changes the pH of the cytoplasm to catalyze sucrose.

2. Which of the following statements is true for mouse cells grown in culture?
   A. They do not normally have the ability to break down sucrose.
   B. They make invertase but only in low levels.
   C. Fusion with other cells reduces the ability of cells to produce invertase.
   D. High concentrations of sucrose are lethal.

3. Based on the results in Experiment 2, which of the following could be true?
   I. Invertase diffused from the lysosomes of cell type A into the lysosomes of cell type B.
   II. The lysosomes of cell type A fused with the lysosomes of cell type B.
   III. Invertase destroyed cell type B and only allowed cell type A to survive.

A. I only
B. II only
C. I and II only
D. III only

4. Another sugar, mannose, was added to mouse cells, and mannose crystals formed inside lysosomes. Similar to sucrose crystals, the mannose crystals disappeared in a few days after the sugar was removed from the medium. If invertase were added to the culture immediately after mannose was removed, what would you predict would happen?
   A. The mannose crystals would disappear in less than two days.
   B. The mannose crystals would disappear within a few days.
   C. Sucrose crystals would form.
   D. Mannose crystals would appear in the cytoplasm.

The following are independent of each other.

5. A cell is isolated that does not contain a nucleus. Which of the following organelles might it contain?
   A. mitochondria
   B. flagella
   C. Golgi
   D. endoplasmic reticulum

6. In eukaryotic cells, DNA replication
    takes place in
    I. the nucleus
    II. the cytoplasm
    III. the mitochondria

A. I only
B. II only
C. I and II only
D. I and III only

Chapter 11
Plasma Membrane and Transport

A. Introduction

One of the defining characteristics of life outlined in Chapter 1 was the need for every living thing to maintain *homeostasis*, the regulation of a specific internal environment regardless of external conditions. One way cells accomplish this is via a *plasma* or *cell membrane*. The membrane functions in two ways:

◆ it forms a barrier between the cell and its surroundings.

◆ it allows for transport of specific molecules and ions into and out of the cell.

The plasma membrane is the key to the survival of the cell and of the organism. In this chapter, we will investigate the structure of the membrane and consider how it functions to maintain homeostasis.

B. Structure

The cell membrane is made up of two different types of molecules, *lipids* and *proteins* (you may wish to review the basic structures of these molecules from Chapter 2). We will focus on the lipids in this section and discuss proteins later.

The cell membrane is composed mostly of phospholipids. Recall that phospholipids contain two regions; a polar head (comprised of a phosphate group) and a nonpolar tail (made up of two fatty acid chains). The head region is *hydrophilic* (water loving) and the tail is *hydrophobic* (water hating). This poses a problem for the molecule in the aqueous environment of the cell. The lipids solve this problem by forming a *lipid bilayer*: the hydrophobic tails associate to exclude water, while the hydrophilic heads are left exposed to the watery external and internal environments. (see Figure 11.1).

The plasma membrane also contains glycolipids and sterols (such as cholesterol). Proteins that span the membrane (*transmembrane proteins*) are responsible for transport of molecules and ions.

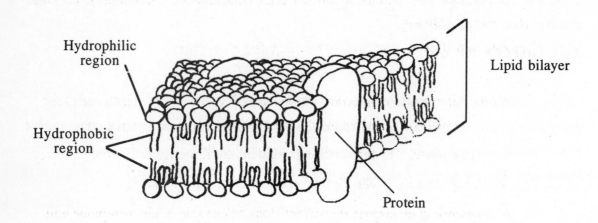

Hydrophilic region

Lipid bilayer

Hydrophobic region

Protein

Figure 11.1: Cross section of the plasma membrane

C. The Fluid Mosaic Model

Our understanding of the structure of the plasma membrane can best be described using the *Fluid Mosaic Model*. The model states that the membrane is not a static network of lipids and proteins, but rather a dynamic matrix that is constantly in motion. In other words, it is fluid. The molecules do not pack together to form a solid layer. Since different types of molecules (i.e. lipids and proteins) make up the membrane, it is said to be mosaic.

D.   Diffusion

Before we begin a discussion of transport, we must consider how molecules and ions move in a liquid. This process is called *diffusion.*

Molecules and ions dissolved in a liquid are called *solutes* and are constantly moving in a random fashion. If the solute is more highly concentrated in one area of the liquid, a *concentration gradient* is formed. Due to random movement, the solutes will move, or diffuse, down the concentration gradient: in other words, the molecules and ions will move from an area of high concentration to an area of low concentration. This will occur until the solute is evenly distributed throughout the liquid and equilibrium is achieved. The particles will continue to move, but the concentration will not change. This is called *dynamic equilibrium.*

The rate of diffusion is influenced by many factors, such as:

- *the "steepness" of the concentration gradient*: Steeper gradients will cause faster diffusion, and, as the gradient decreases, the diffusion slows.

- *temperature*: The higher the temperature, the faster the diffusion.

- *size of the solute*: Smaller molecules and ions move faster.

- *presence of an electrical gradient*: Ions on one side of the membrane will help attract solutes with the opposite charge, thereby increasing the steepness of the concentration gradient of the solute.

- *presence of a pressure gradient*: Pressure can increase the gradient of a solute.

Transport across membranes can occur by diffusion. Certain solutes that are small, nonpolar and "lippidy," such as O_2, can diffuses freely across the membrane. All other molecules cannot cross the cell membrane by diffusion, but can cross by the other methods discussed in this chapter. However, the principles of diffusion, especially the notion of concentration gradients, are crucial to most of these other methods of transport.

E.   Osmosis

Osmosis is closely related to diffusion. It is the diffusion of water across biological membranes. It may be easiest to understand this process if you keep in mind that water is not only a solvent, but also a molecule itself that can have a concentration gradient. As the concentration of solutes increase, the concentration of water decreases. In the cell, the concentration gradient of water is influenced by the total number of molecules of all solutes present on both sides of the membrane. The movement of water in response to this gradient is not referred as diffusion, but as osmosis.

The direction of water movement is influenced by *tonicity*, the relative concentration of solutes in two liquids. When solutes are in equal concentrations, the liquids are said to be *isotonic*, and there will be no net movement of water molecules. If the concentrations of solutes are not equal, water will move from the *hypotonic* solution (less solutes) to the *hypertonic* solution (more solutes). If the cell cannot adjust to the difference in solute concentrations between the cytoplasm and the external environment, the cell will burst (if placed in a hypotonic solution) or shrivel (if placed in a hypertonic solution).

A phenomenon related to osmosis is *bulk flow*, the movement of water unrelated to a membrane or concentration gradient. It can be due to many factors including pressure gradients, as seen in kidney cells.

F.   Selective Transport

Transmembrane proteins permit certain molecules to pass through the lipid bilayer. This type of transport is highly specific for molecules and ions Therefore, the cell needs many different kinds of transport proteins.

In general, all transport proteins function in a similar fashion. The molecule to be transported first binds to the protein. This causes the protein to change its shape. In essence, it "closes" behind the molecules and "opens" to the opposite side of the membrane (remember, molecules can be transported in either direction: from the inside out or from the outside in). This is often referred to as a *gated channel*. Once the protein has allowed the molecule to pass through the lipid bilayer, the molecule is released.

There are two types of selective transport (see Fig. 11.2):

♦ *passive transport* (or *facilitated diffusion*): Transmembrane proteins facilitate the diffusion of a solute down its concentration gradient. Remember our discussion earlier: this process will continue until an equilibrium is reached. However, this rarely happens. For example, once a molecule is transported into a cell, it is usually metabolized right away. Therefore, the concentration gradient does not change and the molecule will continue to diffuse into the cell.

♦ *active transport*: Molecules can be pumped across the cell membrane against their concentration gradient, i.e. from an area of low concentration to an area of high concentration. Since this is not the normal behavior for molecules, active transport requires energy, usually in the form of ATP. Once ATP binds, it alters the conformation of the transmembrane protein and the molecule can bind. The molecule is transported across the membrane and is released. The protein returns to its original conformation, preventing the molecule from making the return trip across the membrane.

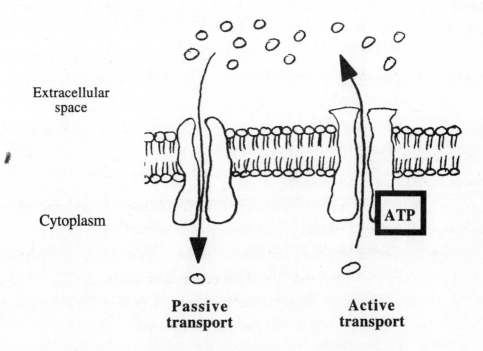

Figure 11.2: Selective Transport

G. Bulk Transport

Bulk transport is not used for selective transport of particular molecules but rather, as its name implies, for transporting large amounts of various molecules, and, in some cases, even whole cells. There are two main types of bulk transport (see Figure 11.3):

♦ *exocytosis*: Exocytosis is used to transport molecules out of the cell. In this process, cytoplasmic vesicles (see Chapter 10) move to the plasma membrane and fuse with it. The membrane from the vesicles become incorporated in the plasma membrane, and the contents of the vesicles are released to the external surroundings of the cell.

♦ *endocytosis*: The converse of exocytosis is endocytosis. In this process, the plasma membrane "sinks" inward and forms a vesicle around particles and fluids on the extracellular side of the membrane. The newly formed vesicle pinches off from the membrane. The contents are transported to various places into the cytoplasm and may be stored for later use. There are three types of endocytosis:

  • *pinocytosis*: This type of endocytosis refers to the flow of liquid droplets.

  • *receptor mediated endocytosis*: This type of transport involves molecules binding to specific receptors clustered at the cell surface. This triggers endocytosis of the molecules. As seen in electron micrographs, the receptors bunch up in the membrane as it sinks into the cytoplasm. Often these structures are called *coated pits*.

  • *phagocytosis*: Phagocytosis is usually found in free living cells, such as amoebas. However, it also occurs in multicellular organisms: the best example of this is white blood cells, such as macrophages, in the human immune system (see Chapter 15). In phagocytosis, the cell membrane wraps around an extracellular object, forming a large vesicle that usually fuses with lysosomes in the cytoplasm. The contents of the vesicle are then digested. Phagocytosis is distinguished from other types of endocytosis by the size and amount of material taken in, and the drastic movement and changes that occur in the cell to engulf the object.

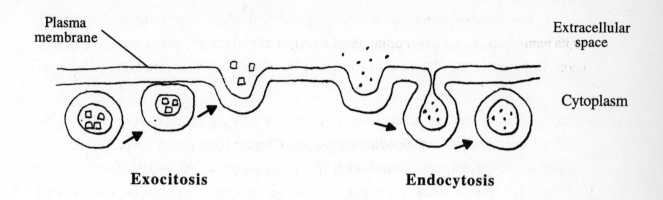

Figure 11.3: Bulk transport

Chapter 11 Problems

Passage 11.1 (Questions 1-4)

The *sodium-potassium (Na⁺/K⁺)* *pump* is a critical element for many processes of the cell. For example, it is responsible for a neuron's ability to transmit messages. The pump transports sodium out of the cell using energy from ATP (the extracellular matrix has a higher concentration of sodium than the intracellular space). The pump also imports potassium, which is more highly concentrated inside the cell than outside. The pump is an example of a *cotransport* *system*. Sodium binds to the transport protein and is exported. Once the sodium ion is released, a potassium ion binds and is transported into the cell (actually, for every three sodium ions pumped out of the cell, two potassium ions are pumped in). Thus, a sodium and potassium gradient are established and maintained across the membrane. Since the ions are being transported in opposite directions, this type of pump is called *antiport*.

The sodium gradient established by the Na⁺/K⁺ pump can be used in many ways. Another cotransport system, the *Na⁺/glucose pump*, is active in human gut epithelial cells, and results in the uptake of glucose. Due to its concentration gradient, sodium diffuses into the cells through the Na⁺/glucose pump and

transports glucose with it (this is called *symport*). The glucose is processed by the cells and can be used to generate energy.

1. The mechanism used by the Na⁺/K⁺ pump can best be described as
   A. bulk transport
   B. osmosis
   C. facilitated diffusion
   D. active transport

2. The mechanism used by the Na⁺/glucose pump can best be described as
   A. bulk transport
   B. osmosis
   C. facilitated diffusion
   D. active transport

3. If a sodium gradient is formed, whereby there is a vast excess of sodium outside the cell, which is the most likely result?
   A. An electrical gradient is also formed.
   B. A magnetic gradient is also formed.
   C. Other positively charged ions will enter the cell.
   D. Negatively charged ions will enter the cell.

4. A poison was found that prevents binding of sodium to the Na⁺/K⁺

pump. What would be the most likely consequence of this poison?

I. potassium would not be pumped into the cell

II. glucose would not be pumped into the cell

III. nerve impulses would not be transmitted

A. I only
B. III only
C. I and II
D. I, II and III

5. In cells where only the Na^+/K^+ pump and the $Na^+/$glucose pump were functional, and where there were high concentrations of glucose and potassium outside the cell, what would you expect to happen?

A. There would be a build up of sodium inside the cell.

B. There would be a build up of potassium inside the cell.

C. There would be an equilibrium of sodium inside and outside of the cell.

D. There would be an equilibrium of glucose inside and outside of the cell.

Questions 6-7 are independent of any passages and independent of each other.

6. A certain transmembrane protein has its amino terminus at the exterior of the cell, carboxy terminus in the cytoplasm and everything in between embedded in the membrane. Which of the following statements is true?

A. The amino terminus must be hydrophobic.

B. Much of the protein is hydrophobic.

C. The protein probably transports sodium.

D. The protein must have a neutral charge.

7. A single celled microorganism isolated from the Atlantic ocean was accidentally cultured in a medium formulated for fresh water microorganism. What probably happened to the organism?

A. The cell shriveled up and died due to exocitosis of salt.

B. The cell swelled and burst due to osmosis of water.

C. The cell died because the membrane transport proteins would not function properly in the new environment.

D. The cell would try to take up as much sodium as possible via endocytosis from the medium.

Chapter 12
Mitosis

A. Introduction

Reproduction is a crucial, and complex, process. As we have seen in Chapter 5, DNA has a method of reproducing itself, called replication. In Chapter 18, we will discuss the process of human reproduction. In this chapter, we will focus on the cellular level of reproduction: how eukaryotic cells divide.

On the cellular level, the parent cell needs to copy the DNA and give enough cytoplasmic components (enzymes, organelles, etc.) to the daughter cells to ensure their survival. There are two types of cellular division, *mitosis* and *meiosis*. Mitosis occurs in the body, or *somatic*, cells, and meiosis occurs in the reproductive, or *germ*, cells. Although the outcomes of these two processes are different, their mechanisms are very similar. Meiosis will be covered in Chapter 18, and mitosis will be discussed here.

B. The Cell Cycle

In the life of a cell, mitosis is only one phase in a cycle. All the phases that describe the activities of the cell are part of *the cell cycle* (see Figure 12.1). This cycle consists of:

- *G_1 (gap) phase*, the phase prior to DNA replication in which cellular activities occur.

- *S phase (synthesis)*, when the DNA replicates.

- *G_2, a second gap*, which occurs after S.

♦ *M phase (mitosis)*, when the cell divides.

G_1, S and G_2 are collectively known as *interphase*. Some cells, such as neurons, function but do not cycle and do not divide. They arrest at a stage in the cell cycle known as G_0.

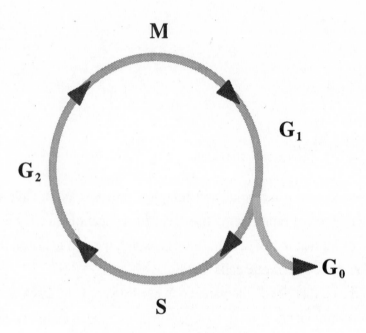

Figure 12.1: The Cell Cycle

The time it takes for a cell to go through the cell cycle is characteristic of the cell type. Check points within the cycle ensure that the cell is ready to continue on to the next phase. The cell will not be allowed to continue if certain events are not completed. For example, a check point in G_2 ensures that the cell is physically big enough to divide in M phase. If the cell has not grown to a critical size, the cell will be arrested in G_2 until it is ready to proceed. In many types of cancer, these check points are disabled, and cells divide in an uncontrolled fashion.

C. The Stages of Mitosis

Four distinct stages have traditionally been observed in the process of mitosis: *prophase, metaphase, anaphase* and *telophase*. An illustration of these stages is depicted in Figure 12.1, and a description of each follows.

D. Prophase

Perhaps the most striking event in prophase is the condensation of the chromosomes into thread like structures that are visible under the microscope. Recall that DNA replication has already taken place by this point in the cell cycle. However, the duplicated strands of DNA are still physically connected. At the chromosomal level, the duplicated strands (called *sister chromatids*) are attached at the region called the *centromere*. The *kinetochore* is associated with each sister chromatid at the centromere (see Figure 12.2).

During *spindle formation*, the microtubules in the cell disassemble and reassemble into the spindle, and the nucleus begins to break down. Once the nuclear envelope has disassembled, one end of each microtubule attaches to a kinetochore while the other end connects to one of two areas in the cell called the *microtubule organizing centers (MTOC)* The MTOC are located on opposite sides, or *poles*, of the cell. In some cells, a barrel shaped structure called a *centriole* is associated with each MTOC.

E. Metaphase

At metaphase, the chromosomes become fully condensed. The main function of metaphase is to ensure each cell gets the correct chromosome complement. After the nuclear membrane has disassembled completely in prophase, and the spindle has assembled, the microtubules pull the chromosomes toward both poles. Since the chromosomes contain two kinetochores, one associated with each chromatid, the chromosomes are pulled toward opposite poles at the same time. The chromatids are still physically connected, so this pulling action results in the chromosomes aligning in the middle of the cell, between the two poles. This also orients the sister chromatids: one to each pole. This region of the cell is often called the *metaphase plate*.

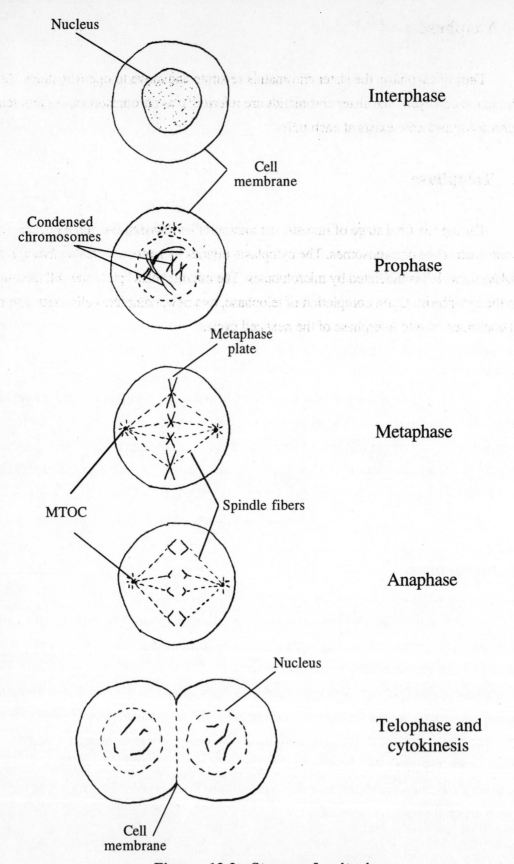

Figure 12.2: Stages of mitosis

F. Anaphase

During anaphase, the sister chromatids separate and move to opposite poles. At this point in the cell cycle, the sister chromatids are referred to as chromosomes. A complete set of chromosomes now exists at each pole.

G. Telophase

During the final stage of mitosis, the microtubules disassemble and a nucleus forms around each set of chromosomes. The cytoplasm divides by a process called *cleavage* or *cytokinesis* which is mediated by microtubules. The microtubules "pull" the cell membrane into the cytoplasm. Upon completion of telophase, two new, complete cells exist, and each cell continues on into interphase of the next cell cycle.

Chapter 12 Problems

Passage 12.1 (Questions 1-4)

Cells will often delay entry into mitosis when the DNA has not completed replication, or when the cell is not yet big enough to divide. In yeast, many proteins and enzymes are known which control the cell's ability to detect unreplicated DNA and to determine exactly how big the cell is. This allows for control of the cell cycle.

You wish to study these cell cycle control proteins in detail. You grow yeast cells and then expose them to a chemical mutagen, know to cause mutations in the DNA. You then examine the cells to see if they exhibit any abnormal growth patterns, indicating cell cycle control proteins may have been mutated. Each mutant cell you obtain has only one mutation in one protein.

Experiment 1:
You expose your cells to a drug which speeds up the cell cycle, but you grow the cells in a nutrient poor medium. This medium normally prevents the cells from growing quickly, although DNA replication still occurs at a normal pace. Most cells take a long time to enter into mitosis. However, you isolate several cells that do not delay entry into mitosis. You call these mutants 1, 2, 3, etc.

Experiment 2:
You add a drug to your yeast cells which does not allow replication to occur. Most of the yeast cells arrest and do not grow. However, several do enter mitosis. You call these mutants A, B, C, etc.

Experiment 3:
Upon careful examination of your mutants, you find a few that allow cells to enter mitosis when either the cell is small or when the DNA has not completed replication. These mutants you call by both previous names (e.g. 5C, 9G, etc.).

Using this data, you try to determine where in the cell cycle these mutations are exerting their influence, and hence, where their normal counterparts act.

1. At what stage in the cell cycle is mutant 8 most likely defective?
    A. G_1
    B. S
    C. G_2
    D. M

2. At what stage in the cell cycle is mutant D most likely defective?
    A. G_1
    B. S
    C. G_2
    D. M

3. At what stage in the cell cycle is mutant 9G most likely defective?
   A. G_1
   B. S
   C. G_2
   D. must be at more than one stage

4. Under your experimental conditions, you find that your mutants quickly die out after a few generations. However, when you culture them without drugs they typically do well. Which of the following mutants would probably die off more quickly than the others under your experimental conditions?
   A. 1
   B. A
   C. 5C
   D. All will die off at the same rate.

Questions 5-6 are independent of any passages and independent of each other.

5. A sensitive instrument called a microspectrophotometer can accurately determine the exact mass of DNA in cells. In a culture of diploid cells, the instrument was used to measure DNA in the cells at various stages of the cell cycle. The lowest amount measured was 3.2 picograms (pg) of DNA, while the highest was 6.4 pg. In one cell, 4.8 pg was measured. In what stage of the cell cycle was this particular cell?
   A. G_1
   B. S
   C. G
   D. M

6. The drug colchicine prevents microtubules from assembling. If this drug was added to a culture of cells undergoing mitosis, in which phase would the cells be blocked?
   A. prophase
   B. metaphase
   C. anaphase
   D. telophase

SECTION 4
VERTEBRATE ANATOMY
AND PHYSIOLOGY

Anatomy and physiology are disciplines usually studied together that deal with the structure and function of multicellular organisms. *Anatomy* is the science that deals with biological *structures* (sometimes called morphology, literally, "the study of form"). How are the parts of an organism arranged, and what are their designs? *Physiology* is the science that explores the *functioning* of these biological structures. What does each part of an organism do, and how is it accomplished?

Central to the study of anatomy and physiology is a hierarchical way of looking at biological entities. The cell is the fundamental unit of life, even though it has many component parts, so it would not be improper to talk about the anatomy and physiology of the cell itself. Traditionally, however, these terms are more commonly reserved for the study of multicellular organisms, namely animals. We will direct our study at the anatomy and physiology of vertebrate animals (animals with "backbones") because these are the organisms emphasized on the MCAT. Since humans are vertebrates, it is convenient and reasonable to use human anatomy and physiology as an example of vertebrate systems in general. Remember, however, that you may be asked questions about other vertebrates (including other mammals, birds, reptiles, and fish), and, to the extent it is relevant, any major differences that exist between these and human systems will be emphasized.

Returning to the theme of hierarchy, the structure and function of a multicellular animal may be approached on many levels, from the simplest to the most complex. As noted before, the cell is the fundamental living unit, and the general functioning of the cell itself is the subject of previous chapters. In an animal, cells undergo *differentiation* and become *specialized* -- all of the cells in an animal's body are not the same, and the first chapter in this section deals with the major types of cells that exist in vertebrate bodies. Groups of specialized cells working together towards a common function are referred to as *tissues*, also discussed in Chapter 13. A structure performing a specific function that is made up of more than one tissue type is referred to as an *organ,* and groups of organs functioning in concert are said to be *organ systems.* The remaining chapters in this section deal with the various organ systems in the vertebrate body. These are grouped together due to similarities in structure, function, or both. Ultimately, all of the organ systems functioning together will create and sustain the *organism* itself, which is the highest level of hierarchy with which we need be concerned here. All of an animal's systems must function harmoniously in order for *homeostasis* to be maintained. Homeostasis is the maintenance of the relative constancy of the internal environment of an organism (i.e., temperature, pH, water balance, etc.), and must be preserved if the organism is to remain healthy. A disruption in homeostasis may lead to disease and ultimately death.

Chapter 13
Specialized Eukaryotic Cells and Tissues

A. Introduction

While all cells share the same fundamental properties, cells in a multicellular animal become specialized to enable them to participate in different functions. Cells that find themselves in a human heart will have to be different structurally than cells found in the brain, due to the different functions these organs perform. Groups of similarly specialized cells working together towards a common function, along with any associated extracellular material, are called *tissues*. While experts can distinguish almost 200 types of human cells, these are usually grouped into four tissue types, each of which performs a basic function. These tissue types are *epithelial*, *connective*, *muscle*, and *nervous*.

B. Epithelial Tissues and Cells

Epithelial tissue covers all of the surfaces of the body that come into contact with the environment. This includes the outer surface of the skin, as well as the linings of the respiratory, digestive, and urogenital tracts. Some epithelial cells are specialized to secrete *mucus* (which acts as a lubricant and protects inner surfaces from infection), while others often cluster together to form *glands* (structures that synthesize and secrete specific substances, often enzymes or hormones). Since epithelial tissue exists wherever the body comes into contact with the environment, it serves a *protective* role and also regulates the *absorption* of materials (as in the digestive and respiratory systems) and their *excretion* (as in the respiratory system and sweat glands). Any particular epithelial tissue is classified according to the shape and arrangement of its cells:

- ◆ *Squamous* epithelium consists of cells that are thin and flattened; typically, substances diffuse through these cells rather easily.

127

- *Cuboidal* epithelium is made up of cube-shaped cells.
- *Columnar* epithelium is composed of elongated, rectangular cells.
- *Simple* epithelium contains cells arranged in a single layer.
- *Stratified* epithelium contains cells arranged in sheets several layers thick.

The epithelial tissue that makes up the outer layer of the skin is *stratified squamous epithelium*, while the nutrient-absorbing tissue of the small intestine is *simple columnar epithelium*.

Epithelial tissues of all types are generally attached to underlying connective tissue by a *basement membrane*, a non-living extracellular conglomeration of proteins and carbohydrates that is secreted by the epithelial cells themselves. Apart from the basement membrane, epithelial tissues generally contain little non-cellular material and are usually continuously turned over. An example of this is the epithelium of the skin, whose cells are constantly shed and replaced by new ones.

C. Connective Tissues and Cells

Connective tissues have the most varied structures and functions of any of the four tissue types. In general, they support and connect the other three tissue types, and may play a role in fat storage, the immune response, and the transportation of materials throughout the body. The organization of connective tissue differs from that of epithelial tissue in that connective tissue cells are almost always separated from each other and exist surrounded by an extracellular material known as the *matrix*. The matrix, which is secreted by the cells of the connective tissue, consists of *ground material* that may contain embedded *fibers*. Connective tissues are usually categorized according to the nature of the matrix in which the cells exist.

Many specific cell types may be found in different connective tissues:

- *Fibroblasts* are probably the most common type of connective tissue cell. As their name suggests, they secrete proteinaceous fibers into the surrounding matrix. Fibroblasts can produce two basic types of fibers, which will largely determine the character of the matrix surrounding them. *Collagenous* or connecting fibers are composed of the protein collagen arranged in long bundles. They are very strong and resist forces applied to them, and thus are abundant in connective tissues such as bone, cartilage, tendons, ligaments, and the lower layers of skin. *Elastic* fibers are largely made up of the protein *elastin*. As their name implies, they are "elastic" (stretchable without being harmed). These fibers can be found in the walls of arteries and the air passages of the respiratory system.

♦ *Mast cells* are also abundant, but are usually located near blood vessels. They secrete substances into the blood, such as *heparin* (which prevents blood clotting) and *histamine* (often responsible for allergic reactions).

♦ *Macrophages* are important connective tissue cells that are able to actively move around the body, and are specialized for the process of *phagocytosis*. Sometimes called scavenger cells, they can engulf and destroy foreign particles, including pathogens, and thus are important defenses against infection. Since they are mobile, they may be found moving between different connective tissue types, often residing temporarily in the lymphatic system and in tissue fluid.

With the abundance of cells and fibers involved, many types of connective tissues are recognized. Each has a particular role to play in the body. We will list and explore the highlights of each major type.

♦ *Loose connective tissue:* Composed mainly of fibroblasts that secrete both collagenous and elastin fibers, the matrix takes on a gel-like consistency. Loose connective tissue is often found below epithelium; it attaches the skin to underlying organs, binds organs together, and fills the spaces between muscles and bones. *Adipose* tissue is a specialized form of loose connective tissue that stores fat; fat provides energy reserves and insulation, and cushions sensitive body parts.

♦ *Dense connective tissue:* Also consisting mainly of fibroblasts, dense connective tissue has fewer cells and a matrix thickly permeated with collagenous fibers. With its great strength, dense connective tissue largely comprises *tendons* (which attach muscles to bones) and *ligaments* (which bind bones to other bones).

♦ *Cartilage:* Cartilage is a very rigid connective tissue. It is composed of cells called *chondrocytes* surrounded by a matrix abundant in collagenous fibers embedded in a gel-like ground substance. Due to its rigidity, cartilage plays a role in supporting many body structures. It can be found in rings as the major supporting structure of the trachea, and in the ears and nose. It associates with many bones, including the vertebrae and the knees.

♦ *Bone:* Bone is even more rigid than cartilage, and provides the major structural framework for the entire body. Bone cells, or *osteocytes*, exist in cavities separated by a matrix rich in collagen. Bone gains most of its amazing strength, however, from the presence of large amounts of mineral salts, mainly calcium phosphate, in the matrix. In addition to providing major structural support for the body as a whole, bones function to anchor muscles and protect vital organs (as with the sternum and cranium). Bones also contain *marrow* that produces blood cells.

♦ *Blood and Lymph:* Blood and lymph are connective tissues in which the ground material of the matrix is a liquid called *plasma*. A variety of specialized cells including *red blood cells* (*erythrocytes*) and *white blood cells* (*leukocytes*) circulate through the body in these tissues by way of the blood and lymphatic vessels. These tissues are involved in the transport of substances throughout the body and in defense against infection.

D. Muscle Tissues and Cells

Muscle tissue has one major function and is comprised of only one type of cell. Muscle cells are specialized cells that have the ability to contract; thus muscle tissue is exclusively involved with movement of one kind or another. Muscle tissues are grouped into three major types based on the appearance of the tissue and its interaction with the nervous system.

♦ *Skeletal muscle:* Skeletal muscles have a striped or *striated* appearance and are controlled voluntarily, or consciously. These muscles are almost always connected to bones, directly or via tendons. Skeletal muscles make up between 20 and 40% of the mass of the entire body, and usually exist in antagonistic pairs. All of the muscles under conscious control, and therefore the ones we usually think about, are skeletal muscles. Examples are the biceps and triceps in the upper arm.

♦ *Cardiac muscle:* Cardiac muscle tissue is found only in the heart, and has the distinction of being the only muscle tissue in the body that appears striated but is controlled involuntarily. Also called the myocardium, the importance of this type of muscle tissue cannot be overstated; if it fails to function properly for only a few minutes, death can occur. If a portion of the myocardium does not receive a sufficient supply of oxygen, a myocardial infarction, or "heart attack", may result.

♦ *Smooth muscle:* Smooth muscle, as its name implies, does not appear striped, but looks uniformly smooth, and is always controlled involuntarily. Due to this fact, we are often unaware of the actions of smooth muscles within our bodies. Smooth muscle surrounds the walls of hollow internal organs, such as those in the digestive and urogenital systems. Rhythmic contractions of smooth muscles provide the driving force for the unidirectional passage of food through the gastrointestinal tract (called *peristalsis*), and are largely responsible for blood circulation in veins, where the blood pressure originating from the heart has all but dissipated.

E. Nervous Tissues and Cells

Nervous tissue is composed mainly of cells called *neurons*, which are highly specialized. They sense certain aspects of their surroundings and respond by transmitting electrical impulses. Nervous tissue also contains *neuroglial* (or *glial*) cells that play several roles, including support, insulation, and transport of nutrients to neurons. The functioning of neurons will be explored in detail in the next chapter, but let us now observe that all neurons follow a generalized structural plan. They typically consist of a centralized *cell body*, which contains the nucleus; several cytoplasmic extensions called *dendrites*, which receive information from other cells; and an *axon* (also called a nerve fiber), a long extension through which impulses travel away from the cell body, bound for another cell (see Figure 13.1). The axons of many neurons are surrounded by specialized neuroglial cells called *Schwann cells*, each of which wraps itself around a portion of the axon in such a way that little cytoplasm is present, and multiple layers of cell membrane encircle the axon. Schwann cell membranes are largely composed of a protein called *myelin,* which is a lipoprotein and thus very hydrophobic. These layers of cell membranes form a *myelin sheath* around an axon. Narrow gaps occur in the myelin sheath between each Schwann cell and are referred to as *nodes of Ranvier*. Axons surrounded by a myelin sheath are referred to as myelinated nerve fibers. The sheath functions to electrically insulate the axon and allow impulses to travel at much greater speeds than would be possible in unmyelinated fibers.

A *nerve* is simply a collection or bundle of neurons. Nervous tissue is found in the brain and spinal cord, which together make up the central nervous system, and in the peripheral nerves, which originate from the central nervous system and make up the peripheral nervous system. Nervous pathways, in general, go in two directions. *Sensory* nerves bring information (a *stimulus*) from the sensory organs towards the central nervous system. After the brain processes this information, it usually sends signals through *motor* nerves to effector organs (muscles and glands) which can bring about an appropriate response. The multiplicity of connections between neurons, muscles, and glands allows the nervous system to coordinate, regulate, monitor, and integrate many body functions, and makes it possible for us to obtain, process, and react to meaningful information about our environment. More details of the physiology of the nervous system can be found in the next chapter.

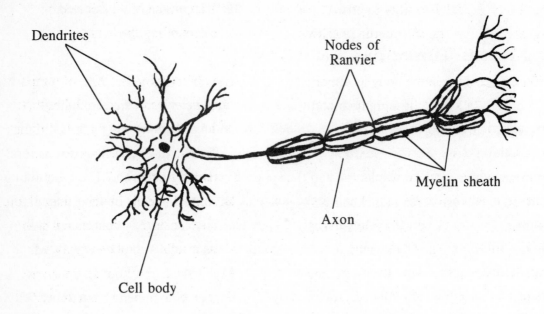

Figure 13.1: The neuron

Chapter 13 Problems

Passage 13.1 (Questions 1-5)

Cancer is a disease in which cells begin to divide when they shouldn't, producing masses of cells called tumors. Cancerous tumors are called "malignant" ones because of their ability to grow aggressively, invade surrounding healthy tissue, and "metastasize", or spread to different locations in the body as tumor cells break off, travel through the blood or lymph, and establish new tumors.

Cancer is generally caused by environmental agents known as "carcinogens", which include chemicals (such as those found in cigarette smoke) and radiation (like the UV rays of sunlight) that mutate cells, causing them to become cancerous.

Tumors that originate from epithelial cells are generally known as carcinomas, and it is estimated that about 90% of all human cancers are carcinomas. Tumors that originate from muscle tissue are called "sarcomas", and tumors can also originate from nervous and connective tissues. Epithelial tissue exists in various locations in the body, including the skin, the mucous membranes lining the lungs and gastrointestinal tract, and the linings surrounding major organs.

1. A person who develops cancer from constantly smoking cigarettes would be most likely to develop a:
   A. Carcinoma of the skin.
   B. Carcinoma of a mucous membrane.
   C. Sarcoma of the diaphragm.
   D. Carcinoma of the epithelium surrounding the heart.

2. The observation that 90% of human cancers are carcinomas implies that:
   A. Most carcinogens, like UV light, penetrate very deeply into underlying tissues.
   B. Epithelial cells by their very nature are more susceptible to mutation than cells of other tissue types.
   C. Cigarette smoking causes more tumors in humans than does UV light.
   D. Most carcinogens do not penetrate tissues very deeply.

3. A lab worker in Alaska develops a carcinoma of the skin. This particular worker is very dedicated, and almost never leaves the lab. The tumor is most likely the result of:
   A. Excessive cigarette smoking by coworkers.
   B. Excessive ingestion of toxic chemicals.
   C. Exposure to radiation from

133

phosphorus-32, a radioactive
isotope the worker routinely uses.

D. Exposure to ultraviolet rays of
sunlight.

4. Which of the following statements is
correct?

A. A tumor located in the liver must
be a sarcoma.

B. A tumor located in a muscle must
be a sarcoma.

C. A tumor composed of epithelial
cells must be located in an epithelial
tissue.

D. A tumor in the breast could
theoretically consist of cells of any
tissue type.

5. Cancer cells can often secrete a
substance that has the ability to
dissolve basement membranes. This
could account for the ability of the
cells of a malignant tumor to:

A. Invade adjacent tissue.

B. Divide rapidly.

C. Stop dividing.

D. Become carcinogenic.

Questions 6-10 are independent of any
passage and independent of each other.

6. Which of the following tissues is not
considered a connective tissue?

A. Blood

B. Bone

C. Lymph

D. Muscle

7. A particular muscle is under
involuntary control, but appears
striated. It is most likely to be:

A. The myocardium, the muscular
portion of the heart.

B. The muscle(s) that surrounds the
esophagus and causes peristalsis.

C. The biceps, the muscle that moves
the forearm.

D. The diaphragm, the muscle that
allows breathing to occur.

8. Which of the following tissue types is
involved with communication using
electrical energy?

A. Epithelial

B. Connective

C. Muscular

D. Nervous

9. The pancreatic cells that manufacture
and secrete the hormone insulin are of
what tissue type?

A. Epithelial

B. Connective

C. Muscular

D. Nervous

10. Arteries are constantly expanding and
contracting due to the force of blood
pumped from the heart, the "blood
pressure". One would expect the walls
of arteries to be composed largely of:

A. Cartilage.

B. Connective tissue containing mainly collagen fibers.

C. Connective tissue containing mainly elastin fibers.

D. Muscular tissue.

Chapter 14
The Nervous and Endocrine Systems

A. Introduction

The nervous and endocrine systems are often considered together because they are both involved with communication and send signals from one part of the body to another. Each system sends its messages by different mechanisms, however, and the two systems have correspondingly different, though complementary, structures and functions. The nervous system is designed for very quick communication and uses electrochemical impulses to transmit information through nervous tissue. The endocrine system performs relatively more slowly, and uses chemical *hormones*, which usually circulate in the blood, to convey messages from a point of origin to a group of target cells. Together, the two systems act to coordinate and regulate the activities of the body as a whole, including the major functions of receiving, processing, and reacting to sensory stimuli, as well as the maintenance of homeostasis.

B. Physiology of the Nerve Impulse

All of the cells in the body have an electric potential difference across their plasma membrane. This means that the inside of each cell is negatively charged with respect to the outside and this difference in voltage, just like a chemical concentration gradient, can be used to do cellular work. The potential difference across a cell membrane (usually about -70 mV) is referred to as the *resting potential*, and exists due to the maintenance of unequal concentrations of positively and negatively charged ions inside and outside of the cell. In addition, a transmembrane protein, the *sodium-potassium pump*, constantly uses active transport to move sodium (Na^+) ions out of the cell and potassium (K^+) ions into the cell, resulting in an electrochemical gradient of sodium and potassium ions across the cell membrane. There is always much more sodium outside of the cell than inside, and potassium is in greater concentration internally. While all cells exist in this state of disequilibrium, it is especially important for the functioning of nervous and muscular tissue cells. The resting potential is maintained due to the impermeability of the cell membrane to any charged atoms or molecules because of its hydrophobic nature (see Chapter 11). Thus, the only way for ions to traverse the membrane is through protein channels which tend to be very specific for a particular type of ion. Since these channels can be open or closed, they are referred to as *gated*, and we will be most interested in the *gated sodium channels* and *gated potassium channels*.

In a resting neuron (refer to Figure 13.1 for structure), almost all of the gated channels are closed. When a proper *stimulus* is present, the neuron reacts by opening the gated sodium channels in the region being stimulated (usually a dendrite). The result is a sudden influx of positively charged sodium ions, which follow their electrochemical concentration gradient and cause the membrane to become *depolarized*. This is a temporary state during which the polarity of the potential difference is reversed, and the inside of the cell becomes positively charged with respect to the outside. This movement of charges and subsequent depolarization is a form of electrical energy, and causes the gated potassium channels to open. As you would expect, the result is a movement of potassium ions from the inside to the outside of the cell, restoring the resting potential in a process known as *repolarization*. The gated channels of both types then close, and the Na^+/K^+ pump restores the concentrations of these ions to their original states. All of these changes taken together are called the *action potential*, and requires only about a thousandth of a second to occur. An important feature of the action potential is its ability to cause similar changes in adjacent regions of the cell; the net result is the unidirectional propagation of a *nerve impulse* down the neuron. After the passage of a nerve impulse through any portion of a neuron, there is a brief *refractory period*, during which the cell is "resetting" itself to be able to receive another stimulus and is unexcitable for a short period of time (about 1/2,500 of a second).

C. Synaptic Transmission

Signals must travel from one neuron to another, but neurons are separated by a space called the *synapse*, or *synaptic cleft*. The nerve impulse cannot "jump" across the synapse, so a different mechanism must be used to propagate the signal from the axon of the presynaptic cell to a dendrite of the postsynaptic cell. This is done using *neurotransmitters*, chemicals that can diffuse across the synapse and stimulate the postsynaptic cells by interacting with specialized receptors located there. Neurotransmitters are synthesized and stored in tiny vesicles near the end of each axon; as the nerve impulse approaches this location, gated channels for calcium (Ca^{++}) open, allowing calcium ions to diffuse into the cell. This event causes the storage vesicles to fuse with the plasma membrane, and the neurotransmitter molecules are released into the synaptic space. When they couple with their corresponding receptors, an action potential may be triggered in the postsynaptic cell, stimulating a new nerve impulse (see Figure 14.1). After neurotransmitter molecules exert their action, they must be quickly removed as the neuron gets ready to receive another signal. Sometimes they are enzymatically broken down, and in other cases they are reabsorbed by the presynaptic axon to be "recycled" and used again later. To sum up, the propagation of the nerve impulse and subsequent stimulation of adjacent neurons by neurotransmitters explains how electrical signals travel through nerves.

Acetylcholine is the major neurotransmitter used to stimulate the contraction of skeletal muscles. Others, such as *seratonin* and *dopamine*, function primarily in the brain and are involved with emotional responses and "higher brain functions".

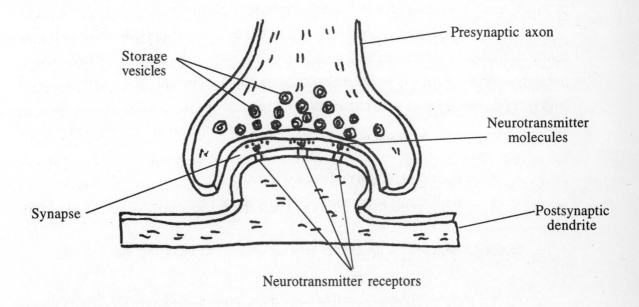

Figure 14.1: Synaptic transmission

D. General Organization of the Vertebrate Nervous System

The nervous system is composed almost exclusively of nervous tissue, as you would expect. The system is divided into two major subdivisions:

♦ *Central nervous system (CNS)* : consists of the *brain* and *spinal cord*.

♦ *Peripheral nervous system (PNS)* : consists of all nerves that carry information to and away from the CNS.

Neurons in peripheral nerves can be classified functionally:

♦ *sensory neurons* carry signals towards the CNS.

♦ *motor neurons* carry signals from the CNS to an *effector* organ.

Sensory pathways begin with neurons containing specialized *sensory receptors*, which are able to gather information about both the external and internal environments of the body. This information is sent to the CNS where it is processed and integrated, and a decision is made about an appropriate response. That response is carried out through motor pathways that stimulate an effector, usually a muscle or gland.

As noted previously, a nerve is simply a bundle of neurons held together by connective tissue. If a nerve consists exclusively of sensory neurons, it is referred to as a *sensory nerve*; likewise, a *motor nerve* contains only motor neurons. Many nerves contain both types and are referred to as mixed nerves. Peripheral nerves can also be classified anatomically, depending upon where they are connected to the central nervous system:

♦ *spinal nerves* originate from the spinal cord.

♦ *cranial nerves* are connected directly to the brain.

Motor pathways in the peripheral nervous system can be further subdivided:

♦ *somatic* (voluntary) nerves control the movement of voluntary skeletal muscles.

♦ *autonomic* (involuntary) nerves control those functions which occur "automatically", such as the regulation of breathing and heartrate, and the stimulation of glands and smooth muscles.

Furthermore, the autonomic system can be divided again into two subsystems. While the interactions between these two systems (and the endocrine system) are often complex, stimulation usually has the following typical effects:

- *the parasympathetic* division slows the rate of heartbeat and respiration, as occurs after eating.
- *the sympathetic* division has the opposite effect, and is often cited for its ability to contribute to the "fight or flight" reaction.

E. Structure and Function of the Central Nervous System

Both the brain and spinal cord are protected by bones (the skull, or cranium, and the vertebrae, respectively) and membranes called *meninges*. Cerebrospinal fluid exists between layers of the meninges for further cushioning. The spinal cord functions as an intermediary between the brain and the spinal nerves, allowing bi-directional communication along its length. Neurons that exist solely within the spinal cord or brain are referred to as *interneurons*, and can be involved in many functions. The brain is the most important and complex organ of the nervous system, and while we are far from a complete understanding of the way it works, we can list its most important component parts and assign to each particular functions (see Figure 14.2).

- *brainstem:* The brainstem connects directly with the spinal cord. It is remarkably similar in all vertebrates, and regulates essential functions such as heartrate and respiration. Often the brainstem is referred to as the *medulla oblongata*, although technically the medulla oblongata is only one part of the brainstem.
- *cerebellum:* Located near the base of the brain and dorsal to the brainstem, the cerebellum is responsible for the complex coordination of muscular movements and the maintenance of balance. It is especially large and important in birds, as it plays a crucial role in the coordination of flight.
- *diencephalon:* Located just above and ventral to the brainstem, the diencephalon consists of several parts and is associated with various functions. The *thalamus* is involved with the selective sorting and relaying of sensory information to the cerebral cortex. The *hypothalamus* is important in the maintenance of homeostasis, specifically regulating body temperature, water/solute balance, and sensations of hunger and thirst,

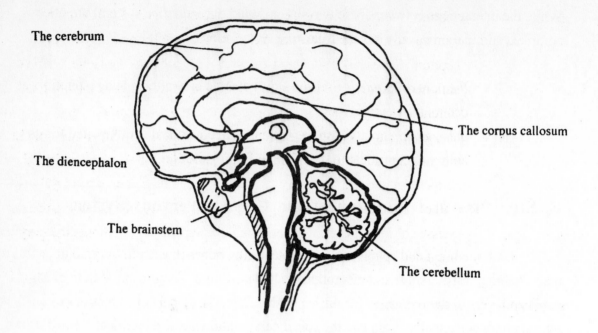

The cerebrum

The corpus callosum

The diencephalon

The brainstem

The cerebellum

Figure 14.2: The brain

among other parameters. It is able to produce hormones to aid in its functioning, and therefore is sometimes referred to as a gland. Both the hypothalamus and the thalamus, in association with certain portions of the cerebrum, also comprise what is known as the *limbic system*. The limbic system seems to be associated with the generation of emotions and the control of certain basic behavioral responses. For example, by responding to thoughts or circumstances with a feeling of anger, aggressive behavior might be initiated. Emotions are thought to have evolved precisely for this purpose; for example, fear signals danger, and an organism may have a better chance of survival if it flees a threatening situation. The limbic system also plays a major role in sexual stimulation and behavior, clearly another important function if a species is to remain in existence.

♦ *cerebrum:* The cerebrum is comprised of two *hemispheres* connected by a structure called the *corpus callosum*. The *cerebral cortex* is a relatively thin layer of tissue that forms the outer surface of the cerebrum. In general, the cerebrum is responsible for the most complex nervous functions in an organism. In all vertebrates, this includes the integration of the sensory reception, processing, and motor response functions which we have already mentioned. The cerebral cortex is the most variable portion of the brain in different vertebrates. Fishes and amphibians have no cerebral cortex whatsoever, and even birds and reptiles possess only a rudimentary one. In lower mammals it is more apparent, culminating with the large and folded structure characteristic of primates and humans. The cortex is responsible for all of the so-called "higher brain functions" of humans, including the processes of thought and reasoning, and the capacity for complex memory storage, learning, and language.

F. Sensory Perception

Since there are potentially many forms in which information can be gathered, several distinct types of receptors have evolved, each specialized to react to a particular stimulus in the environment. Five major types of receptors are recognized in humans.

- *chemoreceptors:* Chemoreceptors are sensitive to the quality and concentrations of chemical substances, and are the major receptors for the senses of taste and smell.
- *photoreceptors:* Sensitive to the quality and intensity of light, photoreceptors are responsible for our sense of vision.
- *mechanoreceptors:* Mechanoreceptors are sensitive to physical pressure, and are involved with several human senses, including hearing, touch, and our ability to determine the relative positions of different parts of our body (*kinesthesis*).
- *thermoreceptors:* Sensitive to changes in temperature, these are involved in our sense of touch.
- *pain receptors:* These receptors are sensitive to tissue damage, and are also involved in our sense of touch.

Other organisms, for example sharks, have electroreceptors that enable them to sense and react to an electric field. Still other organisms possess magnetoreceptors, which allow them to be aware of the earth's magnetic field. Humans apparently evolved without the need for these other sensory abilities.

In humans, senses can be subdivided into two categories. The *somatic senses* receive information from receptors located on the skin (the sense of touch), as well as from receptors in muscles, joints, and various other internal locations (called *proprioception*). The *special senses* are those whose receptors are collected into large, complex sensory organs located in the head, and include taste, smell, hearing, equilibrium, and vision (sight). We will now list these senses, describing the types of receptors and the major structures and functions involved.

◆ *touch:* The sense of touch is actually mediated through a complex association of different types of receptors located on the skin. A combination of mechanoreceptors, thermoreceptors, and pain receptors collects information that we perceive as a single sensation containing all three types of information.

◆ *proprioception:* While not traditionally classified as a human sense, most of us realize that we obtain sensations giving us information about the interior of our bodies. For example, we can tell if many of our muscles are contracted or relaxed (including the perception of our own heartbeat and breathing), and we can certainly feel internal pain! As with touch, different types of receptors at various internal locations are responsible for this "sense".

◆ *smell (olfaction):* The sense of smell is the product of specialized chemoreceptors, sometimes referred to as olfactory receptors, located in the nasal cavity. It is estimated that these sensitive receptors allow sensations of approximately 10,000 different aromas. Along with the sense of taste, it is thought that the olfactory sense evolved mainly to aid in food selection. Some other vertebrates, for example the bloodhound, have an extremely well developed and powerful sense of smell, approximately 40 times more sensitive than a human's.

◆ *taste:* The sense of taste, like that of smell, is made possible by the presence of specialized chemoreceptors; in the case of taste, however, these receptors are located on so-called taste buds on the tongue. Taste receptors are far less sensitive than olfactory receptors, as there are only four fundamental taste sensations that can be perceived: sweet, sour, salty, and bitter. Various taste sensations result from different combinations of the four basic ones. The overall sensation produced by the consumption of food has a strong olfactory component. You can prove this by eating while holding your nose; whatever you are ingesting suddenly becomes rather "tasteless"!

◆ *hearing:* The sense of hearing is made possible by the existence of the *ear*, a complex organ comprised of an external, middle, and inner section (see Figure 14.3). The stimulus for the sensation of hearing is the physical vibration of the molecules of the medium contacting the ear, usually air, in the form of sound waves. The external ear collects and transmits sound waves from the environment to the ear's interior. The middle ear consists of the *tympanic membrane* (eardrum), which protects the interior of the ear and transmits vibrations of the air to the three ear bones, or *ossicles*, also located in this region. The names of the three ossicles are the *hammer*, the *anvil*, and the *stirrup* (or more technically the *malleus*, the *incus*, and the *stapes*). The vibrations are transmitted to a structure in the inner ear called the *cochlea* via the ossicles. The cochlea is a fluid filled compartment that contains the *organ of Corti*, a patch of tissue with many specialized mechanoreceptors. These hearing receptors are stimulated when the cochlear fluid vibrates, sending information to the brain via the *auditory nerves*. The human ear can distinguish frequencies in the range of 20 to 20,000 cycles/second. Other vertebrates can hear higher or lower pitched sounds.

◆ *equilibrium:* The sense of equilibrium is again not traditionally looked upon as a human sense, but we should recognize it as one. This sense provides information regarding the movement and orientation of the head in space. As with hearing, specialized mechanoreceptors located in the ear are responsible for the sensations, but the fluid that stimulates these receptors is located in the *semicircular canals* of the inner ear. Like proprioception, equilibrium may be a sense we take for granted!

◆ *vision (sight):* The organ of vision is the *eye*, a complex structure with many component parts that functions in a very similar way to a conventional camera (see Figure 14.4). Light enters the eye through the transparent, protective *cornea*, and then through the *lens*, which focuses the light into an inverted image on the *retina*, located at the back of the eyeball. The amount of light entering the eye is controlled by the *iris* (the colored portion of the eye), a muscular structure that changes the size of the *pupil*, the opening in the iris. The retina contains the photoreceptors, which are classified into two categories based on their shape and function. *Rods*, responsible for "night vision", contain the pigment *rhodopsin*, and are more light sensitive than the *cones*, which are responsible for color vision. Dim light does not stimulate the cones, but it does affect the rods; that is why we can distinguish shapes but not colors in dim light. Stimulated photoreceptors send information to the brain via the *optic nerves*. Most nocturnal vertebrates have retinas that contain rods only, in large quantities, so that while they can see well at night, they lack color vision almost entirely.

This survey of our senses reveals that instead of the traditional five, humans have at least seven different senses and possibly more (depending upon how they are classified).

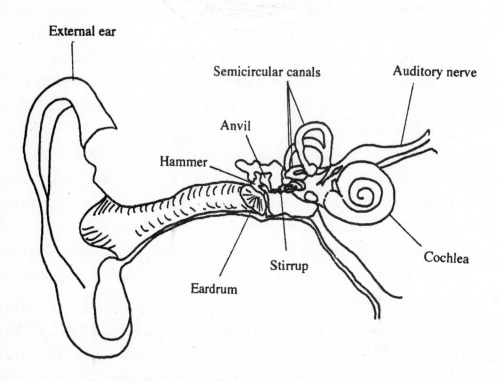

Figure 14.3: The ear

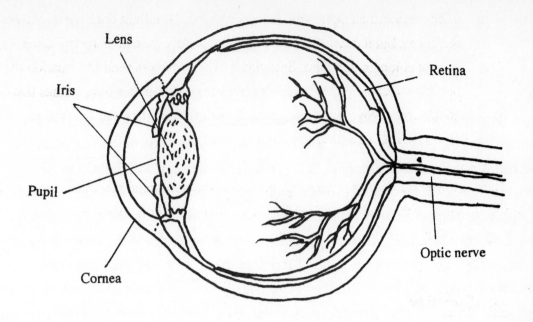

Lens

Iris

Pupil

Cornea

Retina

Optic nerve

Figure 14.4: The eye

G. The Endocrine System

As we noted at the beginning of the chapter, the endocrine system is related to the nervous system and the two act in concert. The endocrine system sends messages from one part of the body to another using chemical *hormones*. These hormones are manufactured and secreted by *endocrine glands* into the bloodstream, through which they travel and ultimately have certain effects on specific *target* cells, tissues, or organs.

As we noted in the last chapter, glands are composed of specialized epithelial tissue, and usually function in the production of one or more particular hormones. Hormones themselves can be divided into two classes based upon their chemical nature and corresponding mechanism of action:

♦ *steroid hormones* are lipids, usually synthesized from cholesterol, that consist of complex ring structures.

◆ *nonsteroid hormones* include amines, short peptides, and protein hormones; these are related in that they are constructed from amino acids, either by their modification or polymerization.

Hormones are able to act selectively on certain target cells due to the presence or absence of specific protein *receptors*, which exist either inside or on the surface of the target cell. If a cell contains a receptor for a particular hormone, it will respond to the message; if it lacks that receptor, it will be unaffected by the hormone's presence. While both classes of hormones function in a fundamentally similar fashion, steroid hormones have a different mechanism of action than nonsteroid hormones due to the chemical differences that exist between the groups. Since steroid hormones are relatively small lipids, they are soluble in the plasma membrane and can pass relatively easily into all of the body's cells. They will exert their action, however, only when they enter cells that contain the appropriate *intracellular* receptor, with which they then bind. The hormone-receptor complex thus formed is now able to act directly on the DNA in the nucleus, altering gene expression to cause the production of different cellular products (usually enzymes or other proteins). The result is some change in the properties, characteristics, or abilities of the cell. Nonsteroid hormones, in general, cannot diffuse across the plasma membrane and therefore must interact with *membrane* receptors. Receptors of this type are usually transmembrane proteins that contain a hormone-binding domain outside of the cell and another domain inside of the cell that changes its shape when the hormone is bound. It subsequently causes other changes in the cell, usually by activating enzymes through a chemical intermediary. Since the hormone is not causing the changes directly, the intermediary is often referred to as a *second messenger* (the hormone being the "first messenger"). While many such *signal transduction* pathways exist, a common one involves *cyclic AMP (cAMP)* as the second messenger.

H. Major Endocrine Glands and Hormones

Now that we understand the basic ideas about what hormones are and how they work, we can list the major endocrine glands, the hormones they produce, and the effects they can cause in the body.

◆ *pituitary gland and hypothalamus:* The pituitary gland is located just below the hypothalamus, at the base of the brain. The hypothalamus-pituitary complex is a major point of interface and coordination between the endocrine and nervous systems. As noted before, the hypothalamus, in addition to functioning in the central nervous system, produces many hormones. Most of these are hormones that control the secretions of the anterior and posterior pituitary gland. Two hormones produced by the hypothalamus are stored and ultimately released by the posterior pituitary.

- *antidiuretic hormone (ADH)*, sometimes referred to as *vasopressin*, regulates the ability of the kidneys to reabsorb water, and plays a major role in the body's overall water balance.
- *oxytocin* functions mainly in females to stimulate the release of milk from mammary glands after childbirth.

Six major hormones are generated and secreted by the anterior lobe of the pituitary.

- *growth hormone (GH)*, sometimes called *somatotropin*, stimulates cells to grow in size and number by causing certain metabolic changes.
- *prolactin (PRL)* causes changes mainly in females, promoting the growth of breast tissue and the secretion of milk after childbirth.

The other four hormones produced by the pituitary gland function in regulating the action of other endocrine glands, and are therefore often called *tropic* hormones.

- *thyroid-stimulating hormone (TSH)* stimulates the thyroid gland.
- *adrenocorticotropic hormone (ACTH)* controls the production of the hormones of the adrenal cortex.
- *follicle-stimulating hormone (FSH)* and *luteinizing hormone (LH)* influence the regulation and hormone production of the primary reproductive organs in both males and females.

♦ *thyroid gland: Thyroxine (T4)* is the major hormone secreted by the thyroid gland, located in the neck. T4 consists of an amino acid complexed with the mineral iodine, and acts to increase the rate of metabolism (respiration) of all body cells. The thyroid gland also produces *triiodothyronine (T3)*, which functions similarly to T4, and *calcitonin*, which regulates the blood levels of the minerals calcium and phosphorus, which are important for healthy bone formation.

♦ *parathyroid glands:* Located on the surface of the thyroid gland, these tiny structures produce only one hormone, *parathyroid hormone (PTH)*, which is sometimes referred to as *parathormone*. PTH functions in conjunction with calcitonin and vitamin D to precisely regulate the levels of calcium, and less importantly phosphorus, in the blood and various body regions. Since calcium is involved in a wide variety of vital functions (nerve and muscle transmission, bone formation, and blood clotting), its regulation is clearly important for the normal functioning of the body.

♦ *adrenal glands:* The adrenal glands are located on the surface of the kidneys, and are subdivided into two parts, the adrenal *cortex* and the adrenal *medulla*, which are actually distinct glands that secrete different hormones. The adrenal cortex produces two major hormones, *aldosterone* and *cortisol*, both steroids. Aldosterone plays a major role in the regulation of sodium and potassium levels, vital in nerve transmission, via the action of the kidneys. Cortisol raises the level of glucose in the blood by stimulating gluconeogenic pathways (especially the production of glucose from proteins and fats) during periods of stress, and apparently plays an additional role in the regulation of the inflammatory and immune responses. The adrenal medulla secretes two hormones, *epinephrine* (often called *adrenalin*) and *norepinephrine* (*noradrenalin*). These hormones are released in conjunction with sympathetic nervous stimulation, and play a role in increasing heart and respiration rates, while additionally raising the blood glucose level, in preparation for potential intense activity.

♦ *pancreas:* The pancreas is the largest gland in the body. In the vicinity of the stomach and attached to the small intestine by connective tissue, it has exocrine as well as endocrine functions. Its exocrine function consists of its ability to produce the major digestive enzymes and release them, through the pancreatic duct, into the duodenum of the small intestine. The endocrine portion of the gland, which is comprised of cell clusters called *islets of Langerhans*, produces and secretes two major hormones, *insulin* and *glucagon*. Both are intimately involved with the maintenance of a relatively constant level of glucose in the blood. Insulin lowers blood glucose concentrations by allowing cells to take up and utilize glucose for fuel, while glucagon has the opposite effect. It reacts to low blood sugar levels by promoting the breakdown of glycogen in the liver and its release as glucose into the blood. Disorders involving these hormones include *diabetes* and *hypoglycemia*.

♦ *ovaries and testes:* These are the primary reproductive organs in females and males, respectively, and in addition to their gamete-producing activities, they also secrete steroid hormones. In females, the ovaries secrete *estrogen* and *progesterone*, which control sexual development, the menstrual cycle, and certain aspects of pregnancy. In males, the testes produce *testosterone*, which stimulates sperm production, controls sexual development, and is responsible for the male secondary sexual characteristics (growth of facial hair, etc.).

♦ *other endocrine activity:* The *pineal gland* secretes *melatonin*, which may play a role in the normal sleep cycle as well as helping to regulate the female reproductive cycle. The *thymus gland* secretes *thymosin*, which helps lymphocytes to mature. Digestive organs, the kidneys, and the heart are all capable of secreting hormones with varying effects.

Chapter 14 Problems

Passage 14.1 (Questions 1-5)

Both the nervous and endocrine systems are involved with communication among body parts, but they exert their actions by different methods. The nervous system uses electrochemical impulses to convey messages through nervous tissue at high speeds, while the endocrine system uses chemical hormones that are released into the blood and directly interact with their target cells. There is some evidence that the nervous amd endocrine systems are evolutionarily related.

Hormones can be of two major types chemically: protein (including amines and peptides) or steroid. Each type of hormone normally exerts its effects differently. Protein hormones, such as insulin, adrenalin, ADH, and gonadotropin-releasing hormone (GnRH) interact with a membrane bound extracellular receptor on their target cells, which causes changes inside of the cell. This usually leads to the activation or inhibition of enzymes through a second-messenger system utilizing cyclic AMP (cAMP) as the second messenger. Steroid hormones such as testosterone, estrogen, and cortisol can diffuse through cell membranes, and usually act by affecting gene expression, but only after interacting with an intracellular receptor.

McCune-Albright syndrome is a genetic disease in which cAMP is synthesized in large quantities even when a signalling hormone is not present; it results in the over-secretion of many hormones, and increased effects of many hormones on their target cells.

1. Target cells of someone who suffers from McCune-Albright syndrome are likely to overreact to the presence of a hormone or respond to a hormone message even when the hormone is not present. Which of the following hormones would not cause overreaction or false message reception in an affected individual?

   A. Insulin
   B. ADH
   C. Testosterone
   D. Adrenalin

2. Some evidence that the nervous and endocrine systems are evolutionarily related comes from the fact that certain molecules function similarly to hormones during transmission of nerve impulses. Which of the following types of molecules fits this description?

   A. The sodium potassium pump
   B. Gated potassium channels
   C. Neurotransmitters
   D. Neurotransmitter receptors

3. The major connection between the nervous and endocrine systems that allows them to coordinate their activities is represented by:
   A. The cerbral cortex directly stimulating the thyroid gland.
   B. The brainstem controlling heart and breathing rate, which is also controlled by adrenalin.
   C. The ability of the cerebellum to coordinate the actions of several endocrine glands.
   D. The intimate connection between the hypothalamus and pituitary gland.

4. Testosterone is a steroid hormone; its release from the testes in males is controlled by gonadotropin-releasing hormone (GnRH). Which of the following statements is true?
   A. Both of these hormones affect target cells using a second messenger system.
   B. An individual with McCune-Albright syndrome is likely to over-produce testosterone.
   C. An individual with McCune-Albright syndrome is likely to under-produce testosterone.
   D. An individual with McCune-Albright syndrome would produce normal amounts of testosterone, but the target cells responding to testosterone would overreact to the message.

5. Stanozolol is a synthetic steroid that resembles testosterone in its chemistry and action. It is often the drug athletes are ingesting when they are said to be on "steroids". Which of the following statements is true of Stanozolol?
   A. It is likely to exert its effects by binding to an external receptor and triggering a second messenger system.
   B. It is likely to be found in all cells of the body after being ingested.
   C. It will likely only be found in muscle cells after being ingested.
   D. It would affect an individual with McCune-Albright syndrome more drastically than a normal individual.

Questions 6-10 are independent of any passage and independent of each other.

6. Often drinking excessive quantities of beer can lead to dehydration later. This can be explained because alcohol inhibits the hormone:
   A. ADH.
   B. Adrenalin.
   C. Norepinephrine.
   D. Glucagon.

7. An action potential is initially triggered by an influx of _____ ions that causes depolarization of the membrane.
   A. Potassium
   B. Sodium
   C. Calcium
   D. Neurotransmitter

8. The brainstem is most likely involved in what type of activities?
   A. Coordination of intricate body movements
   B. Thought and memory
   C. Control of breathing and heartrate
   D. Control of emotions and sexual impulses

9. Which of the following statements is true regarding the sense of hearing?
   A. Sound waves cause vibrations of ossicles, which are transmitted to chemoreceptors in the cochlea.
   B. The type of receptors responsible for sensing vibrations that allow hearing are mechanoreceoptors.

   C. Since hearing is normally caused by the vibration of air molecules creating sound waves, one could not hear underwater.
   D. The stimulus for hearing is chemical in nature.

10. Some people who have a deficiencey of vitamin A exhibit symptoms of night blindness. This condition allows normal sight during the day (in bright light) but virtual blindness when it becomes dark, when people without the condition could at least make out shapes and outlines. It is likely that this deficiency is causing its effects by:
   A. blocking the passage of information down the optic nerve to the brain.
   B. interfering with t he functioning of the cones.
   C. interfering with the functioning of the rods.
   D. interfering with the functioning of all photoreceptors.

Chapter 15
The Cardiovascular and Lymphatic Systems and the Immune Response

A. Introduction

The cardiovascular and lymphatic systems are related in that they both play a role in the movement of substances throughout the body. This transportation system is often referred to as *circulation* (sometimes the term circulatory system is used synonymously with cardiovascular system). The two systems are physically linked, but play different roles in the overall functioning of the body. The major job of the cardiovascular system is to transport nutrients and oxygen from the respiratory and digestive systems to all the cells of the body, and to deliver cellular wastes such as carbon dioxide and urea to their respective points of elimination. Hormones and other important molecules are also transported in the blood. This system functions in the maintenance of homeostasis by helping to stabilize the temperature, pH, and osmotic balance of the body, as well as playing a part in the complex system of defense against disease. The major roles of the lymphatic system include the drainage and return to the cardiovascular system of excess tissue fluid and the absorption of fat from the digestive system. In addition, the immune response, the body's major defense system against specific disease-causing agents, occurs largely in the lymphatic system.

B. General Organization of the Cardiovascular System

The cardiovascular system can be thought of as comprised of three major components: *blood*, the fluid connective tissue in which the many substances to be transported are dissolved; blood *vessels*, through which the blood circulates; and a muscular *heart*, which is the pump that provides the driving force for the movement of blood through the vessels. Let us consider each of these "parts" in more detail.

155

C. The Blood

As noted previously, blood is considered a connective tissue, and like all connective tissues is composed of cells separated by an intercellular matrix, referred to as *plasma*. All blood cells are manufactured in the *bone marrow* from unspecialized *stem cells*, and ultimately differentiate into a variety of cells with different functions and characteristics.

- *red blood cells (erythrocytes):* Erythrocytes, specialized for the transport of oxygen, are the most plentiful type of blood cell, gaining their red color from large quantities of the protein *hemoglobin*. Hemoglobin contains iron, and binds reversibly to oxygen. Red blood cells are unique among body cells in that they lack a nucleus, which limits their lifetime to a few months. This means that they, like other blood cells, must constantly be produced by the bone marrow. Erythrocytes are also characterized by their unique shape, which resembles a biconcave disk.

- *white blood cells (leukocytes):* White blood cells are involved with some aspect of the body's defense system. There are many types of leukocytes, which can be divided into two major groups based upon their general morphology.

  - *granulocytes* have granular cytoplasm, and include the *neutrophils*, *eosinophils*, and *basophils*.
  - *agranulocytes* (which lack cytoplasmic granules) are of two major types, *monocytes* and *lymphocytes*.

  Neutrophils, monocytes, and *macrophages* (large cells that develop from monocytes) are involved in the process of *phagocytosis* (the ingestion and subsequent digestion of foreign agents that enter the body). Eosinophils help to control *inflammation* (discussed later), while basophils release heparin (which inhibits blood clotting) and histamine (which is involved in allergic reactions). Lymphocytes are involved in *specific immunity*, which will be discussed later.

- *platelets (thrombocytes):* Platelets are not truly cells, but fragments of giant cells which break apart and enter the circulation. They play an essential role in blood clotting and repairing breaks in blood vessels. Blood clotting is a complex process requiring a cascade of reactions involving at least fifteen different plasma proteins. When a blood vessel break is detected, the end result is the activation of one of these proteins into *fibrin*, an insoluble protein which clumps and binds together platelets, forming a clot that covers the wound.

♦ *plasma:* Plasma is the liquid matrix of the blood, in which all the other components are either suspended or dissolved. Plasma is largely made up of water, with many solutes dissolved in it. The dissolved substances include nutrients (amino acids, monosaccharides, and small lipids); gases (oxygen, carbon dioxide, and nitrogen); wastes (urea, uric acid, ketones, etc.); and a wide variety of simple ions, or electrolytes, which influence the pH and osmotic pressure of the blood and tissue fluids. Also found dissolved in the plasma are a variety of proteins, called *plasma proteins*, which are involved in several processes including clotting, immune reactions, and the maintenance of osmotic balance.

D. Blood Types and Transfusion Compatibilities

The membranes of red blood cells contain certain markers, or *antigens*, which may be of different types. Furthermore, there are several major antigenic groups. The most important of these is the so-called *ABO antigen group*, which is based on the presence or absence of two major antigens, referred to as A and B. Any particular red blood cell can contain only one of four possible combinations of antigens from this group: A only, B only, A and B, or neither. A person whose erythrocytes contain only antigen A has type A blood; likewise, if only antigen B is present, an individual's blood type is B. If both A and B antigens are present, a person is said to have type AB blood, while type O refers to the absence of both antigens. Another blood group is referred to as the *Rh group*. Individuals whose red blood cells express the Rh factor (antigen) are Rh⁺, while those who lack it are Rh⁻. This is what is meant when a person's blood type is expressed, for example, as O positive: their red blood cells do not contain antigens A or B (from the ABO group), but do contain the Rh antigen.

E. The Blood Vessels

The blood vessels are the tubes through which blood passes as it moves from one part of the body to another. They represent a closed system that allows substances to travel to or from any body cell, with the heart as the central pumping organ that allows circulation to occur. Blood vessels are of three major types.

- *arteries:* Arteries are major vessels that carry blood away from the heart. Arterioles are smaller branches of arteries that ultimately lead to *capillaries* or *capillary beds*. Since the blood in arteries and arterioles has recently been pumped into them by the heart, it is under considerable pressure, and the walls of arteries are thickened to withstand this *blood pressure*. They consist of a layer of specialized epithelium called *endothelium*, and are reinforced by smooth muscle and connective tissue rich in elastin.

- *capillaries:* Capillaries are the smallest and most permeable of the blood vessels, and it is here that the major function of the cardiovascular system is carried out. Composed of a layer of endothelium only one cell thick, the walls of capillaries allow the diffusion of materials between the blood and the tissue fluid surrounding body cells. This includes the diffusion of nutrients and oxygen into cells, and the diffusion of carbon dioxide and other waste molecules out of cells. In addition, plasma fluid is forced through capillary walls due to the pressure of the blood. Most of this fluid is reabsorbed by the venules which are connected to the other end of the capillaries, but some fluid remains in the intercellular spaces. This fluid is normally returned to the cardiovascular system via the lymphatic system.

- *veins:* After blood passes through an artery, arteriole, and capillary, the exchange of substances between blood and tissue is complete. The blood must now be returned to the heart, and this is accomplished by its passage through venules (small veins connected to capillaries) and veins. Veins are major vessels that carry blood towards the heart. By this point, most of the initial blood pressure created by the heart has dissipated, so blood flow through veins occurs by contraction of muscles surrounding veins. Valves ensure a unidirectional flow of blood through the veins towards the heart.

F. Structure and Function of the Heart, and the Path of Circulation

The human heart consists of four chambers: the right and left *atria* (located in the upper region), which receive blood from veins, and the right and left *ventricles* (located in the lower region), which are the major pumping portions of the heart and propel blood into arteries (see Figure 15.1). The wall of the heart is largely composed of cardiac muscle, often called the *myocardium*, and the two sides are separated by a thick structure called the

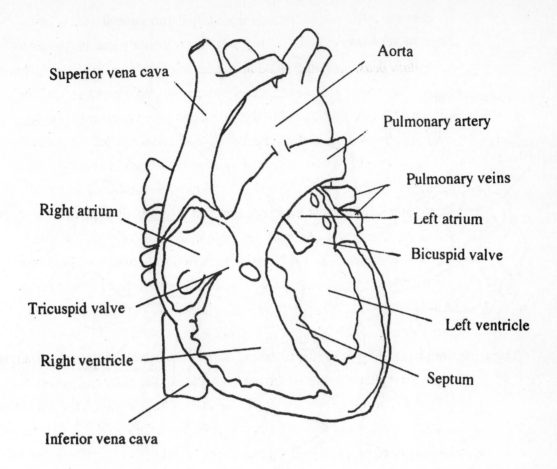

Figure 15.1: Structure of the heart

septum. The entire heart is surrounded by a fluid-filled sac, the *pericardium*, which serves a protective role.

If we were to follow the path blood takes as it travels throughout the body, we would find that it always flows in one direction, and that we can trace the major vessels through which it flows and their connections with the heart (see Figure 15.2). Arbitrarily starting in the left ventricle, the most powerful pumping region of the heart, oxygen-rich blood is forced into the *aorta*, the largest artery in the body, under considerable pressure. The aorta quickly divides and subdivides, ultimately supplying oxygenated blood to all of the body's tissues via capillaries. As the deoxygenated blood returns towards the heart, venules ultimately merge into two major veins, the superior and inferior *vena cava*, which enter the heart's right atrium. Blood passes into the right ventricle through the

159

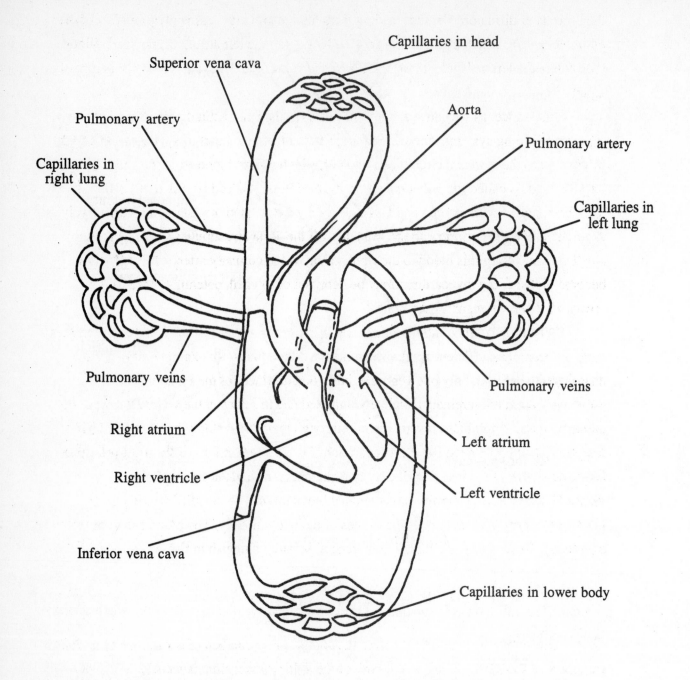

Superior vena cava

Capillaries in head

Pulmonary artery

Aorta

Pulmonary artery

Capillaries in
right lung

Capillaries in
left lung

Pulmonary veins

Pulmonary veins

Right atrium

Left atrium

Right ventricle

Left ventricle

Inferior vena cava

Capillaries in lower body

Figure 15.2: Path of circulation

tricuspid valve, and is pumped out again into the *pulmonary artery*. Notice that the blood present in the pulmonary artery is oxygen-poor, not oxygen-rich as it is in most other arteries. The pulmonary artery branches into two smaller arteries, one leading to each lung, and ultimately terminates in capillary beds surrounding the *alveoli*, or air sacs, of the lungs. It is here that oxygen enters the blood from the lungs, and carbon dioxide leaves, both by the process of diffusion. Venules leading from these capillaries ultimately join to form the *pulmonary vein*, which deposits oxygenated blood into the left atrium of the heart. Blood then enters the left ventricle through the *bicuspid* valve, and the cycle is ready to begin again.

In essence, as we can see from this analysis, the heart actually consists of two separate pumping systems: one which pumps blood from the heart to the tissues and back, referred to as the *systemic* circuit; and another, which pumps blood from the heart to the lungs and back, called the *pulmonary* circuit. In addition, the cells of the myocardium itself must be supplied with oxygen and nutrients if they are to continue functioning effectively. A small vessel, the *coronary* artery, branches off the aorta and supplies the myocardium; *cardiac* veins return this blood to the right atrium. If the coronary artery or its branches become blocked, the myocardium may be deprived of oxygen, potentially resulting in a *myocardial infarction*, or "heart attack".

While the hearts of all mammals and birds are structurally similar, lower vertebrates have different, less efficient heart arrangements. Amphibians, for example, have a three-chambered heart with only one ventricle, but blood destined for the systemic and pulmonary circulation remains relatively unmixed due to ridges in the ventricular wall. In addition, many amphibians respire directly through their moist skin (in addition to their lungs), lessening the need for strict separation. Fish, by contrast, have the most primitive hearts of all, usually consisting of only two chambers, a single atrium and a single ventricle. The ventricle pumps deoxygenated blood directly to the gills, where gas exchange occurs, and then on to the tissues of the body directly. The blood pressure eventually dissipates, and circulation in general is rather sluggish in fish.

G. The Cardiac Cycle and Blood Pressure

One complete heartbeat involves the complex coordination of the actions of all four chambers of the heart, during which both of the atria contract simultaneously (while the ventricles are relaxing), followed by the contraction of both ventricles (while the atria are relaxed). These events are called the *cardiac cycle*, and can be traced electrically using an *electrocardiogram* (ECG). The heart is able to "excite itself", i. e., no external nervous stimulus is necessary to initiate the depolarization of the myocardium. Instead, a specialized region of the heart called the *sinoatrial (S-A) node* initiates impulses at a rate of 70-80 times/minute in an adult. Since it is responsible for the generation of the heartbeat, the S-A node, located in the right atrium, is often referred to as the *pacemaker*. The depolarization spreads across the muscle cells of the atria, causing them to contract, and another critical region, the *atrioventricular (A-V) node*, is stimulated. The A-V node is the only electrical connection between the ventricles and the atria; by the time it transmits the "message" to the cells of the ventricles signaling them to contract, the atria have relaxed. An ECG tracing of the cardiac cycle graphically displays these events in detail (see Figure 15.3).

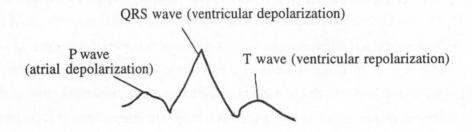

QRS wave (ventricular depolarization)

P wave
(atrial depolarization)

T wave (ventricular repolarization)

Figure 15.3: An electrocardiogram (ECG) tracing of a single heartbeat

Although stimulation from the nervous system is not necessary to initiate the heartbeat, it is important in the regulation of the heartrate. This rate must change, for example, during physical exertion. The *cardiac center* of the brain is located in the medulla oblongata of the brainstem; it is able to analyze the levels of carbon dioxide and oxygen in the blood indirectly by sensing blood pH. The heartrate can subsequently be affected through parasympathetic stimulation (decreasing the rate) or sympathetic stimulation (increasing the rate) of the S-A node by motor nerves as is appropriate. (Similar mechanisms usually cause an accompanying change in the rate of respiration.) Additionally, certain hormones have an effect on the heartrate, most notably epinephrine, which causes the rate to increase in response to stressful situations.

As noted earlier, the contraction of the left ventricle forces blood into the aorta, and is responsible for the pressure of blood against the walls of the arteries. This force is what we usually refer to as *blood pressure*, although the pressure of blood can be measured anywhere in the circulatory system. Traditionally, the blood pressure is measured at an artery in the arm by a device that expresses the pressure in terms of its ability to raise a column of mercury (in units of mm Hg). Blood pressure is usually expressed as two numbers: one represents the *systolic* pressure, the highest pressure which occurs as the ventricles contract, with the other representing the *diastolic* pressure, the lowest pressure occurring as the ventricles relax. Normal blood pressure is considered to be 120/80 in an adult male, although many factors can influence an individual's blood pressure at a given time. Chronic high blood pressure, or *hypertension*, can be a significant health threat as it puts undue stress on the cardiovascular system.

H. General Structure and Function of the Lymphatic System

As noted earlier, the lymphatic system is intimately connected with the cardiovascular system. Its major functions include the drainage and return of tissue fluid to the cardiovascular system and the protection of the body against infection.

As discussed previously, plasma fluid is forced into intercellular spaces near the capillaries by the pressure of blood, and not all of it is reabsorbed into the exiting venule. Lymphatic capillaries, which originate all over the body in tissues, collect this fluid, which is now referred to as *lymph*. (*Lacteals* are specialized lymphatic capillaries that begin in the microvilli of the small intestine and are the primary site of lipid absorption.) The lymph is transported via lymphatic vessels and ducts, which ultimately empty their contents back into the cardiovascular system at the *subclavian veins,* which drain the arms. As with venous circulation, lymph is not under high pressure, and must rely on smooth and skeletal muscular contractions, along with a system of valves, to ensure proper unidirectional flow. In addition to the lymphatic vessels, several lymphatic organs exist that play roles in specific lymphatic functions. The three most important of these are:

- ♦ *lymph nodes:* Located at various positions in the lymphatic system, lymph nodes are masses of tissue through which lymph flows and is cleansed in the process. Two major types of white blood cells collect and function in the nodes: *macrophages*, which ingest foreign particles through phagocytosis, and *lymphocytes*, which are responsible for the immune response (covered in more detail shortly). Thus the lymph nodes act as filters that remove pathogens and foreign particles before they return to the general circulation.
- ♦ *thymus gland:* Located in the lower neck, the thymus stores certain lymphocytes that were produced in the bone marrow. The thymus produces the hormone *thymosin*, which helps to differentiate these lymphocytes into functional *T lymphocytes* or *T cells*. These T cells then migrate into the lymph nodes and play a role in immunity.
- ♦ *spleen:* Located in the abdominal cavity, the spleen structurally and functionally resembles a giant lymph node. Unlike the nodes, however, it

163

also contains blood. Loaded with macrophages and lymphocytes, the spleen is active in destroying foreign invaders as well as damaged or nonfunctional red blood cells.

I. Protection From Infection: Non-specific Defenses

The body is in constant contact with pathogens, microorganisms that can cause disease. These are mainly bacteria and viruses, although some pathogens are protozoa, fungi, or even worms. In any event, the body possesses two major lines of defense to protect itself, the *non-specific* and *specific* defenses. The non-specific defenses protect the body from pathogens in general, while the specific defenses, often called the *immune response*, target and destroy one particular type of pathogen that may be infecting the body at any given time. We will focus on the specific defense shortly.

The non-specific defenses include any physical or chemical barriers able to prevent the colonization of the body by pathogens (*infection*). The skin and mucous membranes provide a continuous surface in direct contact with the environment that should physically prevent the entrance of pathogens. Intact skin is more reliable than the mucous membranes, however, which often must function in the exchange of materials with the environment and tend to be more permeable. Because of this vulnerability, the mucous membranes secrete mucus, a sticky substance designed to trap pathogens before they can breach the membrane. Even so, some microorganisms are able to enter the body through intact mucous membranes, especially in the respiratory tract. Additionally, skin may be punctured or cut so that it is no longer intact, making an inviting target of entry for potential pathogens.

Chemical non-specific defenses include the following:

♦ *enzymes,* such as lysozyme, can kill bacterial cells and are present in tears and saliva.
♦ *perspiration,* secreted from sweat glands, creates osmotically unfavorable conditions for bacterial growth due its high salt concentration.
♦ *acidic conditions* in the stomach kill most of the bacteria ingested in food before they can proliferate.
♦ *interferons* are small proteins effective only against viruses that are released by virally infected cells to signal their neighbors to prepare for invasion.

If a pathogen manages to breach these first lines of defense and enters the body (usually at the skin or mucous membranes), it must deal with the second line of non-specific defenses: *phagocytosis* and *inflammation*. As noted previously, phagocytes are neutrophils and macrophages that can engulf and digest foreign invaders. If pathogens enter through damaged tissue (as with a skin wound), phagocytosis is coupled to a more dramatic inflammatory response. Damaged cells release chemicals that have multiple effects:

- *blood supply* to the area is increased and clots often form, isolating the damaged area.
- *phagocytic cells* are recruited and enter the region, digesting the invaders they find.
- *local temperature* may rise, inhibiting the growth of pathogenic bacteria.

The inflammatory response, while usually painful, is certainly beneficial: it is designed to disable intruders and promote tissue repair before the pathogens can enter the bloodstream. If this defense fails, a systemic infection may result, and the final line of defense is the immune response.

J. The Immune Response

The immune response is also called the specific defense system because it is a reaction to a particular type of pathogen and is effective only against that pathogen. The immune response is only activated if a pathogen breaches the non-specific defenses and enters the circulation, creating a *systemic* infection. Two types of lymphocytes are involved in the immune response: *T lymphocytes* (or *T cells*) and *B lymphocytes* (or *B cells*). Both are produced by the bone marrow. B cells remain and mature in the marrow, while the T cells migrate to the thymus to continue their maturation. Both cell types eventually move to the lymphatic system and collect in the lymph nodes and spleen (some lymphocytes also circulate in the blood). While both types of lymphocytes are part of the immune response, they approach their respective tasks in different ways.

K. Antibody-Mediated Immunity

B-cells are responsible for *antibody-mediated* or *humoral* immunity. When each individual B cell matures, it begins to express on its surface a single type of *antibody*, a protein molecule composed of four polypeptide chains (see Figure 15.4). The amazing aspect of this phenomenon is that every B cell displays a different antibody; more than a million (up to 100 million) unique B cells are thus present at any time in an individual. Molecules on the surface of pathogens, known as *antigens*, bind specifically with existing antibodies. With such a vast diversity of B cells and antibodies in the system, it is overwhelmingly likely that there will be an antibody present to react with any antigen that enters the body. When this antigen/antibody binding takes place, the B cell displaying the antibody is said to be *stimulated* or *activated*, and a series of changes rapidly ensues. The B cell quickly proliferates by mitosis, making more and more B cells, each able to express the same antibody; since each of these cells is a genetic clone of the original, this entire process is often referred to as *clonal selection and expansion*. Members of the new population of identical B cells soon begin to differentiate into two types of cells with different functions: *plasma* B cells and *memory* B cells.

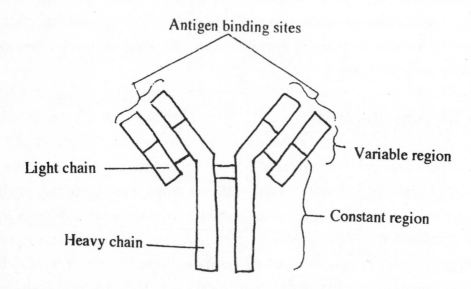

Figure 15.4: Structure of an antibody molecule

Plasma cells are specialized to manufacture and release huge quantities of the antibody that initially responded to the antigen. These antibodies can now bind with virtually all of the stimulating antigen, and, by doing so, they rid the body of the antigen-containing invader in two ways. The binding of the antibody to the antigen may disable the intruder directly. More commonly, the antibody/antigen complex is phagocytized or targeted by a system of plasma proteins known as the *complement* system. Complement proteins make holes in the membranes of targeted cells, causing them to lyse and die.

Memory cells, which also have the ability to produce antibodies, persist for long periods of time, sometimes the entire lifetime of an individual. If the same antigen is encountered again in the future, the immediate large scale production of antibodies disables the pathogen before it can cause significant effects. This phenomenon accounts for the ability of the body to acquire active immunity against a specific disease and is the reason why, after an individual contracts a disease once, he or she is often immune to future infection. It is also the rationale behind the effectiveness of *vaccination* (*immunization*).

An antibody protein is composed of four polypeptides, each of which has a constant region and a variable region (see Figure 15.4). It is the variable region that differs from antibody to antibody, providing the specificity of the B cell response. Since antibodies are proteins, the amazing diversity of antibodies that exists in any person presents an apparent mystery. Every polypeptide manufactured by a cell must have a corresponding gene to supply the instructions, but there are only about 100,000 genes in the entire human genome. How can over a million different antibodies be produced when it seems there are not enough genes to encode them? It has been established that a unique process called *somatic recombination* provides the answer. The segments of DNA that encode the variable regions of each chain are broken up into several hundred "modules". In any particular B cell, several of the modules are selected and ordered randomly as DNA is cut and rejoined together; this unique combination of modules is then transcribed and translated into a unique antibody. This "shuffling" of DNA segments accounts for the vast diversity of observed antibodies and the paradox of their existence.

L. Cell-mediated immunity

While B cells and the antibodies they produce play a vital role in the immune response, they do not act alone. As noted above, T lymphocytes, or T cells, constitute another part of the specific defense system. Lymphocytes normally do not react with "self" cells, that is, those that belong in the body. This is due to the presence of a group of proteins present on all "self" cells called the *major histocompatibility complex (MHC),* which lymphocytes are able to recognize. The MHC proteins also play a role in the functioning of T cells. A T cell cannot interact with an antigen unless that antigen is "presented" by one of the body's own cells that has become infected by the pathogen. For example, if a virus infects a cell, the viral antigens will not be freely circulating in the blood or lymph to be detected by B cells or antibodies. However, the infected cell displays new antigens on its surface. Like B cells, each T cell displays a surface antigen receptor, similar to an antibody, that can bind and recognize only one type of antigen. When a T cell encounters a cell presenting an antigen along with the MHC complex, the T cell becomes stimulated. Thus, T cells are responsible for *cell-mediated immunity*.

There are several classes of T cells, each of which performs a different function in the cell-mediated response. T cells, like B cells, rapidly divide and differentiate after being stimulated, creating cells of the following types:

- *effector or cytotoxic* T cells act by directly attacking and destroying the infected cell, and also release chemicals called *lymphokines* which attract and stimulate macrophages.
- *memory* T cells have the same function as do memory B cells.
- *helper* T cells release chemicals called *interleukins* after being stimulated. These chemicals act to increase the activities of both cytotoxic T cells and B cells, ensuring a speedy and potent response to infection. (It is these helper T cells that are infected by the HIV virus in AIDS, causing a general suppression of the immune response.)
- *suppressor T cells* seem to play a role in shutting off the immune response after the pathogen has been eliminated, but this process is not yet completely understood.

Chapter 15 Problems

Passage 15.1 (Questions 1-5)

Considering the amazing quantities and diversity of pathogens that exist in the environment, vertebrates had to develop a complex defense system, or they would have perished. In humans, as in most animals, there are multiple lines of defense against potential pathogens. The integumentary membranes (skin and mucous membranes) provide a physical barrier to pathogens. If these are compromised, the inflammatory response is stimulated, during which neutrophils and macrophages phagocytize foreign invaders nonspecifically.

If an infection becomes systemic, the immune response is the last resort. Lymphocytes, specialized white blood cells that mainly reside in the lymph nodes, specifically attack pathogens in the blood and lymph. B lymphocytes are responsible for antibody-mediated immunity, which involves the reaction of protein antibody molecules with antigenic markers on the pathogen. T lymphocytes are responsible for cell-mediated immunity, during which antigens are presented to T cells by antigen presenting cells of the human body, often macrophages or virally infected cells.

Several diseases can cause the immune system to become weakened or almost completely destroyed. AIDS (Acquired Immune Deficiency Syndrome) is a disease caused by the HIV virus, which attacks helper T cells that normally produce chemicals (interleukins) that stimulate the entire immune system. While functional cytotoxic T cells and plasma B cells can be created, their general activity is low due to lack of interleukin stimulation. Type I diabetes mellitus is an example of an autoimmune disease, in which lymphocytes attack normal body cells, in this case the insulin producing cells of the pancreas. Perhaps the most devastating immune disease is called severe combined immune deficiency (SCID); individuals with this luckily rare condition have virtually no functioning lymphocytes, and often must live in vinyl bubbles to completely cut them off from any contact with pathogens.

1. What do the diseases AIDS and SCID have in common?
   A. In both cases, functional antibodies cannot be produced.
   B. In both cases, any secondary infection must cause death.
   C. In both cases, T cells are either absent or relatively inactive.
   D. Both diseases are caused by viral infection.

2. During HIV infection:
   A. Bacteria infect helper T cells, leading to compromised immunity.
   B. Functional antibodies to antigens on the HIV virus are produced.
   C. All T cells in the body are destroyed by the virus.
   D. HIV can be found infecting B cells.

3. Which of the following statements is true of the inflammatory response?
   A. B lymphocytes are important during inflammation, as they specifically phagocytize foreign invaders.
   B. Phagocytic white blood cells act nonspecifically to phagocytize invaders.
   C. It does nothing to actually destroy pathogens that enter the body; it only stops them from spreading to other regions of the body.
   D. Red blood cells must be involved in phagocytosis, since swelling and redness are caused by massive amounts of red blood cells entering the inflamed area.

4. Which physical barrier would be most susceptible to infection?
   A. Intact skin
   B. The respiratory mucous membrane
   C. Infection never occurs through skin or mucous membranes.

D. They both present an equivalent barrier to pathogens.

5. Which of the following statements is true regarding the immune response?
   A. B cells can only be stimulated if antigen is presented to them by an antigen presenting cell.
   B. T cells can only be stimulated if antigen is presented to them by an antigen presenting cell.
   C. Macrophages exert their action by producing antibodies.
   D. Macrophages are very specific, and can only phagocytize pathogens of a single type.

Questions 6-10 are independent of any passage and independent of each other.

6. By definition, which type of blood vessel must be connected to a ventricle of the heart?
   A. An artery
   B. A vein
   C. A capillary
   D. Any of the above could be connected to a heart ventricle.

7. Which of the following statements is true regarding the blood?
   A. White blood cells contain hemoglobin, and are involved in oxygen transport.
   B. Blood cells are all made in bone

marrow.

C. Red blood cells contain
hemoglobin, and are primarily
involved with creating blood
clots.

D. Platelets contain hemoglobin, and
are responsible for oxygen
transport in the blood.

8. Blood located in which major vessel
would contain the highest
concentration of oxygen?
A. Superior vena cava
B. Aorta
C. Pulmonary vein
D. Pulmonary artery

9. Which of the following statements is
true regarding capillaries?

A. In a capillary bed, nutrients and
oxygen diffuse into cells.

B. In a capillary bed, plasma is often
forced into spaces between cells,
and is ultimately picked up by a
lymphatic capillary to be returned
to the general circulation.

C. In a capillary bed, urea and carbon
dioxide diffuse into the blood.

D. All of the above are true of
capillary beds.

10. Hemoglobin is a _____ that
requires the presence of the mineral
_____ to function properly.
A. Protein; iodine
B. Lipid; iron
C. Protein; iron
D. Protein; chromium

Chapter 16
The Digestive, Respiratory, and Urinary Systems: Absorption and Excretion

A. Introduction

Many of us would not ordinarily consider the digestive, respiratory, and urinary systems to be closely related. There are certainly differences between these systems and the functions they perform. The digestive system is primarily concerned with the breakdown and absorption of nutrients found in the food we eat, which the body uses for energy and as raw material for building macromolecules. The respiratory system is involved with the process of gas exchange, allowing oxygen to enter the body and carbon dioxide to be released to the environment. The urinary system functions primarily in ridding the body of other metabolic wastes (most importantly urea), and is also vital in the maintenance of the water/solute balance of the body. So what is it that these systems have in common? If you think about each of the functions mentioned above, a common theme emerges: each of these systems is involved with the *absorption* (input) or *excretion* (output) of needed substances or metabolic wastes, respectively. While each system deals with various substances in different ways, absorption and excretion represent the fundamental processes by which various substances are exchanged between the cells of our bodies and the external environment.

B. Structure and Function of the Digestive System

Since humans and all vertebrates are heterotrophs, we must obtain food from the environment by eating plant or animal tissue. This food contains nutrients, which are needed to supply energy, raw materials for building new molecules, and other substances the body requires but cannot synthesize. Since the material we must consume is often in complex form, it must be chemically broken down into its simpler components before it can enter the body and be used by cells. Thus the digestive system's primary functions are the *ingestion* (taking in), *digestion* (breaking down), and *absorption* (actual entry into the bloodstream) of the nutrients found in food.

While the digestive system consists of many organs, each performing a different function, it in essence is a long tube through which food moves in one direction (see Figure 16.1). The following discussion refers to the human digestive system; while fundamentally similar in all vertebrates, keep in mind that specific differences may exist in different types of organisms.

- ◆ *mouth:* Food initially enters the body through the mouth, the cavity that begins the digestive tract. The actions of the teeth in the process of chewing (mastication) begin the physical breakdown of food, while the salivary glands, located near the base of the tongue, secrete *saliva* into the mouth. This saliva contains *salivary amylase*, an enzyme which breaks down starch into maltose (a disaccharide), and causes the food to become more liquid in consistency. Thus food is both physically and chemically altered while in the mouth.

- ◆ *pharynx, the esophagus, and swallowing:* When food has been sufficiently chewed and mixed with saliva, it is now referred to as a *bolus* and can be swallowed. Swallowing is a muscular reflex action that causes the rapid movement of the bolus through the pharynx, or throat, and into the esophagus. Since the paths of food and air cross in the pharynx, the *epiglottis*, a flap of tissue, moves during the process of swallowing so that it covers the *glottis*, or entrance to the *trachea* (windpipe), to prevent choking. The esophagus carries food from the pharynx to the stomach. Rhythmic contractions of the smooth muscle that surrounds the esophagus result in the unidirectional movement of food towards the stomach, a process called *peristalsis*.

- ◆ *stomach*: The stomach serves several functions. First, it stores food until it can be processed further by the small intestine. Epithelial cells of the stomach wall secrete gastric juice, a combination of hydrochloric acid (HCl), mucus, and *pepsinogen* (an enzyme precursor). The epithelium of the stomach also secretes a hormone, *gastrin*, which controls the secretion of gastric juice. The HCl causes the pH of the stomach to be extremely low, usually with a value of about 2, and these acidic conditions kill many ingested bacterial cells and help to physically dissolve the food further. In

addition, the acidic conditions cause pepsinogen to be converted into
pepsin, an enzyme that begins to chemically break down proteins.
Contractions of the muscular stomach walls cause a churning action which
contributes to the continuing physical breakdown of the bolus, until it exists
in a homogeneous, semi-liquid state. This partially digested food, referred
to as *chyme*, is now ready for further processing. The *pyloric sphincter* is a
strong muscle that guards the entrance to the small intestine, and allows
chyme to slowly enter.

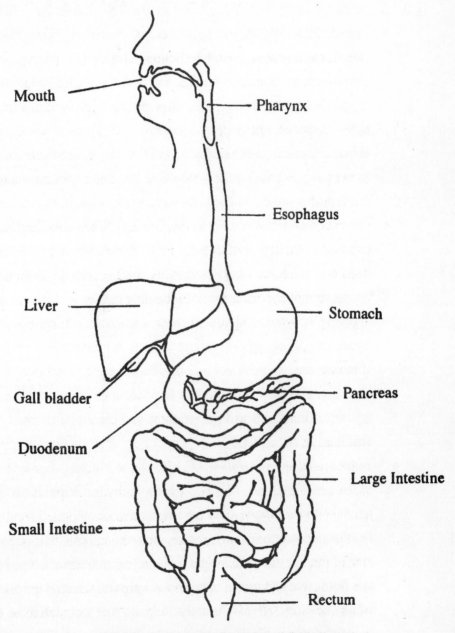

**Figure 16.1:The human digestive
system**

♦ *small intestine - digestion:* Most of the "action" of digestion occurs in the small intestine. It is here that the chemical breakdown of complex carbohydrates, proteins, and fats is completed. The small intestine is also the site of absorption of the products of digestion into the bloodstream. Chemical digestion is completed in the first portion of the small intestine, the *duodenum.* Enzymes manufactured by the pancreas attack undigested nutrients, and bile manufactured by the liver aids in the process. Specifically, the pancreas produces pancreatic *amylase,* which breaks down starch into maltose, *trypsin* and other proteolytic enzymes, which break down proteins into amino acids, and *lipases,* which hydrolyze fats, yielding glycerol and fatty acids. These enzymes are dissolved in pancreatic juice and enter the duodenum via the pancreatic duct. These juices also have the ability to neutralize the acid entering the duodenum from the stomach. The liver produces *bile,* which is stored in the gall bladder; it travels to the duodenum via the bile duct and participates in digestion by emulsifying fats, which otherwise would not be appreciably soluble and would not be fully exposed to the action of lipases. Finally, the epithelium of the small intestine itself also produces enzymes that break disaccharides into monosaccharides. As you might expect, hormones regulate the production and secretion of digestive enzymes and bile. *Secretin* and *cholecystokinin* are secreted by the duodenal epithelium in response to acid and the presence of nutrients, and stimulate the pancreas and gall bladder to release their products. When digestion is complete, monosaccharides, amino acids, fatty acids, and glycerol, along with various vitamins and minerals, are ready to be absorbed into the blood.

♦ *small intestine - absorption:* Absorption of nutrients occurs in the remainder of the small intestine, which is anatomically broken into two parts, the *jejunum* and the *ileum.* These portions are adapted in several ways to facilitate absorption; many of these adaptations exist to increase the surface area of the intestinal wall, which will allow nutrient absorption to take place at a faster rate and to increase total absorption. Firstly, the length of the small intestine is great, approximately six meters in humans. In order to fit in the abdominal cavity, it must be greatly coiled. Additionally, the walls of the small intestine project fingerlike folds, known as *villi,* whose surface

area is increased even further by the presence of tiny cellular projections
known as *microvilli*. All in all, the total absorptive surface area of the small
intestine is over three hundred square meters! Monosaccharides, amino
acids, and small fatty acids enter capillaries in the villi by both facilitated
diffusion and active transport. Mineral electrolytes also enter the
bloodstream directly, usually by active transport, and water follows by
osmosis. Larger fatty acids, glycerol, and cholesterol do not enter the
capillaries of the villi, but instead are combined and packaged into
lipoprotein particles called *chylomicrons*, which enter a *lacteal*. The lacteal is
a small lymphatic vessel, and the chylomicrons ultimately enter the blood by
way of the lymphatic system.

♦ *large intestine:* Following the small intestine is the large intestine, so named
because its diameter is greater than that of the small intestine. Its surface
area is comparatively small, however, and by the time material reaches the
large intestine, most of the nutrients have already been absorbed. The large
intestine is anatomically divided into two parts, the pouchlike *cecum*, which
represents the beginning of the organ, and the much longer *colon*, which
has the shape of an inverted "U". (The *appendix*, a small pouch which
apparently plays no role in digestion, is also located near the cecum.) There
is a large population of symbiotic mutualistic bacteria, mostly *Escherichia
coli*, which reside in the colon of humans and many other vertebrates. They
are sustained by particles of food which could not be digested by their host,
and find the warm temperature of the colon ideal for their growth. In return,
they synthesize certain vitamins and amino acids, most notably vitamin K,
which is involved in proper blood clotting. The major digestive role of the
large intestine is to reabsorb water that is still in the digestive tract before the
remaining waste material is eliminated. To facilitate this, any remaining salts
are also absorbed here. The resulting waste, or *feces*, should be relatively
solid, and consists of indigestible materials including cellulose fibers, some
water, and many bacterial cells. It is stored in the *rectum* until it is
eliminated by defecation through the *anus*. (You should note that this
elimination is not properly referred to as excretion, as the materials present
in the feces have simply passed through, but never entered, the body.)

♦ *pancreas and liver -- accessory organs:* We noted above that the pancreas
and liver are important in the overall process of digestion. They are referred
to as accessory organs, however, because food never actually passes

through them. Instead, they function by producing necessary substances and secreting them into the digestive tract. To reiterate, the pancreas produces digestive enzymes dissolved in an alkaline fluid which is emptied into the duodenum. The liver produces bile, which is stored in the gall bladder and enters the duodenum to help with the digestion of fats. While both organs have other functions, their roles in digestion cannot be overstated. (Remember that the pancreas also plays a major role, along with the liver, in controlling the level of blood glucose, as we discussed in Chapter 14.)

C. Nutrition

In this chapter, we alluded to some of the major types of nutrients. The detailed structures of many of these were discussed in Chapter 2. We will now consider each in more detail with respect to the needs they fulfill in the body.

- ♦ *carbohydrates:* Carbohydrates are a group of molecules based on the *monosaccharide*, or simple sugar, subunit. We can consume them in complex form as *polysaccharides* like starch, or in simple forms, as mono- or disaccharide sugars. Carbohydrates are prevalent in plant tissues such as fruits and grains, and function mainly to provide the body with energy.
- ♦ *proteins:* Proteins are polymers of *amino acids*. They are abundant in animal foods like meat, and are necessary largely to supply amino acid building blocks for the construction of the body's own proteins. Since they can be converted to glucose or fat, they can also provide energy in times of need. Eight amino acids must be ingested and are referred to as *essential*, but the body can synthesize the other needed twelve. A *complete* protein source contains all twenty of the necessary amino acids.
- ♦ *fats:* Fats are lipids composed of one molecule of *glycerol* attached to three *fatty acid* chains. They are often abundant in animal products, and play several roles in the body, including their primary function in long-term energy storage. Fats are also important in the synthesis of cell membranes and certain hormones. The body needs but cannot manufacture certain polyunsaturated fatty acids, which therefore must be consumed and are referred to as *essential* fatty acids.
- ♦ *vitamins:* Vitamins are essential organic compounds that the body cannot

synthesize but needs for a wide variety of purposes. Many act as *coenzymes* in metabolic pathways, and are usually required in relatively small amounts. Others act as *antioxidants*, protecting important molecules from oxidation and damage by free radicals and thus potentially playing a role in the prevention of cancer. Vitamins are often classified according to their solubility properties; A, D, E, and K are fat soluble, while the many vitamins in the B complex and C dissolve readily in water. The required vitamins can usually be obtained from a variety of plant and animal sources, although supplementation is a common practice, especially if the diet is deficient.

◆ *minerals:* Like vitamins, minerals are essential substances the body must obtain from the environment and are used for a variety of functions. Unlike vitamins, however, minerals are inorganic, usually elemental, substances that are often ingested as ionic salts; thus they dissociate in water and are often referred to as electrolytes. Examples of important minerals are calcium, phosphorus, sodium, potassium, chloride, and iodine. As with vitamins, these can usually be obtained in sufficient quantities from a normal diet, but are sometimes supplemented due to other factors.

◆ *water:* No discussion of nutrition would be complete without a mention of water, probably the most essential nutrient. While we likely take it for granted, water is vital in many ways to the functioning of the body. As the major solvent present in our cells, it accounts for much of the mass of the entire organism, and is especially important as a part of the blood and lymph. Dehydration, if severe enough, will inevitably lead to death. While the body can "manufacture" a certain amount of water as it engages in metabolic reactions, water must be ingested to ensure an adequate supply.

D. General Structure and Function of the Respiratory System

We noted in our discussion of digestion that humans, along with other vertebrates, are heterotrophs, and thus must obtain organic molecules from the environment to supply them with energy. That energy is released by a process of oxidation called *cellular respiration*, which requires oxygen and produces carbon dioxide. This means that organisms such as humans have a constant need to obtain oxygen and rid themselves of carbon dioxide. Since both of these substances exist as gases under physiological conditions, a system that allows gas exchange must be present. The process of breathing, or *respiration*, refers to the constant exchange of oxygen and carbon dioxide between the organism and the environment, and is the major function of the respiratory system. The major structures of the respiratory system are, in essence, a series of tubes that ultimately connects with capillaries of the circulatory system (see Figure 16.2). The following discussion refers to the human respiratory system; important differences exist in other vertebrates, especially fish, and will be addressed subsequently.

♦ *nasal passages, the pharynx, and the trachea:* During normal breathing, air enters the body through the nostrils and nasal passages, travels through the pharynx, and enters the trachea, or windpipe. The trachea is a strong tube strengthened by rings of cartilage which maintain its structural integrity. The *larynx*, or upper region of the trachea, contains the vocal cords, which humans use to make sounds.

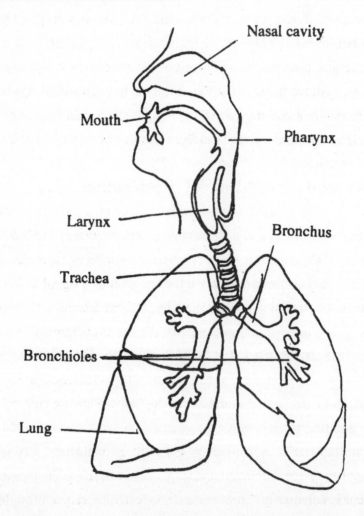

Figure 16.2: The human respiratory system

- *bronchi and bronchioles:* The trachea divides into two bronchi (singular, *bronchus*) inside the *lungs*. Each bronchus further subdivides again and again, creating many smaller tubes called bronchioles.
- *alveoli:* The smallest bronchioles terminate in tiny air sacs called alveoli (singular, *alveolus*). Each alveolus is thin-walled and surrounded by capillaries from the cardiovascular system. The barrier is so thin that gases can diffuse freely directly across the alveolar wall into or out of the blood. A human's two lungs contain about 300 million alveoli, with an exchange surface area of approximately 75 square meters.

The entire inner surface of the respiratory system is composed of epithelial tissue which secretes mucus; it is therefore called a *mucous membrane*. Since the alveoli have such thin walls, the respiratory system is potentially susceptible to the entry of pathogens, and the mucus secreted by the bronchial tubes and trachea acts to trap any pathogens or foreign particles before they can reach the exchange surfaces. Many of the cells of the mucous membrane also contain *cilia*, small projections which beat in one direction, causing a current of mucus to move towards the top of the trachea. This flow, known as the *ciliary escalator*, ensures that material trapped by the mucus is removed from the system, protecting the delicate respiratory surfaces from harm.

E. Mechanics and Regulation of Respiration

Breathing, or respiration, consists of two complementary processes: *inhalation* or *inspiration*, during which air enters the lungs, and *exhalation* or *expiration*, during which air leaves the lungs. Inspiration occurs when the brain sends a signal to the *diaphragm*, a sheet-like muscle at the base of the thoracic cavity, and the *intercostal* muscles, located between the ribs. When the diaphragm contracts, the overall volume of the thoracic cavity increases, causing the air pressure in the lungs to decrease. Air automatically flows into the lungs due to the external air pressure. When the diaphragm relaxes, the thoracic cavity returns to its initial size, and air is forced out of the lungs. Thus we can see that inspiration is active while expiration is passive.

The respiratory rate is controlled by centers in the brainstem, which normally send out rhythmic impulses to the diaphragm causing a regular cycle of inspiration and expiration to occur involuntarily. (To some extent, breathing can be brought under conscious control.) The respiratory center neurons are also sensitive to information about the chemical composition of the blood, and this allows them to alter the rate of breathing when conditions dictate, as during exercise or physical/emotional stress. The respiratory neurons are mainly sensitive to the pH of the blood (the concentration of H^+ ions, which as we shall soon see, is intimately related to the concentration of carbon dioxide). As metabolic activity increases, the levels of carbon dioxide and hydrogen ions in the blood rise, triggering an increase in the rate of breathing to restore normal levels of these substances. Whenever carbon dioxide concentration increases, oxygen concentration decreases, so there is really no need for the brain to monitor both parameters. There are receptors called the *aortic* and *carotid bodies*, however, which are sensitive to the levels of oxygen in the blood; they transmit this information to the respiratory centers of the brain, enabling "fine-tuning" of the system.

F. Transport of Gases in the Blood

Oxygen diffuses into the blood from the air, but oxygen is not extremely soluble in the plasma of the blood. Therefore, vertebrates have hemoglobin, a protein with a high affinity for oxygen so sufficient oxygen can be transported to meet metabolic demands. Hemoglobin consists of four polypeptide chains combined with an iron-containing heme group. Hemoglobin, which is red in color, is packed into red blood cells, and allows them to play their role in the transport of oxygen around the body. It is also responsible for the red color of blood.

Carbon dioxide is somewhat more soluble in the plasma than oxygen, but much of it reacts with water in the blood to form carbonic acid, H_2CO_3, which subsequently dissociates to form bicarbonate ions and free hydrogen ions. This is why increased levels of carbon dioxide increase the acidity (H+ concentration) of the blood. Since carbon dioxide can exist in the blood in these different forms, it also plays a major role in buffering the blood against pH changes, a major aspect of homeostasis.

G. Gas Exchange in Fishes

Since fish live in a watery environment, they do not have lungs that function like those of higher vertebrates. Fish usually have *gills*, surfaces over which water flows that are vascularized and allow gas exchange. Water can dissolve far less oxygen than air, however, and fish are able to survive with this low oxygen concentration for two major reasons. Firstly, in general, the metabolic rates of fishes are much lower than those of higher vertebrates, so they require less oxygen. Secondly, fishes have developed a *countercurrent* system in which the blood passing through the gills travels in a direction opposite to the flow of water over the gills. This allows for the extraction of almost all the available oxygen from the water. Fish have different ways of moving water over their gill surfaces; many have a flaplike *operculum* which slowly moves water across the gills; others use their mouths to gulp water, or swim quickly with their mouths open to facilitate higher oxygen intake. Only when animals made the transition from water to land was it practical for the modern lung to evolve.

H. General Structure and Function of the Urinary System

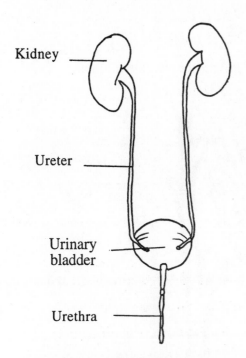

**Figure 16.3: The human
urinary system**

The urinary system is a special excretory system that plays several roles in maintaining homeostasis. A primary function is the excretion of *urea*, a major nitrogen-containing waste product derived from the catabolism of amino acids. More generally, this system regulates the chemical composition and pH of the blood by analyzing and adjusting the levels of major ions (including H+), nutrients, and other important substances in the blood. Finally, the urinary system is responsible for maintaining the proper amount of water in the body, a major determining factor in the concentrations of all solutes present in an organism. Anatomically, the urinary system consists of the following (see Figure 16.3):

- ◆ *kidneys:* The kidneys, located dorsally behind the stomach and liver, are the major organs of the urinary system. They filter blood, analyze its composition, and form urine that will ultimately be expelled from the body. Each kidney is divided into an outer *cortex* region, and an inner *medulla*.
- ◆ *ureters:* These tubes transport urine from each kidney to the urinary bladder.
- ◆ *urinary bladder:* This sac-like structure stores the urine until enough of it has collected to be expelled.
- ◆ *urethra:* The urethra is the tube through which the urine ultimately exits the body.

I. The Nephron and Urine Formation

The functional unit of the kidney is called the *nephron*, and each kidney contains about a million nephrons (see Figure 16.4). *Renal* arteries supply each kidney with blood; after entering the kidney, they branch and subdivide so that each nephron is supplied with arterial blood through a tiny *afferent* arteriole. The arteriole feeds a capillary bed referred to as the *glomerulus*. Constriction of the arterioles causes the blood pressure to be especially

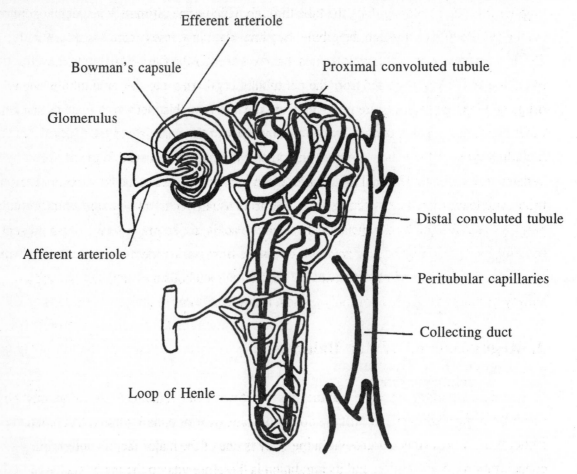

Figure 16.4: The nephron

high in this region, and the glomerular capillaries are extremely permeable, causing a significant portion of the plasma, along with its dissolved substances, to be forced out of the arteriole. This *filtrate* collects in *Bowman's capsule*, a cuplike structure which leads to the *renal tubule*. As the filtrate passes through the tubule, its composition will be altered, ultimately forming urine. During the process of filtration, blood cells and large protein molecules cannot pass through the capillary walls, and thus do not leave the blood, but instead leave the capillary bed through an *efferent* (leaving) arteriole. This vessel subdivides again into a set of *peritubular* capillaries, which surround and interact with the renal tubule. This complex arrangement allows the filtrate in the tubule to exchange materials with the blood as urine formation proceeds. The peritubular capillaries merge to form a venule which ultimately joins many others and exits the kidney as a renal vein.

The renal tubule has three main sections: the *proximal convoluted tubule*; a long, "U"-shaped section called the *Loop of Henle*; and the *distal convoluted tubule*, which empties into the *collecting duct*, the tube through which urine ultimately leaves the nephron. As the filtrate moves through the tubule, two important processes occur simultaneously. During *secretion*, some of the molecules that did not enter the filtrate but are still in the blood are actively transported from the peritubular capillaries into the renal tubule. Many drugs and toxic substances are removed from the blood by this method. *Reabsorption* is the other major process that occurs, by which a majority of the materials in the filtrate, including most of the water, glucose, and other nutrients, are returned to the blood. Whatever remains in the renal tubule after these transport processes occur becomes the urine, and leaves via the collecting duct. The urine usually consists of water which contains *urea* (a waste formed by the metabolism of amino acids) as the major solute. Also present in lesser quantities may be *uric acid* (which results from nucleotide metabolism), *creatinine* (from the metabolism of creatine), *ketones* (from the metabolism of fatty acids), and a variety of other substances normally present in trace amounts.

J. Regulation of Water Balance

It is important to realize that the amount of water that remains in the urine must be carefully controlled to ensure that we do not become over or underhydrated. As noted earlier, the amount of water present in the body is one of the major factors determining concentrations of all solutes, and its regulation is therefore vital to the maintenance of homeostasis. Additionally, as land creatures, we are in constant danger of losing water to the environment, and mechanisms of excreting urine that is hypertonic to our body fluids have thus evolved for purposes of water conservation. Depending on the circumstances, of course, we also may need to create urine that is hypotonic to body fluids, for example, after we have consumed a large amount of water. How is the nephron able to regulate the amount of water that leaves in the urine?

Firstly, as the filtrate passes through the proximal convoluted tubule, its volume is drastically reduced as sodium ions, glucose, and amino acids are actively transported out, causing water to follow passively by osmosis. In addition, negatively charged ions return to the blood due to the electrical imbalance created by active transport of positive ions. All of these substances are readily picked up by the peritubular capillaries and returned to the blood. As the filtrate begins its passage through the loop of Henle, its composition is altered more dramatically. Both active transport and diffusion of both Na^+ and urea make the area surrounding the loop extremely hypertonic to the filtrate; however, the walls of the ascending branch of the loop and the collecting duct itself are impermeable to water. So as salt is removed from the filtrate and water is not allowed to follow, the urine becomes very dilute (hypotonic). If nothing else was to happen, this would be the end of the process and urine would always be very dilute. Remember, however, that it is the lack of permeability of the collecting duct wall that prevents water from diffusing out of the duct. If the wall could be made permeable to water, it would rapidly move by osmosis out of the urine and back into the surrounding area to be ultimately returned to the blood, causing a concentrated, hypertonic urine to be excreted. As you've probably guessed, there is a way of controlling the permeability of the wall of the collecting duct to water, and thus of regulating the concentration of the urine. This mechanism depends on the action of the hormone *ADH* (*antidiuretic hormone*), which increases the permeability of the walls of the collecting duct to water, promoting the formation of a concentrated urine.

As we discussed in an earlier chapter, ADH is manufactured by the hypothalamus and stored and secreted by the pituitary gland in the brain. The hypothalamus monitors the osmotic composition of the blood and the blood pressure, and triggers a release of ADH when necessary. If the blood is dilute, as might occur after drinking a lot of fluids, the hypothalamus decreases ADH production, so more water is excreted in the urine. Conversely, if the body is dehydrated, the osmotic pressure of the blood increases, and the hypothalamus steps up ADH production, causing more water to be retained.

The hormone aldosterone, secreted by the adrenal cortex, triggers the nephron to increase reabsorption of sodium ions as well as increase secretion of potassium. Thus, the electrolyte balance of the body is also controlled by the nephron. In addition, the nephron participates in the regulation of pH by secreting hydrogen ions into the urine. All in all, the kidney really is an amazing organ, which performs and controls many processes leading to an incredibly fine-tuned regulation of body fluid composition.

K. Other Excretory Processes

While we have explored the major excretory processes carried out by the respiratory and urinary systems, other organs and systems are also involved with excretion. For example, the liver produces pigments called *biliverdin* and *bilirubin* as it breaks down the heme portion of hemoglobin during the process of red blood cell destruction. These pigments are stored in the gall bladder and released with the bile, and are thus referred to as *bile pigments*. They ultimately leave the body in the feces.

Another example would be the *sweat* produced by *sweat glands* embedded in the skin. While sweat is mostly water and functions in cooling the body, it also contains small amounts of electrolytes, urea, and uric acid. Sweating is thus an excretory function.

Chapter 16 Problems

Passage 16.1 (Questions 1-2)

Some individuals do not produce sufficient amounts of the enzyme lactase to digest the sugar lactose, present in milk and dairy products, and are referred to as "lactose intolerant". Lactose is a disaccharide, which must be broken down by lactase into its constituent monosaccharides, glucose and galactose, before it can be absorbed. If not broken down, it remains in the small intestines and is passed along into the large intestine, a place it does not belong, with waste materials. The results can range from dehydration and diarrhea to intestinal cramps and bloating. The pain and bloating often experienced by the lactose intolerant after lactose ingestion are caused by intestinal bacteria that metabolize the lactose to which they are normally not exposed. Products of this fermentation include organic acids and various gases. Some products are available to allow lactose intolerant individuals to eat lactose containing products, and are meant to be ingested just before eating milk or dairy products.

1. Which of the following is a reasonable explanation of the observation that lactose intolerant individuals become dehydrated after lactose consumption?

A. The presence of lactose in the large intestine inhibits the pituitary gland from releasing the hormone ADH.

B. Large amounts of lactose in the large intestine increase the osmotic pressure, causing water to be retained there and eliminated with wastes, whereas it would normally be reabsorbed into the blood.

C. Because they cannot drink milk, lactose intolerant individuals are deprived of an important water source.

D. The presence of lactose in the large intestine causes more frequent urination.

2. What is the likely nature of the products that, if taken before lactose ingestion, will inhibit the symptoms of lactose intolerant individuals?

A. They are likely antibiotics that kill the bacteria in the intestine so that they cannot metabolize the sugar.

B. They probably contain the enzyme lactase, which will end up in the small intestine and allow lactose digestion.

C. They are probably cocktails of various drugs that inhibit urination and help to ease the pain.

D. They are likely drugs that allow the small intestine to absorb undigested lactose.

Passage 16.2 (Questions 3-5)

After glucose is absorbed by the small intestine, it is transported to the liver, where many "decisions" are made regarding its fate. These decisions are hormonally effected, and include release of some glucose into the blood, storage of some as glycogen, and conversion of some to fat.

The hormones insulin and glucagon are produced by the pancreas; insulin is produced in response to high blood sugar, as after a meal, and tells body cells to take up glucose from the blood, while notifying the liver to store or convert any excess. Glucagon targets the liver when blood sugar is low, telling it to break down some glycogen and release it into the blood as glucose. The interaction of these hormones acts like a thermostat to maintain a relatively constant blood glucose concentration.

In individuals with diabetes mellitus type I, insulin is no longer produced by the pancreas, and must be supplemented by intravenous injection, or the afflicted individual will eventually die.

3. Why must insulin be injected intravenously, while other enzymes

such as lactase can be taken orally, by pill.

A. Insulin is a protein; if it was taken by mouth, it would be broken down into its constituent amino acids, and would never enter the blood.

B. Since insulin affects glucose concentrations, if it were ingested it would halt the absorption of glucose by the small intestine.

C. If insulin was taken in pill form, it would interact with glucagon secreted by the pancreas in the small intestine, and the two would "neutralize" each other.

D. None of the above answers is reasonable.

4. All of the following symptoms might be associated with untreated diabetes mellitus type I except:

A. Extremely high blood glucose.

B. Extremely low blood glucose.

C. The excretion of glucose in the urine.

D. Dehydration due to water loss in the urine.

5. Sometimes if the administration of glucose is not timed properly, insulin is injected but an individual does not eat for a prolonged period of time. This can lead to insulin shock, during which a person loses consciousness and can die. The probable cause of

189

insulin shock is:

A. The injected insulin causes the blood sugar to become so low that glucose is not available to fuel the body's needs.

B. The injected insulin causes so much glucose to be released into the blood that the surge of energy can cause heart rhythm irregularities.

C. The injected insulin suppresses hunger, so that the person does not realize they should eat.

D. Injected insulin causes the inhibition of glucagon synthesis, so no glycogen can be broken down to glucose by the liver.

Questions 6-10 are independent of any passage and independent of each other.

---

6. Which of the following parameters does the brain monitor most closely in regulating the rate of respiration?

A. The concentration of oxygen in the blood.

B. The heartrate.

C. The concentration of carbon dioxide in the blood and the blood pH.

D. The concentration of lactic acid in the blood.

7. If release of the hormone ADH was inhibited, the result would be:

A. Large volumes of concentrated urine

B. Large volumes of dilute urine

C. Small volumes of concentrated urine

D. Small volumes of dilute urine

8. The contraction of the _____ causes active inhalation, and is normally involuntarily controlled by respiratory centers located in the _____.

A. Diaphragm; brainstem

B. Diaphragm; cerebellum

C. Rectus abdominus; brainstem

D. Rectus abdominus; cerebellum

9. All of the following substances would be found in the glomerular filtrate of the nephron before reabsorption except:

A. Urea

B. Glucose

C. Amino acids

D. Large plasma proteins

10. Which of the following is an organ that plays a role in digestion, but never has any food actually pass through it?

A. The large intestine

B. The stomach

C. The pancreas

D. The colon

Chapter 17
The Integumentary, Skeletal, and Muscular Systems: Protection, Support, and Movement

A. Introduction

In this chapter, we will explore three systems that have a close physical connection, and are related in that none of them could function properly without the help of the others. While this is true of all body systems in the widest sense, the integumentary, muscular, and skeletal systems share a particularly intimate connection. The integumentary system, whose major organ is the skin, is responsible for a wide variety of functions, including protection from infection; absorption and excretion (in the sense that organs of the system line all exchange surfaces); temperature regulation; and sensory contact with the environment (in the sense that many sensory receptors, discussed earlier, are located in the skin). Skin is often directly connected to muscles, the major organs of the muscular system. Muscles have but one function: to contract, causing movement. While there are many types of movements, major movements of the body entail the connection of muscles to bones (often via tendons). In fact, it is bones that voluntary muscles cause to move when we raise our arms or lift our legs. In addition, bones, the major organs of the skeletal system, provide the major structural framework of the body. Without bones, there would be no means of supporting the rest of the organism.

B. Organization of the Integumentary System

The major organs of the integumentary system are technically referred to as *membranes*. We tend to think of organs as discrete entities within the body, but remember that, by definition, organs simply consist of at least two tissue types functioning together towards a common purpose. Looked at this way, the skin, perhaps the most important of these membranes, certainly qualifies as an organ. All of the membranes of the

191

integumentary system line body surfaces or internal cavities, and three major types can be identified and described.

♦ *serous membranes:* Serous membranes are organs that line internal body cavities which lack any connection with the outside environment, and often surround and line other internal organs. They typically have a simple structure, consisting of a single layer of epithelial tissue attached to a thin layer of loose connective tissue. Examples of serous membranes would be the membranes lining the thoracic and abdominal cavities.

♦ *mucous membranes:* Mucous membranes, to which we have referred previously, are organs which line internal body cavities that are continuous with the external environment. This includes the inner surfaces of all organs of the digestive tract, the respiratory system, and the urinary and reproductive systems. Like serous membranes, mucous membranes are composed of a combination of epithelial and connective tissues. Mucous membranes get their name from the fact that the cells of these organs secrete *mucus*, a substance that serves to lubricate the surface of the membrane and protect the organism from infection.

♦ *cutaneous membrane:* The cutaneous membrane lines the external surfaces of the body and is also the technical term for the skin. Since the skin is the most complex and versatile organ of the integumentary system, we will explore it in more detail.

C. The Cutaneous Membrane: the "Skin"

As noted in the introduction, the skin plays a variety of roles vital to the continuing health of the organism. In previous chapters we examined the excretion of sweat, and the sensory nerve endings located in the skin that help us to gather information about the world around us. Similarly, we noted the role of the skin as a non-specific barrier acting in general defense against infection by pathogens. The skin also plays a major role in thermoregulation, a topic we will consider shortly. Since we have already discussed the many functions associated with the skin, we should now address its structure (see Figure 17.1). The skin can be seen as composed of three layers, each with a unique composition.

♦ *epidermis:* This outermost layer of the skin is composed exclusively of stratified squamous epithelial tissue. Recall from Chapter 13 that stratified epithelium is many layers thick, and this has an interesting consequence for the skin. Since only epithelial cells are present, there is no supply of blood to nourish the epidermis. A single layer of cells that lies close to the dermis

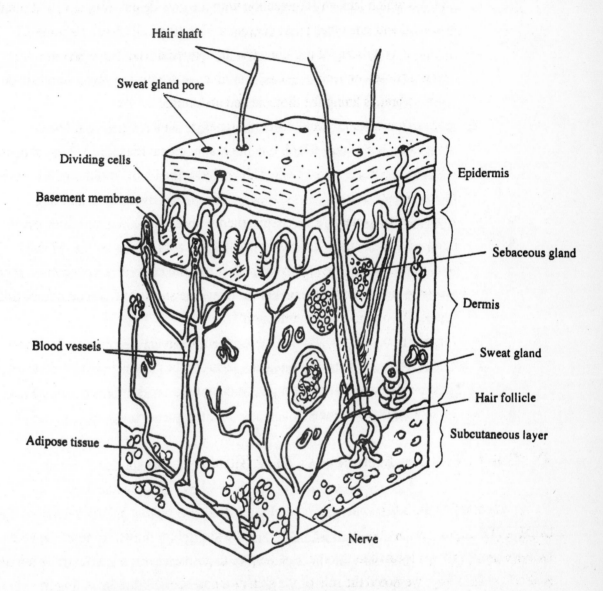

Figure 17.1: The cutaneous membrane (skin)

is nourished by capillaries found in the thicker lower layer. These cells are able to undergo mitosis and continually produce new cells. As the new cells are pushed outward, further and further from the blood supply, they become deprived of oxygen and nutrients and die. During this process, the dying cells begin to produce and store large amounts of the fibrous protein *keratin*, which acts as a "sealant". Thus the outer epidermis consists of many layers of tightly packed dead cells containing large amounts of keratin, making the epithelium impermeable to water. Deeper down in the epidermis lie cells which produce the pigment *melanin*, giving skin its color. The presence of melanin and keratin in the epidermis allows it to protect underlying skin layers from water gain/loss, potential damage from ultraviolet radiation, and mechanical damage. The epidermis is connected to the underlying dermis by a *basement membrane*.

♦ *dermis:* The dermis is generally three to four times thicker than the epidermis, and is composed of dense connective tissue containing collagen and elastin fibers. This allows the skin to be both strong and pliable. A major function of the dermis is to anchor the epidermis to underlying structures. The dermis also contains blood vessels, some muscular tissue (smooth muscle associated with involuntary movements of the skin and secretions of glands), and nervous tissue (acting in either a sensory or motor capacity). Also located in the dermis are several types of accessory structures:

- *hair follicles* are composed of epidermal cells protruding into the dermis. As a hair begins to grow, the cells being pushed outward, like other epidermal cells, die and become keratinized. Thus what we perceive as hair is really a shaft of dead, highly proteinaceous cells. Only mammals have true hair, and its function is to act as an insulator. Humans are the only mammalian species in which hair does not cover almost the entire body in large quantities.

- *sebaceous glands* produce and release *sebum*, an oily substance that is often secreted into hair follicles. Sebum functions to lubricate the hair and skin; in certain individuals, however, bacterial infection of sebaceous glands can result in *acne*, a condition in which the skin is covered by inflamed, raised lesions.

- *sweat glands* produce *sweat*, usually to cool the body during conditions of high temperature or physical exertion. As we noted in the last chapter, while sweat is mainly water, it may also contain electrolytes and wastes such as urea, so sweating is also considered an excretory process.

♦ *subcutaneous layer:* The subcutaneous layer is a relatively thin basal portion of the skin. It is composed almost exclusively of loose connective tissue which functions in binding the entire skin to the underlying skeletal muscles. Much of this connective tissue is adipose tissue, which as we noted earlier functions in the storage of fat; its location in the subcutaneous layer allows it to contribute to temperature regulation by acting as an insulator against loss of heat. The subcutaneous layer also contains blood vessels that nourish the skin.

D. Thermoregulation

All vertebrates create a certain amount of heat as a by-product of their metabolic reactions. In addition, the rate of metabolism is to an extent determined by the temperature of an organism's body, so that temperature cannot vary greatly without metabolic consequences. This is because enzymes are affected by temperature: the colder their environment, the slower the reactions they catalyze will proceed. As temperatures rise, the reactions speed up, but only until a certain point at which the enzyme loses its structural integrity, or *denatures*, and can no longer function properly. So all animals must exist within a temperature range that allows their enzymes to function, and at a reasonable rate.

Vertebrates can be classified based upon the major source of heat that allows their bodies to remain within a reasonable temperature range, and according to whether or not they have the ability to actively regulate their temperature and keep it at an almost constant level. *Ectotherms* absorb most of the heat used to warm their bodies from the environment, while *endotherms* use the heat they generate themselves, during metabolic reactions. *Poikilotherms* have little ability to regulate their body temperatures by internal mechanisms, and are often referred to as "cold-blooded". What this really means is that their body temperature varies with the environmental temperature. *Homeotherms*, often referred to as "warm-blooded", are able to maintain their internal temperatures in a very narrow range that is generally high and advantageous for their metabolic activities. Almost all endotherms are also homeotherms, and almost all ectotherms are poikiolotherms. Mammals and birds are the most obvious examples of homeothermic endotherms, while fishes and reptiles are examples of poikilothermic ectotherms. Since fishes live in a watery environment, the external temperature does not vary much, and therefore their body temperatures remain relatively constant, albeit low. Their metabolic processes are similarly slow. Reptiles must absorb heat from the environment, usually by basking on a rock to "get some sun". This raises their body temperature to ensure a reasonable metabolic rate. At night, the temperature of their bodies falls, their metabolism slows, and they become almost completely inactive. Humans, of course, are endotherms and homeotherms, using our relatively high metabolic rates to create heat and to keep our body temperature at a very constant 37^0C (98.6^0F). Just how do we achieve this thermal constancy?

The hypothalamus, a portion of the brain we encountered in Chapter 14, contains a thermostat set to maintain the body temperature at 37^0C. It receives information about the temperature of various parts of the body from internal receptors, and about the external conditions from the temperature sensors located in the skin (part of the sense of touch, see Chapter 13). If it is very hot outside, and the body temperature begins to rise above the thermostat "set-point", a variety of responses help restore the internal temperature to normal. *Vasodilation* (widening of blood vessels in the skin) increases the blood flow and accelerates the transfer of heat away from the body. In addition, sweat glands are stimulated to excrete sweat; this cools the body because internal heat is used to evaporate the liquid sweat. (Dogs rely more on the evaporation of saliva, which they expose to the environment by "panting".) These mechanisms function in concert to ensure that the body remains at a safe temperature. They are, however, not foolproof. Sweating becomes less effective as the ambient humidity rises; on an extremely hot and humid day, sweat will be produced but will not evaporate, leaving you wet, but still hot! In addition, profuse sweating causes excessive water and electrolyte loss, which must be replaced. Likewise, vasodilation becomes less effective as the temperature rises, and if the external temperature is higher than body temperature, the body may begin to gain heat from the environment! In these cases, it is often advisable for humans to resort to extreme measures -- air conditioners, cool showers, or swimming pools!

The hypothalamus also acts when extreme cold causes the internal temperature to drop below normal. In this case, *vasoconstriction* (narrowing of blood vessels) reduces the blood supply to the skin, thus lowering the rate of heat loss. In addition, the insulating hairs of the skin become erect and trap warm air, and the layer of adipose tissue in the subcutaneous layer serves as an efficient barrier to heat loss. Overall metabolic rate rises as well, so more heat will be produced. This can be accomplished in a number of ways.

- *involuntary contraction of muscles* ("shivering") creates heat, as do the voluntary movements we often perform when cold (walking, rubbing hands together, etc.).
- *hormones* such as adrenaline may be secreted, signaling the release of glucose into the blood and the increase of heart and respiratory rates.
- In extreme cases, the thyroid gland may step up its production of thyroxine, which increases overall cellular respiration by directly stimulating

mitochondria.

Of course, if it becomes too cold or low temperatures persist for too long, these mechanisms will not be adequate, and death will occur. As a final note, this explains why it is especially dangerous to get wet when cold. This can be thought of as sweating at the wrong time; heat is removed from the body as water evaporates from the skin. *Hypothermia* (a state of reduced body temperature with noticeable negative effects) can occur at temperatures as high as 50^0F if an individual is wet.

E. Functions and Organization of the Skeletal System

The major function of the skeletal system is to provide support for the body. In addition, it plays roles in:

♦ storage of calcium.

♦ production of blood cells.

♦ facilitation of movement.

♦ protection of important organs.

Individual *bones*, composed mainly of connective tissue, are the organs of the skeletal system. The skeletal system is divided into the *axial* and *appendicular* portions. The axial skeleton consists of the *skull, hyoid bone, thoracic cage*, and *vertebral column*. The appendicular skeleton consists of the *pectoral girdle* and the *upper limbs* (arms), and the *pelvic girdle* and the *lower limbs* (legs). There are usually a total of 206 bones in the human body, and most of these can be found in the skull, hands, and feet.

F. Classification and Structure of Bones

Bones are classified according to their shape (*long, short, flat*, or *irregular*). A long bone such as the *humerus* is often used to illustrate the major structures of a bone (see Figure 17.2). The shaft, or longest portion of the bone, is referred to as the *diaphysis*, and at each end of the diaphysis lies an enlarged part called an *epiphysis*, which functions in articulating with other bones. The portion of each epiphysis that connects with another bone is covered by *articular cartilage*. The entire bone is covered by the *periosteum*, a fibrous tissue which allows an entrance and exit for blood vessels and nerves, and provides a site for the attachment of *tendons* (which connect muscles to bones) and *ligaments* (which

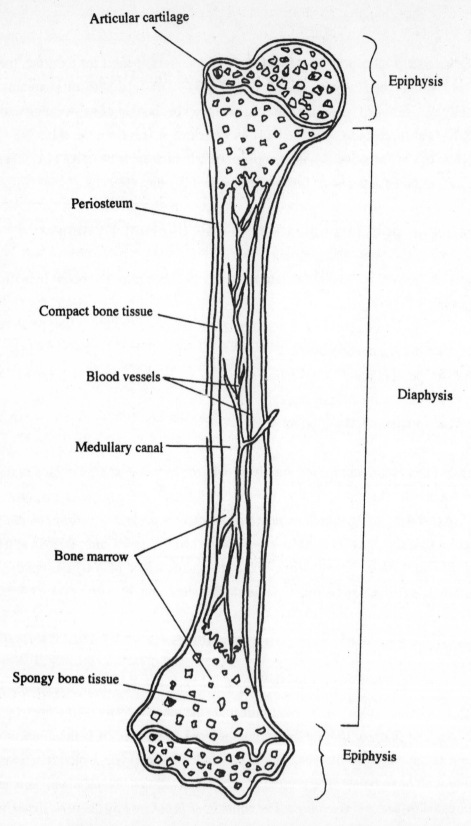

Figure 17.2: Structure of a long bone, the humerus

attach bones to other bones). It is also involved in the formation and repair of bone tissue. The hardened part of the diaphysis consists of *compact bone* tissue, while the epiphyses are made up of *spongy bone* tissue. The compact bone of the diaphysis encloses a cylindrical space called the *medullary canal*, which contains blood vessels, nerves, and the *bone marrow*, a soft connective tissue involved in the production of blood cells.

Bone connective tissue, as we noted in Chapter 13, consists of cells called osteocytes which exist in cavities (*lacunae*) separated by a collagenous matrix. The matrix also contains large amounts of inorganic mineral salts, mainly in the form of *hydroxyapatite* (calcium phosphate), which gives bone tissue its great hardness. In the case of compact bone, the cavities are arranged in concentric circles around *Haversian (osteonic) canals*, which contain blood vessels to nourish the osteocytes. Osteocytes concentrically clustered around a Haversian canal form units called *Haversian (osteonic) systems*. Many of these units join together in an orientation that confers resistance to pressure, and make up the substance of the compact bone tissue. In spongy bone, the osteocytes are not clustered around Haversian canals, but instead rest within the spaces formed by the *trabeculae*, bony plates that are irregularly connected and cause spongy bone tissue to be strong but light.

G. Growth and Development of Bones

Most bones are *endochondral* bones, which initially develop as cartilage that is gradually replaced by bone tissue in the process of *endochondral ossification*. (Other bones, mainly in the skull, are termed *intermembranous* and develop from layers of non-cartilagenous connective tissue.) An endochondral bone grows in length due to the mitotic activity of cells in an *epiphyseal disk*, located between an epiphysis and the diaphysis. Ultimately, the disk itself becomes ossified, and no further growth can occur. During an individual's entire life, however, bones are continually "remodeled", as bone tissue is continually *resorbed* and new tissue *deposited*. Many factors are necessary for the proper growth and development of bones, including vitamins A, C and D, the minerals calcium and phosphorus, and growth and thyroid hormones.

H. Bone Articulations (Joints)

Joints exist wherever bones meet, and are classified according to the means by which the bones are bound together. Most joints where movement occurs are classified as *synovial joints*. Here, bones are held together by the *joint capsule* (which is strengthened by the presence of ligaments). Between the bones involved exists a *joint cavity*, which is surrounded by the inner surfaces of the capsule. These surfaces are lined with a specialized type of integumentary membrane, the *synovial membrane*, which secretes *synovial fluid* that acts as a lubricant so that the bones do not crunch against each other.

I. Functions and Organization of the Muscular System

The major function of the muscular system is to allow movement. As we noted in Chapter 13, muscle tissue can be classified as one of three major types: skeletal, smooth, or cardiac. Individual *muscles*, composed of a particular type of muscular tissue as well as connective and nervous tissue, are the organs of the muscular system. *Skeletal muscles* are responsible for the movements of bones and are under voluntary control. *Smooth muscles* facilitate the movement of substances through the body (e. g. food in the digestive tract or blood in a vein), *while cardiac muscle* (the myocardium) is found exclusively in the heart and provides the driving force for the movement of blood in the cardiovascular system. Both cardiac and smooth muscles are under involuntary control. By weight, muscle tissue, particularly skeletal muscle, is the most prevalent tissue in the body.

J. Structure and Actions of Skeletal Muscles

An individual skeletal muscle is composed of thousands of *muscle fibers*, and each muscle fiber is actually a single, specialized muscle cell shaped like a long cylinder, up to several centimeters in length (see Figure 17.3)! Muscle cells contain multiple nuclei and mitochondria, and a specialized plasma membrane called the *sarcolemma*, which can become depolarized and carry an action potential similar to the action potential of a neuron. Perhaps the most striking feature of the muscle fiber is the presence of thousands of long subunits called *myofibrils*, surrounded by a tubular membrane system called the *sarcoplasmic reticulum* (equivalent to the endoplasmic reticulum of a non-muscle cell). Another membranous network of tubes, the *transverse tubules*, are invaginations of the sarcolemma that permeate the fiber, allowing an action potential to quickly spread to interior regions of each muscle cell. The functional unit of the myofibril is the *sarcomere*, each of which is composed of *thin filaments* made of the protein *actin* associated with *thick filaments* made up of the protein *myosin*. Repeating sarcomeres cause a skeletal muscle to take on its characteristic striated appearance. The sarcomere contains light regions (called I bands), composed exclusively of thin filaments anchored directly to a proteinaceous *Z line*, and darker regions (called A bands), which consist of thick filaments which overlap thin filaments. The thick filaments are indirectly connected to the Z lines, and the region from one Z line to the next is a complete sarcomere (see Figure 17.4).

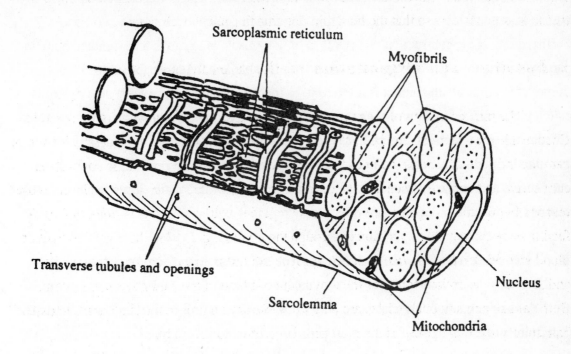

Figure 17.3: A muscle fiber

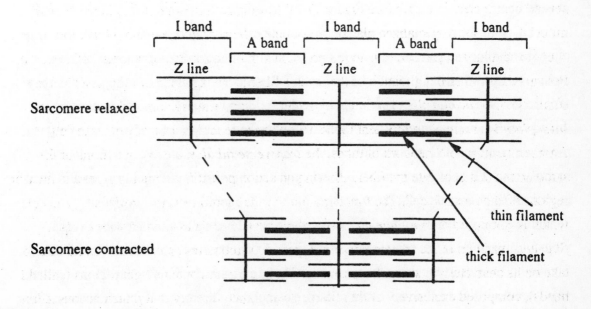

Figure 17.4: The sarcomere

Each muscle is surrounded by layers of fibrous connective tissue referred to as *fascia*. Extensions of the fascia form *tendons*, the structures that connect skeletal muscles to bones. In order to do its job, a skeletal muscle must be attached to at least two bones. Furthermore, if the contraction (shortening) of the muscle is to move a designated bone in a particular direction, one attachment must be immovable and the other movable. The immovable point of attachment is referred to as the *origin*, and the movable attachment is called the *insertion*. Thus when the muscle contracts, it produces a movement by "pulling on" the bone to which it is inserted. Muscles generally work in opposing pairs referred to as *antagonistic*; this means that since the only action a muscle can perform is contraction, one muscle acts to move a bone in a particular direction, while its antagonistic partner must contract to move it in the opposite direction.

K. The Mechanism and Regulation of Muscle Contraction

As noted previously, the sarcomere is the functional unit of muscle contraction. The thin filaments are composed of globular actin protein subunits polymerized to form a long chain, two of which are wrapped around each other to form the filament. Thick filaments, on the other hand, are composed of two myosin chains wrapped around each other; each chain is a long, fibrous protein, with an exposed globular "head" at its end and many globular "cross-bridges" protruding along its length. Given the arrangement of thick and thin filaments in the sarcomere, how can we explain and understand the contraction of a muscle fiber?

One of the remarkable aspects of muscle fiber contraction is that although the entire muscle fiber becomes shorter during contraction, nothing actually gets shorter at the molecular level. Instead, the myosin and actin filaments slide past each other, so that they take up less space, in a process explained by the "sliding filament" model. According to this model, when the muscle fiber is stimulated, the head and cross-bridges on the myosin molecule approach and interact with binding sites on the actin molecule. The head hydrolyzes ATP, which provides the energy by which the myosin cross-bridges and head propel the thin filament closer to the center of the sarcomere. Repeated cycles of attachment, movement, and breakage cause the actin filaments to slide past the myosin molecules, so that, at full contraction, the Z lines, which are directly attached to the thin filaments, are almost touching the myosin heads (see Figure 17.4). Thus as the sarcomere gets "smaller", due to changes in the relative positions of the thick and thin filaments, the myofibril as a whole is seen to contract, pulling the bone to which it is attached.

Since skeletal muscles contract in response to voluntary signals from the nervous system, we must explain the mechanism by which the course of events detailed above is set into action and controlled. As we observed in Chapter 14, motor neurons are nervous tissue cells in pathways leading from the brain to an effector organ, usually a muscle. The axon of a motor neuron interacts with the sarcolemma of a muscle cell at the *neuromuscular junction*, which resembles a neuronal synapse in many ways. Often a motor neuron is connected to several muscle fibers, which it stimulates to contract simultaneously. The motor neuron and all its associated muscle fibers are referred to as a *motor unit*. The axon releases the neurotransmitter *acetylcholine* in response to an incoming action potential, which binds to postsynaptic receptors on the muscle cell sarcolemma, triggering a depolarization of the sarcolemma which quickly spreads throughout the muscle fiber by way of the transverse tubules. The acetylcholine is quickly degraded by the enzyme *acetylcholinesterase* in order to "reset" the system for the next signal. How does the depolarization of the membrane lead to contraction?

Two other groups of proteins are involved in the regulatory process. *Tropomyosin* molecules are long and thin, and are associated with globular *troponin* molecules. When the muscle fiber is relaxed, the tropomyosin interacts with the actin filaments so that the binding sites for myosin cross-bridge formation are covered. When the membrane is depolarized, electrical changes occur that cause gated channels for the positively charged ion calcium to open in the membrane of the sarcoplasmic reticulum (SR). Since large amounts of calcium are stored inside the SR, it quickly rushes out into the cytoplasm (often called the *sarcoplasm*) of the muscle cell. Calcium subsequently binds to troponin, causing a conformational change which shifts tropomyosin off the myosin binding sites of the thin filaments, allowing cross-bridge formation, ATP hydrolysis, and the sliding of the filaments. When the sarcolemma is repolarized, calcium is pumped back into the sarcoplasmic reticulum by active transport, the muscle fiber relaxes, and the cycle is ready to begin again.

L. Skeletal Muscles and Energy Supply

As noted above, ATP supplies the energy for a muscle fiber to contract. Since muscular contraction often requires large amounts of energy, especially under extreme exertion, the supply of ATP that can be generated by aerobic cellular respiration is sometimes not enough to fuel the muscle's needs. Under these circumstances, alternate means of generating ATP must be found, or muscle contraction will cease. Firstly, muscles store additional fuel in the form of glycogen, which can be quickly mobilized when energy is needed. Muscles also store another high energy compound called *creatine phosphate*, which reacts with ADP to regenerate ATP by donating a phosphate group. Thus as the ATP supply dwindles, it can be quickly "restocked" by creatine phosphate. If energy demands are still not being met, the body uses its last alternative: the anaerobic process of fermentation begins in the muscle cells. As noted earlier, glucose can be broken down by humans in the process of fermentation to produce two molecules of lactic acid (lactate). While extremely inefficient, the process can provide extra ATP for short periods of time. Since lactic acid is toxic, however, when the "emergency" need for energy is over it must be reconverted to glucose in a process known as *gluconeogenesis*. This process requires energy, which is usually supplied by aerobic respiration. The amount of energy required to dispose of the lactic acid that has been produced corresponds to the so-called "oxygen debt", and explains why heavy breathing often continues even when activity has ceased.

M. Smooth and Cardiac Muscles

In general, the mechanisms of contraction of both smooth and cardiac muscles resemble those of skeletal muscles. Several important differences in both structure and function, however, are apparent. Smooth muscles contain both actin and myosin filaments, but they are more randomly arranged and are not positioned into sarcomeres. Smooth muscle cells also:

♦ lack transverse tubules.

♦ have only a single nucleus

♦ have poorly developed sarcoplasmic reticula.

♦ contain the protein *calmodulin* instead of troponin which serves essentially the same function by binding to calcium.

♦ are stimulated only by the autonomic division of the nervous system.

♦ can recognize the neurotransmitter *norepinephrine* (*noradrenalin*) as well as acetylcholine. in addition, smooth muscles are often stimulated to contract by hormones.

Cardiac muscle is located exclusively in the heart, and is unique in being the only muscle that is both striated and involuntarily controlled. Its contraction is virtually identical to that of skeletal muscle, as might be expected from the presence of sarcomeres. However, the ends of the muscle cells of the myocardium are connected by *intercalated disks*, which help hold the cells together and allow muscle impulses to travel rapidly from cell to cell. Unlike skeletal muscle, cardiac muscle is self exciting, and when one portion of the muscle is stimulated, the depolarization quickly travels to other fibers, causing the entire muscle to contract as a unit. The initial stimulation for a single "heartbeat" comes from the *sinoatrial node*, or "pacemaker".

Chapter 17 Problems

Passage 17.1 (Questions 1-2)

Psoriasis is a chronic skin disease in which afflicted individuals develop red patches with a scale-like appearance. The cause of psoriasis is a relatively simple one, but it is difficult to treat. The epidermal cells of an individual with psoriasis are dividing 5-10 times more frequently than they should be! This accounts for the excessive accumulation of cells that leads to the symptoms, as they cannot be sloughed off quickly enough to prevent buildup.

1. Which of the following statements is true of the cells making up the scaly patches of a psoriasis sufferer?
   A. The cells are alive and contain large quantities of melanin.
   B. The cells are dead and highly keratinized.
   C. The cells are far from the dermis, but blood vessels from the dermis grow towards the surface of the skin and supply them with nutrients, or else they could not continue to divide.
   D. The cells are dead and contain large quantities of collagen.

2. What type of drugs might be effective in severe cases of psoriasis?
   A. Collagen creams designed to moisturize the skin
   B. Antibiotics that can kill the bacteria responsible for the problem
   C. Anticancer drugs that systemically inhibit mitosis
   D. Drugs that inhibit the formation of sebum, and have also been used to effectively treat acne

Passage 17.2 (Questions 2-4)

At the neuromuscular junction of a skeletal muscle, neurotransmitters must contact receptors on the muscle fiber sarcolemma to transmit the signal for muscle contraction. That neurotransmitter must subsequently be enzymatically broken down, so that it is removed from the receptor, "resetting it" to receive another message. Many "chemical weapons" are in fact inhibitors of the enzyme necessary to break down the neurotransmitter in question, causing it to remain attached to the receptor indefinitely.

3. The enzyme inhibited by most chemical weapons is probably:
   A. Acetylcholinesterase
   B. Acetylcholine
   C. Seratonase
   D. ATPase

4. Which of the following would probably result after poisoning by one of the agents described in the passage?
   A. The heart would stop, since no messages from the nervous system could signal it to contract.
   B. A person would begin to lose the ability to actively move, and would ultimately die from the failure of the diaphragm to contract, causing suffocation.
   C. The person would suffer from mental confusion, as messages could not be sent within the brain itself.
   D. All muscular functioning in the body would cease.

Questions 5-10 are independent of any passage and independent of each other.

5. Under which conditions would normal human body cooling mechanisms work best?
   A. Temperature 80^0 F, humidity 95%
   B. Temperature 80^0 F, humidity 35%
   C. Temperature 100^0 F, humidity 50%
   D. Cooling mechanisms are unaffected by the humidity and/or temperature, and will work just as efficiently under all of the stated conditions.

6. Which of the following connective tissues bind muscles to bones?
   A. Ligaments
   B. Articular cartilage
   C. Tendons
   D. Adipose tissue

7. The release of which ion from the sarcoplasmic reticulum of a muscle fiber directly stimulates muscle contraction?
   A. Sodium
   B. Potassium
   C. Calcium
   D. Phosphorus

8. Which layer of the skin consists mainly of vascularized adipose tissue?
   A. Epidermis
   B. Dermis
   C. Subcutaneous layer
   D. None of the above

9. Hair follicles are located physically in the _____, but hair consists of _____ cells.
   A. Epidermis; dermal
   B. Dermis; epidermal
   C. Subcutaneous layer; epidermal
   D. Subcutaneous layer; dermal

10. Which of the following is not necessary for muscle contraction according to the sliding filament model?

A. ATP
B. Calcium ions
C. Creatine phosphate
D. Troponin molecules

Chapter 18
Reproductive Systems, Gametogenesis, and Early Development

A. Introduction

Almost all vertebrates reproduce sexually, and sexual life cycles always entail two complementary processes: *meiosis* and *fertilization*. Meiosis is a type of cell division which produces genetically *haploid (n)* cells, or *gametes*, from *diploid (2n)* precursor cells. These gametes, the *sperm* and *eggs* (or *ova*) in males and females, respectively, unite in the process of fertilization to produce a new diploid individual, a *zygote*. This zygote then undergoes a series of changes which constitute its *development* into a mature adult form. The reproductive systems of males and females contain the structures and perform the functions that make these events possible.

Reproductive systems are unique in that they are not necessary to promote and facilitate the life of the individual organism. Their ultimate function is simply to ensure that new individuals can be produced. Specifically, this means that they are involved in the processes of gamete production and delivery, and the maintenance of the life of a developing individual. As usual, we will explore sexual reproduction and development in the context of the human process, realizing that while the fundamentals are similar in most vertebrates, differences exist in specific strategies between the vertebrate classes.

(Please note: some of the terminology used in this chapter, especially with reference to meiosis, presupposes a general knowledge of basic genetic principles and terms. Review Chapter 19 if you are uncomfortable with these concepts.)

B. Structure and Function of the Male Reproductive System

The male reproductive system is composed of the primary sex organs, the *testes*, and a variety of accessory organs that function in the transportation and maintenance of

209

sperm cells (see Figure 18.1). The testes play the major role in production of functional sperm cells, and also secrete the major male sex hormone, *testosterone*. We will first examine the testes, and then consider the contributions of the accessory organs.

♦ *testes:* The testes (singular: testis) are the primary sex organs, or *gonads*, in males (see Figure 18.2). The testes are suspended in a sac called the *scrotum*, which allows them to lie just outside the body. For a variety of reasons, sperm formation is facilitated by the slightly lower temperature of the scrotum, and inhibited by normal body temperature. Sperm are actually produced in coiled *seminiferous tubules*, which fill most of the volume of each testis. Epithelial cells lining the tubules ultimately differentiate into *primary spermatocytes*, each of which undergoes meiosis (refer to the part on meiosis later in this chapter) to produce four haploid *spermatids* (immature sperm cells). Other cells located in the tubules, the *Sertoli cells*, function to nourish the developing sperm cells during this time. It is interesting to note that sperm production begins during adolescence, and continues throughout a male's entire life! Spermatids begin to mature while still in the testis, and the process continues as they move to the *epididymis*.

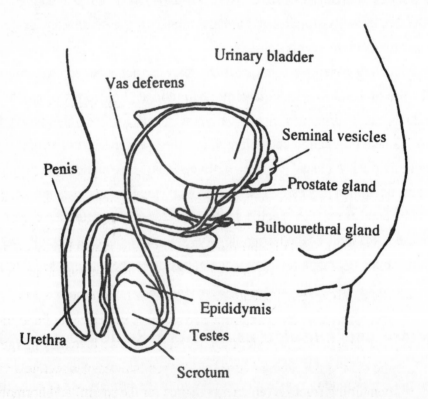

Figure 18.1: The male reproductive system

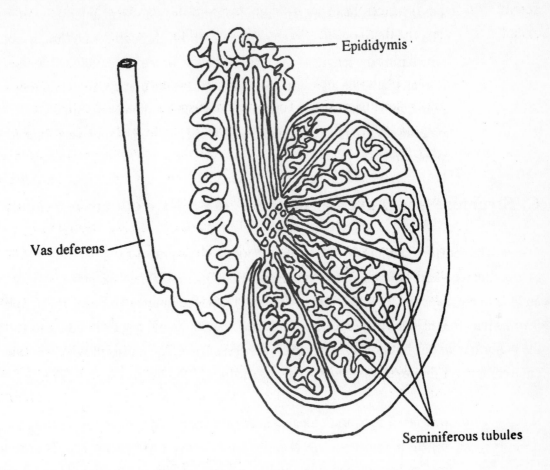

Figure 18.2: A testis (internal view)

♦ *epididymis:* The epididymis is a coiled tube that lies just above each testis. Here sperm complete their differentiation, acquiring a distinctive shape and the ability to move. A mature sperm cell consists of a head, which contains the nucleus with the chromosomes; the body, which harbors mitochondria for energy production; and a tail, which allows the sperm to "swim".

♦ *vas deferens:* Each epididymis is connected to a tube called the vas deferens (plural: vasa deferentia), in which many sperm are stored and transported. The vasa deferentia enter the abdominal cavity where they merge and join the duct of the *seminal vesicles*. The seminal vesicles secrete a viscous fluid containing fructose (an energy source for the sperm) and hormones that will stimulate the female system when the sperm are deposited. The sperm then travel through the *prostate gland*, which secretes an alkaline fluid into the *semen* to enhance sperm motility. Ultimately, the sperm enter the *urethra*. The sperm, immersed in semen, exit the body through the urethra, a tube which runs the length of the *penis*, the male organ of sexual intercourse. (Recall that urine also exits the body through the urethra; in males, the reproductive and urinary systems are intimately connected. Special precautions exist that prevent the conduction of both semen and urine at the same time.)

C. Structure and Function of the Female Reproductive System

The female reproductive system is composed of the primary sex organs, the *ovaries*, and a variety of other important organs that function in the transport of egg cells and the maintenance of the life of the developing fetus (see Figures 18.3 and 18.4). The *ovaries* play the major role of producing and releasing functional egg cells, and also secrete the major female sex hormones, *estrogen and progesterone*. The *uterus* provides a suitable environment for the development of a new organism.

- ◆ *ovaries:* The ovaries, located in the abdominal cavity, are the primary sex organs in females. Cells called *primary oocytes* will eventually give rise to mature haploid egg cells through meiosis, similar to sperm production in males. Unlike sperm production, however, all of the primary oocytes a female will ever produce are formed by birth, and all are arrested in prophase of meiosis I. They are surrounded by a structure called the *ovarian follicle*, whose cells provide nutrition for the developing egg. At the onset of puberty, a follicle ruptures and an oocyte is released approximately once every 28 days in a process called *ovulation*; the first meiotic division is completed just before the oocyte is released. Meiosis II will only take place if the egg is fertilized. Females stop releasing eggs at *menopause*, which normally occurs at around age 50.
- ◆ *oviducts:* After ovulation, the newly released oocyte is swept into a tube called the oviduct or *Fallopian tubes*, located near the ovary. The egg travels through the oviduct towards the *uterus* due to smooth muscle contractions. If fertilization occurs, it must happen in the oviduct; whether or not it becomes fertilized, the egg will eventually reach the *uterus*.

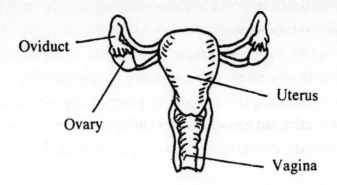

Figure 18.3: The female reproductive system

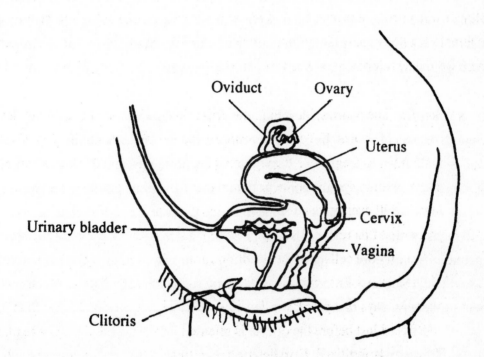

Figure 18.4: The female repoductive system (internal view)

♦ *uterus:* A fertilized egg begins dividing during its journey and will implant
itself into the uterine wall (called the *endometrium*). Here it will continue to
develop and grow, the details of which will be discussed later. If the egg

has not been fertilized, it will eventually be expelled from the uterus with most of the uterine lining during *menstruation*.

♦ *vagina:* The vagina is a muscular tube which connects the uterus to the external environment. It therefore serves a dual function: it is the female organ of sexual intercourse, which allows the penis to enter and deposit sperm, and it also functions as the birth canal, through which the fetus will emerge when it is born. The *cervix* is the muscle surrounding the opening of the uterus into the vagina.

D. Hormone Production and Regulation in Males and Females

As we noted previously, in addition to their roles in creating gametes, the testes and ovaries also produce and secrete the major male and female sex hormones.

Testosterone production begins in males during early embryonic development, and is responsible for the development of an embryo as a male rather than a female. After birth, the production of testosterone is inhibited until about the age of ten, when a surge in its production triggers the onset of puberty. The testosterone produced during this period stimulates the testes to begin producing sperm. It is also responsible for the development of the male secondary sexual characteristics, including the development of facial and body hair, deepening of the voice, and the growth of muscle tissue. The production of testosterone is at all times controlled by various pituitary hormones and the hypothalamus.

In females, the hypothalamus controls the release of various pituitary hormones which interact with estrogen and progesterone to create the *menstrual cycle*, the period from ovulation to menstruation that occurs on a monthly basis. As in males, the onset of puberty follows increased secretion of sex hormones, and, in addition to initiating the menstrual cycle, causes the development of the female secondary sexual characteristics, which include enlargement of the hips and breasts.

E. Sexual Response and Stimulation

In males, sexual excitation causes *erection* of the penis due to an influx of blood into the erectile tissue which occupies most of the volume of the penis. Erection is accompanied by the secretion of small amounts of seminal fluid from the *bulbourethral (Cowper's) glands*, which functions as a lubricant in anticipation of sexual intercourse. If sensory receptors on the penis receive continued stimulation, various muscles involuntarily contract causing the forceful *ejaculation* of sperm through the vasa deferentia and urethra, experienced as a series of pleasant sensations referred to as *orgasm*.

While females may also experience orgasm, it is not necessary in order for conception to take place. The *clitoris*, which is developmentally homologous to the penis, is the organ of sexual stimulation in females. When arousal occurs, pleasant sensations are accompanied by the secretion into the vagina of a lubricating fluid, and muscular contractions occur similar to those in males.

F. Meiosis and Gametogenesis

Meiosis is the process of cell division that allows haploid cells to be created from diploid parent cells. It occurs only in sexual reproduction, only in the primary sex organs, and only for the purpose of gamete production, or *gametogenesis*. Meiosis is similar to mitosis (see Chapter 12), but two complete division cycles take place instead of one, and four haploid cells are produced as opposed to two diploid cells.

Meiosis consists of the following stages and events (see Figure 18.5):

- ◆ *prophase I:* During this phase, chromosomes condense, the nuclear envelope breaks down, and spindle formation begins.
- ◆ *metaphase I*: At this stage, homologous chromosome pairs line up on the cell's equator; this is the major difference between meiosis and mitosis!
- ◆ *anaphase I*: The homologous chromosomes separate and begin to move towards the opposite poles of the cell.
- ◆ *telophase I:* Nuclear membranes may or may not form and cytokinesis may or may not occur; regardless, the haploid sets of chromosomes have been separated, and are now ready to proceed through meiosis II.
- ◆ *prophase II:* During this phase, chromosomes condense, the nuclear envelope breaks down, and spindle formation begins again.
- ◆ *metaphase II*: At this stage, chromosomes (which still consist of two chromatids) line up randomly on the cell's equator.
- ◆ *anaphase II*: The chromatids separate and begin to move towards the opposite poles of the cell.
- ◆ *telophase II:* As meiosis draws to a close, sets of haploid genomes become enclosed by new nuclear membranes, the chromosomes begin to decondense, and the spindle apparatus is disassembled.

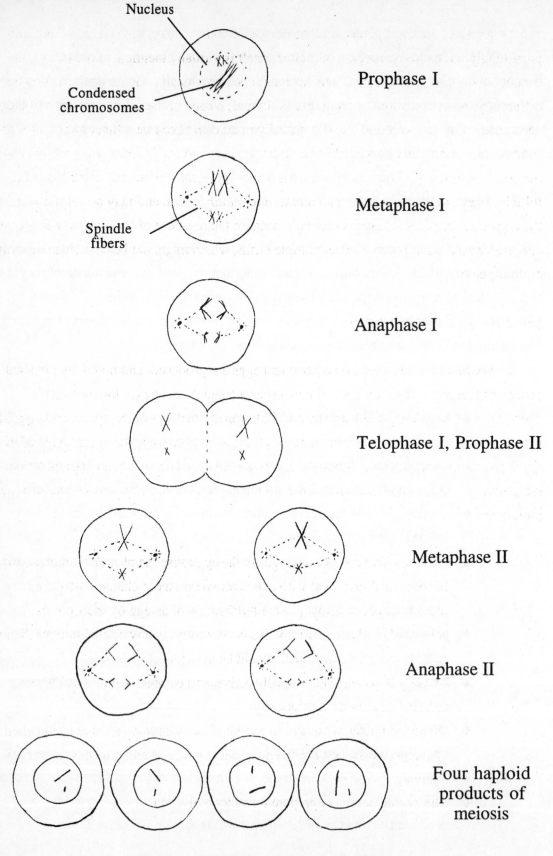

Figure 18.5: The stages of meiosis

As noted earlier, the result of meiotic cell division is four haploid cells from each parental diploid cell. The process of meiosis itself is virtually identical in the two sexes, except for the timing of the divisions (as mentioned previously). Gametogenesis proceeds differently, however, in males and females. In males, each of the newly created haploid cells, referred to as spermatids, will eventually mature and become a functional sperm cell. In females, on the other hand, only one of the four haploid cells produced by meiosis will become a mature egg. The other three cells do not grow and are pushed to the side of the follicle. They are visible microscopically as *dark polar bodies*, and play no further role in the reproductive process. This is probably because the presence of four functional eggs at one time would virtually guarantee multiple births, which might not be desirable depending on the species.

G. Early Development

We have already seen how sperm and eggs are produced, and noted the physical processes that allow them to meet. When a sperm contacts an egg (in the oviduct), a chemical reaction takes place between molecules on the surfaces of the sperm and egg. This binding signals the sperm to release enzymes that begin to dissolve the outer layers of the egg's protective coating, and ultimately allows the fusion of the sperm and egg plasma membranes. The sperm nucleus now enters the cytoplasm of the egg, and several changes rapidly ensue:

- ◆ Electrical and physical changes in the egg cause the plasma membrane to become unable to bind with any other sperm; these changes are called blocks to "polyspermy", or the fertilization of an egg by multiple sperm cells. It should be clear why this is necessary, as any cell with more than a diploid set of chromosomes would be inviable.
- ◆ The egg becomes metabolically active, and completes meiosis II. Protein synthesis increases dramatically.
- ◆ When the nuclei of the sperm and egg fuse, a diploid cell is created called a zygote. Now the cell has the potential to continue along its developmental pathway.
- ◆ The zygote begins to prepare for mitotic division.

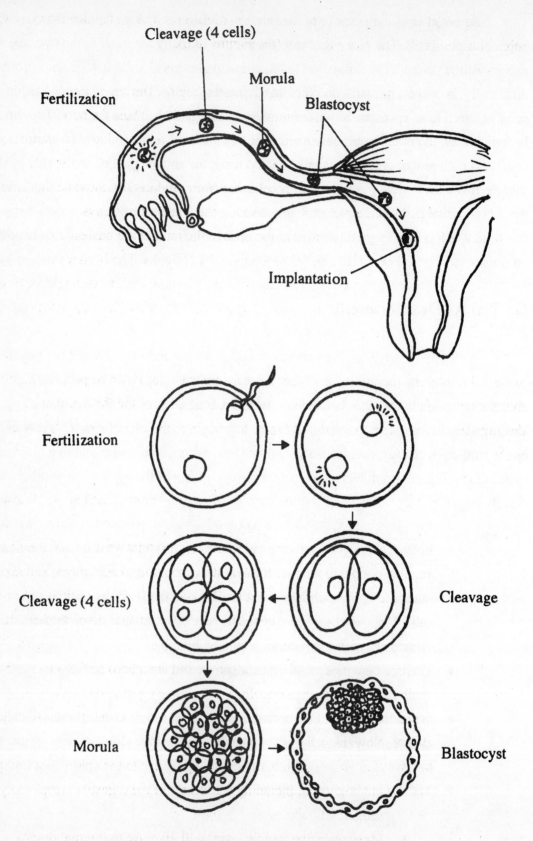

Figure 18.6: Early developmental events

After fertilization occurs, the egg continues its journey towards the uterus, and more changes take place along the way (see Figure 18.6).

♦ *cleavage*, a modified form of mitosis, begins. During cleavage, mitotic cell divisions are not accompanied by cell growth. Thus, the number of cells is increasing, but the overall volume is not increasing. This is because no nutrients are yet available to provide energy for growth processes.

♦ *a morula*, or solid ball of cells, has been produced by the time the dividing cells reach the uterus. This usually takes about three days.

♦ *a blastocyst* is formed as the cells of the morula are pushed towards the periphery, and consists of a hollow ball of cells. The blastocyst forms after about six days, and is often called the blastula in other vertebrate species.

♦ *implantation* of the blastocyst into the uterine wall (the endometrium) occurs towards the end of the first week.

After implantation, the cell mass that has implanted itself can be properly referred to as the *embryo*. The embryonic stage lasts until the beginning of the third month of development. This is the most crucial period for proper formation of major structures, and many important changes occur during embryonic development.

♦ The *placenta* forms between the embryo and mother, and allows transport of nutrients and oxygen to the embryo for energy production. The placental connection also allows the transport of embryonic wastes from the embryo to the blood stream of the mother. It is important to note that while small substances such as those mentioned above freely diffuse across the placenta, it is not a direct connection, and the circulation of mother and embryo remain separate.

♦ *Gastrulation* changes the overall shape of the embryo so that it resembles a three-layered disc, the *gastrula*. Three primary germ layers are formed by this process, each of which will eventually give rise to different structures in the adult organism:

    ● *Endoderm*, the inner layer, will give rise to the epithelium lining all inner cavities, including the linings of the digestive, respiratory, and urogenital tracts.

    ● *Mesoderm*, the middle layer, will give rise to internal organs, muscle and connective tissues, and the majority of internal structures.

- *Ectoderm*, the outer layer, will give rise to the nervous system and the skin.

♦ The embryo becomes enclosed in a fluid filled sac, the *amnion*, surrounded by an amniotic membrane and several other membranes.

By the end of the embryonic period, roughly the *first trimester*, *organogenesis* and *morphogenesis* (the development of major organs and body shape, respectively) are basically complete. From the third month forward until birth (the second and third trimesters), the developing organism is referred to as the *fetus*. While the fetal stage lasts the longest, the overall body plan has already been laid out, and most of the time spent as a fetus involves the growth and maturation of existing structures. After a total of approximately nine months, labor begins as the uterus begins to contract and the amnionic membrane ruptures. The baby passes through the dilated cervix and vagina, and enters the world as a new individual.

Chapter 18 Problems

Passage 18.1 (Questions 1-4)

Several genetic disorders are caused by trisomies or monosomies, the presence of one too many or one too few of a particular chromosome, respectively. Some such conditions include Down syndrome, which is caused by the presence of 3 copies of chromosome 21 (trisomy 21); Turner's syndrome, caused by the presence of only one sex chromosome (monosomy X, denoted XO); and Klinefelter's syndrome, caused by the presence of an extra sex chromosome (XXY).

Individuals with Down syndrome are somewhat mentally retarded, exhibit characteristic facial features, and suffer from a wide variety of chronic health problems. Turner's individuals appear female, and may suffer slight retardation while Klinefelter's individuals appear male, and likewise may be somewhat retarded. While nondisjunction occurs randomly, no adults with trisomies or monosomies involving any chromosomes other than the sex chromosomes and chromosome 21 are ever observed; if such a condition occurs, it causes miscarriage or early death.

The major cause of trisomies and monosomies is nondisjunction (failure to separate) of homologous chromosomes or chromatids during meiosis, so that gametes are created with 2 copies or no copies of a particular chromosome (when there should be one of each).

1. Which of the following cases of nondisjunction could lead to the development of an individual with Turner's syndrome?
   A. Failure of the X and Y chromosome. to separate during meiosis I in the father
   B. Failure of the two X chromosomes to separate during meiosis I in the mother.
   C. Failure of the two Y chromatids to separate during meiosis II in the father.
   D. All of the above events could lead to Turner's syndrome.

2. The observations that Turner's individuals appear female and Klinefelter's individuals appear male may give us information about sex determination in humans. From this information, we can tell that:
   A. Sex is determined by the number of X chromosomes (1=male, 2=female).
   B. Sex is determined by the presence or absence of the Y chromosome.
   C. Sex is determined by the egg, and not the sperm.

D. Any of the above are consistent with the observations.

3. The fact that trisomies of only chromosome 21 and the sex chromosomes are observed in adults implies that:

   A. Chromosome 21 and the sex chromosomes are more prone to nondisjunction.

   B. Trisomies or monosomies of any other chromosomes have such detrimental effects that they do not allow development and cause death.

   C. There are no genes for fundamental life processes located on chromosome 21.

   D. Both B and C are correct.

4. The older a woman gets, the greater the chances that she will give birth to a Down syndrome child. Which of the following statements is true?

   A. Only the mother (through the egg) can cause Down syndrome in a child; the father (through the sperm) cannot.

   B. Older eggs have a greater chance of undergoing nondisjunction, since all of a females eggs are present at birth, and meiosis is only completed after fertilization.

   C. The age of a man is completely irrelevant with respect to the chances of his sperm contributing

to the formation of a Down syndrome child.

   D. Both B and C are correct.

Questions 5-10 are independent of any passage and independent of each other.

---

5. Which of the following statements is true regarding twin formation?

   A. Identical twins result from the fertilization of one egg by two sperm.

   B. Fraternal twins result when two eggs are mistakenly released at once, and each is fertilized by one sperm.

   C. Fraternal twins result when one egg is fertilized by one sperm, and the developing embryo splits apart, each part being able to grow into a new individual.

   D. Identical twins are not really genetically identical.

6. Fertilization normally takes place in which structure of the female reproductive system?

   A. The vagina
   B. The uterus
   C. The oviduct
   D. The ovary

7. Which of the following statements is true regarding the male and female reproductive and urinary systems?

A. In both males and females, the urethra carries urine, and also functions in the reproductive system, in males for the delivery of sperm and in females as the orifice that accepts the sperm.

B. In males, sperm and urine ultimately leave the body through the same tube, the urethra.

C. In females, the ureters play a role in oogenesis, so the two systems are interconnected, but in a different way than occurs in males.

D. None of the above statements is true.

8. In the 1960s, a drug called thalidomide, ironically prescribed for morning sickness, was responsible for the malformation of several babies. In general, at what time during pregnancy would it be most dangerous to take a drug that is toxic or harmful to the developing child?

A. During the zygote stage

B. Before implantation

C. During the embryonic stage

D. During the fetal stage

9. Which embryonic germ layer ultimately gives rise to the structures of the nervous system?

A. Endoderm

B. Mesoderm

C. Ectoderm

D. Gastroderm

10. In most marine vertebrates (fish), physical copulation does not occur; instead, eggs and sperm are simply released into the water, where they can meet and fertilization may occur. Humans have various blocks to polyspermy, and fishes have similar mechanisms to prevent fertilization of an egg by more than one sperm. In addition, their method of fertilization probably requires:

A. The release of far greater amounts of eggs by females.

B. Mechanisms to prevent the fertilization of more than one egg by a single sperm.

C. Mechanisms to avoid potential cross-species fertilization, which would be counterproductive since members of different species are genetically incompatible.

D. Both A and C are correct.

SECTION 5
GENETICS AND EVOLUTION

The topics of genetics and evolution are intimately linked together. Not only do they complement each other, but they are central to our current understanding of all aspects of biology. These two topics unite and unify the various fields of biology, including molecular biology, microbiology, and anatomy and physiology. Therefore, the study of genetics and evolution is an absolute necessity for all students of biology.

In addition, the field of genetics is rapidly advancing. This has important consequences in many areas, not the least of which is medicine. Genetics has aided our understanding of cancer, inherited diseases, reproduction, infectious diseases, and much more. In the future, we will rely heavily on genetics to help us diagnose and treat a host of medical conditions.

Chapter 19
Genetics

A. Introduction

During the American Civil War, and at about the time Darwin was proposing his theory of evolution (see Chapter 20), a monk in what is now the Czech Republic was growing peas in the Abby gardens. Gregor Mendel was using them to unlock the secrets of inheritance.

No one prior to Mendel had undertaken a systematic study to gain insight into how traits are passed from one generation to the next. Breeders of plants and animals were well aware of certain characteristics of inheritance, but there was no theory or explanation of how traits were transmitted from parent to offspring. Mendel advanced our knowledge of the field tremendously, and his principles and theories have been shown to be valid over and over again. We still use his methodologies today.

Mendel was successful for several reasons. First, his choice of the garden pea provided him with an ideal model system. The traits Mendel observed in the peas were easy to score and only had two variations; for example, flowers were either white or purple, plants were either tall or short, and seeds were either wrinkled or round. Plants with different traits could be interbred and huge numbers of progeny could be obtained for analysis. But, perhaps more importantly than his choice of a model system, Mendel kept meticulous records, and he used mathematics to analyze his data.

B. Dominant and Recessive Traits

Mendel began his experiments with pure breeding strains. These were strains that had been bred for many generations so their progeny always exhibited the same traits, and these traits were always exactly the same in the parents and offspring. In his experiments, he crossed two pure breeding strains that differed only in one trait. The two original strains in this type of cross are called the *parental generation*, or *P*. The resulting progeny are called the *first filial generation*, or F_1. Mendel noticed that the F_1 plants displayed only one of the traits from the parents. When Mendel allowed the F_1 plants to self fertilize, they produced the *second filial generation* (F_2). In this generation, some of the F_2 plants had the same trait as the F_1 plants (and hence of one of the P plants), but some had the trait not seen in the F_1 generation (but seen in the other P strain).

Mendel proposed that one trait was masking the expression of the other trait in the F_1 generation but the masked trait could reappear in the F_2. He called the trait that was always expressed *dominant* and the trait that could be masked *recessive*.

For example, when Mendel crossed plants that produced yellow seeds with plants that produced green seeds, all the F_1 plants produced only yellow seeds. After self crossing the F_1 plants, some of the F_2 plants produced yellow seeds, and some produced green seeds. Specifically, Mendel found that about three quarters of the F_2 plants displayed the dominant trait (yellow seeds) and one quarter showed the recessive trait (green seeds). Another way to phrase this is to say there was a 3:1 ratio of yellow to green seeds in the F_2. Mendel found that each of the traits he looked at behaved exactly the same way. All had one variation that was dominant in the F_1 generation, and all showed a 3:1 ratio of dominant to recessive expression in the F_2 generation.

C. The Principle of Segregation

Mendel concluded that each plant contained two "factors" for each trait that could be inherited by the progeny. Each parent contributed one factor to the offspring. If the progeny received at least one factor that was dominant, the offspring would show that trait. Only offspring inheriting two recessive factors would show that characteristic. Since the two factors remain distinct and do not blend, Mendel called this the *Principle of Segregation*.

Mendel did not know what these factors were, but today we can explain his observations on a molecular level. Mendel's "factors" are *genes*, and the different varieties of the genes (purple vs. white flowers, for example) are called *alleles*. Mendel's observations, particularly his Principle of Segregation, are easily explained with our knowledge of meiosis (see Chapter 18). During meiosis, the pairs of homologous chromosomes (those that carry the same information, or the same genes) line up and one chromosome of the pair moves to one pole of the cell while the other moves to the opposite pole. Therefore, one allele will be distributed to each new cell.

D. Phenotypes and Genotypes

If you think about alleles and how they are expressed, you may realize that a dominant trait can be expressed in two ways: if an individual carries two copies of a dominant allele, or if it carries one copy of the dominant allele and one copy of the recessive allele. The only way to display the recessive trait is if two copies of the recessive allele are present. We use two terms in genetics to distinguish between what alleles an individual carries and what trait is expressed. *Genotype* refers to the exact alleles present, and *phenotype* is the trait that is observed. If the two alleles present are the same (either both dominant or both recessive), the condition is called *homozygous*. If two different alleles are present in the genotype (the dominant and the recessive), the condition is called *heterozygous*.

We are now ready to examine the inheritance of traits on a molecular level and to discuss some advanced topics in genetics. Be sure you understand the basics before you move on.

E. Monohybrid Crosses

When only one trait in a cross is examined, the mating is called a *monohybrid cross*. We can represent the cross in a simple manner and make predictions about the outcome. In crosses, the dominant allele is usually represented by a capital letter and the recessive allele is represented by the lower case. In addition, the dominant allele is used to represent the gene itself. For example, since yellow is dominant to green seeds, the letter *Y* is chosen to represent the gene for seed color. The dominant allele is *Y* while the recessive allele is represented as *y*. Recall that Mendel used only pure breeding strains in his experiments. Therefore, all his parental plants were homozygous.

If we consider the example from above, where Mendel crossed plants having yellow seeds with those having green seeds, we can represent the cross as follows:

P: *YY* X *yy*

Each parent will contribute one allele (through the gametes) to the offspring. From the homozygous dominant parent, the only allele that can be passed on to the offspring will be Y, while in the homozygous recessive parent, only a y allele can be transmitted. Therefore, all the offspring will be Yy. Remember that Mendel self crossed the F_1 progeny to obtain the F_2. The results of this cross are shown below:

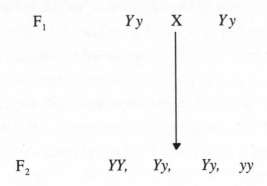

There are three genotypes in the F_2 generation (YY, Yy, and yy) but only two phenotypes (yellow and green seeds). Moreover, there is a 3:1 ratio of yellow to green seeds.

How can you determine the genotypes of the progeny from a cross? Typically, a matrix can be arranged to predict the outcomes of a cross. This matrix is called a *Punnett square*. On one side of the square, all the possible gametes from one parent are listed, while on the other side, all the gametes from the other parent are listed. The gametes are then combined in the boxes. Consider our example of the parental cross (P) above:

	Y (P gamete)	Y (P gamete)
y (P gamete)	Yy (F₁ progeny)	Yy (F₁ progeny)
y (P gamete)	Yy (F₁ progeny)	Yy (F₁ progeny)

All the progeny (the F_1 generation) are genotypically heterozygotes, and each has a yellow phenotype. When the F_1 individuals are crossed, the Punnett square looks like this:

	Y (F$_1$ gamete)	y (F$_1$ gamete)
Y (F$_1$ gamete)	YY (F$_2$ progeny)	Yy (F$_2$ progeny)
y (F$_1$ gamete)	Yy (F$_2$ progeny)	yy (F$_2$ progeny)

The F$_2$ generation shows three genotypes: one quarter homozygous dominant (*YY*), one quarter homozygous recessive (*yy*) and one half heterozygous (*Yy*). The corresponding phenotypes are three quarters yellow and one quarter green, or a 3:1 ratio.

F. Test Crosses

Since the homozygous dominant genotype and the heterozygous genotype both express the same phenotype, we cannot be certain of the genotype of a plant that produces yellow seeds. We can determine its genotype by crossing it with a homozygous recessive plant, a true breeding plant that produces green seeds (genotype *yy*). This is called a *test cross*. The following two Punnett squares illustrate what progeny we would obtain from a test cross involving a homozygous dominant (left) or a heterozygote (right):

	Y	Y
y	Yy	Yy
y	Yy	Yy

	Y	y
y	Yy	yy
y	Yy	yy

If the yellow seed strain is homozygous dominant, all the progeny from the test cross will have the yellow phenotype. However, if the yellow seed strain is heterozygous, half of the progeny from the test cross will have yellow seeds and half will have green seeds. In this manner, test crosses can be very valuable in determining the exact genotype of individuals who express the dominant phenotype.

G. Sex Linked Traits

In humans, sex is determined by the inheritance of two X chromosomes (female) or an X and Y (male). Much information is carried on the X chromosome. This creates a unique situation regarding dominant and recessive genes on this chromosome. In females, the expression of one recessive allele can, of course, be hidden by the expression of a dominant allele on the other X chromosome. But in males, if only one recessive allele is inherited, the trait is expressed. This condition, where only one allele is present and will be expressed, is called the *hemizygous* condition.

When working out crosses with genes carried on the X chromosome, the X and Y chromosome must both be represented. For example, the trait for color blindness is a recessive X linked trait (we will represent it as X^c). If a heterozygous female ($X X^c$) marries a normal man (XY), the probability that their children will show the trait can be determined using a Punnett square:

	X	X^c
X	XX	XX^c
Y	XY	X^cY

Half of the sons will be colorblind, and half of the daughters will be heterozygotes, or *carriers* of the condition.

We call traits carried on the X chromosome *sex linked* traits. Traits not carried on the X or Y chromosome are called *autosomal* traits. Y linked traits are called *Hollandric* traits. However, due to the lack of genes on the Y chromosome, this type of inheritance is not well characterized and is disputed by many researchers.

H. Dihybrid Crosses

We can also examine crosses with two different traits (a *dihybrid cross*) to see how the traits are inherited by the progeny. Consider a cross between two pure breeding strains, one with yellow seeds and purple flowers, and one with green seeds and white flowers (yellow is dominant to green and purple is dominant to white). We can represent the cross like this:

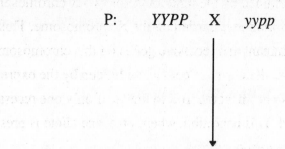

P: *YYPP*   X   *yypp*

F₁   all progeny will have the genotype YyPp
with the phenotype yellow seeds and purple flowers

When the F₁ generation is self-crossed, we can set up a Punnett square of all possible combinations of gametes. Look carefully at the F₁ genotype. Each gamete must contain one allele for the gene for seed color and one allele for the gene for flower color. The analysis would look like this:

	YP	**Yp**	**yP**	**yp**
YP	YYPP	YYPp	YyPP	YyPp
Yp	YYPp	YYpp	YyPp	Yypp
yP	YyPP	YyPp	yyPP	yyPp
yp	YyPy	Yypp	yyPp	yypp

By counting all the squares and combining the phenotypes, you should see that 9/16 of the progeny will have yellow seeds and purple flowers, 3/16 will have yellow seeds and white flowers, 3/16 will have green seeds and purple flowers, and 1/16 will have green seeds and purple flowers. Thus, the phenotypic ratio for a dihybrid cross is 9:3:3:1.

I.   Principle of Independent Assortment and Linkage

Mendel's second theory, the *principle of independent assortment*, came from his observations of dihybrid crosses. As you can see in the example above, the distribution of alleles for one trait in the gametes does not influence the distribution of alleles for the second trait. In other words, during meiosis, the alleles segregate, or assort, independently of each other. The traits will be distributed equally in the gametes.

This principle is violated when two genes are physically *linked*, or joined, on the same chromosome. When this occurs, the alleles for two different traits do not assort independently, but instead are inherited together.

J.   Exceptions to Mendelian Inheritance

Most traits are not inherited in a simple dominant/recessive fashion. In fact, most genes have more than two alleles, and most traits are influenced by more than one gene. It can be very confusing. We will not go into an in-depth discussion of all these exceptions, but we will list the most common variations in the dominant/recessive inheritance pattern:

- ♦ *multiple alleles*: more than two alleles exist for a gene. The most common example of this is blood type in humans: the ABO system. Three different alleles exist, designated I^A , I^B and i.

- ♦ *incomplete* (or *partial*) *dominance*: the heterozygote displays a phenotype that is intermediate to the phenotypes of the two homozygotes. Flower color in snapdragons is a classic example of this. When two pure breeding plants are crossed, one that has red flowers and one that has white, all the F_1 progeny have pink flowers. When the F_1 plants are crossed, one quarter have red flowers, one half develop pink flowers, and one quarter have white flowers.

- ♦ *codominance*: the heterozygote exhibits both phenotypes of the homozygotes. We can go back to the ABO blood types for an example of codominance. The i allele is always recessive, so individuals who are $I^A i$ are blood type A, $I^B i$ are blood type B, and ii are blood type O. Homozygotes $I^A I^A$ and $I^B I^B$ are A and B, respectively. However, when an individual inherits the alleles $I^A I^B$, that individual expresses both phenotypes, and is said to be blood type AB.

- ♦ *gene interaction*: two genes interact to affect the phenotype of one trait. A novel phenotype will be produced by this interaction. *Polygenic traits* are characteristics that are caused by many genes acting together. For example, skin color is a polygenic trait.

♦ *epistasis*: one gene interferes with the phenotypic expression of another gene. This differs from gene interaction in that no new phenotype is produced. A related phenomenon is *pleiotropy*. This refers to one gene affecting many traits. One example of this would be the genetic disorder Sickle Cell anemia. Individuals with this disease have a mutation in the gene encoding hemoglobin, but have many different organs and systems affected.

K. Environmental Effects on Gene Expression

The development and expression of traits also depends on the external and internal environment. The frequency with which a certain trait is expressed in a population is called *penetrance*, and the extent to which a phenotype is expressed in an individual is called *expressivity*.

The external environment can influence phenotypes. For example, Himalayan rabbits have mostly white fur, while black coat color is found only on the extremities (ears, paws, nose and tail). The gene that produces pigment in the fur is only active at low temperatures, producing the unusual pattern.

Internal factors can influence the expression of genes. Age will often influence the expression of a gene, such as is seen with the development of Huntington's disease in humans. Sex can also determine phenotypes. This is most evident in the preponderance of baldness in human males.

Other factors, such as behavior and intelligence, are also heavily influenced by environment. Although there is currently a debate among scientists (one that may not end for a long time), it is evident that these traits are determined by both "nature" (genetics) and "nurture" (environment).

Chapter 19 Problems

Passage 19.1 (Questions 1-6)

     In the fruit fly, *Drosophila melanogaster*, many different genes influence eye color. Mutations in any one of these genes will change the color of the eyes. Normally, flies have brick red eyes (this is called the *wild type* condition). The inheritance patterns of these variations has been extensively studied. The results of some crosses are described below.

Cross 1:
Wild type flies were crossed with brown eyed flies. The F_1 progeny all had red eyes. When the F_1 were crossed with each other, 3/4 of the F_2 had red eyes and 1/4 had brown eyes.

Cross 2:
Wild type females were crossed with white eyed males. All of the F_1's had red eyes. In the F_2 generation, all of the females had red eyes, while half of the males had red eyes and half had white eyes.

Cross 3.
Brown eyed flies were crossed with scarlet eyed flies (scarlet is known to be an autosomal recessive trait). All of the F_1 progeny had red eyes. The F_2 progeny showed a ratio of 9:3:3:1 red to brown to scarlet to white.

Cross 4:
Another mutation affecting the eye, called Bar, does not affect color. Instead, it affects the shape of the eye, changing it from the normal round phenotype to an elongated, oval shape. Wild type flies were crossed with Bar eyed flies. Half of the F_1 progeny had Bar shaped eyes and half had wild type eyes. When the wild type F_1 flies were crossed with the Bar eyed F_1 flies, the F_2 generation showed the same phenotypes as the F_1 generation: half were wild type, half had Bar eyes.

1. The inheritance pattern of brown eyes fits with which of the following mechanisms?
   A. autosomal recessive
   B. autosomal dominant
   C. sex-linked recessive
   D. sex-linked dominant

2. The inheritance pattern of white eyes fits with which of the following mechanisms?
   A. autosomal recessive
   B. autosomal dominant
   C. sex-linked recessive
   D. sex-linked dominant

3. The inheritance pattern of Bar eyes fits with which of the following mechanisms?
   A. autosomal recessive
   B. auttsomal dominant
   C. sex-linked recessive
   D. sex-linked dominant

4. What is the best way to describe the genotype of the Bar eyed mutants in the parental generation in cross 4?
   A. homozygous dominant
   B. homozygous recessive
   C. heterozygous
   D. hemizygous

5. To determine the genotype of the red F_2 individuals in cross 1, a test cross could be done. What should be the genotype of the flies used in the test cross? Assume the symbol b^+ indicates the wild type allele for the brown gene, while b indicates the mutation.
   A. b^+b^+
   B. bb
   C. b^+b
   D. $X^b X^b$ and/or $X^b Y$

6. The relationship between brown and scarlet eye color is an example of

A. codominance.
B. incomplete dominance.
C. gene interaction.
D. epistasis.

Questions 7-8 are independent of any passage and independent of each other.

7. A couple has a child with cystic fibrosis, an autosomal recessive disease. Neither parent has the disease. Another child is born, who is unaffected. What is the probability that this unaffected child is a carrier of cystic fibrosis?
   A. 1/4
   B. 1/2
   C. 2/3
   D. 3/4

8. A woman with blood type AB marries a man with blood type B. Which of the following blood types could not be found in their children?
   A. A
   B. B
   C. AB
   D. O

Chapter 20
Evolution

A. Introduction

Evolution is perhaps the most important concept in biology. As discussed before, it is one of the unifying principles of biology. Indeed, most scientists would list it as <u>the</u> unifying topic. It has often been said that nothing in biology makes sense without evolution.

The theory of evolution is not disputed among scientists. Observations and evidence collected and examined over the past 150 years supports this theory as much as, or even more than, other theories such as the atomic theory, the cell theory or the theory of gravity. However, the exact mechanisms of evolution, the details of how it occurred and continues to occur, are, in deed, disputed. This is the challenge and excitement facing researchers today.

Evolution is refuted by some nonscientists, mostly fundamentalist, who believe in *creationism*, the idea that all living things arose through divine creation in their present forms. A few points are important to understand in this debate:

- ◆ Science cannot prove or disprove the existence of God. Faith is not in the realm of science. We can, however, gather evidence to support or refute scientific questions, such as whether or not evolution occurred. In this case, we can no longer ignore or disregard this process. It is, in scientific terms, a fact.

- ◆ Many religions, including the Catholic and Protestant churches and all but the most conservative Jewish sects, recognize and do not dispute the major tenants of evolution. Most believe, however, that humans are special in that a divine creator has given us something, a soul or free will, that sets us apart from all other living things.

♦ Evolutionary theories do not address the origins of the earth or necessarily the beginnings of life. *Evolution* is defined as, and is used to describe, change with time.

There are many aspects of and ways to study evolution. We will only discuss some of the basics in this chapter.

B. Charles Darwin

The person usually cited as the key figure in our understanding and development of the theory of evolution is Charles Darwin. He was not the first to propose the idea of evolution, but he was the first to provide extensive support for the process, and he also postulated a mechanism for how evolution occurred.

Darwin's ideas were born on a five year voyage he took around the world aboard the H.M.S. *Beagle*, beginning in 1831. Darwin was the ship's naturalist, and he made extensive observations and collected specimens, most notably from up and down both coasts of South America and from the Galapagos islands, located off the coast of Equador. His book, *On the Origin of Species by Means of Natural Selection*, was published 22 years after his return to England. Several observations helped Darwin formulate his theory. These include:

♦ *overproduction*: Darwin noted that plants and animals produce many offspring, more than the number necessary for their own replacement. In other words, to replace themselves in a population, a mating pair of sexually reproducing organisms need only have two offspring. The production of large amounts of offspring means that growth will occur in an exponential fashion, creating a huge population in only several generations. In reality, however, this exponential growth is not seen. Many factors limit the population size, some which are discussed below.

♦ *variation:* No two individuals are exactly the same. There is always some variation, something that is different, among individuals. In addition, these variations can be passed on from parent to offspring, as shown through selective breeding of domesticated plants and animals. Darwin did not know the mechanisms behind this process (and Mendel's work was not recognized at the time), but it was obvious that traits were inherited.

◆ *competition:* All species require certain resources in order to survive. Some things, such as soil, food and water, are in limited quantities in the environment. Therefore, different species compete for their use. In addition, a population reproducing geometrically will put individuals of the same species in competition with one another.

◆ *survival and reproduction of the fittest:* Competition results in the survival of some organisms over others. Certain variations will contribute to this survival, and individuals who posses these traits are more likely to reach reproductive maturity. Therefore, the offspring of these individuals will inherit these traits and will have a better chance at survival. In this way, beneficial traits are selected and eventually will increase with frequency in the population.

Thus we can see that overproduction produces a large number of individuals, each having different variations. Competition between species and among individuals of the same species results in survival of the fittest. The best of each generation reproduce and pass on these traits to the next generation. From these observations, Darwin postulated a mechanism that would explain how these factors contribute to evolution. This process is known as *natural selection* and is the cornerstone of the theory of evolution.

C. Causes of Evolution: Natural Selection, Mutation, and Gene Flow

Darwin's notion of natural selection is not necessarily the only cause of evolution, but it is the key that unifies the theory. Two other important factors are *mutation* and *gene flow*. Before we begin our discussion of these three processes, it is important to note that evolution occurs in populations, not individuals. A *population* is defined as a group of individuals of the same species occupying a given area. Therefore, the remainder of our discussion will focus on populations of individuals, and how changes arise in these populations.

♦ *natural selection:* Natural selection is the result of the interaction of environment and individual variations. When environmental conditions change, selective pressure is placed on a population. Only organisms possessing beneficial variations that allow them to exist in the different environment will survive and reproduce. It is important to understand that natural selection can only work with the variations already present in the population. New variations cannot be produced to help organisms survive. For example, during the evolution of terrestrial vertebrates, the ancestral species was a tetrapod (possessing four legs). Therefore, all terrestrial vertebrates have "four legs." Human evolution involved a transition from walking on "all fours" to walking erect, and an alteration of the forelimbs into arms and hands. Natural selection did not create this situation, but made due with the materials it had to work with. Made due, you say? Aren't humans pretty well off? Well, yes, but ask anyone who's ever had back or knee problems, and they'll tell you these structures are far from perfect. For all intents and purposes, our intellect and logic allowed us to survive, not our physical strength and prowess. Natural selection is responsible for both.

♦ *mutation:* As we discussed above, Darwin was not aware of how variations arose or how traits were inherited, as the field of genetics would not take shape for decades after his death. Today, genetics is central to our understanding of evolution. In Chapter 6, we discussed how mutations alter protein production. This alteration produces new alleles, or variations of genes that may result in a change in the phenotype of an organism. New alleles may change the genetic make up of the population, and this may lead to evolution.

♦ *gene flow:* Gene flow is described as the movement of alleles from one population to another. This movement could cause changes in the population, either by eliminating variation (as some organisms may leave the population) or by enhancing it (as some organisms enter the population).

Although mutation and gene flow play critical roles, natural selection is cited as the main cause of evolution. As you may have already deduced, the three are not mutually exclusive, and, indeed, natural selection often involves mutation and gene flow. Perhaps the most important thing to remember is that evolution is due to both environment and genetic variation within species. Natural selection is the result of the interaction of these factors and produces changes in the population.

D. Adaptation

When selective pressures are placed on populations, natural selection causes certain traits to become more "fit" than others. The variations with the greatest survival value will become more common in each successive generation. Genetic traits that give organisms a better chance at survival will be selected for, and traits that reduce the fitness of individuals will be selected against. This process is known as *adaptation*. Although there are many different definitions of this word, it has a specific meaning in evolutionary theory, and refers to genetics. Adaptation is a change in the genetics of a population with time. An individual cannot change its genetic makeup. Therefore, in evolutionary terms, an individual cannot adapt, only a population can.

Recall that earlier we defined evolution as a change with time, and here we are applying the same definition to adaptation. Evolution is used more often to describe the accumulation of changes or the formation of a new species via the processes of natural selection and adaptation.

E. Population Genetics

The modern definition of evolution is specific: evolution is defined as the change in allelic frequencies in a population with time. A change in the allelic frequency for one gene does not necessarily result in what we think of evolution, but rather, if changes occur in many genes, the result may be evolution. We usually refer to all of the genes, and all of the alleles, in a population as the *gene pool*. Thus, the diversity and variation of every population can be ascertained by examining the gene pool.

Recall from Chapter 19 that alleles are different varieties of genes caused by mutations in the DNA. To understand evolution, we must understand the genetics of a population, not just of an individual. In 1908, two researchers, G. H. Hardy and G. Weinberg, set out to understand this via the use of mathematics. They reasoned that, if no genetic changes were taking place over time, then a population would be in equilibrium and would not change. If this were true, the frequency of each allele in a population could be calculated rather easily. Knowing the frequency of each allele would allow for the description of the genotypic frequencies within the population as well.

For example, consider a genetic trait with two alleles, the dominant allele *A* and the recessive allele, *a*. Since there are only two alleles of this gene in the population, the sum of the frequency of the two alleles must be one. If we assign symbols to these frequencies (i.e. the frequency of *A* can be represented by *p*, and the frequency of *a* can be represented by *q*), then we can express this idea as:

$$p + q = 1$$

Furthermore, if we know *p* and *q*, we can calculate the frequencies of the various genotypes. If mating is random in a population, then this mating can be expressed as the probability of alleles coming together in any combination. Mathematically we can express this as (p + q) X (p + q). Since p + q = 1, the product of this equation also equals 1. With some algebraic manipulation, this equation becomes

$$p^2 + 2pq + q^2 = 1$$

Each term represents one genotype; specifically, the frequency of the homozygous dominant (*AA*) in the population is expressed by the term p^2, the homozygous recessive (*aa*), q^2, and the heterozygote (*Aa*) *2pq*.

For example, if *p* = 0.85, then we could calculate *q* (1 - 0.85 = 0.15). In addition, we could calculate the frequency in the population of *AA* (0.085 X 0.85 = 0.72), *Aa* (2 X 0.85 X 0.15 = 0.26) and *aa* (0.15 X 0.15 = 0.02). If we consider a population of 1000 individuals, we would predict that 0.72 X 1000, or 720, would be of the genotype *AA*, 0.26 X 1000, or 260, would be *Aa*, and 0.02 X 1000, or 20, would be *aa*.

We can also determine the frequency of the alleles given raw numbers in the population. For example, if, in a population, 800 individuals were found to be of the genotype *AA*, 160 were *Aa*, and 40 were *aa*, then we can calculate allelic frequencies given the formulae:

$$\text{frequency of } A = p = \frac{\text{total number of } A \text{ alleles}}{\text{total number of alleles}}$$

$$\text{frequency of } a = q = \frac{\text{total number of } a \text{ alleles}}{\text{total number of alleles}}$$

The total number of *A* alleles in a population is expressed as

$$(2 \text{ X \# of } AA) + (\text{\# of } Aa)$$

as homozygous dominant individuals have 2 *A* alleles, and heterozygotes have only 1 *A* allele. Similarly, total number of *a* alleles in a population is expressed as

$$(2 \text{ X \# of } aa) + (\text{\# of } Aa)$$

as homozygous recessive individuals have 2 *a* alleles, and heterozygotes have only 1 *a* allele. The total number of alleles in the population is equal to

$$2 \text{ X \# of individuals}$$

as each individual in the population has two alleles for every gene, including the gene of interest. Thus, our equation to find p becomes:

$$p = \frac{(2 \text{ X } 800) + (160)}{2 \text{ X } 1000} = 0.88$$

We can similarly determine q, or we can remember that $p + q = 1$. Therefore $q = 0.12$.

Also remember that genes can have more than two alleles. Similar equations can be used to describe the frequencies in this case. If all the alleles of a gene occur in the same proportions for many generations, these alleles are called *balanced polymorphisms*. However, if the allelic frequencies are seen to change from one generation to the next, the population is not in equilibrium.

F.   Hardy-Weinberg Equilibrium

The relationships described above, and the equations that describe them, are known as the *Hardy-Weinberg equilibrium*. But this brings us to an important point: if a population is in Hardy-Weinberg equilibrium, the allelic frequencies are not changing and therefore evolution could not occur. Hardy and Weinberg identified five tenants that, when violated, would result in the equilibrium being disturbed and, thus, a shift in the allelic frequencies, which may result in evolution. The five principles necessary to maintain Hardy Weinberg equilibrium in a population are:

- *no mutation:* Mutation would cause the production of new alleles in a population and thus change allelic frequencies.

- *no migration:* Migration, either immigration or emigration, would result in the exchange of alleles between populations, thus changing allelic frequencies.

- *no selection:* If particular alleles were selected for, then the frequency of these alleles would increase over time. Similarly, if alleles were selected against, their frequency would be reduced over time.

- *large population:* With small populations, the allelic frequencies can change by chance due to random fluctuations in the gene pool.

- *random mating:* If mating is not random, then some alleles would increase in frequency while others would decrease. Usually random mating is violated when sexual selection is in play, which we will discuss shortly.

As you may have guessed, most populations violate at least one of these tenets. However, the principles and equations of Hardy-Weinberg equilibrium are still useful in describing and studying a population.

One notable violation of Hardy-Weinberg equilibrium is population size. Several processes have been helpful in understanding genetics of small populations. Some of these include:

- *genetic drift:* Random chance will cause fluctuations in allelic frequencies. Smaller populations are more susceptible to these chance events, and frequencies can change significantly. For example, natural disasters can decimate small populations. If, by random chance, all the individuals with a certain variation were killed during a hurricane, then the allelic frequency of that trait would be dramatically reduced. Larger populations would not face such drastic changes.

- *bottlenecks:* When the size of a population is dramatically reduced, usually due to disease or natural disaster, alleles may be lost. The population may be able to recover and increase in number. However, the genetic variation has been reduced and cannot be restored. This is the problem with endangered species today. Although we have protected many species that were on the verge of extinction, diversity has been reduced. If the environment changes, there may not be enough variation within the population to allow the species to survive. Bottlenecks (and genetic drift) can be helped by gene flow. With endangered species, zoos will often exchange animals for mating purposes to increase genetic diversity.

♦ *founder effect:* When a few individuals from a population form their own new population, the only genetic variation that exists is what these individuals bring. In essence, they do not bring the whole gene pool to the new population, but rather only a fraction of it. Again, this will reduce diversity and variation.

G. Selection

Often, when Hardy-Weinberg equilibrium is violated, natural selection is occurring which will shift allelic frequencies. We can identify four different types of selection which alter these frequencies in different ways.

♦ *directional selection:* Sometimes one allele, or a combination of alleles from different genes, provide an adaptive advantage for an organism. Since these organisms are more likely to survive and reproduce, the frequencies of these advantageous alleles will increase. Directional selection is when the allelic frequency shifts in a steady, constant direction. For example, pesticide resistance in insects is due to alleles which provide protection against these chemicals. Thus, all insects that survive will carry these alleles and will pass them onto their progeny. Soon, all the individuals in a population will have these alleles.

♦ *stabilizing selection:* In this type of selection, an intermediate form of an allele or trait is favored over the extremes. A good example of this is with human birth weight. The average weight of a new born is 7 pounds. Much lower than this results in medical problems and infant mortality. Much higher and the mother will have difficulty carrying and delivering the child.

♦ *disruptive selection:* Disruptive selection occurs when environmental conditions favor the two extremes of the trait. In this case, the population will, in essence, be split into two. Given enough time, evolution may result in two different species.

♦ *sexual selection:* When competition occurs between individuals of the same sex over mating rights, it is often times the bigger, more aggressive animal, or the animal with the more pleasing appearance or courtship display that is allowed to mate. Therefore, these alleles will be passed on to the next generation. Sexual selection has also been implemented in *sexual dimorphism*, the dramatic difference seen between members of the opposite sexes in the same species (for example, the beautifully plumed peacock and his drab counterpart, the peahen.)

H. Evidence for evolution

We have discussed why evolutionary theory arose, the mechanisms that may be responsible for evolution, and a mathematical theory to identify when evolution is occurring. But we still have not investigated one important question: How do we know evolution occurred? Most evidence supporting evolution can be classified in one of the following categories:

♦ *comparative anatomy*: This involves careful comparison of body parts in different organisms. For example, all mammals have hair or fur and have mammary glands used to produce milk to feed their young. Further investigation reveals that mammals also have similar bone structures. These data imply that all mammals had an ancestral relationship. If we further examine the bone structure in mammals, birds, reptiles and amphibians, we can also see amazing similarities, again indicating that even these diverse organisms came from a common ancestral species.

♦ *comparative biochemistry:* Recent advances in biochemical analysis, including protein and DNA sequencing, have allowed for detailed investigations into comparisons of species at the molecular level. This type of comparison reveals differences in sequences that can be used to determine how similar two species are. The rate of change in sequences has also been used as a *molecular clock* to calculate the time of divergence between two species.

♦ *vestigial structures:* Organs or body parts that have no functional value to an organism are called vestigial structures. Since they are present but have no function, they are probably remnants of structures from an ancestral species. For instance, the *appendix* in humans is an example of a vestigial structure. It is the remains of the *cecum*, a structure that acts as a storage chamber in animals that eat a diet high in cellulose. Another example is the pelvic girdle found in whales. This structure has no function and, with time, has been reduced in size and even disconnected from the spine. However, it remains, and gives us evidence that ancestral whales were once land dwelling creatures with hind limbs.

♦ *embryonic development:* This is perhaps the most curious and fascinating category we will discuss. When vertebrates are examined, the stages of embryonic development are strikingly similar. Even in organisms as different as turtles and chickens and humans, the form of the developing embryo, and the structures of the embryo, are almost identical. In fact, at one point in human development, *gill slits* are apparent. It is argued that these similarities are evidence for a common ancestor for all vertebrates.

♦ *natural distribution of living things*: By examining where living things exist in the world, we can compare similarities and differences among the species. This has lead to some interesting findings. For example, species of monkeys in the western hemisphere resemble each other more closely than they resemble species of monkeys in Europe or Africa or Asia. This indicates that, although all monkeys had a common ancestor, geographic separation (different continents) allowed evolution of monkeys in different ways (see the discussion of reproductive isolation below).

♦ *fossil evidence:* Probably the most important category of evidence for evolution is the fossil record. Various methods, most notably *radioactive dating*, can determine the age of particular rocks. Embedded in these rocks are fossils, preserved specimens of once living organisms. What we know from fossils is that organisms that were alive in the past do not closely resemble organisms alive today, and many species are extinct. What we can see in these fossils are similarities with plants and animals that are alive today, but that these creatures have changed over time. One of the best examples of this is the horse. Fossil evidence over the past 60 million years documents the changes in the horse, including its overall size, hoof structure and jaw and tooth patterns.

♦ *selective breeding (artificial selection):* Humans have been cultivating plants and animals for thousands of years. We have selected certain traits and attributes in these organisms and breed organisms to retain and enhance traits that are useful and beneficial to us. This process of selective breeding or artificial selection is quite amazing. For example, the vegetables familiar to us as cabbage, cauliflower, broccoli, brussel sprouts and kale are all different variations of the same plant. Similarly, dogs, from Chihuahuas to Great Danes, all belong to the same species and were selectively bred from wolves. If humans can exert this type of selective pressure to create so many different varieties from one species, an intuitive leap will tell you it can occur in nature as well.

I. Speciation

Natural selection can cause one species to evolve into two or more species. How can this occur? Speciation requires *reproductive isolation*, the situation whereby one population of a species becomes isolated and can reproduce only with the individuals in that population (remember the premises of Hardy-Weinberg). The different environment of the isolated species will pose different selective pressures on the population, and, given enough time, natural selection may result in evolution of a new species.

Two types of isolation are generally recognized:

♦ *allopatric:* When species are divided by a physical barrier, they have undergone allopatric isolation. The most prominent type of allopatric isolation is *geographic isolation*: Volcanoes, tectonic plate shift, formation of new rivers, species blown by storms to island, etc. can cause geographic isolation. This type of isolation is probably the most common form of reproductive isolation, and, consequently, the most important.

♦ *sympatric:* When no physical barrier divides a population, reproductive isolation can still occur. In this case, daughter species arise within the home range of an existing species. One type of sympatric isolation is *behavioral isolation*. In this case, a genetic variation may arise within a species that causes behavioral changes. For example, changes may cause some individuals to feed at night. Eventually, these individuals will become nocturnal, essentially isolating themselves from the diurnal individuals. Adaptation may cause changes in eyesight, coloration, and other traits to allow these organism to survive. This may lead to speciation. Another example of sympatric isolation is *physiological and anatomical isolation*: Variations in physical attributes may prevent breeding among individuals within a population, which may eventually lead to speciation. Consider one example from above: although all dogs are the same species, they can be very different. The Chihuahua will find it difficult, if not impossible, to mate with the Great Dane due to differences in their sizes. Thus, given enough time, the two strains may eventually evolve into two different species.

J. Types of Evolution

When we examine evolution as a process, we see certain patterns. It is helpful to discuss evolution in terms of these patterns to answer questions and make comparisons. These patterns include:

- ◆ *divergent evolution*: This process refers to what is normally thought of as evolution, and what we have been discussing thus far. Divergent evolution occurs when individuals from one population evolve differently. This, as discussed above, can lead to speciation. For example, the brown bear and the polar bear had a common ancestor. Migration of the bears, leading to geographic isolation, resulted in adaptation to different environments. Divergent evolution often results in individuals having *homologous structures*, structures that have been adapted differently to perform different functions. For example, the forelimbs in vertebrates evolved into arms (humans), wings (bats) and fins (whales).

- ◆ *convergent evolution:* When environments are similar or identical, the same selective pressures will be placed on the organisms that live in these environments. Therefore, different species in one environment (or two similar environments) will evolve similar structures to function in the environment. These structures are called *analogous structures*. One striking example of this is seen in sharks (fish), whales (mammals) and penguins (birds): although very distantly related, all have developed similar structures (fins) that allow them to function in the same environment (the ocean).

♦ *coevolution:* Organisms that share an environment often evolve together due to the selective pressures placed on one or more species in the environment. Thus, one species often changes in response to the change in another species. For example, if rabbits were the main food source for one population of foxes, and the rabbits adapted to become faster runners allowing them to avoid the foxes, then the foxes must adapt and become faster runners in order to continue using the rabbits as a food source.

Chapter 20 Problems

Passage 20.1 (Questions 1-4)

    The ability to taste phenylthiocarbamide (PTC) is determined by the T gene. Homozygous dominant individuals (TT) experience PTC as a very strong and unpleasant taste. Heterozygotes (Tt) can taste PTC but experience it as a much weaker taste do not find it quite as offensive. Homozygous recessive individuals (tt) cannot taste PTC at all. As a class assignment, students were tested for their ability to taste PTC, and were asked to test their parents as well. The class data was pooled and the results are shown in the following table:

Ability to taste PTC	Students	Parents
Strong taste	6	11
Weak taste	4	14
No taste	10	15

The class then examined the data and calculated allelic and genotypic frequencies, based on the formulas related to Hardy-Weinberg equilibrium.

1. What is the allelic frequency of T in the students?
   A. 0.40
   B. 0.60
   C. 0.16
   D. 0.36

2. In the parents, what proportion have the ability to taste PTC?
   A. 0.28
   B. 0.35
   C. 0.63
   D. 1.00

3. In the parents, what is the value of q?
   A. 0.45
   B. 0.55
   C. 0.28
   D. 0.35

4. Is this population in Hardy-Weinberg equilibrium for the ability to taste PTC?
   A. Yes, as the allelic frequencies are relatively the same in each generation.
   B. No, as strong tasters do not occur with the same frequency in each generation.
   C. No, as the values of p and q in the student generation are not equal.
   D. No, as the values of p and q are not the same in each generation.

Questions 5-6 are independent of any
passage and independent of each other.

5. Cystic fibrosis, a recessive genetic
   disease, occurs in a particular
   population in approximately 1 of
   every 2,000 births. What is the
   frequency of carriers in this
   population?
   A. 0.0224
   B. 0.9776
   C. 0.0219
   D. 0.0438

6. Many species of marsupials (found
   mainly in Australia) share similarities
   to species of placental mammals
   (found in most other regions of the
   world) even though they are not very
   closely related. This is an example of:
   A. divergent evolution.
   B. convergent evolution.
   C. vestigial structures.
   D. sympatric speciation.

Solutions

Chapter 1 Solutions

1. A.

No direct evidence is presented to confirm that HHV8 causes KS, although it appears to be associated with the disease. Answer B is not the best choice as observation 1 was based on a 2 year study: those who tested positive for HHV8 may have developed KS at a later date. A statement about all syphilis patients developing KS is not valid, even if HHV8 is truly the cause of the disease: only a certain percentage would be predicted to develop the disease. And, conversely, it cannot be stated that all hemophiliacs are safe from the disease either.

2. C.

KS is prevalent in individuals with HIV and syphilis, two sexually transmitted diseases. Although HIV can also be contracted through blood transfusions, it appears HHV8 cannot due the hemophiliac data in observation 2. Casual contact and airborne transmission can also be ruled out as HHV8 antibodies are rarely found in HIV negative blood donors.

3. B.

No evidence is given that transplant patients had or didn't have HHV8, so the virus as a cause of KS cannot be ruled out based on this statement. However, since these transplant patients have a weakened immune system, as is found in AIDS, it appears KS thrives under this condition.

4. B.

Although some may argue that one characteristic of life is the storage of genetic information in the form of DNA, numerous viruses do contain DNA. Also, one outstanding feature of many viruses is their rapid mutation rate. However, all viruses need the cellular machinery to replicate: they cannot reproduce on their own.

Chapter 2 Solutions

1. A.

RNA, a nucleic acid, is the only molecule listed which contains phosphorus (in the phosphate group portion of the nucleotide). Thus radioactive phosphorus will not show up in proteins, glucose (a carbohydrate), or amino acids (protein subunits).

2. C.

Both RNA and proteins contain nitrogen, RNA in the nitrogenous base portion of the nucleotide, and proteins in the amino group of every amino acid. A and B are not correct because they exclude RNA or proteins. D is incorrect because fatty acids, constituents of triglycerides, do not contain nitrogen.

3. C.

Both cholesterol and phospholipids contain carbon, as do all of the major biomolecules we discussed, as they are organic. Therefore, radioactive carbon would show up in all the biomolecules we mentioned.

4. B.

We are told that arginine is an amino acid, and amino acids are the building blocks of proteins. DNA and RNA are made up of nucleotides, while fatty acids are long chain hydrocarbons that are not considered polymers, and certainly are not formed from amino acids.

5. D.

This question combines aspects of both of the preceding experiments in an attempt to cause confusion. Arginine simply allows the cells to grow, as they could not make proteins without it. However, since neither arginine nor any other amino acids contain phosphorus, no proteins, whether they contain arginine or not, should be labeled. The only remaining choice recognizes that both RNA and phospholipids contain phosphorus, in the phosphate group that each contains as part of its structure.

6. C.

The human digestive system can only absorb sugars in the form of monosaccharides. Galactose is the only monosaccharide listed (glucose and fructose are the others). Lactose, maltose, and sucrose are all disaccharides, and must be enzymatically split before absorption.

7. D.

One of the major differences between DNA and RNA is that RNA contains the five-carbon sugar ribose, while DNA contains the five-carbon sugar deoxyribose. Both DNA and RNA contain phosphate groups, and both contain adenine and guanine. (RNA contains the pyrimidine base uracil instead of the pyrimidine base thymine.)

8. B.

Protein primary structure refers only to the linear order of amino acids. Secondary and tertiary folding are characteristics of all proteins, and involve interactions between various amino acids and ultimately cause specific three-dimensional folding. Both A and D are incorrect for related reasons; some proteins consist of more than one polypeptide chain, and it is only these proteins that exhibit quaternary folding (the association of multiple polypeptides). All proteins contain amino acids, by definition, so C cannot be correct.

9. C.

The major factor that determines whether or not a triglyceride will be solid or liquid at room temperature is the level of saturation of the fatty acids it contains. A completely saturated triglyceride is completely "filled" with hydrogen atoms, and is therefore linear in shape. This allows the molecules to pack closely and easily together, which results in a solid phase physical structure. We would call this type of molecule a "fat" or "saturated fat". A point of unsaturation occurs where a carbon-carbon double bond exists, and hydrogen atoms could potentially be added by hydrogenation. The more points of unsaturation, the more "kinks", or bends, the fatty acid will have. This makes packing together difficult, and we obtain a liquid, usually called an "oil".

10. A.

Cellulose is the only polysaccharide, or complex carbohydrate, listed. Lactose is a disaccharide, and ribose is a monosaccharide.

Chapter 3 Solutions

1. **A.**

We can tell that this is true because the ranges of activity depicted by the graph do not overlap. Therefore, no pH value exists at which both enzymes will be even slightly active. It is assumed that the general pH values are known for the stomach and small intestine, approximately 2 and 8 respectively. Therefore, the graph confirms that pancreatic amylase will have no activity at pH 2 (choice B), but that this is the optimum for pepsin (not 8.5, as is suggested in choice C.) The graph additionally shows that pancreatic amylase loses all activity at pH 7, so that it could not function in an acidic environment. Since the passage tells us that pancreatic amylase functions in the small intestine, choice D must be incorrect.

2. **C.**

The key here is to understand that trypsin, like pancreatic amylase, functions in the small intestine, and therefore must have a similar optimal pH as does pancreatic amylase. The graph shows that optimum as 8.5. For the same reasons stated above for pepsin and pancreatic amylase, pepsin and trypsin could never work under similar conditions (choice B). Additionally, both choices A and D must be incorrect because they demand that trypsin could function at pH 2 and 0 (the pH of 1M HCl, which you should at least know is acidic).

3. **B.**

Since humans are endotherms and maintain a constant body temperature of approximately 37^0 C (98.6^0 F), all human enzymes should share this optimal temperature. Curves A and C depict very different optimal temperatures.

4. **A.**

Since sharks are fish, they are ectothermic and will assume the temperature of their environment. While there is no way for you to know exactly what this value is, it is certainly colder than 37^0 C, and the optimal temperature of the enzyme shown in graph A, about 12^0 C (about 50^0 F), is reasonable for cool water, since you have to pick one choice. D cannot be true; everything that is alive must contain a DNA polymerase!!

5. **D.**

Denaturation implies that the enzyme has lost all function because its shape has significantly changed. According to the graph, enzyme B has no activity below 17^0 C or above 43^0 C. Therefore, choice A is incorrect because this is the optimal temperature. Both choices B and C are out of the activity range, but cold temperatures do not cause denaturation, they simply cause a slowing of the reaction rate based on general kinetic principles until it is ultimately zero. Only high temperatures will cause denaturation, so choice D (50^0 C) must be correct.

6. A.

From the information given, we can tell that the optimal temperature and pH for the enzyme in question is 37 degrees C, pH 6 (the values at which the reaction proceeds to completion most quickly). As with the previous passage, the high temperature rules out any shark enzymes (choices B and D), and the mildly acidic pH could only exist in the mouth, not the small intestine (which is mildly alkaline).

7. C.

A human enzyme would likely become denatured at 60^0 C, as we saw in the last passage, and this would account for the lack of activity (the failure of the blue color to disappear implies that the starch remains present forever, since the enzyme cannot break it down). Choice A does not make sense, since heat will always tend to destabilize chemical bonds. Choice B could not be correct, because the IKI is still active; it is responsible for the blue color. Logically, this leaves out choice D, too.

8. B.

The explanation is the same as in question 6.

9. D.

This question is simply testing your general knowledge of how an enzyme functions in the context of this passage. Namely, an enzyme always functions by lowering the activation energy of a reaction (usually by providing a surface at the active site that puts the reactant(s) in a proper orientation and proximity). A is incorrect since it states the opposite of this idea. Choice B reflects what would happen if we were to facilitate a reaction by adding heat; the whole point of enzymes is to facilitate the reaction at a temperature that would not be harmful to life. With regard to choice C, an enzyme or any catalyst can never alter the change in free energy during a reaction, it can only affect the rate of that reaction! (This is a basic principle of thermodynamics and enzyme function).

10. D.

Again, this question is simply testing your general knowledge of how an enzyme functions in the context of this passage. The optimal pH and temperature for any enzyme will reflect the environment in which it normally functions; that is, in fact, why the optimal values are optimal! Choice B must be incorrect, because when an enzyme is denatured, it has no activity, the exact opposite of optimal functioning. Two other ideas you are expected to know regarding the general mechanism of enzyme action are the following: the active site of an enzyme is typically composed of only a few amino acids, and the enzyme is "recyclable", or not irreversibly changed by participating in the reaction. These ideas invalidate choices A and C.

Chapter 4 Solutions

1. **C.**

Ethanol fermentation produces two products from the pyruvic acid made during glycolysis: ethanol and carbon dioxide. Logically, then, the pH at which the most carbon dioxide is produced will be the same pH at which the most ethanol is produced.

2. **B.**

If aerobic respiration is occurring, it should not affect the net amount of gas present because for every molecule of oxygen that is used up, a molecule of carbon dioxide will be produced. Thus the net production of gas will accurately reflect the carbon dioxide produced by fermentation. The passage clearly states that fermentation and aerobic respiration can occur simultaneously, so choice C must be incorrect. Choice D must be wrong because carbon dioxide is never used up or created by glycolysis.

3. **C.**

The passage tells us that yeast are fungi, which are eukaryotic and in addition to a nucleus must possess mitochondria. In general, in all eukaryotic organisms, glycolysis and fermentation reactions occur in the cytoplasm, while the Krebs cycle and electron transport

occur in the mitochondria. Choice D must be incorrect; if aerobic respiration occurs, the Krebs cycle must be a part of it.

4. **B.**

It is true that aerobic respiration is much more efficient (36 molecules of ATP harvested per glucose molecule) than fermentation (2 ATP molecules harvested per glucose molecule). The net amount of ATP produced by either process, however, will depend on the number of glucose molecules used by each pathway. If 50 glucose molecules are fermented, for example, the net yield of ATP will be 100 molecules. If, at the same time, 2 molecules of glucose were broken down by respiration, the net yield of ATP would be 72 molecules. Both choices C and D must be incorrect, since the passage clearly states that the two processes can take place simultaneously and that fermentation can take place in the presence of oxygen.

5. **C.**

We have already established that yeast have mitochondria and can carry out aerobic respiration, so they must contain an electron transport chain in the inner mitochondrial membrane (these ideas leave out choices A and D). However, we know that fermentation involves only glycolysis plus the fermentation reactions, which do not take place in the mitochondria and do not involve electron transport. Choice B is impossible since carbon dioxide is a waste product of the Krebs cycle or fermentation, and will not require energy to be made; it would certainly never be produced by electron transport.

6. **B**.

The important information to remember when answering both questions 6 and 7 is the following. First, with cyanide poisoning, electron transport stops completely; this causes a buildup of NADH, and the ultimate shutdown of all previous processes, including the Krebs cycle and glycolysis, due to the unavailability of NAD+. Cyanide poisoning would therefore not allow any oxygen to be used up or carbon dioxide to be manufactured. In addition, no energy is released, as all processes are stopped. Since ATP synthase is still functioning, the proton gradient will eventually disappear, causing the pH in the intermembrane space to rise dramatically, as equilibrium with the matrix is reached. With 2,4-dinitrophenol, or any uncoupler, electron transport continues, and so do oxygen consumption and carbon dioxide evolution. Since the membrane is leaky to protons, they will flow back to the matrix without making ATP; the energy released will be dissipated as heat, which accounts for the increased body temperature. To the extent the proton gradient is relieved,

the pH will rise in the intermembrane space. With an ATP synthase inhibitor like oligomycin, again, oxygen will continue to be used and carbon dioxide produced, as electron transport will continue. Since protons cannot re-enter the matrix, however, the gradient will become steeper and steeper, and the pH in the intermembrane space will drop dramatically as it becomes very acidic.

So, the high body temperature of the person from observation 1, coupled with continued oxygen consumption and the relatively unchanged or alkaline pH of the intermembrane space, identifies the poisoning agent as an uncoupler.

7. **C**.

Refer to the information from question 6. The dropping pH in the intermembrane space alone allows identification of this toxin as an ATP synthase inhibitor.

8. **B**.

Again, refer to the information from question 6. NADH will build up as electron transport is discontinued, as it has no place to give up electrons. NAD+ and FAD, the oxidized forms of coenzymes, will eventually decrease in amount until there are none left. Carbon dioxide will ultimately stop being produced, so its concentration will not change very much.

9. **B.**

We know that uncouplers function by allowing the inner mitochondrial membrane to become permeable to protons, and we know from question six that energy is released but not used (harvested as ATP); it is simply dissipated as heat. Choice A is incorrect because uncouplers decrease the formation of ATP; choice C is incorrect because it describes a cyanide-like poison that shuts down electron transport.

Choice D makes little sense; if anything, an uncoupler would cause the metabolic rate to rise.

10. **A.**

Again referring to the information from question 6, cyanide poisoning is the only situation we mentioned where glycolysis (and the Krebs cycle) will ultimately cease to function, due to the unavailability of oxidized coenzymes.

Chapter 5 Solutions

1. B.

Detection of radioactive phosphate in the pellet indicates the bacteria now contain the DNA of the bacteriophage. Radioactive sulfur in the supernatant suggests the protein of the phage did not enter the cell. Since the bacteria took up something from the phage, answer D is unlikely, as it does appear the phage infected the cell.

2. C.

The experiment verified that the DNA of the phage entered the cell. Therefore, the bacteria were indeed infected. It is not likely the protein coats are necessary for further functioning of the phage as they never entered the cell. It is also unlikely the radioactive phosphate would immediately kill the cells (after all, phage were propagated in bacteria grown in medium containing the isotope). The most likely answer is that the phage would reproduce as normal.

3. D.

Answer D is the only choice that makes any sense. All the other answers defeat the purpose of the experiment: a competitive inhibitor would prevent the phage from entering the cells at all; breaking apart the cell membrane would cause the contents of the cell to be released, where they would be found in the supernatant, along with the components of the phage that did not infect the cell; a mutant phage that could not bind to the cell would probably not infect the cell.

4. A.

Bacteriophages work by making the target cell do something it could not do before. Fertilization results in a new type of cell and is the beginning of a developmental cycle, not the best analogy to the phage experiment. Consuming enzymes would not fundamentally change an organism. Although the T2 experiment used radioactivity, not all experiments involving radioactive isotopes examine the same phenomenon.

5. C.

After one round of replication, all the DNA was found to be intermediate in density, with one strand containing the light isotope and one containing the heavy isotope. A second round of replication would mean that these intermediate DNA double strands would now serve as the template strands. The resulting copies would contain the light isotope. Therefore, from the template strand containing the heavy isotope, the resulting double strand would be intermediate, and from the template containing the light isotope, the double strand would contain only the light isotope. This would result in half the

DNA being intermediate and half being light.

6. **C.**

Only the bases in a nucleotide contain nitrogen.

7. **D.**

Conservative replication implies that the template strands remain together and the copied strands form the new double stranded DNA molecule. If this were true, then the template strands would contain only ^{15}N, the heavy isotope, and the copy strands would contain only ^{14}N, the light isotope.

8. **A.**

Okazaki fragments are generated during replication of the lagging strand. Therefore, they would contain only ^{14}N.

9. **A.**

Since G-C base pairs contain three hydrogen bonds, whereas A-T base pairs contain only two, the G-C pairing would require more energy, and hence a higher temperature, to disrupt. Extending this idea, long chains of DNA require different temperatures to denature depending on how many G-C pairs they have relative to A-T base pairs. Since there is no difference in the number of hydrogen bonds between a DNA-DNA double strand and a DNA-RNA double strand with the same sequence (A-U base pairs only contain two, just like A-T), there would be no difference in the temperature necessary to denature them.

10. **B.**

Chromosomes contain DNA and proteins. It is necessary to keep the DNA intact during isolation for further experiments, so adding DNase would not be wise. Since chromosomes do not contain RNA or lipids, reagents used to degrade these components are not necessary. However, to purify the DNA, proteins must be removed. Proteases are often used to accomplish this.

11. **A.**

Since RNA contains U instead of T, the answers using T can be eliminated automatically. This question stresses the property of base pairing that requires the strands to be in the opposite orientation (antiparallel). Therefore, although the sequence UAGGCGAUUC (response B) matches the DNA sequence as written, the 5' and 3' ends are not in the correct orientation. If the sequence was reversed, as in answer A, the two strands would complementary base pair.

Chapter 6 Solutions

1. **A.**

   Starting at the first nucleotide and reading every three nucleotides as a codon, the predicted amino acid sequence can be deduced. The translation of this sequence requires the use of the genetic code (see Figure 6.3).

2. **B.**

   A single nucleotide substitution in the sequence will result in a single amino acid change in the resulting protein (refer to the genetic code). The protein will still be translated, so response A is not true. We cannot infer from the sequencing information or from the family history that the mutation will not allow the heart to develop properly, so response C is incorrect. In addition, we are told the protein functions as a single polypeptide chain, so response D is also incorrect.

3. **C.**

   The mutation in the sequence of the gene causes a termination codon to be inserted. This stops the translation of the protein. Since it occurs early in the sequence (the 25th amino acid out of 283 total), the protein will almost certainly not function.

4. **B.**

   If the corresponding tRNA was mutated to now allow incorporation of the normal amino acid into the sequence, the protein would function correctly. Responses A and C would not allow for insertion of the correct amino acid at the critical position in the protein, and response D would not guarantee correction of the mutation. As a matter of fact, it would cause more mutations.

5. **D.**

   Using the genetic code in Figure 6.3, all of the mRNA sequences can be found to code for the same amino acid sequence.

6. **A.**

   Poly A tails regulate the degradation of the transcripts. They are not required for any of the other functions listed in answers B, C and D.

7. **D.**

   Recall that the mRNA transcript is manufactured in the 5' to 3' direction, meaning the DNA is copied in the 3' to 5' direction. Also, the mRNA is the complement of the DNA template, not an exact copy of it.

Chapter 7 Solutions

1. A.

All the bacteria were infected by the phage and lysed. The other conditions, whether true or not, deal with growth or death of bacteria and would not cause lysis of the bacteria. Therefore, the plate would remain cloudy. Only lysis causes the plates to appear clear.

2. C.

The control in this experiment (condition 1) rules out answers A and B. If UV light killed the bacteria, as suggested in D (and as can happen, depending on conditions), then all the bacteria would die. (Although it is possible that only a small percentage would die, it would be highly unlikely that this lethality would show a plaque pattern.) C is the only plausible answer, and we know that UV light can induce lysogenic strains to become lytic.

3. D.

Under both conditions, infection and induction, lysis would occur. Therefore, on average for these experimental conditions, infection would produce 20 plaques per plate and induction would produce 50 plaques per plate, for a total of 70 plaques per plate.

4. B.

Once induction occurs, viral particles are produced that can go on to infect other bacterial cells. Therefore, the isolation of bacteriophage from cultures would not support the theory of autolysis. Answer A is possible in the realm of either theory, C would not distinguish between the two, and D has nothing to do with either theory, as bacteria that grow well at 37^0C will not grow at 4^0C.

5. C.

The action of the analogs is at the level of reverse transcription. If the reverse transcriptase mutates to no longer allow incorporation of the analogs, then the virus can continue on its normal path. It is unlikely the body would mount an immune response to these analogs (choice B) as these analogs are so similar to normal nucleotides. Although the outer protein coat can and does mutate (choice A), this has nothing to do with the analogs. And the virus must incorporate into the host chromosome, so choice D is also incorrect.

6. D.

Antibody production against reverse transcriptase would not prevent the virus from entering the cell. All other conditions would allow the immune system to make antibodies against the

intact virus, as it exists outside the cells
where the immune system can detect it.

Chapter 8 Solutions

1. C.

The experiment shows that a soluble factor released by *P. aeruginosa* is probably present in the supernatant (the medium which was then used to grow *B. cepacia*). This factor induced the production of survival molecules in *B. cepacia*. Therefore, we know that *P. aeruginosa* can communicate with *B. cepacia*. We are given no experimental evidence to indicate if *B. cepacia* is able to communicate with *P. aeruginosa* .

2. A.

Since *B. cepacia* were grown in the liquid medium after the *P. aeruginosa* had been removed by centrifugation, a soluble factor, probably a protein, must have been present. No direct cell-to-cell contact could have taken place. In addition, we have no direct evidence that *B. cepacia* secreted any proteins.

3. C.

Nerve cells communicate chemically by releasing factors into the synapse between each other. Hormones are released from one gland and travel to a target tissue or organ where they are detected by receptors. Both systems use communication systems similar to the release of protein from one bacterial cell and detection by another.

4. C.

It is important to control this experiment. This can be accomplished by incubating *B. cepacia* in medium that had not been used to grow another strain of bacteria. In this manner, we could directly see the effects of *P. aeruginosa* on *B. cepacia*.

5. D.

The most likely answer to this question is that the *P. aeruginosa* were defective in secretion. If they had mutations in any other system, they would be unlikely to survive and reproduce.

6. C.

Five hours would mean ten doublings, which would result in 1×10^8 cells.

7. B.

DNA replication (response A) would probably continue to occur by utilizing preexisting enzymes. Damage to the glycocalxy (response D) would not necessarily mean the cell would die. However, production of new pili or repair of flagella (B and C) would almost certainly require protein synthesis and therefore could not occur in the presence of this type of antibiotic.

Chapter 9 Solutions

1. **B.**

   The graphs clearly show that, when the fungal species is present, the production of sugar is greatly increased and growth of the algae is decreased. Since sugar is made, the algae has no problem using the radioactive isotope of carbon.

2. **C.**

   It appears that the presence of the fungus decreases the growth of the algae, and forces it to produce more sugar. However, the algae does not necessarily appear to be harmed by this interaction.

3. **A.**

   Since there is less sugar production, but not less growth of the algae, it appears that dehydration causes photosynthesis to decrease.

4. **D.**

   It appears that the lichen need abundant supplies of water in order to thrive. Desert conditions would probably not supply enough water.

Chapter 10 Solutions

would destroy one cell type, so III is not a possibility.

1. **C.**

Since the sucrose crystals appeared in the lysosomes of the cell, the invertase had to have been internalized in order to catalyze the reaction of the crystals into monosaccharides. Given the circumstances, none of the other answers are appropriate.

2. **B.**

Since we are told that the sucrose crystals are broken down within several days of sucrose being eliminated from the medium, it appears that the cells have the ability to produce invertase, but probably in low levels.

3. **C.**

Either conditions I or II would explain the results seen in Experiment 2. There is no indication that invertase

4. **B.**

Recall that enzymes are specific for their substrates. Invertase would probably not catalyze the break down of mannose. Therefore, even in the presence of invertase, the mannose crystals would take several days to be eliminated from the cells.

5. **B.**

Cells that do not contain nuclei are prokaryotes, such as bacteria, and do not contain most other organelles. However, bacteria may contain flagella, which aids in locomotion.

6. **D.**

Recall that both the nucleus and mitochondria contain DNA. Therefore, replication can take place in both organelles.

Chapter 11 Solutions

1. D.

Since the pump is transporting ions against their concentration gradients, and as it requires ATP to do so, this process is considered active transport. Recall that bulk transport is not specific for molecules or ions, osmosis is the diffusion of water, and facilitated diffusion is possible due to concentration gradients and is a passive process.

2. C.

The Na^+/glucose pump uses the concentration gradient established by the Na^+/K^+ pump. It is therefore considered facilitated diffusion.

3. A.

The only logical answer is that an electrical gradient will form. In general other ions, be they positive or negative, will not be transported based on sodium concentration. And a magnetic gradient? What's that?

4. D.

All of the choices would be possible results of preventing transport of sodium.

5. B.

Under these conditions, sodium transport out of the cell (by the Na^+/K^+ pump) and its import (via the Na^+/glucose pump) would not be affected, so both of these pumps would be functional, and there would be no build up of sodium inside the cell (choice A). Equilibrium of sodium and/or glucose (choices C and D, respectively) may occur, but this is unlikely as the pumps will continue to work. However, if no other pump is active, there would be a build up of potassium inside the cell.

6. B.

This is the best answer of the choices given. The amino terminus is probably not hydrophobic (choice A) as it is located extracellularly, where there is a great abundance of water. We are given no good reason to assume the protein transports sodium, so choice C is not the best. Transmembrane proteins do not necessarily carry any particular charge, and do not have to be neutral, so answer D is not correct. Answer B relies on your knowledge of the composition of the cell membrane, specifically the lipid component. For a protein to span the membrane, it must be compatible with the environment of the membrane, which is hydrophobic.

7. B.

The microorganism is adapted to life in a high salt environment. Remember that water can freely diffuse across cell membranes. Therefore, the tonicity of the organism was probably well suited to its environment. Placing the cell in the fresh water medium, which was hypotonic to the cell, would have caused water to rush into the cell, thereby lysing it.

Chapter 12 Solutions

1. **C.**

Inability to detect whether the cell was large enough to divide would occur at G_2.

2. **B.**

The cell should not be allowed into G_2 if all the DNA has not yet been replicated. Therefore, the mutation probably occured in S phase.

3. **D.**

It appears that these mutants exert their controls at two different stages in the cell cycle, perhaps at both S and G_2.

4. **C.**

Each mutant would eventually die out under the experimental conditions. However, the mutants that are defective at both checkpoints would probably die out most quickly.

5. **B.**

The amount of DNA in the cell was intermediate to the amount in a cell before DNA replication (3.2 pg, in G_1) and a cell after DNA replication (6.4 pg, in G_2). Therefore, the cell had to be undergoing replication of the DNA and therefore had to be in S phase. Cells in mitosis (M) would contain either 6.4 pg (prior to telophase) or 3.2 pg (just after telophase) of DNA, but never any amount in-between.

6. **B.**

If microtubules cannot assemble, then the chromosomes cannot move via the spindle fibers. Mitosis would proceed up until that point. Therefore, the cells would enter metaphase but never reach anaphase.

Chapter 13 Solutions

1. B.

Since cigarette smoke is inhaled, it is most likely to contact the mucous membrane of the lungs, whose outer layer is composed of epithelium.

2. D.

Since carcinogens, whether chemicals or radiation, are contacting the body from the environment, and we know that epithelium is always the tissue that separates the body from the environment, we would expect the carcinogens to initially contact epithelium. If they penetrated tissue deeply, all types of cancers would be equally prevalent; the fact that carcinomas make up 90% of all cancers implies that after the carcinogen contacts the epithelium, it generally does not penetrate much deeper. There is no reason to believe that choice B is correct, and choice C is irrelevant to the question.

3. C.

The cause of a carcinoma of the skin would most likely be radiation exposure from the environment, or contact with the skin by carcinogenic chemicals. Since the worker lives in Alaska and rarely goes outside, it is unlikely that excessive exposure to sunlight is the culprit, and radiation from the isotope is a more likely causative agent. Cigarette smoke or ingestion of chemicals would likely affect mucous membranes or internal body parts.

4. D.

Due to the possibility of metastasis, a tumor that originated in one part of the body from a particular type of cell may "spread" to virtually any body location, producing a new tumor there. The tumor, however, will still be made up of the type of cells from which it originally grew.

5. A.

Since the basement membrane holds epithelium to underlying tissue, it would have to be penetrated by any cells wishing to invade another tissue. It has nothing to do with cell division (leaving out choices B and C) and choice D doesn't make sense -- the cells themselves cannot be carcinogens. The carcinogen is the environmental agent that caused the mutation in the first place.

6. D.

Choices A, B, and C all refer to tissues composed of cells and ground material, and all are listed as connective tissues. Muscle tissue is made up of muscle cells, with little intercellular material, and muscle tissue is one of the four fundamental tissue types.

7. **A.**

The only muscle in the body that is involuntary and striated is cardiac muscle, and its only location is in the heart. Smooth muscle is involuntary and unstriated, as is described by choice B. Skeletal muscle is under voluntary control and appears striated, as is described by choice C. The diaphragm is under both involuntary and voluntary control, and is considered a skeletal muscle.

8. **D.**

Nervous tissue is the only tissue type involved with communication using electricity. Muscle tissues use electricity, but for movement; connective and epithelial tissues are not involved with communication, and certainly not by using electricity.

9. **A.**

All glands are composed of glandular epithelium, and all hormone producing structures are classified as glands.

10. **C.**

Elastin fibers allow stretching, which clearly must take place in the walls of the arteries. Collagen confers strength and is not stretchable; cartilage is even harder and more unyielding. While a small amount muscle tissue may exist in the walls of arteries, it is not significant with regard to the question.

Chapter 14 Solutions

1. **C.**

Since testosterone is identified in the passage as a steroid hormone, it does not stimulate cells by using cAMP or a second messenger system, and thus should not affect cells abnormally in an individual with the disease. The other three hormones are all identified as proteins, which would use cAMP and thus affect cells abnormally in an individual with McCune-Albright syndrome.

2. **C.**

Hormones are chemical messengers that are produced by a gland, travel to their target cells, and send a message to those cells by interacting with a receptor. While neurotransmitters travel only a short distance, they are secreted by presynaptic dendrites, diffuse across the synaptic cleft, and interact with receptors on the postsynaptic axon, signaling that cell to initiate an action potential. The parallel with hormones is striking. Choices A and B refer to intermembrane proteins that allow transport through a plasma membrane. Choice D refers to proteins that would be more analogous to hormone receptors.

3. **D.**

The hypothalamus, which is composed mainly of nervous tissue and is considered a part of the brain, can also produce hormones, and controls the actions of the pituitary gland almost directly. The pituitary then controls the actions of all other glands in the body. Choices A and C are simply false statements, that may confuse you due to the presence of familiar sounding terminology. While choice B is a true statement, it does not demonstrate any general connection between the two systems, and certainly not one as important as the hypothalamus-pituitary connection.

4. **B.**

Since the release of testosterone is controlled by GnRH, which is identified in the passage as a protein hormone, the cells that secrete testosterone will overreact to the message and secrete excess quantities of testosterone. Choice D describes the opposite of the truth; we know from question one that once produced, testosterone will not have any abnormal effects on target cells. Its presence in large quantities, however, may cause abnormal effects. Choice A is not true because testosterone, being a steroid, does not function using a second-messenger system.

5. **B.**

Steroid hormones diffuse freely through plasma membranes and thus should be found in all cells. They only cause effects, however, in the cells that contain the appropriate intracellular receptor. A is incorrect because it implies a mode of action that would be employed by a protein hormone. D is also incorrect; for the same reason testosterone will not affect the cells of an individual with McCune-Albright syndrome abnormally, no steroid hormone will, including Stanozolol.

6. **A.**

ADH (antidiuretic hormone) tells the walls of the collecting duct and distal convoluted tubules of the nephron to become permeable to water, allowing it to avoid being excreted in the urine. If it is inhibited, the urine will contain excessive water, causing dehydration. The other hormones listed do not directly affect water balance.

7. **B.**

As positively charged sodium ions quickly diffuse into a neuron through a gated channel, the interior of the cell becomes electrically positive with respect to the outside (depolarization). Potassium is involved in repolarization as it flows out of cells (choice A) and calcium is involved with neurotransmitter release (choice C). Neurotransmitters themselves never actually enter cells, and they are certainly not ions (choice D).

8. **C.**

The brainstem controls autonomic activities such as breathing and heartrate. Choice A is describing the actions of the cerebellum; choice B is describing actions of the cerebral cortex; and choice D is describing actions of the diencephalon.

9. **B.**

Mechanoreceptors react to physical stimulation, and are in fact the receptors for the sense of hearing. Choice A would be correct if "chemoreceptors" was replaced by "mechanoreceptors"; likewise, choice D is incorrect as it implies a chemical stimulus that would be picked up by chemoreceptors. Choice C is incorrect, because sound waves, which are simply vibrations of molecules, can occur in any medium. (Sound would be impossible in a vacuum.)

10. **C.**

The rods are responsible for night vision, or the ability to discern shapes and outlines without color in dim light. If they are inhibited, "night blindenss" will occur. If the cones were inhibited, color vision would be affected (choice B). Choices A and D would result in the blocking of all visual information, causing total blindness.

Chapter 15 Solutions

1. C

Individuals afflicted by SCID have no T cells, while those with AIDS have T cells whose function has been compromised. Choice A is incorrect because the passage tells us that individuals with AIDS can in fact make antibodies (this is the basis for many common HIV tests). No information from the passage supports choice B or choice D.

2. B

As noted in question 1, individuals with AIDS can and do make antibodies to the HIV virus; they simply cannot do it efficiently enough to ward off the disease. A is incorrect because it is a viral infection that occurs, not a bacterial one. Choices C and D are incorrect because the passage does not support them; it implies that T cells are left alive, and it does not say that HIV infects any cell type except helper T cells.

3. B

The passage tells us that the inflammatory response acts only in a nonspecific fashion, which leaves out choice A as a possibility. The major blood cells involved in inflammation are the neutrophils and macrophages, which phagocytize foreign invaders. Choices C and D are not supported by the passage: it

says that phagocytes do destroy invaders, and never mentions red blood cells. Red blood cells would never be involved in phagocytosis!

4. B

Intact skin, which contains an epithelial layer that is quite thick, is a much better barrier to infection than the respiratory mucous membrane, where most infections are acquired. While the passage does not state this directly, you are expected to be able to reason it through. Since gas exchange occurs across the surface of the respiratory membrane, it must be extremely thin, and could never be as good a barrier as intact skin. Choice C is not true and is not supported by the passage.

5. B

The passage states this specifically. B cells can react to circulating antigens, so choice A is incorrect. Choices C and D are incorrect, because the passage tells us that macrophages act by phagocytosis, and also that they are nonspecific.

6. A

Since we know that the proper definition of an artery is a vessel that takes blood away from the heart, and that the ventricle pumps blood away from the heart, vessels attached to ventricles must be arteries.

7. **B.**

All blood cells are initially produced in the bone marrow! White blood cells do not contain hemoglobin (choice A); red blood cells are not involved with blood clotting (choice C); and platelets do not contain hemoglobin or transport oxygen.

8. **C.**

Since the pulmonary vein is returning blood to the heart that has just been oxygenated by the lungs, it must contain the highest concentration of oxygen. All of the other vessels mentioned contain varying amounts of oxygen. This question attempts to confuse you because of the general misperception that arteries always contain higher oxygen levels than do veins.

9. **D.**

All of the statements are true.

10. **C.**

Hemoglobin is a protein that must complex with iron in order to perform its function, which is to carry oxygen in red blood cells. Iodine is complexed with the thyroid hormone thyroxin (choice A); hemoglobin is certainly not a lipid (choice B); and chromium is a mineral that interacts with insulin as part of the glucose tolerance factor.

Chapter 16 Solutions

1. B.

The normal function of the large intestine is to reabsorb water from the digestive system into the blood; the presence of large amounts of any chemical not usually present will inhibit this function, and allow more water than normal to be eliminated with the feces. This also contributes to diarrhea. None of the other choices make sense, and none are supported by the passage.

2. B.

These supplements actually do contain the enzyme lactase; since it is a normal digestive enzyme, it will not be broken down by the proteases present in the digestive system as most other proteins would. Choice A would have far reaching consequences, as the bacteria of the colon are mutualistic and play an important role in homeostasis. Choice C is unlikely and unsupported by the passage. While choice D is tempting, only monosaccharides may ever be absorbed by the small intestines -- this has to do with their size and the lack of any machinery to transport them across the small intestinal wall.

3. A.

Since insulin is a protein and should never normally be found in the digestive tract, it would in fact be digested and useless if taken orally. Both choices B and C are unreasonable and unsupported by the passage; you should be aware that glucagon should never be present in the digestive tract. Thus choice D is also ruled out.

4. B.

If diabetes type I is untreated, no insulin exists to reduce the blood sugar, causing it to build up to extremely high levels, so much so that it upsets the osmotic balance between the cells and blood, causing water to leave the cells, enter the blood, and be excreted. The tremendous amounts of glucose also tax the kidneys' mechanism for reabsorbing it, so some is excreted in the urine.

5. A.

Since the job of insulin is to reduce the blood sugar, excess insulin will do just that, by any means it can. Choice B describes the opposite effect, and therefore must be discarded. Both choices C and D are unreasonable and unsupported by the passage.

6. C.

Since the carbon dioxide concentration is so closely linked with the pH of the blood, the brain uses these parameters to gather information about the actions to take to control the respiratory rate. While the concentration of oxygen could be monitored logically (and is, by the carotid and aortic bodies), this is a fine tuning measure, and is not a major source of regulation (choice A). Choice B is incorrect, because the heartrate is regulated by similar mechanisms as the respiration rate; one does not directly affect the other. Choice D is unsupported by the passage, and untrue.

7. B.

Since ADH controls the permeability of the walls of the collecting duct of the nephron to water, its absence would cause water to be excreted in large quantities in the urine. This would eventually lead to dehydration.

8. A.

The diaphragm is the sheetlike muscle that separates the thoracic and abdominal cavities; its contraction, regulated by the brainstem, is largely responsible for inhalation. The rectus abdominus is an abdominal muscle that moves the body; the cerebellum is involved with the coordination of movement.

9. D.

All relatively small molecules initially enter the filtrate, even if they are nutrients; plasma proteins are too large to diffuse across the capillary wall. Glucose and amino acids will normally be completely reabsorbed, leaving urea to be excreted in the urine.

10. C.

The pancreas, known as an accessory digestive organ, is vital to digestion because it manufactures and secretes most of the major digestive enzymes that function in the small intestine. Food never enters it, however, as it is not a part of the gastrointestinal tract. Food does pass through all of the other organs.

Chapter 17 Solutions

1. B.

Like all outer epithelial cells, the cells of a psoriasis blemish are dead and highly keratinized, which is what gives them the scaly appearance. All of the other choices do not make sense, and are not supported by the passage.

2. C.

Since the problem here is excess cell division (which must be by mitosis), anti-cancer drugs that inhibit cell division should be effective (although there are side effects). While collagen is an important component of the dermis, it has nothing to do with psoriasis or the epidermis (choice A). Choice B would only be valid in the case of a bacterial infection, and none exists in this case. Sebum-inhibiting drugs do work against acne, but again, this is due to bacterial infection and is not applicable to psoriasis (choice D).

3. A.

It is expected that you are aware that the neurotransmitter acetylcholine is virtually the only important one that acts at the neuromuscular junctions of skeletal muscles. Acetylcholinesterase is the enzyme that normally degrades it, and if this is inhibited, paralysis will occur. Choice B is incorrect as it refers to the neurotransmitter itself (but might trick you if you weren't careful). Choices C and D are unsupported by the passage.

4. B.

Since only muscles stimulated by acetylcholine will be affected, choice D cannot be true. The heart requires no nervous stimulation to keep beating, and the brain uses different neurotransmitters than acetylcholine (choices A and C).

5. B.

The major cooling mechanisms are sweating and vasodilation. The efficiency of sweating decreases as the humidity increases, and vasodilation becomes less effective as the temperature rises, and counterproductive if it rises above body temperature. So, the conditions with the lowest humidity and temperature would allow the most efficient functioning.

6. C.

All of the tissues listed are connective tissues. Ligaments, however, are involved in the connection of bones to other bones (choice A); articular cartilage occurs also at bone/bone connections (choice B); and adipose tissue is not involved in truly "connecting" things together, although it may be present in a wide variety of locations.

7. C.

Calcium is stored in the sarcoplasmic reticulum of muscle cells, and as the muscle cell becomes depolarized, it is released into the sarcoplasm, where it directly stimulates troponin to initiate contraction. Sodium and potassium are involved only in the nervous signal that depolarizes the sarcolemma (choices A and B), and phosphorus is not relevant in this context.

8. **C.**

The subcutaneous layer is mainly composed of connective adipose tissue, which requires a steady blood supply. The epidermis is composed solely of epithelial cells (choice A), and the dermis contains all tissue types, but little fat (choice B).

9. **B.**

Hairs are composed of epithelial cells being pushed outward by a dividing lower layer, and the further they get from the nutrient supply they die and are keratinized. The follicle itself, however, is located physically in the dermis, where it is protected from bacterial infection, etc.

10. **C.**

ATP is directly necessary to provide energy, calcium is necessary to activate the complex, and troponin is necessary to bind to calcium and participate in activation. Creatine phosphate is often present, and functions to "recharge" ADP to ATP, but it is not required for contraction.

Chapter 18 Solutions

1. **D**.

All of these events could lead to the production of a Turner's individual in the following ways. If the X and Y chromosomes fail to separate in the father at meiosis I, some of the resulting gametes will contain both X and Y, and some will contain no sex chromosomes. If the latter type joins with a normal egg, an XO individual will result. Likewise, failure of the X's to separate during meiosis I in the mother would lead to some eggs containing two X chromosomes, and some containing none; if the latter combined with a normal male sperm carrying an X chromosome, Turner's would result. Finally, if the two chromatids of the replicated Y chromosome failed to separate during meiosis II, some gametes would end up with two Y chromosomes, and some with no sex chromosomes; if the latter combined with a normal female egg, an XO individual would be produced.

2. **B**.

Since we know that normal human males are chromosomally XY and females are XX, it would not be unreasonable to put forth either of the following hypotheses: 1.) Sex is determined by the number of X chromosomes present; or 2.) Sex is determined by the presence or the absence of the Y chromosome. Consider that Turner's individuals appear female, and yet only possess one X, while those with Klinefelter's syndrome appear male, and yet contain two X's. However, they do contain a Y, while the Turner's individuals do not. Thus, we can postulate that sex is in fact normally determined by the presence or absence of the Y chromosome (which is known to be the case). Choice C is incorrect; since the Y chromosome determines sex, it is the sperm, and thus the father, that contributes the information about the sex of the offspring.

3. **D**.

The passage clearly states that nondisjunction is random, so choice A is ruled out. It also states that if other trisomies or monosomies exist, they are either miscarried or die early; this implies that the effects of such events are extremely detrimental (choice B is true). C also must be true, because if there were genes for fundamental life processes on chromosome 21, Down syndrome individuals could not live to adulthood.

4. **D**.

Question one has established that nondisjunction in either parent can in fact lead to Down syndrome, and there is no reason to believe that it can not, so choice A must be incorrect. It is true that a female is born with all the eggs she will ever release already formed, but arrested in the early stages of meiosis; the longer they remain in her body, the greater the chances that mutations will occur which might result in non-disjunction (choice B is correct). In addition, males would have the same probability of creating an aberrant sperm at any time in their lives, since sperm are made and turned over continuously until death (C is correct).

5. **B.**

Identical twins result when one egg is fertilized by one sperm, as normal, but for some reason the two cells that result after the zygote divides become separated; at this early stage, each of the cells can go on to produce a complete individual. Fraternal twins are created when two eggs are mistakenly released, and are fertilized by separate sperm. Thus identical twins are in fact genetically identical, while fraternal twins are no more genetically related than any siblings. Of course, identical twins are not identical in all of their characteristics, due to the influence of the environment on development. Choice B is the only answer consistent with this information.

6. **C.**

Fertilization normally takes place in the oviduct (choice C is correct), and cleavage begins as the zygote begins to travel towards the uterus, where implantation occurs (choice B is not). The ovary functions solely in the release of eggs and production of hormones, and the vagina functions as the receptacle for the penis, and the birth canal, excluding both choices A and D.

7. **B.**

In males, the sperm and urine do in fact share the urethra as a common pathway out of the body. In females, the urinary and reproductive systems are completely separate anatomically and physiologically; superficially they seem connected due to their external openings in the same general vicinity (choices A, C and D are incorrect).

8. **C.**

The worst effects of any teratogenic (birth-defect causing) drug would occur during the embryonic stage (week two to the end of month two). This is because all of the major events of organogenesis, germ tissue formation, and differentiation occur during this stage. If the drugs were ingested earlier than implantation (choices A and B), the negative effects would likely terminate the zygote or morula before it could implant, or might not harm them at all, depending on the drug. While drugs can certainly harm a fetus, it is usually less severe because all of the major organs have been formed and the general body layout is complete by this stage (choice D).

9. **C.**

The ectoderm gives rise to the skin and the nervous system. The endoderm gives rise to the internal mucous membranes and the gut (choice A). The mesoderm gives rise to most major organs (not in the nervous system), muscles, etc. (choice B). There is no such thing as the gastroderm (choice D).

10. **D.**

Since the eggs and sperm released into the water by fish must find each other virtually "by chance", eggs (and sperm) must be released in very large quantities to ensure that some fertilization occurs (choice A is correct). In addition, since so many species of fish release their eggs and sperm in this fashion (not to mention hundreds of marine invertebrates), species-specific identification methods must exist that allow only sperm and eggs from the same species to attempt to join. While it is theoretically possible for the sperm of one species to fertilize the egg of another, this would be counterproductive so mechanisms have evolved to prevent it (Choice C is correct). Choice B is incorrect as it is impossible for a sperm to fertilize more than one egg in any environment.

Chapter 19 Solutions

1. **A.**

Since the F_1 progeny all are phenotypically similar to one parent (they have red eyes), and the F_2 generation displays a phenotypic ratio of 3:1 red: brown, the brown trait must be recessive. Furthermore, since the pattern does not indicate a difference in heritablity in males and females, it must also be an autosomal trait.

2. **C.**

The pattern seen is consistent with a sex-linked recessive trait. Genotypically, the F_1 generation consists of all females heterozygote for the trait (as they inherit one X from the male parent and one from the female parent) and all males will be hemizygous for the normal (wild type) allele (as they can only inherit the X from the female parent). In the F_2 generation, the F_1 females will contribute the wild type allele to half the male progeny and the white allele to the other half, resulting in the phenotypes reflecting the genotypes. However, the male F_1's only have a wild type allele, which will be passed on to the females in the F_2 generation, so all these flies will have red eyes, regardless of what allele they inherit maternally. To extend your knowledge and understanding, determine what would happen if the reciprocal cross was done (white eyed females crossed with red eyed males in the parental generation).

3. **B.**

Since half of the progeny in a cross between affected and unaffected individuals display the mutant phenotype, this condition is autosomal dominant.

4. **C.**

As stated before, the mutation is dominant, but if one parent was homozygous for the allele, all the progeny would show the mutant phenotype. Only a heterozygote could produce unaffected progeny.

5. **B.**

Recall that a test cross is used to confirm the genotype of an individual. The test cross is done with individuals that are homozygous recessive for the allele. When the individual with the unknown genotype is mated to the homozygous recessive individual, only two outcomes are possible: all the progeny are phenotypically dominant (indicated the unknown genotype is homozygous dominant) or half the progeny are phenotypically dominant and half are recessive (indicating the unknown individual was a heterozygote).

6. C.

Codominance and incomplete dominance (choices A and B) refer to interactions among alleles for one gene. In this situation, we are looking at the relationship between two genes, and how the alleles for one trait affect the expression of the other trait. Gene interaction and epistasis (choices C and D) describe relationships between genes; however, gene interactions result in new phenotypes (e.g. the white phenotype) whereas epistasis results in one phenotype expressed over another. If epistasis were taking place, the ratio of 9:3:3:1, the typical ratio expected in a dihybrid cross, would change to 9:4:3, if brown was epistatic to scarlet. The genotype representing the 1 in the above ratio is *bb/scsc* (both alleles at both genes recessive). If brown masks scarlet, as in epistasis, this genotype would phenotypically be brown. If a gene interaction occurs, a new phenotype would result (white).

7. C.

The parents must be heterozygotes. They have a 1/4 chance of having a child with the disease, and a 3/4 chance of having an unaffected child. Since we know one child is unaffected, we can eliminate the homozygous recessive genotype, and we are left with only two possibilities: the child is homozygous dominant or heterozygous. If a Punnett square of the cross is examined, there is a 2/3 chance the unaffected child will be a carrier.

8. D.

The woman will have the genotype $I^A I^B$, while the man could have either genotype $I^B I^B$ or $I^B i$. Therefore, the only phenotype that could not be produced in the offspring would be blood type O, which, genotypically, is *ii*, which would require the mother to contribute an *i* allele, which she does not have.

Chapter 20 Solutions

1. **A.**

According to the equations given in the chapter, the allelic frequency (p) of the dominant allele is

$$\frac{(2 \times 6) + 4}{2 \times 10} = 0.40.$$

2. **C.**

The question does not specify whether the parents have a weak or strong taste of PTC, only that they can taste it. Therefore, the proportion that can taste it is $\frac{11 + 14}{40} = 0.63$.

3. **B.**

Recall that q is the frequency of the recessive allele, in this case t. Using the formulas in the chapter (similar to Question 1), we find that q = 0.55.

4. **D.**

Remember that a population is said to be in Hardy-Weinberg equilibrium if allelic frequencies do not change. Here we see that the values of p and q are different from one generation to the next. It does not require that the genotypic frequencies be the same in each generation (response B).

5. **D.**

You are given the frequency of affected individuals, 1 in 2,000, or 0.0005. This is the frequency of the genotype aa, which is equal to q^2. Therefor, q is equal to 0.0224. Since we know q we also know p ($1 - q = 0.9776$). In a population, carriers are heterozygotes, individuals who carry the allele but are not affected by it. The formula to calculate the frequency of heterozygotes is $2pq$. therefore, the frequency of carriers in this population is 0.0438.

6. **B.**

Convergent evolution is the notion that different species evolved similar attributes in similar environments, even though they are not closely related.

SECTION 5
READING COMPREHENSION

Chapter 21
Introduction

The reading comprehension portion of the MCAT is 85 minutes long and consists of about 9 passages, each about 500 words long and each with about 7 questions. The subject matter of a passage can be almost anything, but the most common themes are politics, history, culture, and science.

Most people find the passages difficult because the subject matter is dry and unfamiliar. Obscure subject matter is chosen so that your reading comprehension will be tested, not your knowledge of a particular subject. Also the more esoteric the subject the more likely everyone taking the test will be on an even playing field. However, because the material must still be accessible to laymen, you won't find any tracts on subtle issues of philosophy or abstract mathematics. In fact, if you read books on current affairs and the Op/Ed page of the newspaper, then the style of writing used in the MCAT passages will be familiar and you probably won't find the reading comprehension section particularly difficult.

The passages use a formal, compact style. They are typically taken from articles in academic journals, but they are rarely reprinted verbatim. Usually the chosen article is heavily edited until it is honed down to the required length. The formal style of the piece is retained but much of the "fluff" is removed. The editing process condenses the article to about one-third its original length. Thus, an MCAT passage contains about three times as much information for its length as does the original article. This is why the passages are similar to the writing on the Op/Ed page of a newspaper. After all, a person writing a piece for the Op/Ed page must express all his ideas in about 500 words, and he must use a formal (grammatical) style to convince people that he is well educated.

In addition to being dry and unfamiliar, MCAT passages often start in the middle of an explanation, so there is no point of reference. Furthermore, the passages are untitled, so you have to hit the ground running.

Chapter 22
Reading Methods

Reading styles are subjective—there is no best method for approaching the passages. There are as many "systems" for reading the passages as there are test-prep books—all "authoritatively" promoting their method, while contradicting some aspect of another. A reading technique that is natural for one person can be awkward and unnatural for another person. However, it's hard to believe that many of the methods advocated in certain books could help anyone. Be that as it may, we'll will throw in our own two-cents worth—though not so dogmatically.

Some books recommend speed reading the passages. This is a mistake. Speed reading is designed for ordinary, nontechnical material. Because this material is filled with "fluff," you can skim over the nonessential parts and still get the gist—and often more—of the passage. As mentioned before, however, MCAT passages are dense. Some are actual quoted articles (when the writers of the MCAT find one that is sufficiently compact). Most often, however, they are based on articles that have been condensed to about one-third their original length. During this process no essential information is lost, just the "fluff" is cut. This is why speed reading will not work here—the passages contain too much information. Furthermore, the bulk of the time is spent answering the questions, not reading the passages. You should, however, read somewhat faster than you normally do, but not to the point that your comprehension suffers. You will have to experiment to find your optimum pace.

Many books recommend that the questions be read before the passage. This strikes us as a cruel joke. In some of these books it seems that many of the methods, such as this one, are advocated merely to give the reader the feeling that he is getting the "inside stuff" on how to ace the test. After being presented with this method, the student may think "Hey, that really makes sense. Now I will know exactly what to look for." But there are two big problems with this method. First, some of the questions are a paragraph long, and reading a question twice can use up precious time. Second, there are usually seven questions per passage, and psychologists have shown that we can hold in our minds a maximum of about three thoughts at any one time (some of us have trouble simply remembering phone numbers). After reading all seven questions, the student will turn to the passage with his mind clouded by half-remembered thoughts. This will at best waste his time and distract him. More likely it will turn the passage into a disjointed mass of information.

However, one technique that you may find helpful is to preview the passage by reading the first sentence of each paragraph. Generally, the topic of a paragraph is contained in the first sentence. Reading the first sentence of each paragraph will give an overview of the passage. The topic sentences act in essence as a summary of the passage. Furthermore, since each passage is only three or four paragraphs long, previewing the topic sentences will not use up an inordinate amount of time. (I don't use this method myself, however. I prefer to see the passage as a completed whole, and to let the passage unveil its main idea to me as I become absorbed in it. I find that when I try to pre-analyze the passage it tends to become disjointed, and I lose my concentration. Nonetheless, as mentioned before, reading methods are subjective, so experiment—this method may work for you.)

Points to Remember

1. Reading styles are subjective—there is no best method for approaching the passages.

2. Don't speed read, or skim, the passage. Instead, read at a faster than usual pace, but not to the point that your comprehension suffers.

3. Don't read the questions before you read the passage.

4. (Optional) Preview the first sentence of each paragraph before you read the passage.

Chapter 23
The Six Questions

A. Introduction

The key to performing well on the passages is not the particular reading technique you use (so long as it's neither speed reading nor pre-reading the questions). Rather the key is to become completely familiar with the question types—there are only six—so that you can anticipate the questions that *might* be asked as you read the passage and answer those that *are* asked more quickly and efficiently. As you become familiar with the six question types, you will gain an intuitive sense for the places from which questions are likely to be drawn. This will give you the same advantage as that claimed by the "pre-reading-the-questions" technique, without the confusion and waste of time. Note, the order in which the questions are asked <u>roughly</u> corresponds to the order in which the main issues are presented in the passage. Early questions should correspond to information given early in the passage, and so on.

The following passage and accompanying questions illustrate the six question types. Read the passage slowly to get a good understanding of the issues.

There are two major systems of criminal procedure in the modern world—the adversarial and the inquisitorial. The former is associated with common law tradition and the latter with civil law tradition. Both systems were historically preceded by
5 the system of private vengeance in which the victim of a crime fashioned his own remedy and administered it privately, either personally or through an agent. The vengeance system was a system of
10 self-help, the essence of which was captured in the slogan "an eye for an eye, a tooth for a tooth." The modern adversarial system is only one historical step removed from the private vengeance system and still retains some of its characteristic features. Thus, for
15 example, even though the right to institute criminal action has now been extended to all members of society and even though the police department has taken over the pretrial investigative functions on behalf of the prosecution, the adversarial system still
20 leaves the defendant to conduct his own pretrial investigation. The trial is still viewed as a duel between two adversaries, refereed by a judge who, at the beginning of the trial has no knowledge of the investigative background of the case. In the final
25 analysis the adversarial system of criminal procedure symbolizes and regularizes the punitive combat.

By contrast, the inquisitorial system begins historically where the adversarial system stopped its development. It is two historical steps removed from
30 the system of private vengeance. Therefore, from the standpoint of legal anthropology, it is historically superior to the adversarial system. Under the inquisitorial system the public investigator has the duty to investigate not just on behalf of the prosecutor
35 but also on behalf of the defendant. Additionally, the public prosecutor has the duty to present to the court not only evidence that may lead to the conviction of the defendant but also evidence that may lead to his exoneration. This system mandates that both parties
40 permit full pretrial discovery of the evidence in their possession. Finally, in an effort to make the trial less like a duel between two adversaries, the inquisitorial system mandates that the judge take an active part in the conduct of the trial, with a role that is both
45 directive and protective.

Fact-finding is at the heart of the inquisitorial system. This system operates on the philosophical premise that in a criminal case the crucial factor is not the legal rule but the facts of the case and that the
50 goal of the entire procedure is to experimentally recreate for the court the commission of the alleged crime.

B. Main Idea Questions

The main idea of a passage typically comes at the end of a paragraph. It tends to be the last—occasionally the first—sentence of the first paragraph. If it's not there, it will probably be the last sentence of the entire passage. Main idea questions are usually the first questions asked.

Some common main idea questions are
- ☐ Which one of the following best expresses the main idea of the passage?
- ☐ The primary purpose of the passage is to . . .
- ☐ In the passage, the author's primary concern is to discuss . . .

Main idea questions are rarely difficult; after all the author wants to clearly communicate her ideas to you. If, however, after the first reading, you don't have a feel for the main idea, review the first and last sentence of each paragraph; these will give you a quick overview of the passage.

Because main idea questions are relatively easy, the MCAT writers try to obscure the correct answer by surrounding it with close answer-choices ("detractors") that either overstate or understate the author's main point. Answer-choices that stress specifics tend to understate the main idea; choices that go beyond the scope of the passage tend to overstate the main idea.

> The answer to a main idea question will summarize the author's argument, yet be neither too specific nor too broad.

In most MCAT passages the author's primary purpose is to persuade the reader to accept her opinion. Occasionally, it is to describe something.

Example: (Refer to passage on page 299.)

The primary purpose of the passage is to

A.   explain why the inquisitorial system is the best system of criminal justice

B.   explain how the adversarial and the inquisitorial systems of criminal justice both evolved from the system of private vengeance

C.   show how the adversarial and inquisitorial systems of criminal justice can both complement and hinder each other's development

D.   analyze two systems of criminal justice and deduce which one is better

The answer to a main idea question will summarize the passage without going beyond it. (A) violates these criteria by *overstating* the scope of the passage. The comparison in the passage is between two specific systems, not between *all* systems. (A) would be a good answer if "best" were replaced with "better." **Beware of extreme words**. (B) violates the criteria by *understating* the scope of the passage. Although the evolution of both the adversarial and the inquisitorial systems is discussed in the passage, it is done to show why one is superior to the other. As to (C), it can be quickly dismissed since it is not mentioned in the passage. Finally, the passage does two things: it presents two systems of criminal justice and shows why one is better than the other. (D) aptly summarizes this, so it is the best answer.

Following is a mini-passage. These exercises are interspersed among the sections of this chapter and are written to the same specifications as actual MCAT passages, but are one-quarter to one-half the length. Because the mini-passages are shorter and designed to test only one issue, they are more tractable than a full passage.

Application: *(Mini-passage)*

As Xenophanes recognized as long ago as the sixth century before Christ, whether or not God made man in His own image, it is certain that man makes gods in his. The gods of Greek mythology first appear in the writings of Homer and Hesiod, and, from the character and actions of these picturesque and, for the most part, friendly beings, we get some idea of the men who made them and brought them to Greece.

But ritual is more fundamental than mythology, and the study of Greek ritual during recent years has shown that, beneath the belief or skepticism with which the Olympians were regarded, lay an older magic, with traditional rites for the promotion of fertility by the celebration of the annual cycle of life and death, and the propitiation of unfriendly ghosts, gods or demons. Some such survivals were doubtless widespread, and, prolonged into classical times, probably made the substance of Eleusinian and Orphic mysteries. Against this dark and dangerous background arose Olympic mythology on the one hand and early philosophy and science on the other.

In classical times the need of a creed higher than the Olympian was felt, and Aeschylus, Sophocles and Plato finally evolved from the pleasant but crude polytheism the idea of a single, supreme and righteous Zeus. But the decay of Olympus led to a revival of old and the invasion of new magic cults among the people, while some philosophers were looking to a vision of the uniformity of nature under divine and universal law.

From Sir William Cecil Dampier, *A Shorter History of Science*, ©1957, Meridian Books.

The main idea of the passage is that
A. Olympic mythology evolved from ancient rituals and gave rise to early philosophy
B. early moves toward viewing nature as ordered by divine and universal law coincided with monotheistic impulses and the disintegration of classical mythology
C. early philosophy followed from classical mythology
D. the practice of science, i.e., empiricism, preceded scientific theory

Most main idea questions are rather easy. This one is not—mainly, because the passage itself is not an easy read. Recall that to find the main idea of a passage, we check the last sentence of the first paragraph; if it's not there, we check the closing of the passage. Reviewing the last sentence of the first paragraph, we see that it hardly presents a statement, let alone the main idea. Turning to the closing line of the passage, however, we find the key to this question. The passage describes a struggle for ascendancy amongst four opposing philosophies: (magic and traditional rites) vs. (Olympic mythology) vs. (monotheism [Zeus]) vs. (early philosophy and science). The closing lines of the passage summarize this and add that Olympic mythology lost out to monotheism (Zeus), while magical cults enjoyed a revival and the germ of universal law was planted. Thus the answer is (B).

As to the other choices, (A) is false. "Olympic mythology [arose] on one hand and early philosophy and science on the other" (closing to paragraph two); thus they initially developed in parallel. (C) is also false. It makes the same type of error as (A). Finally, (D) is not mentioned in the passage.

C. Description Questions

Description questions, as with main idea questions, refer to a point made by the author. However, description questions refer to a minor point or to incidental information, not to the author's main point.

Again, these questions take various forms:
- ☐ According to the passage . . .
- ☐ In line 37, the author mentions . . . for the purpose of . . .
- ☐ The passage suggests that which one of the following would . . .

The answer to a description question must refer <u>directly</u> to a statement in the passage, not to something implied by it. However, the correct answer will paraphrase a statement in the passage, not give an exact quote. In fact, exact quotes ("Same language" traps) are often used to bait wrong answers.

Caution: When answering a description question, you must find the point in the passage from which the question is drawn. Don't rely on memory—too many obfuscating tactics are used with these questions.

Not only must the correct answer refer directly to a statement in the passage, it must refer to the relevant statement. The correct answer will be surrounded by wrong choices which refer directly to the passage but don't address the question. These choices can be tempting because they tend to be quite close to the actual answer.

Once you spot the sentence to which the question refers, you still must read a few sentences before and after it, to put the question in context. If a question refers to line 20, the information needed to answer it can occur anywhere from line 15 to 25. Even if you have spotted the answer in line 20, you should still read a couple more lines to make certain you have the proper perspective.

Example: (Refer to passage on page 299.)

According to the passage, the inquisitorial system differs from the adversarial system in that

A.   it does not make the defendant solely responsible for gathering evidence for his case

B.   it does not require the police department to work on behalf of the prosecution

C.   it requires the prosecution to drop a weak case

D.   a defendant who is innocent would prefer to be tried under the inquisitorial system

This is a description question, so the information needed to answer it must be stated in the passage—though not in the same language as in the answer. The needed information is contained in lines 32–35, which state that the public prosecutor has to investigate on behalf of both society and the defendant. Thus, the defendant is not solely responsible for investigating his case. Furthermore, the paragraph's opening implies that this feature is not found in the adversarial system. This illustrates why you must determine the context of the situation before you can safely answer the question. The answer is (A).

The other choices can be easily dismissed. (B) is the second best answer. Lines 17–19 state that in the adversarial system the police assume the work of the prosecution. Then lines 27–29 state that the inquisitorial system begins where the adversarial system stopped; this implies that in both systems the police work for the prosecution. The passage states that both systems are removed from the system of private vengeance. (C) is probably true, but it is neither stated nor directly implied by the passage. Finally, (D) uses a reference to the passage to make a true but irrelevant statement. People's attitude or preference toward a system is not a part of that system.

Application: *(Mini-passage)*

If dynamic visual graphics, sound effects, and automatic scorekeeping are the features that account for the popularity of video games, why are parents so worried? All of these features seem quite innocent. But another source of concern is that the games available in arcades have, almost without exception, themes of physical aggression.... There has long been the belief that violent content may teach violent behavior. And yet again our society finds a new medium in which to present that content, and yet again the demand is nearly insatiable. And there is evidence that violent video games breed violent behavior, just as violent television shows do....

The effects of video violence are less simple, however, than they at first appeared. The same group of researchers who found negative effects [from certain video games] have more recently found that two-player aggressive video games, whether cooperative or competitive, reduce the level of aggression in children's play....

It may be that the most harmful aspect of the violent video games is that they are solitary in nature. A two-person aggressive game (video boxing, in this study) seems to provide a cathartic or releasing effect for aggression, while a solitary aggressive game (such as Space Invaders) may stimulate further aggression. Perhaps the effects of television in stimulating aggression will also be found to stem partly from the fact that TV viewing typically involves little social interaction.

From Patricia Marks Greenfield, *Mind and Media: The Effects of Television, Video Games, and Computers.* © 1984 by Harvard University Press.

According to the passage, which of the following would be likely to stimulate violent behavior in a child playing a video game?

I.   Watching the computer stage a battle between two opponents

II.   Controlling a character in battle against a computer

III. Challenging another player to a battle in a non-cooperative two-person game

A.   II only

B.   III only

C.   I and II only

D.   II and III only

Item I, True: Stimulation would occur. This choice is qualitatively the same as passively watching violence on television. **Item II, True:** Stimulation would also occur. This is another example of solitary aggression (implied by the second sentence of the last paragraph). **Item III, False:** No stimulation would occur. Two-player aggressive games are "cathartic" (again the needed reference is the second sentence of the last paragraph). The answer is (C).

Often you will be asked to define a word or phrase based on its context. For this type of question, again you must look at a few lines before and after the word. Don't assume that because the word is familiar you know the definition requested. Words often have more than one meaning. And the MCAT often asks for a peculiar or technical meaning of a common word. For example, as a noun *champion* means "the winner," but as a verb *champion* means "to be an advocate for someone." You must consider the word's context to get its correct meaning.

On the MCAT the definition of a word will not use as simple a structure as was used above to define *champion*. One common way the MCAT introduces a defining word or phrase is to place it in <u>apposition</u> to the word being defined.

Don't confuse "apposition" with "opposition": they have antithetical [exactly opposite] meanings. Words or phrases in <u>apposition</u> are placed next to each other, and the second word or phrase defines, clarifies, or gives evidence for the first word or phrase. The second word or phrase will be set off from the first by a comma, semicolon, hyphen, or parentheses. (Note: If a comma is not followed by a linking word—such as *and, for, yet*—then the following phrase is probably appositional.)

Example:

The discussions were acrimonious, frequently degenerating into name-calling contests.

After the comma in this sentence, there is no linking word (such as *and, but, because, although,* etc.). Hence the phrase following the comma is in apposition to *acrimonious*—it defines or further clarifies the word. Now acrimonious means bitter, mean-spirited talk, which would aptly describe a name-calling contest.

Application: *(Mini-passage)*

The technical phenomenon, embracing all the separate techniques, forms a whole.... It is useless to look for differentiations. They do exist, but only secondarily. The common features of the technical phenomenon are so sharply drawn that it is easy to discern that which is the technical phenomenon and that which is not.

... To analyze these common features is tricky, but it is simple to grasp them. Just as there are principles common to things as different as a wireless set and an internal-combustion engine, so the organization of an office and the construction of an aircraft have certain identical features. This identity is the primary mark of that thoroughgoing unity which makes the technical phenomenon a single essence despite the extreme diversity of its appearances.

As a corollary, it is impossible to analyze this or that element out of it—a truth which is today particularly misunderstood. The great tendency of all persons who study techniques is to make distinctions. They distinguish between the different elements of technique, maintaining some and discarding others. They distinguish between technique and the use to which it is put. These distinctions are completely invalid and show only that he who makes them has understood nothing of the technical phenomenon. Its parts are ontologically tied together; in it, use is inseparable from being.

From Jacques Ellul, *The Technological Society*, ©1964 by Alfred A. Knopf, Inc.

The "technical phenomenon" referred to in the opening line can best be defined as

A.   all of the machinery in use today

B.   the abstract idea of the machine

C.   a way of thinking in modern society

D.   what all machines have in common

(A): No, it is clear from the passage that the technical phenomenon is more abstract than that, since it is described in the opening paragraph as uniting all the separate "techniques" (not machines) and as comprising the "features" that such things as an office and an aircraft have in common. (B): No, the passage states that the technical phenomenon is something that includes both techniques and their use (See closing lines of the passage); it is thus broader that just the idea of machinery. (C): **Yes**, this seems to be the best answer; it is broad enough to include both techniques and their uses and abstract enough to go beyond talking only about machines. (D): No, the passage suggests that it is something that techniques have in common and techniques can include airplanes or offices.

D. Writing Technique Questions

All coherent writing has a superstructure or blueprint. When writing, we don't just randomly jot down our thoughts; we organize our ideas and present them in a logical manner. For instance, we may present evidence that builds up to a conclusion but intentionally leave the conclusion unstated, or we may present a position and then contrast it with an opposing position, or we may draw an extended analogy.

There is an endless number of writing techniques that authors use to present their ideas, so we cannot classify every method. However, some techniques are very common to the type of explanatory or opinionated writing found in MCAT passages.

1.   Compare and contrast two positions.

This technique has a number of variations, but the most common and direct method is to develop two ideas or systems (comparing) and then point out why one is better than the other (contrasting).

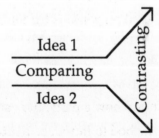

Some common tip-off phrases to this method of analysis are

- By contrast
- Similarly

Some typical questions for these types of passages are

- According to the passage, a central distinction between a woman's presence and a man's presence is:
- In which of the following ways does the author imply that birds and reptiles are similar?

Writing technique questions are similar to main idea questions; except that they ask about how the author <u>presents</u> his ideas, not about the ideas themselves. Generally, you will be given only two writing methods to choose from, but each method will have two or more variations.

Example: (Refer to passage on page 299.)

Which one of the following best describes the organization of the passage?

A. Two systems of criminal justice are compared and contrasted, and one is deemed to be better than the other.

B. One system of criminal justice is presented as better than another. Then evidence is offered to support that claim.

C. Two systems of criminal justice are analyzed, and one specific example is examined in detail.

D. A set of examples is furnished. Then a conclusion is drawn from them.

Clearly the author is comparing and contrasting two criminal justice systems. Indeed, the opening to paragraph two makes this explicit. The author uses a mixed form of comparison and contrast. He opens the passage by developing (comparing) both systems and then shifts to developing just the adversarial system. He opens the second paragraph by contrasting the two criminal justice systems and then further develops just the inquisitorial system. Finally, he closes by again contrasting the two systems and implying that the inquisitorial system is superior.

Only two answer-choices, (A) and (B), have any real merit. They say essentially the same thing—though in different order. Notice in the passage that the author does not indicate which system is better until the end of paragraph one, and he does not make that certain until paragraph two. This contradicts the order given by (B). Hence the answer is (A). (Note: In (A) the order is not specified and therefore is harder to attack, whereas in (B) the order is definite and therefore is easier to attack. Remember that a measured response is harder to attack and therefore is more likely to be the answer.)

2. Show cause and effect.

In this technique, the author typically shows how a particular cause leads to a certain result or set of results. It is not uncommon for this method to introduce a sequence of causes and effects. A causes B, which causes C, which causes D, and so on. Hence B is both the effect of A and the cause of C. For a discussion of the fallacies associated with this technique see Causal Reasoning (page 391). The variations on this rhetorical technique can be illustrated by the following schematics:

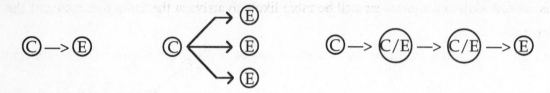

Example: *(Mini-passage)*

Thirdly, I worry about the private automobile. It is a dirty, noisy, wasteful, and lonely means of travel. It pollutes the air, ruins the safety and sociability of the street, and exercises upon the individual a discipline which takes away far more freedom than it gives him. It causes an enormous amount of land to be unnecessarily abstracted from nature and from plant life and to become devoid of any natural function. It explodes cities, grievously impairs the whole institution of neighborliness, fragmentizes and destroys communities. It has already spelled the end of our cities as real cultural and social communities, and has made impossible the construction of any others in their place. Together with the airplane, it has crowded out other, more civilized and more convenient means of transport, leaving older people, infirm people, poor people and children in a worse situation than they were a hundred years ago. It continues to lend a terrible element of fragility to our civilization, placing us in a situation where our life would break down completely if anything ever interfered with the oil supply.

George F. Kennan

Which of the following best describes the organization of the passage?

A. A problem is presented and then a possible solution is discussed.

B. The benefits and demerits of the automobile are compared and contrasted.

C. A topic is presented and a number of its effects are discussed.

D. A set of examples is furnished to support a conclusion.

This passage is laden with effects. Kennan introduces the cause, the automobile, in the opening sentence and from there on presents a series of effects—the automobile pollutes, enslaves, and so on. Hence the answer is (C). Note: (D) is the second-best choice; it is disqualified by two flaws. First, in this context, "examples" is not as precise as "effects." Second, the order is wrong: the conclusion, *"I worry about the private automobile"* is presented first and then the examples: it pollutes, it enslaves, etc.

3.   State a position and then give supporting evidence.

This technique is common with opinionated passages. Equally common is the reverse order. That is, the supporting evidence is presented and then the position or conclusion is stated. And sometimes the evidence will be structured to build up to a conclusion which is then left unstated. If this is done skillfully the reader will be more likely to arrive at the same conclusion as the author.

Following are some typical questions for these types of passages:

- According to the author, which of the following is required for one to become proficient with a computer?
- Which of the following does the author cite as evidence that the bald eagle is in danger of becoming extinct?

E. Extension Questions

Extension questions are the most common. They require you to go beyond what is stated in the passage, asking you to draw an inference from the passage, to make a conclusion based on the passage, or to identify one of the author's tacit assumptions.

You may be asked to draw a conclusion based on the ideas or facts presented:

☐ It can be inferred from the passage that . . .
☐ The passage suggests that . . .

Since extension questions require you to go beyond the passage, the correct answer must say *more* than what is said in the passage. Beware of same language traps with these questions: the correct answer will often both paraphrase and extend a statement in the passage, but it will not directly quote it.

"Same Language" traps: For extension questions, any answer-choice that explicitly refers to or repeats a statement in the passage will probably be wrong.

The correct answer to an extension question will not require a quantum leap in thought, but it will add significantly to the ideas presented in the passage.

Example: (Refer to passage on page 299.)

The author views the prosecution's role in the inquisitorial system as being

A.   an advocate for both society and the defendant

B.   solely responsible for starting a trial

C.   a protector of the legal rule

D.   an aggressive but fair investigator

This is an extension question. So the answer will not be explicitly stated in the passage, but it will be strongly supported by it.

The author states that the prosecutor is duty bound to present any evidence that may prove the defendant innocent and that he must disclose all pretrial evidence (i.e., have no tricks up his sleeve). This is the essence of fair play. So the answer is probably (D).

However, we should check all the choices. (A) overstates the case. Although the prosecutor must disclose any evidence that might show the defendant innocent, the prosecutor is still advocating society's case against the defendant—it must merely be measured advocacy. This is the second-best answer. As for (B), although it is implied that in both systems the right to initiate a case is extended to all people through the prosecutor, it is not stated or implied that this is the only way to start a case. Finally, (C) is not mentioned or implied in the passage. The answer, therefore, is (D).

Application: *(Mini-passage)*

Often, the central problem in any business is that money is needed to make money. The following discusses the sale of equity, which is one response to this problem.

Sale of Capital Stock: a way to obtain capital through the sale of stock to individual investors beyond the scope of one's immediate acquaintances. Periods of high interest rates turn entrepreneurs to this equity market. This involves, of necessity, a dilution of ownership, and many owners are reluctant to take this step for that reason. Whether the owner is wise in declining to use outside equity financing depends upon the firm's long-range prospects. If there is an opportunity for substantial expansion on a continuing basis and if other sources are inadequate, the owner may decide logically to bring in other owners. Owning part of a larger business may be more profitable than owning all of a smaller business.

Small-Business Management, 6th Ed., © 1983 by South-Western Publishing Co.

The passage implies that an owner who chooses not to sell capital stock despite the prospect of continued expansion is

A.   subject to increased regulation

B.   more conservative than is wise under the circumstances

C.   likely to have her ownership of the business diluted

D.   sacrificing security for rapid growth

(A): No. This is not mentioned in the passage. **(B): Yes.** The passage states that *"the owner may decide <u>logically</u> to bring in other owners";* in other words, the owner would be wise to sell stock in this situation. (C): No. By NOT selling stock, the owner retains full ownership. (D) No. Just the opposite: the owner would be sacrificing a measure of security for growth if she did sell stock.

F. Application Questions

Application questions differ from extension questions only in degree. Extension questions ask you to apply what you have learned from the passage to derive new information about the same subject, whereas application questions go one step further, asking you to apply what you have learned from the passage to a different or hypothetical situation.

The following are common application questions:

☐   Which one of the following is the most likely source of the passage?

☐   Which one of the following actions would be most likely to have the same effect as the author's actions?

You may be asked to complete a thought for the author:

☐   The author would most likely agree with which one of the following statements?

☐   Which one of the following sentences would the author be most likely to use to complete the last paragraph of the passage?

To answer an application question, take the author's perspective. Ask yourself: what am I arguing for? what might make my argument stronger? what might make it weaker?

Because these questions go well beyond the passage, they tend to be the most difficult. Furthermore, because application questions and extension questions require a deeper understanding of the passage, skimming (or worse yet, speed reading) the passage is ineffective. Skimming may give you the main idea and structure of the passage, but it is unlikely to give you the subtleties of the author's attitude.

Example: (Refer to passage on page 299.)

Based on the information in the passage, it can be inferred that which one of the following would most logically begin a paragraph immediately following the passage?

A. Because of the inquisitorial system's thoroughness in conducting its pretrial investigation, it can be concluded that a defendant who is innocent would prefer to be tried under the inquisitorial system, whereas a defendant who is guilty would prefer to be tried under the adversarial system.

B. As the preceding analysis shows, the legal system is in a constant state of flux. For now the inquisitorial system is ascendant, but it will probably be soon replaced by another system.

C. The accusatorial system begins where the inquisitorial system ends. So it is three steps removed from the system of private vengeance, and therefore historically superior to it.

D. The criminal justice system has evolved to the point that it no longer seems to be derivative of the system of private vengeance. Modern systems of criminal justice empower all of society with the right to instigate a legal action, and the need for vengeance is satisfied through a surrogate—the public prosecutor.

The author has rather thoroughly presented his position, so the next paragraph would be a natural place for him to summarize it. The passage compares and contrasts two systems of criminal justice, implying that the inquisitorial system is superior. We expect the concluding paragraph to sum up this position. Now all legal theory aside, the system of justice under which an innocent person would choose to be judged would, as a practical matter, pretty much sum up the situation. Hence the answer is (A).

Application: *(Mini-passage)*

The idea of stuff expresses no more than the experience of coming to a limit at which our senses or our instruments are not fine enough to make out the pattern.

Something of the same kind happens when the scientist investigates any unit or pattern so distinct to the naked eye that it has been considered a separate entity. He finds that the more carefully he observes and describes it, the more he is *also* describing the environment in which it moves and other patterns to which it seems inseparably related. As Teilhard de Chardin has so well expressed it, the isolation of individual, atomic patterns "is merely an intellectual dodge."

...Although the ancient cultures of Asia never attained the rigorously exact physical knowledge of the modern West, they grasped in principle many things which are only now occurring to us. Hinduism and Buddhism are impossible to classify as religions, philosophies, sciences, or even mythologies, or again as amalgamations of all four, because departmentalization is foreign to them even in so basic a form as the separation of the spiritual and the material.... Buddhism ... is not a culture but a critique of culture, an enduring nonviolent revolution, or "loyal opposition," to the culture with which it is involved. This gives these ways of liberation something in common with psychotherapy beyond the interest in changing states of consciousness. For the task of the psychotherapist is to bring about a reconciliation between individual feeling and social norms without, however, sacrificing the integrity of the individual.

He tries to help the individual to be himself and to go it alone in the world (of social convention) but not of the world.

From Alan W. Watts, *Psychotherapy East and West*, © 1961 by Pantheon Books, a division of Random House.

What does the passage suggest about the theme of the book from which it is excerpted?

A. The book attempts to understand psychotherapy in the context of different and changing systems of thought.

B. The book argues that psychotherapy unites elements of an exact science with elements of eastern philosophy.

C. The book describes the origins of psychotherapy around the world.

D. The book compares psychotherapy in the West and in the East.

(A): Yes, this is the most accurate inference from the passage. The passage discusses how the more carefully a scientist views and describes something the more he describes the environment in which it moves, and the passage traces similarities between psychotherapy and Eastern systems of (evolving) thought. (B): No, this is too narrow an interpretation of what the whole book would be doing. (C): No, too vague; the passage is too philosophical to be merely a history. (D): No, also too vague, meant to entrap those of you who relied on the title without thinking through the passage.

G. Tone Questions

Tone questions ask you to identify the writer's attitude or perspective. Is the writer's feeling toward the subject positive, negative, or neutral? Does the writer give his own opinion, or does he objectively present the opinions of others?

Before you read the answer-choices, decide whether the writer's tone is positive, negative, or neutral. It is best to do this without referring to the passage.

However, if you did not get a feel for the writer's attitude on the first reading, check the adjectives that he chooses. Adjectives and, to a lesser extent, adverbs express our feelings toward subjects. For instance, if we agree with a person who holds strong feelings about a subject, we may describe his opinions as impassioned. On the other hand, if we disagree with him, we may describe his opinions as excitable, which has the same meaning as "impassioned" but carries a negative connotation.

313

Example: (Refer to passage on page 299.)

The author's attitude toward the adversarial system can best be described as

A.   encouraged that it is far removed from the system of private vengeance

B.   concerned that it does not allow all members of society to instigate legal action

C.   hopeful that it will be replaced by the inquisitorial system

D.   doubtful that it is the best vehicle for justice

The author does not reveal his feelings toward the adversarial system until the end of paragraph one. Clearly the clause "the adversarial system of criminal procedure symbolizes and regularizes the punitive combat" indicates that he has a negative attitude toward the system. This is confirmed in the second paragraph when he states that the inquisitorial system is historically superior to the adversarial system. So he feels that the adversarial system is deficient.

The "two-out-of-five" rule is at work here: only choices (C) and (D) have any real merit. Both are good answers. But which one is better? Intuitively, choice (D) is more likely to be the answer because it is more measured. To decide between two choices attack each: the one that survives is the answer. Now a tone question should be answered from what is directly stated in the passage—not from what it implies. Although the author has reservations toward the adversarial system, at no point does he say that he hopes the inquisitorial system will replace it, he may prefer a third system over both. This eliminates (C); the answer therefore is (D).

The remaining choices are not supported by the passage. (A), using the same language as in the passage, overstates the author's feeling. In lines 11–13, he states that the adversarial system is only *one* step removed from the private vengeance system—not *far* removed. Remember: Be wary of extreme words. (A) would be a better choice if "far" were dropped. (B) makes a false claim. In lines 14–17, the author states that the adversarial system *does* extend the right to initiate legal action to all members of society.

Application: *(Mini-passage)*

An elm in our backyard caught the blight this summer and dropped stone dead, leafless, almost overnight. One weekend it was a normal-looking elm, maybe a little bare in spots but nothing alarming, and the next weekend it was gone, passed over, departed, taken....

The dying of a field mouse, at the jaws of an amiable household cat, is a spectacle I have beheld many times. It used to make me wince.... Nature, I thought, was an abomination.

Recently I've done some thinking about that mouse, and I wonder if his dying is necessarily all that different from the passing of our elm. The main difference, if there is one, would be in the matter of pain. I do not believe that an elm tree has pain receptors, and even so, the blight seems to me a relatively painless way to go. But the mouse dangling tail-down from the teeth of a gray cat is something else again, with pain beyond bearing, you'd think, all over his small body. There are now some plausible reasons for thinking it is not like that at all.... At the instant of being trapped and penetrated by teeth, peptide hormones are released by cells in the hypothalamus and the pituitary gland; instantly these substances, called endorphins, are attached to the surfaces of other cells responsible for pain perception; the hormones have the pharmacologic properties of opium; there is no pain. Thus it is that the mouse seems always to dangle so languidly from the jaws, lies there so quietly when dropped, dies of his injuries without a struggle. If a mouse could shrug, he'd shrug....

Pain is useful for avoidance, for getting away when there's time to get away, but when it is end game, and no way back, pain is likely to be turned off, and the mechanisms for this are wonderfully precise and quick. If I had to design an ecosystem in which creatures had to live off each other and in which dying was an indispensable part of living, I could not think of a better way to manage.
From Lewis Thomas, *On Natural Death,* © 1979 by Lewis Thomas.

Which one of the following would best characterize the author's attitude toward the relationship between pain and death?

A. Dismay at the inherent cruelty of nature

B. Amusement at the irony of the relationship between pain and death

C. Admiration for the ways in which animal life functions in the ecosystem

D. A desire to conduct experiments on animals in order to discover more about the relationship between pain and death

The author's attitude toward the relationship between pain and death evolves through three stages. First, he expresses revulsion at the relationship. This is indicated in the second paragraph by the words *"wince"* and *"abomination."* Then in the third paragraph, he adopts a more analytical attitude and questions his previous judgment. This is indicated by the clause, *"I wonder if his dying is necessarily all that different from the passing of our elm."* And in closing the paragraph, he seems resigned to the fact the relationship is not all that bad. This is indicated by the sentence, *"If a mouse could shrug, he'd shrug."* Finally, in the last paragraph, he comes to express admiration for the relationship between pain and death. This is indicated by the phrase *"wonderfully precise and quick,"* and it is made definite by the closing line, *"If I had to design an ecosystem . . . in which dying was an indispensable part of living, I could not think of a better way to manage."* Thus, the answer is (C).

The other choices are easily ruled out. Choice (A) is perhaps superficially tempting. In the second paragraph the author does express dismay at the ways of nature, but notice that his concerns are in the past tense. He is *now* more understanding, wiser of the ways of nature. As to (B), the author is subtly reverential, never ironical, toward nature. Finally, (D) is not mentioned or alluded to in the passage.

Beware of answer-choices that contain extreme emotions. Remember the passages are taken from academic journals. In the rarefied air of academic circles, strong emotions are considered inappropriate and sophomoric. The writers want to display opinions that are considered and reasonable, not spontaneous and off-the-wall. So if an author's tone is negative, it may be disapproving—not snide. Or if her tone is positive, it may be approving—not ecstatic.

Furthermore, the answers must be indisputable. If the answers were subjective, then the writers of the MCAT would be deluged with letters from angry test takers, complaining that their test-scores are unfair. To avoid such a difficult position, the writers of the MCAT never allow the correct answer to be either controversial or grammatically questionable.

Let's use these theories to answer the following questions.

Example:

Which one of the following characterizes the author's attitude toward John Wilkins' writing style?

A.   ardent advocacy

B.   qualified admiration

C.   dispassionate impartiality

D.   perfunctory dismissal

Even without reference to the passage, this is not a difficult question to answer.

Scholars may advocate each other's work, but they are unlikely to be ardent advocates. Furthermore, the context stretches the meaning of advocacy—to defend someone else's cause or plight. So (A) is unlikely to be the answer.

(B) is the measured response and therefore is probably the answer.

"Dispassionate impartiality" is a rather odd construction; additionally, it is redundant. It could never be the answer to an MCAT question. This eliminates (C).

Remember, scholars want their audience to consider their opinions well thought out, not off-the-wall. But *perfunctory* means "hasty and superficial." So (D) could not be the answer.

Hence, even without the passage we can still find the answer, (B).

Example:

Which one of the following best describes the author's attitude toward scientific techniques?

A. critical

B. hostile

C. idealistic

D. neutral

(A) is one of two measured responses offered. Now a scholar may be critical of a particular scientific technique, but only a crackpot would be critical of *all* scientific techniques—eliminate (A).

"Hostile" is far too negative. Scholars consider such emotions juvenile—eliminate (B).

"Idealistic," on the other hand, is too positive; it sounds pollyannaish—eliminate (C).

(D) is the other measured response, and by elimination it is the answer.

Points to Remember

1. The order of the passage questions <u>roughly</u> corresponds to the order in which the issues are presented in the passage.

2. The six questions are

   Main Idea
   Description
   Writing Technique
   Extension
   Application
   Tone

3. The main idea of a passage is usually stated in the last, sometimes the first, sentence of the first paragraph. If it's not there, it will probably be the last sentence of the entire passage.

4. If after the first reading, you don't have a feel for the main idea, review the first and last sentence of each paragraph.

5. The answer to a description question must refer directly to a statement in the passage, not to something implied by it. However, the correct answer will paraphrase a passage statement, not quote it exactly. In fact, exact quotes are used with these questions to bait wrong answers.

6. When answering a description question, you must find the point in the passage from which the question is drawn.

7. If a description question refers to line 20, the information needed to answer it can occur anywhere from line 15 to 25.

8. Some writing techniques commonly used in the MCAT passages are
   A. Compare and contrast two positions.
   B. Show cause and effect.
   C. State a position; then give supporting evidence.

9. For extension questions, any answer-choice that refers explicitly to or repeats a statement in the passage will probably be wrong.

10. Application questions differ from extension questions only in degree. Extension questions ask you to apply what you have learned from the passage to derive new information about the same subject, whereas application questions go one step further, asking you to apply what you have learned from the passage to a different or hypothetical situation.

11. To answer an application question, take the perspective of the author. Ask yourself: what am I arguing for? what might make my argument stronger? what might make it weaker?

12. Because application questions go well beyond the passage, they tend to be the most difficult.

13. For tone questions, decide whether the writer's tone is positive, negative, or neutral before you look at the answer-choices.

14. If you do not have a feel for the writer's attitude after the first reading, check the adjectives that she chooses.

15. Beware of answer-choices that contain extreme emotions. If an author's tone is negative, it may be disapproving—not snide. Or if her tone is positive, it may be approving—not ecstatic.

16. The answers must be indisputable. A correct answer will never be controversial or grammatically questionable.

Mentor Exercise

From Romania to Germany, from Tallinn to Belgrade, a major historical process—the death of communism—is taking place. The German Democratic Republic no longer exists as a separate
5   state. And the former German Democratic Republic will serve as the first measure of the price a post-Communist society has to pay for entering the normal European orbit. In Yugoslavia we will see whether the federation can survive without communism.
10   One thing seems common to all these countries: dictatorship has been defeated and freedom has won, yet the victory of freedom has not yet meant the triumph of democracy. Democracy is something more than freedom. Democracy is freedom
15   institutionalized, freedom submitted to the limits of the law, freedom functioning as an object of compromise between the major political forces on the scene.
We have freedom, but we still have not achieved
20   the democratic order. That is why this freedom is so fragile. In the years of democratic opposition to communism, we supposed that the easiest thing would be to introduce changes in the economy. In fact, we thought that the march from a planned
25   economy to a market economy would take place within the framework of the bureaucratic system, and that the market within the Communist state would explode the totalitarian structures. Only then would the time come to build the institutions of a civil
30   society; and only at the end, with the completion of the market economy and the civil society, would the time of great political transformations finally arrive.
The opposite happened. First came the big political change, the great shock, which either broke
35   the monopoly and the principle of Communist Party rule or simply pushed the Communists out of power. Then came the creation of civil society, whose institutions were created in great pain, and which had trouble negotiating the empty space of freedom.
40   Only then, as the third moment of change, the final task was undertaken: that of transforming the totalitarian economy into a normal economy where different forms of ownership and different economic actors will live one next to the other.
45   Today we are in a typical moment of transition. No one can say where we are headed. The people of the democratic opposition have the feeling that we won. We taste the sweetness of our victory the same way the Communists, only yesterday our prison
50   guards, taste the bitterness of their defeat. Yet, even as we are conscious of our victory, we feel that we

are, in a strange way, losing. In Bulgaria the Communists have won the parliamentary elections and will govern the country, without losing their
55   social legitimacy. In Romania the National Salvation Front, largely dominated by people from the old Communist bureaucracy, has won. In other countries democratic institutions seem shaky, and the political horizon is cloudy. The masquerade goes on: dozens
60   of groups and parties are created, each announces similar slogans, each accuses its adversaries of all possible sins, and each declares itself representative of the national interest. Personal disputes are more important than disputes over values. Arguments over
65   values are fiercer than arguments over ideas.

1. The author originally thought that the order of events in the transformation of communist society would be represented by which one of the following?

   A. A great political shock would break the totalitarian monopoly, leaving in its wake a civil society whose task would be to change the state-controlled market into a free economy.

   B. The transformation of the economy would destroy totalitarianism, after which a new and different social and political structure would be born.

   C. First the people would freely elect political representatives who would transform the economy, which would then undermine the totalitarian structure.

   D. The change to a democratic state would necessarily undermine totalitarianism, after which a new economic order would be created.

1. This is a description question, so you should locate the point in the passage from which it was drawn. It is the third paragraph. In lines 24–28, the author recalls his expectation that, by introducing the market system, the communist system would topple from within.

   Be careful not to choose (A). It chronicles how the events actually occurred, not how they were *anticipated* to occur. (A) is baited with the words "great shock," "monopoly," and "civil society."

   The answer is (B).

2. Beginning in the second paragraph, the author describes the complicated relationship between "freedom" and "democracy." In the author's view, which one of the following statements best reflects that relationship?

   A. A country can have freedom without having democracy.

   B. If a country has freedom, it necessarily has democracy.

   C. A country can have democracy without having freedom.

   D. A country can never have democracy if it has freedom.

2. This is an extension question, so the answer must say more than what is said in the passage, without requiring a quantum leap in thought. The needed reference is *"Democracy is something more than freedom"* (lines 13–14). Since freedom can exist without democracy, freedom alone does not insure democracy.

   The answer is (A).

3. From the passage, a reader could conclude that which one of the following best describes the author's attitude toward the events that have taken place in communist society?

   A. Relieved that at last the democratic order has surfaced.

   B. Clearly wants to return to the old order.

   C. Disappointed with the nature of the democracy that has emerged.

   D. Surprised that communism was toppled through political rather than economic means.

3. This is a tone question. The key to answering this question is found in the closing comments. There the author states *"The masquerade goes on,"* referring to nascent democracies. So he has reservations about the newly emerging democracies.

   Watch out for (D). Although it is supported by the passage, it is in a supporting paragraph. The ideas in a concluding paragraph take precedence over those in a supporting paragraph.

   The answer is (C).

4. A cynic who has observed political systems in various countries would likely interpret the author's description of the situation at the end of the passage as

    A.   evidence that society is still in the throws of the old totalitarian structure.

    B.   a distorted description of the new political system.

    C.   a fair description of many democratic political systems.

    D.   evidence of the baseness of people.

4. This is an application question. These are like extension questions, but they go well beyond what is stated in the passage. In this case we are asked to interpret the author's comments from a cynic's perspective. Because application questions go well beyond the passage, they are often difficult, as is this one.

Hint: A cynic looks at reality from a negative perspective, usually with a sense of dark irony and hopelessness.

    Don't make the mistake of choosing (D). Although a cynic is likely to make such a statement, it does not address the subject of the passage—political and economic systems. The passage is not about human nature, at least not directly.

The answer is (C).

5. Which one of the following does the author imply may have contributed to the difficulties involved in creating a new democratic order in eastern Europe?

    I.   The people who existed under the totalitarian structure have not had the experience of "negotiating the empty space of freedom."

    II.   Mistaking the order in which political, economic, and social restructuring would occur.

    III.   Excessive self-interest among the new political activists.

    A.   I only

    B.   II only

    C.   I and III only

    D.   I, II, and III

5. This is an extension question. Statement I is true. In lines 37–39, the author implies that the institutions of the new-born, free society were created in great pain because the people lacked experience. Statement II is true. Expectations that the market mechanisms would explode totalitarianism and usher in a new society were dashed, and having to readjust one's expectations certainly makes a situation more difficult. Finally, statement III is true. It summarizes the thrust of the passage's closing lines.

The answer is (D).

6. By stating "even as we are conscious of our victory, we feel that we are, in a strange way, losing" (lines 50–52) the author means that

    A.   some of the old governments are still unwilling to grant freedom at the individual level.

    B.   some of the new governments are not strong enough to exist as a single federation.

    C.   some of the new democratic governments are electing to retain the old political parties.

    D.   no new parties have been created to fill the vacuum created by the victory of freedom.

6. This is a hybrid extension and description question. Because it refers to a specific point in the passage, you must read a few sentences before and after it. The answer can be found in lines 52–65.

The answer is (C).

Exercise

Directions: This passage is followed by a group of questions to be answered based on what is <u>stated</u> or <u>implied</u> in the passage. For some questions, more than one choice could conceivably answer the question. However, choose the <u>best</u> answer; the one that most accurately and completely answers the question. Answers and solutions begin on page 325.

In the United States the per capita costs of schooling have risen almost as fast as the cost of medical treatment. But increased treatment by both doctors and teachers has shown steadily declining
5 results. Medical expenses concentrated on those above forty-five have doubled several times over a period of forty years with a resulting 3 percent increase in the life expectancy of men. The increase in educational expenditures has produced even
10 stranger results; otherwise President Nixon could not have been moved this spring to promise that every child shall soon have the "Right to Read" before leaving school.

In the United States it would take eighty billion
15 dollars per year to provide what educators regard as equal treatment for all in grammar and high school. This is well over twice the $36 billion now being spent. Independent cost projections prepared at HEW and at the University of Florida indicate that by 1974
20 the comparable figures will be $107 billion as against the $45 billion now projected, and these figures wholly omit the enormous costs of what is called "higher education," for which demand is growing even faster. The United States, which spent nearly
25 eighty billion dollars in 1969 for "defense," including its deployment in Vietnam, is obviously too poor to provide equal schooling. The President's committee for the study of school finance should ask not how to support or how to trim such increasing costs, but how
30 they can be avoided.

Equal obligatory schooling must be recognized as at least economically unfeasible. In Latin America the amount of public money spent on each graduate student is between 350 and 1,500 times the amount
35 spent on the median citizen (that is, the citizen who holds the middle ground between the poorest and the richest). In the United States the discrepancy is smaller, but the discrimination is keener. The richest parents, some 10 percent, can afford private
40 education for their children and help them to benefit from foundation grants. But in addition they obtain ten times the per capita amount of public funds if this is compared with the per capita expenditure made on the children of the 10 percent who are poorest. The
45 principal reasons for this are that rich children stay longer in school, that a year in a university is disproportionately more expensive than a year in high school, and that most private universities depend—at least indirectly—on tax-derived finances.

50 Obligatory schooling inevitably polarizes a society; it also grades the nations of the world according to an international caste system. Countries are rated like castes whose educational dignity is determined by the average years of schooling of its
55 citizens, a rating which is closely related to per capita gross national product, and much more painful.

323

1. Which one of the following best expresses the main idea of the passage?

   A. The educational shortcomings of the United States, in contrast to those of Latin America, are merely the result of poor allocation of available resources.
   B. Both education and medical care are severely underfunded.
   C. Obligatory schooling must be scrapped if the goal of educational equality is to be realized.
   D. Obligatory education does not and cannot provide equal education.

2. The author most likely would agree with which one of the following solutions to the problems presented by obligatory education?

   A. Education should not be obligatory at all.
   B. Education should not be obligatory for those who cannot afford it.
   C. More money should be diverted to education for the poorest.
   D. Future spending should be capped.

3. According to the passage, education is like health care in all of the following ways EXCEPT:

   A. It has reached a point of diminishing returns, increased spending no longer results in significant improvement.
   B. It has an inappropriate "more is better" philosophy.
   C. It is unfairly distributed between rich and poor.
   D. The amount of money being spent on older students is increasing.

4. Why does the author consider the results from increased educational expenditures to be "even stranger" than those from increased medical expenditures?

   A. The aging of the population should have had an impact only on medical care, not on education.
   B. The "Right to Read" should be a bare minimum, not a Presidential ideal.
   C. Educational spending has shown even poorer results than spending on health care, despite greater increases.
   D. It inevitably polarizes society.

5. Which one of the following most accurately characterizes the author's attitude with respect to obligatory schooling?

   A. qualified admiration
   B. critical
   C. neutral
   D. resentful

6. By stating "In Latin America the amount of public money spent on each graduate student is between 350 and 1,500 times the amount spent on the median citizen" and "In the United States the discrepancy is smaller" the author implies that

   A. equal education is possible in the United States but not in Latin America.
   B. equal education for all at the graduate level is an unrealistic ideal.
   C. educational spending is more efficient in the United States.
   D. underfunding of lower education is a world-wide problem.

Answers and Solutions to Exercise

1. Which one of the following best expresses the main idea of the passage?

   A. The educational shortcomings of the United States, in contrast to those of Latin America, are merely the result of poor allocation of available resources.
   B. Both education and medical care are severely underfunded.
   C. Obligatory schooling must be scrapped if the goal of educational equality is to be realized.
   D. Obligatory education does not and cannot provide equal education.

The answer to a main idea question will summarize the passage, without going beyond it.

(A) fails to meet these criteria because it makes a false claim. Lines 32–37 imply that the discrepancy in allocation of funds is greater in Latin America. Besides, Latin America is mentioned only in passing, so this is not the main idea.

(B) also makes a false claim. The author implies that increased funding for education is irrelevant, if not counterproductive. In fact, the sentence *"The President's committee for the study of school finance should ask not how to support or how to trim such increasing costs, but how they can be avoided"* implies that he thinks an increase in funding would be counterproductive.

(C) is the second-best answer-choice. The answer to a main idea question should sum up the passage, not make a conjecture about it. Clearly the author has serious reservations about obligatory schooling, but at no point does he state or imply that it should be scrapped. He may believe that it can be modified, or he may be resigned to the fact that, for other reasons, it is necessary. We don't know.

Finally, (D) aptly summarizes the passage, without going beyond it. The key to seeing this is the opening to paragraph three, *"Equal obligatory schooling must be recognized as at least economically unfeasible."* In other words, regardless of any other failings, it cannot succeed economically and therefore cannot provide equal education.

2. The author would most likely agree with which one of the following solutions to the problems presented by obligatory education?

   A. Education should not be obligatory at all.
   B. Education should not be obligatory for those who cannot afford it.
   C. More money should be diverted to education for the poorest.
   D. Future spending should be capped.

This is an application question. These questions tend to be rather difficult, though this one is not. To answer an application question, put yourself in the author's place. If you were arguing his case, which of the solutions would you advocate?

As to (A), although we rejected the recommendation that obligatory education be eliminated as Question 1's answer, it is the answer to Question 2. The author does not merely imply that obligatory education has some shortcomings; he suggests that it is fundamentally flawed. Again this is made clear by the opening to paragraph three, *"Equal obligatory schooling must be recognized as at least economically unfeasible."* Still, there is a possible misunderstanding here: perhaps the author believes that obligatory education is a noble but unrealistic idea. This possibility, however, is dispelled by the closing paragraph in which he states that obligatory education polarizes society and sets up a caste system. Obviously, such a system, if this is true, should be discarded. The answer is (A).

The other choices can be easily dismissed. (B) is incorrect because nothing in the passage suggests that the author would advocate a solution that would polarize society even more. Indeed, at the end of paragraph three, he suggests that the rich already get more than their fair share.

(C) is incorrect because it contradicts the author. Paragraph two is dedicated to showing that the United States is too poor to provide equal schooling. You can't divert money you don't have.

Finally, (D) is the second-best answer-choice. Although the author probably believes that future spending should be restrained or capped, this understates the thrust of his argument. However, he might offer this as a compromise to his opponents.

3. According to the passage, education is like health care in all of the following ways EXCEPT:

A. It has reached a point of diminishing returns, increased spending no longer results in significant improvement.
B. It has an inappropriate "more is better" philosophy.
C. It is unfairly distributed between rich and poor.
D. The amount of money being spent on older students is increasing.

This is a description question, so we must find the place from which it is drawn. It is the first paragraph. The sentence *"But increased treatment by both doctors and teachers has shown steadily declining results"* shows that both have reached a point of diminishing returns. This eliminates (A) and (B). Next, the passage states *"Medical expenses concentrated on those above forty-five have doubled several times"* (lines 5–6) and that the demand and costs of higher education are growing faster than the demand and costs of elementary and high school education. This eliminates (D). Hence, by process of elimination, the answer is (C). We should, however, verify this. In paragraph three, the author does state that there is a "keen" discrepancy in the funding of education between rich and poor, but a survey of the passage shows that at no point does he mention that this is also the case with health care.

4. Why does the author consider the results from increased educational expenditures to be "even stranger" than those from increased medical expenditures?

   A. The aging of the population should have had an impact only on medical care, not on education.
   B. The "Right to Read" should be a bare minimum, not a Presidential ideal.
   C. Educational spending has shown even poorer results than spending on health care, despite greater increases.
   D. It inevitably polarizes society.

This is an extension question. We are asked to interpret a statement by the author. The needed reference is the closing sentence to paragraph one. Remember: extension questions require you to go beyond the passage, so the answer won't be explicitly stated in the reference—we will have to interpret it.

The implication of President Nixon's promise is that despite increased educational funding many children cannot even read when they graduate from school. Hence the answer is (B).

Don't make the mistake of choosing (C). Although at first glance this is a tempting inference, it would be difficult to compare the results of education and medical care directly (how would we do so?). Regardless, the opening line to the passage states that educational costs have risen "almost as fast" as medical costs, not faster.

(A) is incorrect because the passage never mentions the aging of the population.

Many students who cannot solve this question choose (D)—don't. It uses as bait language from the passage, *"inevitably polarizes a society."* Note: The phrase "Right to Read" in (B) is not a same language trap; it is merely part of a paraphrase of the passage. The correct answer to an extension question will often both paraphrase and extend a passage statement but will not quote it directly, as in (D).

5. Which one of the following most accurately characterizes the author's attitude with respect to obligatory schooling?

   A. qualified admiration
   B. critical
   C. neutral
   D. resentful

Like most tone questions this one is rather easy. Although choice (A) is a measured response, the author clearly does not admire the obligatory school system. This eliminates (A); it also eliminates (C). Of the two remaining choices, (B) is the measured response, and it is the answer. Although the author strongly opposes obligatory schooling, "resentful" is too strong and too personal. A scholar would never directly express resentment or envy, even if that is his true feeling.

6. By stating "In Latin America the amount of public money spent on each graduate student is between 350 and 1,500 times the amount spent on the median citizen" and "In the United States the discrepancy is smaller" the author implies that

   A. equal education is possible in the United States but not in Latin America.
   B. equal education for all at the graduate level is an unrealistic ideal.
   C. educational spending is more efficient in the United States.
   D. underfunding of lower education is a world-wide problem.

This is another extension question. By stating that the amount of funding spent on graduate students is more than 350 times the amount spent on the average citizen, the author implies that it would be impossible to equalize the funding. Hence the answer is (B).

None of the other choices have any real merit. (A) is incorrect because the import of the passage is that the rich get better schooling and more public funds in the United States and therefore discrimination is "keener" here (lines 37–38).

(C) is incorrect because it is neither mentioned nor implied by the passage.

(D) is the second-best choice. Although this is implied by the numbers given, it has little to do with the primary purpose of the passage—to show that obligatory education is perhaps not such a good idea.

Chapter 24
Pivotal Words

As mentioned before, each passage contains 400 to 600 words and only six to ten questions, so you will <u>not</u> be tested on most of the material in the passage. Your best reading strategy, therefore, is to identify the places from which questions will most likely be drawn and concentrate your attention there.

Pivotal words can help in this regard. Following are the most common pivotal words.

Pivotal Words

But	**Although**
However	**Yet**
Despite	**Nevertheless**
Nonetheless	**Except**
In contrast	**Even though**

As you may have noticed, these words indicate contrast. Pivotal words warn that the author is about to either make a U-turn or introduce a counter-premise (concession to a minor counterpoint).

Pivotal words are more likely to introduce a new direction than a concession.

The following are two typical outlines for reading passages:

Premise	**Premise**
Conclusion	**Premise**
Premise	**Pivotal Word**
Counter-premise	**Continuation of Pivotal Word**
Restatement of Conclusion	**Conclusion**

Pivotal words mark natural places for questions to be drawn. At a pivotal word, the author changes direction. The MCAT writers form questions at these junctures to test whether you turned with the author or you continued to go straight. Rarely do the MCAT writers let a pivotal word pass without drawing a question from its sentence.

As you read a passage, circle the pivotal words and refer to them when answering the questions.

Let's apply this theory to the passage on criminal justice. For easy reference, the passage is reprinted here in the left-hand column, with explanations in the right-hand column. The pivotal words are marked in bold.

There are two major systems of criminal procedure in the modern world—the adversarial and the inquisitorial. The former is associated with common law tradition and the latter with civil law tradition. Both systems were historically preceded by the system of private vengeance in which the victim of a crime fashioned his own remedy and administered it privately, either personally or through an agent. The vengeance system was a system of self-help, the essence of which was captured in the slogan "an eye for an eye, a tooth for a tooth." The modern adversarial system is only one historical step removed from the private vengeance system and still retains some of its characteristic features. Thus, for example, **even though** the right to institute criminal action has now been extended to all members of society and **even though** the police department has taken over the pretrial investigative functions on behalf of the prosecution, the adversarial system still leaves the defendant to conduct his own pretrial investigation. The trial is still viewed as a duel between two adversaries, refereed by a judge who, at the beginning of the trial has no knowledge of the investigative background of the case. In the final analysis the adversarial system of criminal procedure symbolizes and regularizes the punitive combat.

By contrast, the inquisitorial system begins historically where the adversarial system stopped its development. It is two historical steps removed from the system of private vengeance. Therefore, from the standpoint of legal anthropology, it is historically superior to the adversarial system. Under the inquisitorial system the public investigator has the duty to investigate not just on behalf of the prosecutor **but also** on behalf of the defendant. Additionally, the public prosecutor has the duty to present to the court not only evidence that may lead to the conviction of the defendant **but also** evidence that may lead to his exoneration. This system mandates that both parties permit full pretrial discovery of the evidence in their possession. Finally, in an effort to make the trial less like a duel between two adversaries, the inquisitorial system mandates that the judge take an active part in the conduct of the trial, with a role that is both directive and protective.

Fact-finding is at the heart of the inquisitorial system. This system operates on the philosophical premise that in a criminal case the crucial factor is not the legal rule but the facts of the case and that the goal of the entire procedure is to experimentally recreate for the court the commission of the alleged crime.

Even though—Here "even though" is introducing a concession. In the previous sentence, the author stated that the adversarial system is only one step removed from the private vengeance system. The author uses the two concessions as a hedge against potential criticism that he did not consider that the adversarial system has extended the right to institute criminal action to all members of society and that police departments now perform the pretrial investigation. But the author then states that the adversarial system still leaves the defendant to conduct his own pretrial investigation. This marks a good place from which to draw a question. Many people will misinterpret the two concessions as evidence that the adversarial system is two steps removed from the private vengeance system.

By contrast—In this case the pivotal word is not introducing a concession. Instead it indicates a change in thought: now the author is going to discuss the other criminal justice system. This is a natural place to test whether the student has made the transition and whether he will attribute the properties soon to be introduced to the inquisitorial system, not the adversarial system.

But also—In both places, "but also" indicates neither concession nor change in thought. Instead it is part of the coordinating conjunction "not only . . . but also . . . ." Rather than indicating contrast, it emphasizes the second element of the pair.

Let's see how these pivotal words can help answer the questions in the last section. The first is from the Description Section:

Example:

According to the passage, the inquisitorial system differs from the adversarial system in that

A. it does not make the defendant solely responsible for gathering evidence for his case

B. it does not require the police department to work on behalf of the prosecution

C. it requires the prosecution to drop a weak case

D. a defendant who is innocent would prefer to be tried under the inquisitorial system

The pivotal phrase "by contrast" flags the second paragraph as the place to begin looking. The pivotal phrase "but also" introduces the answer—namely that the prosecutor must also investigate "on behalf of the defendant." The answer is (A).

The next question is from the Writing Techniques Section:

Example:

Which one of the following best describes the organization of the passage?

A. Two systems of criminal justice are compared and contrasted, and one is deemed to be better than the other.

B. One system of criminal justice is presented as better than another. Then evidence is presented to support that claim.

C. Two systems of criminal justice are analyzed, and one specific example is examined in detail.

D. A set of examples is presented. Then a conclusion is drawn from them.

The pivotal phrase "by contrast" gives this question away. The author is comparing and contrasting two criminal justice systems, which the opening pivotal word introduces. Hence the answer is (A).

For our final example, consider the question from the Extension Section:

Example:

The author views the prosecution's role in the inquisitorial system as being

A. an advocate for both society and the defendant

B. solely responsible for starting a trial

C. a protector of the legal rule

D. an aggressive but fair investigator

The information needed to answer this question is introduced by the pivotal phrase, "but also." There it is stated that the prosecutor must present evidence that may exonerate the defendant; that is, he must act fairly. The answer is (D).

Mentor Exercise

Directions: This passage is followed by a group of questions to be answered based on what is <u>stated</u> or <u>implied</u> in the passage. For some questions, more than one choice could conceivably answer the question. However, choose the <u>best</u> answer; the one that most accurately and completely answers the question. Hints, insights, and answers are given in the right-hand column.

The premise with which the multiculturalists begin is unexceptional: that it is important to recognize and to celebrate the wide range of cultures that exist in the United States. In what sounds like a reflection of traditional American pluralism, the multiculturalists argue that we must recognize difference, that difference is legitimate; in its kindlier versions, multiculturalism represents the discovery on the part of minority groups that they can play a part in molding the larger culture even as they are molded by it. And on the campus multiculturalism, defined more locally as the need to recognize cultural variations among students, has tried with some success to talk about how a racially and ethnically diverse student body can enrich everyone's education.

Phillip Green, a political scientist at Smith and a thoughtful proponent of multiculturalism, notes that for a significant portion of the students the politics of identity is all-consuming. Students he says "are unhappy with the thin gruel of rationalism. They require a therapeutic curriculum to overcome not straightforward racism but ignorant stereotyping."

(1) But multiculturalism's hard-liners, who seem to make up the majority of the movement, damn as racism any attempt to draw the myriad of American groups into a common American culture. For these multiculturalists, differences are absolute, irreducible, intractable—occasions not for understanding but for separation. The multiculturalist, it turns out, is not especially interested in the great American hyphen, in the syncretistic (and therefore naturally tolerant) identities that allow Americans to belong to more than a single culture, to be both particularists and universalists.

The time-honored American mixture of assimilation and traditional allegiance is denounced as a danger to racial and gender authenticity. This is an extraordinary reversal of the traditional liberal commitment to a "truth" that transcends parochialisms. In the new race/class/gender formation, universality is replaced by, among other things, feminist science Nubian numerals (as part of an Afro-centric science), and what Marilyn Frankenstein of the University of Massachusetts-Boston describes as "ethno-mathematics," in which the cultural basis of counting comes to the fore.

There are two critical pivotal words in this passage—(1) **But**, and (2) **however**.

(1) **But**. Until this point, the author did not reveal his feeling toward multiculturalism. He presented an objective, if not positive, view of the movement. However, "**But**" introduced an abrupt change in direction (a U-turn). Before he talked about the "kindlier" multiculturalism—to which he appears to be sympathetic. Now he talks about "hard-line" multiculturalism, which he implies is intolerant and divisive.

The pivotal word "**but**" doesn't just change the direction of the passage, it introduces the main idea: that multiculturalism has become an extreme and self-contradictory movement.

The multiculturalists insist on seeing all perspectives as tainted by the perceiver's particular point of view. Impartial knowledge, they argue, is not possible, because ideas are simply the expression of individual identity, or of the unspoken but inescapable assumptions that are inscribed in a culture or a language. The problem, **(2) however,** with this warmed-over Nietzscheanism is that it threatens to leave no ground for anybody to stand on. So the multi-culturalists make a leap, necessary for their own intellectual survival, and proceed to argue that there are some categories, such as race and gender, that do in fact embody an unmistakable knowledge of oppression. Victims are at least epistemologically lucky. Objectivity is a mask for oppression. And so an appalled former 1960s radical complained to me that self-proclaimed witches were teaching classes on witchcraft. "They're not teaching students how to think," she said, "they're telling them what to believe."

1. Which one of the following ideas would a multi-culturalist NOT believe?

   A. That we should recognize and celebrate the differences among the many cultures in the United States.

   B. That we can never know the "truth" because "truth" is always shaped by one's culture.

   C. That "difference" is more important than "sameness."

   D. That different cultures should work to assimilate themselves into the mainstream culture so that eventually there will be no excuse for racism.

2. According to a hard-line multiculturalist, which one of the following groups is most likely to know the "truth" about political reality?

   A. Educated people who have learned how to see reality from many different perspectives.

   B. A minority group that has suffered oppression at the hands of the majority.

   C. High government officials who have privileged access to secret information.

   D. Minorities who through their education have risen above the socioeconomic position occupied by most members of their ethnic group.

(2) **however**. This is the second critical pivotal word. The author opened this paragraph by presenting the multiculturalist's view; now he will criticize their positions.

1. The sentence introduced by the pivotal word **"But"** gives away the answer to this question.

The answer is (E).

2. This is a rather hard extension question.

   Hint: A subjugated minority group has at least the "unmistakable knowledge of oppression" (last paragraph).

   Don't make the mistake of choosing (D). Upper class minorities have simply exchanged one tainted point of view for another—and probably a more tainted one since the adopted position does not allow for knowledge of "oppression."

The answer is (B).

3. The author states that in a "kindlier version" of multiculturalism, minorities discover "that they can play a part in molding the larger culture even as they are molded by it." If no new ethnic groups were incorporated into the American culture for many centuries to come, which one of the following would be the most probable outcome of this "kindlier version"?

A. At some point in the future, there would be only one culture with no observable ethnic differences.

B. Eventually the dominant culture would overwhelm the minority cultures, who would then lose their ethnic identities.

C. The multiplicity of ethnic groups would remain but the characteristics of the different ethnic groups would change.

D. The smaller ethnic groups would remain, and they would retain their ethnic heritage.

4. The author speaks about the "politics of identity" that Phillip Green, a political scientist at Smith, notes is all-consuming for many of the students. Considering the subject of the passage, which one of the following best describes what the author means by "the politics of identity"?

A. The attempt to discover individual identities through political action

B. The political agenda that aspires to create a new pride of identity for Americans

C. The current obsession for therapy groups that help individuals discover their inner selves

D. The trend among minority students to discover their identities in their ethnic groups rather than in their individuality

3. This application question clearly goes well beyond the passage.

If no new ethnic groups were incorporated into the American culture, then the interplay between the larger and smaller groups would continue, with both groups changing, until there would be only one common (and different from any original) group.

The answer is (A).

4. This is an extension question. You may find the classification of the these problems as "application" or "extension" to be somewhat arbitrary or even disagree with a particular classification. As mentioned before, application and extension questions differ only in degree. Question 3 is clearly an application question; by asking you to make a conjecture about the future, it goes well beyond the passage. How to classify Question 4, however, is not so clear. I classified it as an extension question because it seems to be asking merely for the author's true meaning of the phrase "the politics of identity." That is, it stays within the context of the passage.

Don't be led astray by (B); it uses the word "political" to tempt you. Although it is perhaps a good description, it is not within the context of the passage, which focuses on ethnic politics, not national identities through "roots."

The answer is (D).

5. Which one of the following best describes the attitude of the writer toward the multicultural movement?

    A.   Tolerant. It may have some faults, but it is well-meaning overall.

    B.   Critical. A formerly admirable movement has been taken over by radical intellectuals.

    C.   Disinterested. He seems to be presenting an objective report.

    D.   Enthusiastic. The author embraces the multiculturalist movement and is trying to present it in a favorable light.

5. Like most tone questions this one is rather easy.

To get a feel for the author's attitude, check the adjectives he chooses. The author starts by introducing the "kindlier" version of multiculturalism and describes a proponent of multiculturalism, Phillip Green, as "thoughtful." Then he introduces the "hard liners" who "damn" any attempt at cultural assimilation. He feels that the movement has changed; that it has gone bad.

The answer is (B).

6. "Multiculturalist relativism" is the notion that there is no such thing as impartial or objective knowledge. The author seems to be grounding his criticism of this notion on

    A.   the clear evidence that science has indeed discovered "truths" that have been independent of both language and culture.

    B.   the conclusion that relativism leaves one with no clear notions of any one thing that is true.

    C.   the absurdity of claiming that knowledge of oppression is more valid than knowledge of scientific facts.

    D.   the agreement among peoples of all cultures as to certain undeniable truths—e.g., when the sky is clear, day is warmer than night.

6. This is an another extension question.

Hint: The answer can be derived from the pivotal sentence containing "however" (2).

The answer is (B).

Exercise

According to usage and conventions which are at last being <u>questioned</u> but have by no means been overcome, the social presence of a woman is different in kind from that of a man. A man's presence is
5 dependent upon the promise of power which he embodies. If the promise is large and credible his presence is striking. If it is small or incredible, he is found to have little presence. The promised power may be moral, physical, temperamental, economic,
10 social, sexual—but its object is always <u>exterior</u> to the man. A man's presence suggests what he is capable of doing to you or for you. His presence may be fabricated, in the sense that he pretends to be capable of what he is not. But the pretense is always toward a
15 power which he <u>exercises on others</u>.

By contrast, a woman's presence expresses her own attitude to herself, and defines what can and cannot be done to her. Her presence is manifest in her gestures, voices, opinions, expressions, clothes,
20 chosen surroundings, taste—indeed there is nothing she can do which does not contribute to her presence. Presence for a woman is so <u>intrinsic</u> to her person that men tend to think of it as an almost physical emanation, a kind of heat or smell or aura.

25 To be born a woman has been to be born, within an allotted and confined space, into the keeping of men. The social presence of women has developed as a result of their ingenuity in living under such tutelage within such a limited space. But this has
30 been at the cost of a woman's self being split into two. A woman must continually watch herself. Whilst she is walking across a room or whilst she is weeping at the death of her father, she can scarcely avoid envisaging herself walking or weeping. From
35 earliest childhood she has been taught and persuaded to survey herself continually.

And so she comes to consider the *surveyor* and the *surveyed* within her as the two constituent yet always distinct elements of her identity as a woman.

40 She has to survey everything she is and everything she does because how she appears to others, and ultimately how she appears to men, is of crucial importance for what is normally thought of as the success of her life. Her own sense of being in
45 herself is supplanted by a sense of being appreciated as herself by another. Men survey women before treating them. Consequently how a woman appears to a man can determine how she will be treated. To acquire some control over this process, women must
50 contain it and internalize it. That part of a woman's

self which is the surveyor treats the part which is the surveyed so as to demonstrate to others how her whole self would like to be treated. And this exemplary treatment of herself by herself constitutes
55 her presence. Every woman's presence regulates what is and is not "permissible" within her presence. Every one of her actions—whatever its direct purpose or motivation—is also read as an indication of how she would like to be treated. If a woman throws a
60 glass on the floor, this is an example of how she treats her own emotion of anger and so of how she would wish to be treated by others. If a man does the same, his action is only read as an expression of his anger. If a woman makes a good joke this is an
65 example of how she treats the joker in herself and accordingly of how she as joker-woman would like to be treated by others. Only a man can make a good joke for its own sake.

1. According to "usage and conventions," appearance is NECESSARILY a part of reality for

   A. men
   B. women
   C. both men and women
   D. neither men nor women

2. In analyzing a woman's customary "social presence," the author hopes to

   A. justify and reinforce it.
   B. understand and explain it.
   C. expose and discredit it.
   D. demonstrate and criticize it.

3. It can be inferred from the passage that a woman with a Ph.D. in psychology who gives a lecture to a group of students is probably MOST concerned with

   A. whether her students learn the material.
   B. what the males in the audience think of her.
   C. how she comes off as a speaker in psychology.
   D. finding a husband.

4. The passage portrays women as

   A. victims
   B. liars
   C. actresses
   D. politicians

5. Which one of the following is NOT implied by the passage?

   A. Women have split personalities.
   B. Men are not image-conscious.
   C. Good looks are more important to women than to men.
   D. A man is defined by what he does, whereas a woman is defined by how she appears.

6. The primary purpose of the passage is to

   A. compare and contrast woman's presence and place in society with that of man's.
   B. discuss a woman's presence and place in society and to contrast it with a man's presence and place.
   C. illustrate how a woman is oppressed by society.
   D. explain why men are better than women at telling jokes.

Answers and Solutions to Exercise

This passage is filled with pivotal words, some of which are crucial to following the author's train of thought. We will discuss only the critical pivotal words. The first pivotal word, "but" (line 14), introduces a distinction between a man's presence and a woman's: a man's is external, a woman's internal. The second pivotal word, "by contrast," introduces the main idea of the passage. The author opened the passage by defining a man's presence; now she will define a woman's presence. The last pivotal word, "but" (lines 29–31), also introduces a change in thought. Now the author discusses how a woman's presence has split her identity into two parts—the *surveyor* and the *surveyed*. By closing with, *"Only a man can make a good joke for its own sake,"* the author is saying a man can concentrate on the punch line, whereas a woman must concentrate on its delivery.

1. According to "usage and conventions" appearance is NECESSARILY a part of reality for
    A. men
    B. women
    C. both men and women
    D. neither men nor women

This is a description question. The needed reference is contained in lines 20–21: *"there is nothing [a woman] can do which does not contribute to her presence. Presence for a woman is intrinsic to her person . . ."* If something is intrinsic to you, then it necessarily is part of your reality. Hence the answer is (B).

Note the question refers to "usage and conventions" discussed in the passage, not to any other way of viewing the world—such as your own!

2. In analyzing a woman's customary "social presence," the author hopes to
    A. justify and reinforce it.
    B. understand and explain it.
    C. expose and discredit it.
    D. demonstrate and criticize it.

Although the author opens the passage with a hint that she doesn't like the customary sex roles (*"conventions which are at last being questioned"*), the rest of the passage is explanatory and analytical. So (C) and (D) are too strong. The answer is (B).

3. It can be inferred from the passage that a woman with a Ph.D. in psychology who gives a lecture to a group of students is probably MOST concerned with
    A. whether her students learn the material.
    B. what the males in the audience think of her.
    C. how she comes off as a speaker in psychology.
    D. finding a husband.

This is an application question; we are asked to apply what we have learned from the passage to a hypothetical situation.

The best way to analyze this question is to compare the speaker to a joke-teller. The passage paints a portrait of a woman as most concerned with the image she presents to the world. She is not concerned with the speech or joke, *per se*, rather with how she delivers it. *"Only a man can make a good joke for its own sake."* The answer is (C).

Don't make the mistake of choosing (B). Although men have, in the main, molded her self-image, she has gone beyond that; she now measures herself in the abstract: "how will I come off to the ultimately critical audience?" and not "how will actual audience members see me?"

4. The passage portrays women as
   A. victims
   B. liars
   C. actresses
   D. politicians

This description question is a bit tricky because the second-best choice is rather good. Women are concerned with the image they present, so they cannot be themselves—they must act their part. Hence the answer is (C).

You may have been tempted by (A). According to the passage, women are thrown into the role of an actress, "into the keeping of men." So, like victims, they are not responsible for their social position. However, nothing in the passage directly suggests that it is wrong for women to be in this position or that women attempt to refuse this role. According to the passage, therefore, women are not, strictly speaking, victims. (*Victim* means "someone not in control of something injurious happening to him or her.")

5. Which one of the following is NOT implied by the passage?
   A. Women have split personalities.
   B. Men are not image-conscious.
   C. Good looks are more important to women than to men.
   D. A man is defined by what he does, whereas a woman is defined by how she appears.

This is an extension question. The passage discusses the fact that a man may fabricate his image (lines 12–14). This suggests that men *are* conscious of their images, but the passage also states that image is not intrinsic to their personalities, as it is for women. The answer is (B).

6. The primary purpose of the passage is to
   A. compare and contrast a woman's presence and place in society with that of a man's.
   B. discuss a woman's presence and place in society and to contrast it with a man's presence and place.
   C. illustrate how a woman is oppressed by society.
   D. explain why men are better than woman at telling jokes.

This is a rather hard main idea question because the second-best choice, (A), is quite good.

The passage does open with a discussion of a man's presence. But in paragraph two the pivotal phrase "by contrast" introduces a woman's presence; from there the discussion of a man's presence is only in regard to how it affects a woman's. So a woman's presence is the main idea; contrasting it with a man's presence is secondary. (B) gives the proper emphasis to these two purposes.

Chapter 25
The Three Step Method

Now we apply all the methods we have learned to another passage. First let's summarize the reading techniques we have developed and express them in a three-step attack strategy for reading MCAT passages:

THE THREE STEP METHOD

1. **(Optional) Preview the first sentence of each paragraph.**

2. **Read the passage at a faster than usual pace (but not to the point that comprehension suffers). Stay alert to places from which any of the six questions might be drawn:**

    a.) **Main Idea**
    b.) **Description**
    c.) **Writing Technique**
    d.) **Extension**
    e.) **Application**
    f.) **Tone**

3. **Annotate the passage and circle any pivotal words. Then use them as reference points when answering the questions. Following are some common annotation marks (you may want to add to this list):**

    A = Author's Attitude
    C = Complex point
    ? = **Question?** I don't understand this part (you can bet that this area will be
        important to *at least* one question)
    SP = Significant **point**
    ! = **Exclamation!** Strong opinion
    W = Weak, questionable or unsupported argument or premise

Notice how the three-step process proceeds from the general to the specific. The **first step**, previewing the first sentences, gives you an overview of the passage. This will help you answer main idea questions. The **second step**, reading the passage at a slightly faster than usual pace, brings out the passage's structure (i.e., does the author compare and contrast, show cause and effect, etc.). Further, it will clue you into the author's attitude (positive, negative, objective, indifferent, etc.). Finally, the **third step**, circling pivotal words and annotating, will solidify your understanding of the passage and highlight specific details.

The three step method should be viewed as a dynamic, and not a static, process. The steps often overlap and they are not performed in strict order. Comprehending a passage is an ebb and

341

flow process. Analyzing a passage to understand how it is constructed can be compared to dismantling an engine to understand how it was built—you may stop occasionally and reassemble parts of it to review what you just did; then proceed again to dismantle more. Likewise, when reading a passage, you may first read and annotate a paragraph (disassembling it) and then go back and skim to reassemble it. During this process, comprehension proceeds from the global to the specific. This can be represented by an inverted pyramid:

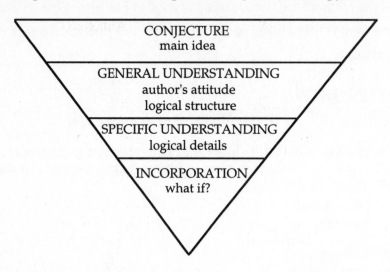

In the conjecture stage, we form a tentative main idea—one which we may have to modify or even reject as we read more deeply into the passage. In the general understanding stage, we develop a feel for the author's tone and discover the schema that she uses to present her ideas. In the specific understanding stage, we fill in the minor gaps in our understanding. Finally, in the incorporation stage, we integrate the ideas presented in the passage into our own thought process. We now understand the ideas sufficiently to defend them, apply them to other situations, or evaluate their validity in a hypothetical situation. Only with complete understanding of the passage can this be done.

Let's apply the three step method to the passage on page 344. Begin by previewing the first sentence of each paragraph:

The sentence *"That placebos can cure everything from dandruff to leprosy is well known"* implies that the passage is about placebos and that they are perhaps cure-alls.

The sentence *"Every drug tested would prove effective if special steps were not taken to neutralize the placebo effect"* gives the first bit of evidence supporting the topic sentence.

The sentence *"Most people feel that the lucky patients in a drug test get the experimental drug because the real drug provides them a chance to be cured"* might be introducing a counter-premise or pivotal point; we won't know until we read the passage.

The sentence *"Placebos regularly cure more than five percent of the patients and would cure considerably more if the doubts associated with the tests were eliminated"* provides more support for the topic sentence.

The sentence *"The actual curing power of placebos probably stems from the faith of the patient in the treatment"* explains why the topic sentence is true.

The sentence *"It may take a while to reach the ten percent level of cure because any newly established program will not have cultivated the word-of-mouth advertising needed to insure its success"* is hard to interpret. This does not help us.

The sentence *"Unfortunately, placebo treatment centers cannot operate as nonprofit businesses"* seems to be off the subject. Again, this does not help us.

In summary, although the last two sentences were not useful, we now have a good idea of what the passage is about: *how* and *why* placebos are effective. We now read the passage—looking for places from which any of the six questions might be drawn, circling the pivotal words, and annotating key points.

Passage begins on the next page.

That placebos can cure everything from dandruff to leprosy is well known. They have a long history of use by witch doctors, faith healers, and even modern physicians, all of whom refuse to admit
5 their efficacy. Modern distribution techniques can bring this most potent of medicines to the aid of everyone, not just those lucky enough to receive placebos in a medical testing program.

Every drug tested would prove effective if
10 special steps were not taken to neutralize the placebo effect. This is why drug tests give half the patients the new medication and half a harmless substitute. These tests prove the value of placebos because approximately five percent of the patients taking
15 them are cured even though the placebos are made from substances that have been carefully selected to be useless.

Most people feel that the lucky patients in a drug test get the experimental drug because the real
20 drug provides them a chance to be cured. **(1) Yet** analysis shows that patients getting the placebo may be the lucky ones because they may be cured without risking any adverse effects the new drug may have. Furthermore, the drug may well be found worthless
25 and to have severe side effects. No harmful side effects result from placebos.

Placebos regularly cure more than five percent of the patients and would cure considerably more if the doubts associated with the tests were eliminated.
30 Cures are principally due to the patient's faith, **(2) yet** the patient must have doubts knowing that he may or may not be given the new drug, which itself may or may not prove to be an effective drug. Since he knows the probability of being given the true drug is
35 about fifty percent, the placebo cure rate would be more than doubled by removing these doubts if cures are directly related to faith.

The actual curing power of placebos probably stems from the faith of the patient in the treatment.
40 This suggests that cure rates in the ten percent range could be expected if patients are given placebos under the guise of a proven cure, even when patients know their problems are incurable.

It may take a while to reach the ten percent
45 level of cure because any newly established program will not have cultivated the word-of-mouth advertising needed to insure its success. One person saying "I was told that my problem was beyond medical help, but they cured me," can direct
50 countless people to the treatment with the required degree of faith. Furthermore, when only terminal illnesses are treated, those not cured tell no one of the failure.

Unfortunately, placebo treatment centers cannot
55 operate as nonprofit businesses. The nonprofit idea was ruled out upon learning that the first rule of public medicine is never to give free medicine. Public health services know that medicine not paid for by patients is often not taken or not effective
60 because the recipient feels the medicine is worth just what it cost him. **(3) Even though** the patients would not know they were taking sugar pills, the placebos cost so little that the patients would have no faith in the treatment. Therefore, though it is against higher
65 principles, treatment centers must charge high fees for placebo treatments. This sacrifice of principles, however, is a small price to pay for the greater good of the patients.

The first item is a main idea question:

1.   Which one of the following best expresses the main idea of the passage?

   A.   Placebo treatment is a proven tool of modern medicine and its expanded use would benefit society's health.

   B.   Because modern technology allows for distribution of drugs on a massive scale, the proven efficacy of the placebo is no longer limited to a privileged few.

   C.   The curative power of the placebo is so strong that it should replace proven drugs because the patients receiving the placebo will then be cured without risking any adverse side effects.

   D.   The price of placebo treatment must be kept artificially high because patients have little faith in inexpensive treatments.

As we found by previewing the topic sentences, the passage is about the efficacy of placebo treatment. Careful reading shows that the passage also promotes expanded use of placebos. Hence the answer is (A).

The other choices can be quickly dismissed. (B) is the second-best choice: the author *does* mention that modern distribution techniques can bring the curative power of placebos to everyone, but he does <u>not</u> fully develop that idea. This answer-choice is tempting because it is contained in the topic paragraph. As to (C), it overstates the author's claim. Although in the third paragraph, the author states that those who receive the placebos may be the lucky ones, this is referring to new, unproven drugs, not to established drugs. As to (D), it, like (B), is mentioned in the passage but is not fully developed. It's tempting because it appears in the last paragraph— a natural place for the conclusion.

The second item is an application question.

2.   Which one of the following is most analogous to the idea presented in the last paragraph?

   A.   Buying a television at a discount house

   B.   Making an additional pledge to charity

   C.   Choosing the most expensive dishwasher in a manufacturer's line

   D.   Waiting until a book comes out in paperback

The information needed to answer this question is heralded by the pivotal phrase "Even though" (lines 61–64). The implication of that sentence is "you get what you pay for." This would motivate one to buy the most expensive item in a manufacturer's line. Hence the answer is (C).

The third item is a description question.

3. According to the passage, when testing a new drug medical researchers give half of the subjects the test drug and half a placebo because

    A. proper statistical controls should be observed.

    B. this method reduces the risk of maiming too many subjects if the drug should prove to be harmful.

    C. all drugs which are tested would prove to be effective otherwise.

    D. most drugs would test positively otherwise.

Since this is a description question, you must refer to the passage to answer it. The opening sentence to paragraph two contains the needed information. That sentence states "<u>Every</u> drug would prove effective if special steps were not taken to neutralize the placebo effect." Hence the answer is (C).

Choice (D) illustrates why you must refer directly to the passage to answer a description question: unless you have a remarkable memory, you will be unsure whether the statement was that **all** or that **most** drugs would prove effective.

The fourth item is an extension question.

4. It can be inferred from the passage that the author might

    A. believe that the benefits of a placebo treatment program that lead patients to believe they were getting a real drug would outweigh the moral issue of lying.

    B. support legislation outlawing the use of placebos.

    C. open up a medical clinic that would treat patients exclusively through placebo methods.

    D. believe that factors other than faith are responsible for the curative power of the placebo.

The answer is (A). One of the first clues to the author's view on this issue is contained in the pivotal clause "yet the patient . . . effective drug" (lines 30–33). Later, in paragraph six, the author nearly advocates that the patient should not be told that he or she might be receiving a placebo. Finally, the closing line of the passage cinches it. There, the author implies that certain principles *can be* sacrificed for the greater good of the patients.

The fifth item is a writing technique question.

5. Which one of the following best describes the organization of the material presented in the passage?

    A. A general proposition is stated; then evidence for its support is given.

    B. Two types of drug treatment—placebo and non-placebo—are compared and contrasted.

    C. A result is stated, its cause is explained, and an application is suggested.

    D. A dilemma is presented and a possible solution is offered.

In the first paragraph the author claims that placebos can cure everything from dandruff to leprosy—this is a result. Then in paragraphs two, three, four, and five, he explains the causes of the result. Finally, he alludes to an application—the placebo treatment centers. The answer is (C).

The sixth item is a tone question.

6. Which one of the following most accurately characterizes the author's attitude toward placebo treatment?

    A. reserved advocacy

    B. feigned objectivity

    C. summary dismissal

    D. perplexed by its effectiveness

This question is a little tricky. Only choices (A) and (B) have any real merit. Although the passage has a detached, third-person style, the author nonetheless *does* present his opinions—namely that placebos work and that their use should be expanded. However, that advocacy is reserved, so the answer is (A).

The other choices can be quickly eliminated:

"Summary dismissal" is not supported by the passage. Besides, a scholar would never summarily dismiss something; he would consider it carefully—or at least give the impression that he has—before rejecting it. This eliminates (C).

Given the human ego, we are unlikely to admit that we don't understand the subject we are writing about. This eliminates (D).

Mentor Exercise

Following the Three Step Method, we preview the first sentence of each paragraph in the passage: (The body of the passage will be presented later.)

The enigmatic opening sentence _"Many readers, I suspect, will take the title of this article [Women, Fire, and Dangerous Things] as suggesting that women, fire, and dangerous things have something in common—say, that women are fiery and dangerous"_ does not give us much of a clue to what the passage is about.

The sentence _"The classical view that categories are based on shared properties is not entirely wrong"_ is more helpful. It tells us the passage is about categorization and that there are at least two theories about it: the classical view, which has merit, and the modern view, which is apparently superior.

The sentence _"Categorization is not a matter to be taken lightly"_ merely confirms the subject of the passage.

Although only one sentence was helpful, previewing did reveal a lot about the passage's subject matter—categorization. Now we read the passage, circling pivotal words, annotating, and noting likely places from which any of the six questions might be drawn. After each paragraph, we will stop to analyze and interpret what the author has presented:

Many readers, I suspect, will take the title of this article [_Women, Fire, and Dangerous Things_] as suggesting that women, fire, and dangerous things have something in common—say, that women are fiery and dangerous. Most feminists I've mentioned it to have loved the title for that reason, though some have hated it for the same reason. But the chain of inference—from conjunction to categorization to commonality—is the norm. The inference is based on the common idea of what it means to be in the same category: things are categorized together on the basis of what they have in common. The idea that categories are defined by common properties is not only our everyday folk theory of what a category is, it is also the principle technical theory—one that has been with us for more than two thousand years.

In this paragraph, the author introduces the subject matter of the passage—categorization. And the pivotal sentence, introduced by "but," explains the classical theory of categorization, albeit rather obtusely. Namely, like things are placed in the same category.

Now we consider the second paragraph:

The classical view that categories are based on shared properties is not entirely wrong. We often do categorize things on that basis. But that is only a small part of the story. In recent years it has become clear that categorization is far more complex than that. A new theory of categorization, called *prototype theory*, has emerged. It shows that human categorization is based on principles that extend far beyond those envisioned in the classical theory. One of our goals is to survey the complexities of the way people really categorize. For example, the title of this book was inspired by the Australian aboriginal language Dyirbal, which has a category, *balan*, that actually includes women, fire, and dangerous things. It also includes birds that are *not* dangerous, as well as exceptional animals, such as the platypus, bandicoot, and echidna. This is not simply a matter of categorization by common properties.

In this paragraph, the second pivotal word—but—is crucial. It introduces the main idea of the passage—the prototype theory of categorization. Now everything that is introduced should be attributed to the prototype theory, <u>not</u> to the classical theory. Wrong answer-choices are likely to be baited with just the opposite.

The author states that the prototype theory goes "far beyond" the classical theory. Although he does not tell us what the prototype theory *is*, he does tell us that it *is not* merely categorization by common properties.

Now we turn to the third paragraph:

Categorization is not a matter to be taken lightly. There is nothing more basic than categorization to our thought, perception, action and speech. Every time we see something as a *kind* of thing, for example, a tree, we are categorizing. Whenever we reason about *kinds* of things—chairs, nations, illnesses, emotions, any kind of thing at all—we are employing categories. Whenever we intentionally perform any *kind* of action, say something as mundane as writing with a pencil, hammering with a hammer, or ironing clothes, we are using categories. The particular action we perform on that occasion is a *kind* of motor activity, that is, it is in a particular category of motor actions. They are never done in exactly the same way, yet despite the differences in particular movements, they are all movements of a kind, and we know how to make movements of that kind. And any time we either produce or understand any utterance of any reasonable length, we are employing dozens if not hundreds of categories: categories of speech sounds, of words, of phrases and clauses, as well as conceptual categories. Without the ability to categorize, we could not function at all, either in the physical world or in our social and intellectual lives.

Though the author does not explicitly state it, this paragraph defines the theory of prototypes. Notice the author likes to use an indirect, even cryptic, method of introducing or switching topics, which makes this a classic MCAT type passage. The MCAT writers have many opportunities here to test whether you are following the author's train of thought.

Now we attack the questions.

1. The author probably chose *Women, Fire, and Dangerous Things* as the title of the article because

    I.   he thought that since the Dyirbal placed all three items in the same category, women, fire, and dangerous things necessarily had something in common.

    II.   he was hoping to draw attention to the fact that because items have been placed in the same category doesn't mean that they necessarily have anything in common

    III.   he wanted to use the Dyirbal classification system as an example of how primitive classifications are not as functional as contemporary Western classification systems.

    A.   I only
    B.   II only
    C.   III only
    D.   II and III only

1. This is an extension question. The second paragraph contains the information needed to answer it. There the author states that women, fire, and dangerous things belong to a category called *balan* in an Australian aboriginal language, which is <u>not</u> simply based on common properties. This eliminates Statement I and confirms Statement II.

The answer is (B).

2. According to the author,

    I.   categorizing is a fundamental activity of people.

    II.   whenever a word refers to a kind of thing, it signifies a category.

    III.   one has to be able to categorize in order to function in our culture.

    A.   I only
    B.   II only
    C.   I and II only
    D.   I, II, and III

2. This is a description question, so we must find the points in the passage from which the statements were drawn. Remember, the answer to a description question will not directly quote a statement from the passage, but it will be closely related to one—often a paraphrase. The needed references for Statements I, II, and III are all contained in the closing paragraph.

The answer is (D).

3. Which one of the following facts would most weaken the significance of the author's title?

    A.   The discovery that all the birds and animals classified as *balan* in Dyirbal are female

    B.   The discovery that the male Dyirbal culture considers females to be both fiery and dangerous

    C.   The discovery that all items in the *balan* category are considered female

    D.   The discovery that neither fire nor women are considered dangerous

3. This is one of the few questions that does not easily fit into any of the six question types. Nevertheless, our work in the arguments section has prepared us for this type of question. Remember: to weaken an argument, attack one or more of its premises. Now the implication of the title is that *women, fire,* and *dangerous things* <u>do not</u> have anything in common. To weaken this implication, the answer should state that all things in the *balan* category <u>have</u> something in common.

The answer is (C).

4. If linguistic experts cannot perceive how women, fire, and dangerous things in the category *balan* have at least one thing in common, it follows that

    A. there probably is something other than shared properties that led to all items in *balan* being placed in that category.
    B. the anthropologists simply weren't able to perceive what the items had in common.
    C. the anthropologists might not have been able to see what the items had in common.
    D. the items do not have anything in common.

4. This is an extension question; we are asked to draw a conclusion based on the passage.

Hint: The thrust of the passage is that commonality is not the only way to categorize things.

The answer is (A).

5. Which one of the following sentences would best complete the last paragraph of the passage?

    A. An understanding of how we categorize is central to any understanding of how we think and how we function, and therefore central to an understanding of what makes us human.
    B. The prototype theory is only the latest in a series of new and improved theories of categorization; undoubtedly even better theories will replace it.
    C. The prototype theory of categories has not only unified a major branch of linguistics, but it has applications to mathematics and physics as well.
    D. An understanding of how the prototype theory of categorization evolved from the classical theory is essential to any understanding of how we think and how we function in society.

5. This is an application question; we are asked to complete a thought for the author.

Most of the third paragraph is introducing the prototype theory of categorization. But in the last sentence the author changes direction somewhat—without any notice, as is typical of his style. Now he is discussing the importance of the ability to categorize. The clause *"Without the ability to categorize, we could not function at all"* indicates that this ability is fundamental to our very being.

Be careful not to choose (D). Although it is probably true, it is too specific: in the final sentence the author is discussing categorization in general.

The answer is (A).

Exercise

Global strategies to control infectious disease have historically included the erection of barriers to international travel and immigration. Keeping people with infectious diseases outside national borders has
5 reemerged as an important public health policy in the human immunodeficiency virus (HIV) epidemic. Between 29 and 50 countries are reported to have introduced border restrictions on HIV-positive foreigners, usually those planning an extended stay in
10 the country, such as students, workers, or seamen.

Travel restrictions have been established primarily by countries in the western Pacific and Mediterranean regions, where HIV seroprevalence is relatively low. However, the country with the
15 broadest policy of testing and excluding foreigners is the United States. From December 1, 1987, when HIV infection was first classified in the United States as a contagious disease, through September 30, 1989, more than 3 million people seeking permanent
20 residence in this country were tested for HIV antibodies. The U.S. policy has been sharply criticized by national and international organizations as being contrary to public health goals and human-rights principles. Many of these organizations are
25 boycotting international meetings in the United States that are vital for the study of prevention, education, and treatment of HIV infection.

The Immigration and Nationality Act requires the Public Health Service to list "dangerous
30 contagious diseases" for which aliens can be excluded from the United States. By 1987 there were seven designated diseases—five of them sexually transmitted (chancroid, gonorrhea, granuloma inguinale, lymphog-ranuloma venereum, and
35 infectious syphilis) and two non-venereal (active tuberculosis and infectious leprosy). On June 8, 1987, in response to a Congressional direction in the Helms Amendment, the Public Health Service added HIV infection to the list of dangerous contagious
40 diseases.

A just and efficacious travel and immigration policy would not exclude people because of their serologic status unless they posed a danger to the community through casual transmission. U.S.
45 regulations should list only active tuberculosis as a contagious infectious disease. We support well-funded programs to protect the health of travelers infected with HIV through appropriate immunizations and prophylactic treatment and to
50 reduce behaviors that may transmit infection.

We recognize that treating patients infected with HIV who immigrate to the United States will incur costs for the public sector. It is inequitable, however, to use cost as a reason to exclude people
55 infected with HIV, for there are no similar exclusionary policies for those with other costly chronic diseases, such as heart disease or cancer.

Rather than arbitrarily restrict the movement of a subgroup of infected people, we must dedicate
60 ourselves to the principles of justice, scientific cooperation, and a global response to the HIV pandemic.

1. According to the passage, countries in the western Pacific have

    A. a very high frequency of HIV-positive immigrants and have a greater reason to be concerned over this issue than other countries.
    B. opposed efforts on the part of Mediterranean states to establish travel restrictions on HIV-positive residents.
    C. a low HIV seroprevalence and, in tandem with Mediterranean regions, have established travel restrictions on HIV-positive foreigners.
    D. continued to obstruct efforts to unify policy concerning immigrant screening.

2. The authors of the passage conclude that

   A. it is unjust to exclude people based on their serological status without the knowledge that they pose a danger to the public.

   B. U.S. regulations should require more stringent testing to be implemented at all major border crossings.

   C. it is the responsibility of the public sector to absorb costs incurred by treatment of immigrants infected with HIV.

   D. the HIV pandemic is largely overstated and that, based on new epidemiological data, screening immigrants is not indicated.

3. It can be inferred from the passage that

   A. more than 3 million HIV-positive people have sought permanent residence in the United States.

   B. countries with a low seroprevalence of HIV have a disproportionate and unjustified concern over the spread of AIDS by immigration.

   C. the United States is more concerned with controlling the number of HIV-positive immigrants than with avoiding criticism from outside its borders.

   D. current law is meeting the demand for prudent handling of a potentially hazardous international issue.

4. Before the Helms Amendment in 1987, seven designated diseases were listed as being cause for denying immigration. We can conclude from the passage that

   A. the authors agree fully with this policy but disagree with adding HIV to the list.

   B. the authors believe that sexual diseases are appropriate reasons for denying immigration but not non-venereal diseases.

   C. the authors disagree with the amendment.

   D. the authors believe that non-venereal diseases are justifiable reasons for exclusion, but not sexually transmitted diseases.

5. In referring to the "costs" incurred by the public (line 54), the authors apparently mean

   A. financial costs.

   B. costs to the public health.

   C. costs in manpower.

   D. costs in international reputation.

Answers and Solutions to Exercise

Previewing the first sentence of each paragraph shows that the passage is about restricting travel of HIV-positive persons and that the authors feel there should be no restrictions. There are two pivotal words: "however" (line 14), and "Rather than" (line 58), which introduces the concluding paragraph.

1. According to the passage, countries in the western Pacific have
   A. a very high frequency of HIV-positive immigrants and have a greater reason to be concerned over this issue than other countries.
   B. opposed efforts on the part of Mediterranean states to establish travel restrictions on HIV-positive residents.
   C. a low HIV seroprevalence and, in tandem with Mediterranean regions, have established travel restrictions on HIV-positive foreigners.
   D. continued to obstruct efforts to unify policy concerning immigrant screening.

This is a description question, so we must find the point in the passage from which the question is drawn. It is the opening sentence to paragraph two. There it is stated that countries in the western Pacific and Mediterranean regions have a low incidence of HIV infection and have introduced border restrictions. The answer, therefore, is (C).

2. The authors of the passage conclude that
   A. it is unjust to exclude people based on their serological status without the knowledge that they pose a danger to the public.
   B. U.S. regulations should require more stringent testing to be implemented at all major border crossings.
   C. it is the responsibility of the public sector to absorb costs incurred by treatment of immigrants infected with HIV.
   D. the HIV pandemic is largely overstated and that, based on new epidemiological data, screening immigrants is not indicated.

This is another description question. The answer is (A). This is directly supported by the opening sentence of paragraph four. Note that (A) is a paraphrase of that sentence.

Be careful with (C). Although this is hinted at in paragraph five, it is never directly stated that the public sector is <u>responsible</u> for these costs, only that it would in fact pick up these costs. Remember: A description question must be answered from what is directly stated in the passage, not from what it implies.

3. It can be inferred from the passage that
   A. more than 3 million HIV-positive people have sought permanent residence in the United States.
   B. countries with a low seroprevalence of HIV have a disproportionate and unjustified concern over the spread of AIDS by immigration.
   C. the United States is more concerned with controlling the number of HIV-positive immigrants than with avoiding criticism from outside its borders.
   D. current law is meeting the demand for prudent handling of a potentially hazardous international issue.

This is an extension question. Lines 21–22 state *"U.S. policy has been sharply criticized by national and international organizations."* Given that this criticism has not caused the United States to change its policies, it must be more concerned with controlling the number of HIV-positive immigrants than with avoiding criticism. The answer, therefore, is (C).

Don't be tempted by (A); it's a same language trap. Every word in it is taken from the passage. However, the passage states that over 3 million people were tested for HIV antibodies (lines 19–21), <u>not</u> that they were tested "positive" for HIV antibodies.

4. Before the Helms Amendment in 1987, seven designated diseases were listed as being cause for denying immigration. We can conclude from the passage that
   A. the authors agree fully with this policy but disagree with adding HIV to the list.
   B. the authors believe that sexual diseases are appropriate reasons for denying immigration but not non-venereal diseases.
   C. the authors disagree with the amendment.
   D. the authors believe that non-venereal diseases are justifiable reasons for exclusion, but not sexually transmitted diseases.

This is another extension question. In lines 44–46, the authors state that only active tuberculosis should be listed as a dangerous contagious disease. We expect that they would oppose adding HIV to the list. The answer is (C).

5. In referring to the "costs" incurred by the public (line 54), the authors apparently mean
   A. financial costs.
   B. costs to the public health.
   C. costs in manpower.
   D. costs in international reputation.

Although governments have ostensibly restricted the immigration of HIV-positive persons out of fear that they may spread the disease, the authors apparently are referring to financial costs, not costs to public health. This is indicated by lines 53–57, where they describe heart disease and cancer as non-contagious and costly, yet still admissible. The answer, therefore, is (A).

Chapter 26
Extra Reading

Most students arrive at [college] using "discrete, concrete, and absolute categories to understand people, knowledge, and values." These students live with a *dualistic* view, seeing "the world in polar
5 terms of we-right-good vs. other-wrong-bad." These students cannot acknowledge the existence of more than one point of view toward any issue. There is one "right" way. And because these absolutes are assumed by or imposed on the individual from
10 external authority, they cannot be personally substantiated or authenticated by experience. These students are slaves to the generalizations of their authorities. An eye for an eye. Capital punishment is apt justice for murder. The Bible says so.

15 Most students break through the dualistic stage to another equally frustrating stage—*multiplicity*. Within this stage, students see a variety of ways to deal with any given topic or problem. However, while these students accept multiple points of view,
20 they are unable to evaluate or justify them. To have an opinion is everyone's right. While students in the dualistic stage are unable to produce evidence to support what they consider to be self-evident absolutes, students in the multiplistic stage are unable
25 to connect instances into coherent generalizations. Every assertion, every point, is valid. In their democracy they are directionless. Capital punishment? What sense is there in answering one murder with another?

30 The third stage of development finds students living in a world of *relativism*. Knowledge is relative: right and wrong depend on the context. No longer recognizing the validity of each individual idea or action, relativists examine everything to find
35 its place in an overall framework. While the multiplist views the world as unconnected, almost random, the relativist seeks always to place phenomena into coherent larger patterns. Students in this stage view the world analytically. They
40 appreciate authority for its expertise, using it to defend their own generalizations. In addition, they accept or reject ostensible authority *after systematically* evaluating its validity. In this stage, however, students resist decision making. Suffering
45 the ambivalence of finding several consistent and

acceptable alternatives, they are almost overwhelmed by diversity and need means for managing it. Capital punishment is appropriate justice—in some instances.

In the final stage students manage diversity
50 through individual *commitment*. Students do not deny relativism. Rather they assert an identity by forming commitments and assuming responsibility for them. They gather personal experience into a coherent framework, abstract principles to guide their
55 actions, and use these principles to discipline and govern their thoughts and actions. The individual has chosen to join a particular community and agrees to live by its tenets. The accused has had the benefit of due process to guard his civil rights, a jury of peers
60 has found him guilty, and the state has the right to end his life. This is a principle my community and I endorse.

1. It can be inferred from the passage that the author would consider which of the following to be good examples of "dualistic thinking"?

   I. People who think "there is a right way and a wrong way to do things"
   II. Teenagers who assume they know more about "the real world" than adults do
   III. People who back our country "right or wrong" when it goes to war

   A. I only
   B. II only
   C. III only
   D. I and III only

GO ON TO THE NEXT PAGE.

2. Students who are "dualistic" thinkers may not be able to support their beliefs convincingly because

    A. most of their beliefs *cannot* be supported by arguments.

    B. they have accepted their "truths" simply because authorities have said these things are "true."

    C. they half-believe and half-disbelieve just about everything.

    D. their teachers almost always think that "dualistic" thinkers are wrong.

3. Which one of the following assertions is supported by the passage?

    A. *Committed* thinkers are not very sure of their positions.

    B. *Relativistic* thinkers have learned how to make sense out of the world and have chosen their own positions in it.

    C. *Multiplicity* thinkers have difficulty understanding the relationships between different points of view.

    D. *Dualistic* thinkers have thought out the reasons for taking their positions.

4. In paragraph two, the author states that in their "democracy" students in the *multiplicity* stage are directionless. The writer describes *multiplicity* students as being in a "democracy" because

    A. there are so many different kinds of people in a democracy.

    B. in an "ideal" democracy, all people are considered equal; by extension, so are their opinions.

    C. Democrats generally do not have a good sense of direction.

    D. although democracies may grant freedom, they are generally acknowledged to be less efficient than more authoritarian forms of government.

5. Which one of the following kinds of thinking is NOT described in the passage?

    A. People who assume that there is no right or wrong in any issue

    B. People who make unreasoned commitments and stick by them

    C. People who believe that right or wrong depends on the situation

    D. People who think that all behavior can be accounted for by cause and effect relationships

6. If students were asked to write essays on the different *concepts* of tragedy as exemplified by Cordelia and Antigone, and they all responded by showing how each character exemplified a traditional definition of tragedy, we could, according to the passage, hypothesize which one of the following about these students?

    A. The students were locked into the relativist stage.

    B. The students had not advanced beyond the dualist stage.

    C. The students had at least achieved the multiplicity stage.

    D. The students had reached the commitment stage.

7. Which one of the following best describes the organization of the passage?

    A. Four methods of thought are compared and contrasted.

    B. It is shown how each of four types of thought evolved from each other.

    C. The evolution of thought from simplistic and provincial through considered and cosmopolitan is illustrated by four stages.

    D. The evolution of thought through four stages is presented, and each stage is illustrated by how it views capital punishment.

GO ON TO THE NEXT PAGE.

A growing taste for shark steaks and shark-fin soup has for the first time in 400 million years put the scourge of the sea at the wrong end of the food chain. Commercial landings of this toothsome fish have
5　doubled every year since 1986, and shark populations are plunging. It is hardly a case of good riddance. Sharks do for gentler fish what lions do for the wildebeest: they check populations by feeding on the weak. Also, sharks apparently do not get cancer and
10　may therefore harbor clues to the nature of that disease.

　　Finally, there is the issue of motherhood. Sharks are viviparous. That is, they bear their young alive and swimming (not sealed in eggs) after
15　gestation periods lasting from nine months to two years. Shark mothers generally give birth to litters of from eight to twelve pups and bear only one litter every other year.

　　This is why sharks have one of the lowest
20　fecundity rates in the ocean. The female cod, for example, spawns annually and lays a few million eggs at a time. If three quarters of the cod were to be fished this year, they could be back in full force in a few years. But if humans took that big of a bite out
25　of the sharks, the population would not recover for 15 years.

　　So, late this summer, if all goes according to plan, the shark will join the bald eagle and the buffalo on the list of managed species. The federal
30　government will cap the U.S. commercial catch at 5,800 metric tons, about half of the 1989 level, and limit sportsmen to two sharks per boat. Another provision discourages finning, the harvesting of shark fins alone, by limiting the weight of fins to 7 percent
35　of that of all the carcasses.

　　Finning got under the skin of environmentalists, and the resulting anger helped to mobilize support for the new regulations. Finning itself is a fairly recent innovation. Shark fins contain noodle-like
40　cartilaginous tissues that Chinese chefs have traditionally used to thicken and flavor soup. Over the past few years rising demand in Hong Kong has made the fins as valuable as the rest of the fish. Long strands are prized, so unusually large fins can be
45　worth considerably more to the fisherman than the average price of about $10 a pound.

　　But can U.S. quotas save shark species that wander the whole Atlantic? The blue shark, for example, migrates into the waters of something like
50　23 countries. John G. Casey, a biologist with the National Marine Fisheries Service Research Center in Narragansett, R.I., admits that international co-ordination will eventually be necessary. But he supports U.S. quotas as a first step in mobilizing
55　other nations. Meanwhile the commercial fishermen

are not waiting for the new rules to take effect. "There's a pre-quota rush on sharks," Casey says, "and it's going on as we speak."

8.　According to the passage, shark populations are at greater risk than cod populations because

　　A.　sharks are now being eaten more than cod.
　　B.　the shark reproduction rate is lower than that of the cod.
　　C.　sharks are quickly becoming fewer in number.
　　D.　sharks are now as scarce as bald eagles and buffalo.

9.　According to the passage, a decrease in shark populations

　　I.　might cause some fish populations to go unchecked.
　　II.　would hamper cancer research.
　　III.　to one-quarter the current level would take over a decade to recover from.

　　A.　II only
　　B.　III only
　　C.　I and III only
　　D.　I and II only

GO ON TO THE NEXT PAGE.

10. If the species *Homo logicus* was determined to be viviparous and to have extremely low fecundity rates on land, we might expect that

    A. *Homo logicus* could overpopulate its niche and should be controlled.
    B. *Homo logicus* might be declared an endangered species.
    C. *Homo logicus* would pose no danger to other species and would itself be in no danger.
    D. None of these events would be expected with certainty.

11. Which one of the following best describes the author's attitude toward the efforts to protect shark populations?

    A. strong advocate
    B. impartial observer
    C. opposed
    D. perplexed

12. It can be inferred from the passage that

    I. research efforts on cancer will be hindered if shark populations are threatened.
    II. U.S. quotas on shark fishing will have limited effectiveness in protecting certain species.
    III. some practices of Chinese chefs have angered environmentalists.

    A. I only
    B. II only
    C. I and II only
    D. II and III only

13. An irony resulting from the announcement that sharks will be placed on the managed species list is

    A. we will now find out less about cancer, so in effect by saving the sharks, we are hurting ourselves.
    B. sharks are far more dangerous to other fish than we are to them.
    C. more chefs are now using the cartilaginous tissues found in shark fins.
    D. more sharks are being killed now than before the announcement.

GO ON TO THE NEXT PAGE.

"A writer's job is to tell the truth," said Hemingway in 1942. No other writer of our time had so fiercely asserted, so pugnaciously defended or so consistently exemplified the writer's obligation to speak truly.

5 His standard of truth-telling remained, moreover, so high and so rigorous that he was ordinarily unwilling to admit secondary evidence, whether literary evidence or evidence picked up from other sources than his own experience. "I only know what I have

10 seen," was a statement which came often to his lips and pen. What he had personally done, or what he knew unforgettably by having gone through one version of it, was what he was interested in telling about. This is not to say that he refused to invent

15 freely. But he always made it a sacrosanct point to invent in terms of what he actually knew from having been there.

→ The primary intent of his writing, from first to last, was to seize and project for the reader what he

20 often called "the way it was." This is a characteristically simple phrase for a concept of extraordinary complexity, and Hemingway's conception of its meaning subtly changed several times in the course of his career—always in the

25 direction of greater complexity. At the core of the concept, however, one can invariably discern the operation of three aesthetic instruments: the sense of place, the sense of fact, and the sense of scene.

The first of these, obviously a strong passion

30 with Hemingway, is the sense of place. "Unless you have geography, background," he once told George Antheil, "you have nothing." You have, that is to say, a dramatic vacuum. Few writers have been more place-conscious. Few have so carefully charted out

35 the geographical ground work of their novels while managing to keep background so conspicuously unobtrusive. Few, accordingly, have been able to record more economically and graphically the way it is when you walk through the streets of Paris in

40 search of breakfast at a corner café . . . Or when, at around six o'clock of a Spanish dawn, you watch the bulls running from the corrals at the Puerta Rochapea through the streets of Pamplona towards the bullring.

"When I woke it was the sound of the rocket

45 exploding that announced the release of the bulls from the corrals at the edge of town. Down below the narrow street was empty. All the balconies were crowded with people. Suddenly a crowd came down the street. They were all running,

50 packed close together. They passed along and up the street toward the bullring and behind them came more men running faster, and then some stragglers who were really running. Behind them was a little bare space, and then the bulls,

55 galloping, tossing their heads up and down. It all went out of sight around the corner. One man fell, rolled to the gutter, and lay quiet. But the bulls

went right on and did not notice him. They were all running together."

60 This landscape is as morning-fresh as a design in India ink on clean white paper. First is the bare white street, seen from above, quiet and empty. Then one sees the first packed clot of runners. Behind these are the thinner ranks of those who move faster

65 because they are closer to the bulls. Then the almost comic stragglers, who are "really running." Brilliantly behind these shines the "little bare space,"

→ a desperate margin for error. Then the clot of running bulls—closing the design, except of course for the

70 man in the gutter making himself, like the designer's initials, as inconspicuous as possible.

14. According to the author, Hemingway's primary purpose in telling a story was

A. to construct a well-told story that the reader would thoroughly enjoy.

B. to construct a story that would reflect truths that were not particular to a specific historical period.

C. to begin from reality but to allow his imagination to roam from "the way it was" to "the way it might have been."

D. to report faithfully reality as Hemingway had experienced it.

GO ON TO THE NEXT PAGE.

15. From the author's comments and the example of the bulls (paragraph 4), what was the most likely reason for which Hemingway took care to include details of place?

    A. He felt that geography in some way illuminated other, more important events.
    B. He thought readers generally did not have enough imagination to visualize the scenes for themselves.
    C. He had no other recourse since he was avoiding the use of other literary sources.
    D. He thought that landscapes were more important than characters to convey "the way it was."

16. One might infer from the passage that Hemingway preferred which one of the following sources for his novels and short stories?

    A. Stories that he had heard from friends or chance acquaintances
    B. Stories that he had read about in newspapers or other secondary sources
    C. Stories that came to him in periods of meditation or in dreams
    D. Stories that he had lived rather than read about

17. It has been suggested that part of Hemingway's genius lies in the way in which he removes himself from his stories in order to let readers experience the stories for themselves. Which of the following elements of the passage support this suggestion?

    I. The comparison of "the designer's initials" to the man who fell and lay in the gutter (lines 56–57) during the running of the bulls
    II. Hemingway's stated intent to project for the reader "the way it was" (line 20)
    III. Hemingway's ability to invent fascinating tales from his own experience

    A. I only
    B. II only
    C. I and II only
    D. I and III only

18. From the passage, one can assume that which of the following statements would best describe Hemingway's attitude toward knowledge?

    A. One can learn about life only by living it fully.
    B. A wise person will read widely in order to learn about life.
    C. Knowledge is a powerful tool that should be reserved only for those who know how to use it.
    D. Experience is a poor teacher.

19. The author calls "the way it was" a "characteristically simple phrase for a concept of extraordinary complexity" (lines 21–22) because

    A. the phrase reflects Hemingway's talent for obscuring ordinary events.
    B. the relationship between simplicity and complexity reflected the relationship between the style and content of Hemingway's writing.
    C. Hemingway became increasingly confused about "the way it was" throughout the course of his career.
    D. Hemingway's obsession for geographic details progressively overshadowed the dramatic element of his stories.

GO ON TO THE NEXT PAGE.

Imagine that we stand on any ordinary seaside pier, and watch the waves rolling in and striking against the iron columns of the pier. Large waves pay very little attention to the columns—they divide right and
5 left and re-unite after passing each column, much as a regiment of soldiers would if a tree stood in their way; it is almost as though the columns had not been
→ there. But the short waves and ripples find the columns of the pier a much more formidable obstacle.
10 When the short waves impinge on the columns, they are reflected back and spread as new ripples in all directions. To use the technical term, they are "scattered." The obstacle provided by the iron columns hardly affects the long waves at all, but
15 scatters the short ripples.

We have been watching a working model of the way in which sunlight struggles through the earth's atmosphere. Between us on earth and outer space the atmosphere interposes innumerable obstacles in the
20 form of molecules of air, tiny droplets of water, and small particles of dust. They are represented by the columns of the pier.

The waves of the sea represent the sunlight. We know that sunlight is a blend of lights of many
25 colors—as we can prove for ourselves by passing it through a prism, or even through a jug of water, or as Nature demonstrates to us when she passes it through the raindrops of a summer shower and produces a rainbow. We also know that light consists of waves,
30 and that the different colors of light are produced by waves of different lengths, red light by long waves and blue light by short waves. The mixture of waves which constitutes sunlight has to struggle through the obstacles it meets in the atmosphere, just as the
35 mixture of waves at the seaside has to struggle past the columns of the pier. And these obstacles treat the
→ light waves much as the columns of the pier treat the sea-waves. The long waves which constitute red light are hardly affected, but the short waves which
40 constitute blue light are scattered in all directions.

Thus, the different constituents of sunlight are treated in different ways as they struggle through the earth's atmosphere. A wave of blue light may be scattered by a dust particle, and turned out of its
45 course. After a time a second dust particle again turns it out of its course, and so on, until finally it enters our eyes by a path as zigzag as that of a flash of lightning. Consequently, the blue waves of the sunlight enter our eyes from all directions. And that
50 is why the sky looks blue.

20. We know from experience that if we look directly at the sun, we will see red light near the sun. This observation is supported by the passage for which one of the following reasons?

A.   It seems reasonable to assume that red light would surround the sun because the sun is basically a large fireball.

B.   It seems reasonable to assume that the other colors of light would either cancel each other or combine to produce red.

C.   It seems reasonable to assume that red light would not be disturbed by the atmospheric particles and would consequently reach us by a relatively direct path from the sun to our eyes.

D.   It is not supported by the passage. The author does not say what color of light should be near the sun, and he provides no reasons that would allow us to assume that the light would be red.

21. Scientists have observed that shorter wavelength light has more energy than longer wavelength light. From this we can conclude that

A.   red light will exert more energy when it hits the surface of the earth than will blue light.

B.   lightning is caused by the collision of blue light with particles in the air.

C.   red light will travel faster than blue light.

D.   blue light has more energy than red light.

GO ON TO THE NEXT PAGE.

22. A scientist makes new observations and learns that water waves of shorter wavelengths spread in all directions not only because they scatter off piers but also because they interact with previously scattered short water waves. Drawing upon the analogy between water waves and light waves, we might hypothesize which of the following?

A. Blue light waves act like ripples that other blue light waves meet and scatter from.

B. Red light waves will be scattered by blue light waves like incoming long water waves are scattered by outgoing ripples.

C. Red light waves can scatter blue light waves, but blue light waves cannot scatter red.

D. The analogy between water and light waves cannot be extended to include the way in which short water waves become ripples and scatter one another.

23. Which one of the following is a reason for assuming that sunlight is constituted of waves of many colors?

A. The mixture of waves that make up sunlight has to struggle through a variety of obstacles in the atmosphere.

B. When passing through water in the atmosphere, sunlight is sometimes broken down into an array of colors.

C. Many different wavelengths of light enter our eyes from all directions.

D. The mere fact that light waves can be scattered is a reason for assuming that sunlight is constituted of waves of different colors.

24. From the information presented in the passage, what can we conclude about the color of the sky on a day with a large quantity of dust in the air?

A. The sky would be even bluer

B. The sky would be redder

C. The sky would not change colors

D. We do not have enough information to determine a change in color

25. We all know that when there is a clear sky, the western sky appears red as the sun sets. From the information presented in the passage, this phenomenon would seem to be explained by which of the following?

I. Light meets more obstacles when passing parallel to the earth's surface than when traveling perpendicular. Consequently, even red light is diffused.

II. The blue light may not make it through the denser pathway of the evening sky, leaving only the long light waves of red.

III. The short red light waves have more energy and are the only waves that can make it through the thick atmosphere of the evening sky.

A. I only

B. II only

C. I and II only

D. II and III only

26. Which one of the following does the author seem to imply?

A. Waves of light and waves of water are identical.

B. Waves of light have the same physical shape as waves of water.

C. Waves of light and waves of water do not have very much in common.

D. Waves of water are only models of waves of light.

363

Answers and Solutions to Extra Reading

Answers to Questions

1.	D	8.	B	15.	A	22.	D
2.	B	9.	C	16.	D	23.	B
3.	C	10.	D	17.	C	24.	D
4.	B	11.	B	18.	A	25.	C
5.	D	12.	B	19.	B	26.	D
6.	B	13.	D	20.	C		
7.	D	14.	D	21.	D		

Questions 1–7

Before we turn to the answers, three pivotal words in the first passage should be noted:

"However" (line 18), "however" (line 44), and "Rather" (line 51).

1. It can be inferred from the passage that the author would consider which of the following to be good examples of "dualistic thinking"?

  I   People who think "there is a right way and a wrong way to do things"
  II. Teenagers who assume they know more about "the real world" than adults do
  III. People who back our country "right or wrong" when it goes to war

  A. I only
  B. II only
  C. III only
  D. I and III only

This is an extension question. Statement I is true. This is the essential characteristic of dualistic (right/wrong) thinkers (lines 3–8). Statement II is false. Dualistic thinkers grant authority (right thinking) to adults and adult figures. This is clear from the sentence, *"These students are slaves to the generalizations of their authorities."* Statement III is true since Dualistic thinkers believe *their* group is right and the *other* group is wrong. (Again, see lines 3–8.) The answer, therefore, is (D).

2. Students who are "dualistic" thinkers may not be able to support their beliefs convincingly because

  A. most of their beliefs *cannot* be supported by arguments.
  B. they have accepted their "truths" simply because authorities have said these things are "true."
  C. they half-believe and half-disbelieve just about everything.
  D. their teachers almost always think that "dualistic" thinkers are wrong.

This is another extension question. Dualistic thinkers probably cannot give cogent arguments for their beliefs since they have adopted them unquestioningly from authority figures; dualistic thinkers do not know (have never thought of) the reasons for which their beliefs are right or wrong. Hence the answer is (B).

3. Which one of the following assertions is supported by the passage?
    A. *Committed* thinkers are not very sure of their positions.
    B. *Relativistic* thinkers have learned how to make sense out of the world and have chosen their own positions in it.
    C. *Multiplicity* thinkers have difficulty understanding the relationships between different points of view.
    D. *Dualistic* thinkers have thought out the reasons for taking their positions.

This is a description question. (A) is false. After carefully thinking through their reasons, committed thinkers are reasonably sure of their position. (B) is also false. Relativistic thinkers make sense of the world, but they have not chosen their position; indeed they cannot even choose a position. (C) is true. Multiplicity thinkers see the world as randomly organized; they can't see the relationships that connect different positions. (See the first pivotal word, "however" [line 18].)

4. In paragraph two, the author states that in their "democracy" students in the *multiplicity* stage are directionless. The writer describes *multiplicity* students as being in a "democracy" because
    A. there are so many different kinds of people in a democracy.
    B. in an "ideal" democracy, all people are considered equal; by extension, so are their opinions.
    C. Democrats generally do not have a good sense of direction.
    D. although democracies may grant freedom, they are generally acknowledged to be less efficient than more authoritarian forms of government.

This is an extension question. Multiplicity students view all opinions as equally valid. They have yet to learn how to rank opinions (truths)—all votes (thoughts) count equally. The answer is (B).

Note, (C) is offered to humor Republicans. The test-makers sometimes run out of tempting wrong choices. Don't dwell on such humorous nonsense.

5. Which one of the following kinds of thinking is NOT described in the passage?
    A. People who assume that there is no right or wrong in any issue
    B. People who make unreasoned commitments and stick by them
    C. People who believe that right or wrong depends on the situation
    D. People who think that all behavior can be accounted for by cause and effect relationships

This is another description question. (A): No, these are the Multiplists. (B): No, Dualists think this way. (C): No, this describes Relativists. Don't confuse (A) and (C). Multiplists acknowledge no right or wrong; whereas Relativists acknowledge a morality, but one that is context dependent. Hence, by process of elimination, we have learned the answer is (D).

6. If students were asked to write essays on the different *concepts* of tragedy as exemplified by Cordelia and Antigone, and they all responded by showing how each character exemplified a traditional definition of tragedy, we could, according to the passage, hypothesize which one of the following about these students?
   A. The students were locked into the relativist stage.
   B. The students had not advanced beyond the dualist stage.
   C. The students had at least achieved the multiplicity stage.
   D. The students had reached the commitment stage.

This is an application question. Since all the students showed how the characters exemplified the *same* concept of "tragedy," they must be working from a common definition of tragedy (the traditional one). They have accepted "authority's" definition of tragedy and have shown how each character fits it. It never occurred to them that there may be other ways to view a tragedy. Hence they are all dualistic thinkers. The answer is (B).

7. Which one of the following best describes the organization of the passage?
   A. Four methods of thought are compared and contrasted.
   B. It is shown how each of four types of thought evolved from each other.
   C. The evolution of thought from simplistic and provincial through considered and cosmopolitan is illustrated by four stages.
   D. The evolution of thought through four stages is presented, and each stage is illustrated by how it views capital punishment.

This is a writing technique question. In each paragraph the author shows how a stage of thought evolved from a previous stage—except the dualistic stage, which starts the analysis. Further, the thought process in each stage is illustrated by how it views capital punishment. Hence the answer is (D).

Be careful not to choose (C). Although dualistic thinking certainly is simplistic and provincial, and committed thinking seems to be considered and cosmopolitan, neither of these judgments is stated nor implied by the passage.

Questions 8–13

8. According to the passage, shark populations are at greater risk than cod populations because
   A. sharks are now being eaten more than cod.
   B. the shark reproduction rate is lower than that of the cod.
   C. sharks are quickly becoming fewer in number.
   D. sharks are now as scarce as bald eagles and buffalo.

This is a description question. Paragraph 3 contains the information needed to answer it. There it is stated that the cod population can replenish itself in a few years, but the shark population would take 15 years. Hence the answer is (B).

Don't make the mistake of choosing (C). Although it is certainly supported by the passage, it does not state how this relates to cod—they too may be decreasing in number. (C) uses the true-but-irrelevant ploy.

366

9. According to the passage, a decrease in shark populations

    I.   might cause some fish populations to go unchecked.
    II.   would hamper cancer research.
    III. to one-quarter the current level would take over a decade to recover from.

    A.   II only
    B.   III only
    C.   I and III only
    D.   I and II only

This is a description question. Statement I is true. It is supported by the analogy drawn between lions and sharks (lines 7–9). This eliminates (A) and (B). Statement II is false. It is too strong an inference to draw from the information in lines 9–11. If sharks were on the verge of extinction, this "could hamper" research. But given that the author does not claim or imply that sharks are near extinction, "would hamper" is too strong. Besides, the author does not state that sharks are being used in research, just that they may be useful in that regard. This eliminates (D). Hence, by process of elimination, we have learned the answer is (C).

10. If the species *Homo logicus* was determined to be viviparous and to have extremely low fecundity rates on land, we might expect that

    A.   *Homo logicus* could overpopulate its niche and should be controlled.
    B.   *Homo logicus* might be declared an endangered species.
    C.   *Homo logicus* would pose no danger to other species and would itself be in no danger.
    D.   None of these events would be expected with certainty.

This is an application question; we are asked to apply what we have learned in the passage to a hypothetical situation. A review of the passage shows that only (B)

and (D) have any real merit. But sharks have survived for 400 million years with an extremely low fecundity rate. This eliminates (B). Hence the answer is (D).

11. Which one of the following best describes the author's attitude toward the efforts to protect shark populations?

    A.   strong advocate
    B.   impartial observer
    C.   opposed
    D.   perplexed

This is a rather easy tone question. The passage has a matter-of-fact or journalistic tone to it. So the answer is (B).

12. It can be inferred from the passage that

    I.   research efforts on cancer will be hindered if shark populations are threatened.
    II.   U.S. quotas on shark fishing will have limited effectiveness in protecting certain species.
    III. some practices of Chinese chefs have angered environmentalists.

    A.   I only
    B.   II only
    C.   I and II only
    D.   II and III only

This is an extension question. Statement I is incorrect. Like Statement II in Question 9, it overstates the case. Statement II is correct. We know from lines 48–50 that some species of sharks migrate into the waters of over 20 countries. U.S. quotas alone cannot "protect" these sharks, even if the quotas reduce the rate of killing in U.S. waters. Statement III is incorrect. The environmentalists are angry at the finning fishermen who are over-fishing the waters, there is nothing in the passage to suggest that this anger is also directed towards the chefs. The answer is (B).

13.   An irony resulting from the announcement that sharks will be placed on the managed species list is
   A.   we will now find out less about cancer, so in effect by saving the sharks, we are hurting ourselves.
   B.   sharks are far more dangerous to other fish than we are to them.
   C.   more chefs are now using the cartilaginous tissues found in shark fins.
   D.   more sharks are being killed now than before the announcement.

By announcing the impending classification, the federal government ironically encourages fishermen to kill as many sharks as they can before the regulations go into effect—stimulating the opposite of what was intended, i.e., the saving of sharks. The answer is (D).

Questions 14–19

14.   According to the author, Hemingway's primary purpose in telling a story was
   A.   to construct a well-told story that the reader would thoroughly enjoy.
   B.   to construct a story that would reflect truths that were not particular to a specific historical period.
   C.   to begin from reality but to allow his imagination to roam from "the way it was" to "the way it might have been."
   D.   to report faithfully reality as Hemingway had experienced it.

This is a description question. (A) is false. The enjoyment of the reader was incidental to Hemingway's primary purpose—truth-telling. (B) is false, though very tempting. The first half of this item *"to construct a story that would reflect truths"* looks very good. The second half, however, spoils it by adding the qualifier *"not particular to a specific historical period."* Reviewing the passage reveals no indication that Hemingway is trying to create any kind of "general truth." In fact, one can argue that Hemingway's emphasis on developing a strong "sense of place" (lines 29–32), and his belief that when trying to tell the truth "I only know what I have seen" (lines 9–10) support the inference that Hemingway sees truth as subjective, not objective. (C) is also false. The passage gives no indication that Hemingway was interested in the way things "might have been." (D) is true. This is clearly the author's interpretation of Hemingway's purpose. Look at the first few sentences of both the first and the second paragraphs. Notice that this question item emphasizes subjective truth, or the truth "as Hemingway had experienced it."

Strategy: In this question, you have two choices—(B) and (D)—which at first glance seem very close. Let's assume you don't understand exactly why a "close second" is wrong. When confronted with this situation, it's a good idea to take a few seconds and try to get into the *Question-Writer's* mindset. What are you missing that the Question-Writer thinks is an important point in this passage? In this case, the Question-Writer is focusing on the subtle point that Hemingway sees his perspective as "subjective," that certain things, true in some places or to some people, may not be true in other places or to other people. In other words, there is no "objective reality."

If intuition is the only way to distinguish between the two close choices, then you should mark them in your test booklet as *close*, perhaps like this $\Big\langle\begin{array}{l}\text{(B)}\\\text{(C)}\\\text{(D)}\end{array}$, to show that you had to choose between them, and move on. If you have trouble with later questions on the same passage, you may want to go back, analyze the passage, and determine the real difference between the earlier "close pair." The Question-Writer may be testing the same question from a different angle, in which case time is well spent pondering the issue.

15. From the author's comments and the example of the bulls (paragraph 4), what was the most likely reason for which Hemingway took care to include details of place?

  A. He felt that geography in some way illuminated other, more important events.
  B. He thought readers generally did not have enough imagination to visualize the scenes for themselves.
  C. He had no other recourse since he was avoiding the use of other literary sources.
  D. He thought that landscapes were more important than characters to convey "the way it was."

This is an extension question. In lines 30–32, Hemingway effectively equates geography with background, and says that without them "you have nothing." In lines 34–37, the author refers to the "geographical groundwork" of Hemingway's novels. Both of these statements imply that details of place set the stage for other, more important events. Hence the answer is (A). Don't try to draw a distinction between "geography," "background," and "landscape." The author uses them interchangeably when referring to details of place. Such latitude with labels is often mimicked by the Question-Writers.

Choice (D) is a close second-best. The author indicates that geography, background, and landscape are quite important to Hemingway. In fact, "first" in the opening to paragraph 3 almost indicates that details of place are the most important aspect of his writing. Looking closely, however, we see that the passage gives no indication of Hemingway's perspective on characters. So no comparison can be made.

16. One might infer from the passage that Hemingway preferred which one of the following sources for his novels and short stories?

  A. Stories that he had heard from friends or chance acquaintances
  B. Stories that he had read about in newspapers or other secondary sources
  C. Stories that came to him in periods of meditation or in dreams
  D. Stories that he had lived rather than read about

Hemingway's primary intent was to project for the reader "the way it was," as seen through his eyes. The answer is (D).

17. It has been suggested that part of Hemingway's genius lies in the way in which he removes himself from his stories in order to let readers experience the stories for themselves. Which of the following elements of the passage support this suggestion?

    I. The comparison of "the designer's initials" to the man who fell and lay in the gutter (lines 56–57) during the running of the bulls

    II. Hemingway's stated intent to project for the reader "the way it was" (line 20)

    III. Hemingway's ability to invent fascinating tales from his own experience

    A. I only
    B. II only
    C. I and II only
    D. I and III only

This is an extension question. Statement I is true. The last line of the passage states that the designer's initials (i.e., the writer's presence) are made as inconspicuous as possible. Statement II is also true. Readers cannot see "the way it was" if they are looking through another medium (the author). Hemingway appears to say, in effect: *"I'm striving to report exactly what happened (and not my opinions about it). The readers must draw their own conclusions."* Statement III is false. In fact, a good case could be made that writing only from personal experience would tend to increase, not decrease, the presence of the writer in his writings. The answer is (C).

18. From the passage, one can assume that which of the following statements would best describe Hemingway's attitude toward knowledge?

    A. One can learn about life only by living it fully.
    B. A wise person will read widely in order to learn about life.
    C. Knowledge is a powerful tool that should be reserved only for those who know how to use it.
    D. Experience is a poor teacher.

This is an application question; we are asked to put ourselves in Hemingway's mind. From Hemingway's statement "I only know what I have seen" and from the author's assertion that Hemingway refused to honor secondary sources, we can infer that he believed one can "know" only through experience. Hence the answer is (A).

19. The author calls "the way it was" a "characteristically simple phrase for a concept of extraordinary complexity" (lines 21–22) because

    A. the phrase reflects Hemingway's talent for obscuring ordinary events.
    B. the relationship between simplicity and complexity reflected the relationship between the style and content of Hemingway's writing.
    C. Hemingway became increasingly confused about "the way it was" throughout the course of his career.
    D. Hemingway's obsession for geographic details progressively overshadowed the dramatic element of his stories.

This is an extension question. The answer is (B). There is a great parallel here. *Phrase* (in the passage) corresponds to *style* (in the answer-choice), and *concept* corresponds to *content*.

20. We know from experience that if we look directly at the sun, we will see red light near the sun. This observation is supported by the passage for which one of the following reasons?

    A. It seems reasonable to assume that red light would surround the sun because the sun is basically a large fireball.

    B. It seems reasonable to assume that the other colors of light would either cancel each other or combine to produce red.

    C. It seems reasonable to assume that red light would not be disturbed by the atmospheric particles and would consequently reach us by a relatively direct path from the sun to our eyes.

    D. It is not supported by the passage. The author does not say what color of light should be near the sun, and he provides no reasons that would allow us to assume that the light would be red.

This is an extension question. According to the passage, red light would not be significantly deflected and consequently would pass through a relatively direct route from the sun to our eyes. Hence the answer is (C).

21. Scientists have observed that shorter wavelength light has more energy than longer wavelength light. From this we can conclude that

    A. red light will exert more energy when it hits the surface of the earth than will blue light.

    B. lightning is caused by the collision of blue light with particles in the air.

    C. red light will travel faster than blue light.

    D. blue light has more energy than red light.

This is another extension question. Since the passage is a science selection, we should expect a lot of extension questions. (A): No, if anything, blue light would exert more energy. (B): No. We can not infer this. The collision of blue light with particles in the air is the reason for a blue sky, not for lightning. (C): No. Speed of light is not mentioned in the passage. (D): Yes. Blue light has a shorter wavelength, consequently it has more energy than red light.

22. A scientist makes new observations and learns that water waves of shorter wavelengths spread in all directions not only because they scatter off piers but also because they interact with previously scattered short water waves. Drawing upon the analogy between water waves and light waves, we might hypothesize which of the following?

    A. Blue light waves act like ripples that other blue light waves meet and scatter from.

    B. Red light waves will be scattered by blue light waves like incoming long water waves are scattered by outgoing ripples.

    C. Red light waves can scatter blue light waves, but blue light waves cannot scatter red.

    D. The analogy between water and light waves cannot be extended to include the way in which short water waves become ripples and scatter one another.

This is an application question since it introduces new information about water waves and asks us to conclude how the behavior of light waves might be similarly affected. Given this information, however, we can justify no conclusion about whether light waves imitate water waves in this new regard. The analogy might hold or it might break down. We don't yet know. (To find out we would have to do an experiment using light.) The answer is (D).

23. Which one of the following is a reason for assuming that sunlight is constituted of waves of many colors?

    A. The mixture of waves that make up sunlight has to struggle through a variety of obstacles in the atmosphere.
    B. When passing through water in the atmosphere, sunlight is sometimes broken down into an array of colors.
    C. Many different wavelengths of light enter our eyes from all directions.
    D. The mere fact that light waves can be scattered is a reason for assuming that sunlight is constituted of waves of different colors.

(A): No. We do not know anything about a "variety" of obstacles; even if we did, we would have no reason to assume that light is constituted of different colors. **(B): Yes.** See lines 23–29. Rainbows occur because light is constituted of many colors. (C): No. This is a distortion of lines 48–50, and it sounds illogical to boot. (D): No. This gives no reason to assume that light is constituted of many colors.

24. From the information presented in the passage, what can we conclude about the color of the sky on a day with a large quantity of dust in the air?

    A. The sky would be even bluer
    B. The sky would be redder
    C. The sky would not change colors
    D. We do not have enough information to determine a change in color

(A): No. Although dust is mentioned as one of the three important obstacles (lines 18–21), we simply do not have enough information to conclude how dust density would change sky color. (B): No. While this idea may fit with the common lore that a lot of dust in the air creates great, red sunsets, the passage itself gives no basis to any conclusion regarding color change. (C):

No. Same reason as in (A) and (B). **(D): Yes.** There is not enough information in the passage to determine a relationship between color change and dust density. The dust may give off a certain color of its own—we can't say for certain.

25. We all know that when there is a clear sky, the western sky appears red as the sun sets. From the information presented in the passage, this phenomenon would seem to be explained by which of the following?

    I. Light meets more obstacles when passing parallel to the earth's surface than when traveling perpendicular. Consequently, even red light is diffused.
    II. The blue light may not make it through the denser pathway of the evening sky, leaving only the long light waves of red.
    III. The short red light waves have more energy and are the only waves that can make it through the thick atmosphere of the evening sky.

    A. I only
    B. II only
    C. I and II only
    D. II and III only

Statement I is true. There are obviously more particles on a horizontal than a vertical path. The glowing red sky is reasonable evidence for some diffusion. Note that Question 24 asks "what can we *conclude*" while this question asks what seems *plausible* (what "would seem to be explained"). So, while we are attempting to make very similar inferences in both questions, what we can do with the data depends, among other things, on the degree of certainty requested. Statement II is true. The path of evening light probably has a greater average density, since it spends more time passing through a zone of thicker atmosphere. It is reasonable to assume this significantly greater density, or the absolute number of particles, might present an obstacle to blue light. Statement III is false. There are two things wrong with this answer: (1) red light waves are not short, relative to blue; (2) we do not know that waves with more energy will more readily pass through obstacles. The passage, in fact, implies just the opposite. The answer is (C).

26.   Which one of the following does the author seem to imply?

    A.   Waves of light and waves of water are identical.
    B.   Waves of light have the same physical shape as waves of water.
    C.   Waves of light and waves of water do not have very much in common.
    D.   Waves of water are only models of waves of light.

(A): No. Water waves offer only a model for light waves. As a model, they are identical in some ways but not in others. (B): No. This is not implied by the passage. What they have in common is the way they act when they impinge on obstacles. (C): No. Waves of water are used as a model because they have much in common with waves of light. **(D): Yes.** See explanation for (A).

SECTION 6
CRITICAL REASONING

Chapter 27
Argument Analysis

A. Introduction

To reason analytically is to break down a thought (passage) into its constituent parts. Then discover how those parts are related to one another and thereby better understand the whole thought (passage).

This process rests on the premise that you are more familiar with (better understand) the parts than the whole thought. For an analogy, we can again use the example, in the chapter *The Three Step Method*, of dismantling an engine to better understand how it works. Once we have separated the starter, generator, radiator, pistons, etc., from the engine, it would be more enlightening if we knew how each of the parts functioned and how they related to one another. This is where premises and conclusions come in. They are the *parts* of an argument. Although the conclusion is often said to follow from the premises, we will study conclusions first, because the first step in analyzing an argument is to identify its conclusion.

Note: In common jargon, an argument means a heated debate between two people. However, as used on the MCAT, a passage argument is a formal presentation of facts and opinions in order to support a position.

B. Conclusions

In most cases, successfully analyzing an argument hinges on determining the conclusion of the argument. The conclusion is the main idea of the argument. It is what the writer is trying to persuade the reader to believe. Most often the conclusion comes at the end of the argument. The writer organizes the facts and his opinions so that they build up to the conclusion. Sometimes, however, the conclusion will come at the beginning of an argument. Rarely does it come in the middle. And occasionally, for rhetorical effect, the conclusion is not even stated.

Example:

The police are the armed guardians of the social order. The blacks are the chief domestic victims of the American social order. <u>A conflict of interest exists, therefore, between the blacks and the police</u>—Eldridge Cleaver, *Soul on Ice*

Here the first two sentences anticipate or setup the conclusion. By changing the grammar slightly, the conclusion can be placed at the beginning of the argument and still sound natural:

> <u>A conflict of interest exists between the blacks and the police</u> because the police are the armed guardians of the social order and the blacks are the chief domestic victims of the American social order.

The conclusion can also be forced into the middle:

> The police are the armed guardians of the social order. <u>So a</u> <u>conflict of interest exists between the blacks and the police</u> because the blacks are the chief domestic victims of the American social order.

It is generally awkward, as in the pervious paragraph, to place the conclusion in the middle of the argument because then it cannot be fully anticipated by what comes before nor fully explained by what comes after. On the rare occasion when a conclusion comes in the middle of an argument, most often either the material that comes before it or the material that comes after it is not essential.

When determining the meaning of a conclusion, be careful not to read any more into it than what the author states. For example, many people will interpret the sentence

"Every Republican is not a conservative"

to mean that some republicans are not conservative.[*] MCAT passages are typically taken from academic journals, and the writers in those journals do not use grammar (logic) that loosely. On the MCAT, the above sentence would mean what it literally states—that no Republican is a conservative.

To illustrate further, consider the meaning of *some* in the sentence "Some of Mary's friends went to the party." It would be unwarranted, based on this statement, to assume that some of Mary's friends did not go to the party. Although it may seem deceiving to say that *some* of Mary's friends went to the party when in fact *all* of them did, it is nonetheless technically consistent with the meaning of *some*.

C. Conclusion Indicators

As mentioned before, the conclusion usually comes at the end of an argument, sometimes at the beginning, but rarely in the middle. Writers use certain words to indicate that the conclusion is about to be stated. Following is a list of the most common conclusion indicators:

CONCLUSION INDICATORS

hence	**therefore**
so	**accordingly**
thus	**consequently**
follows that	**shows that**
conclude that	**implies**
as a result	**means that**

These conclusion flags are very helpful, but you must use them cautiously because many of these words have other functions.

---

[*] To give the sentence that meaning reword it as "Not every republican is a conservative".

Example:

All devout Muslims abstain from alcohol. Steve is a devout Muslim. <u>Thus</u>, he abstains from alcohol.

In this example, "thus" anticipates the conclusion that necessarily follows from the first two sentences. Notice the different function of *thus* in the following sentence.

Example:

The problem is simple when the solution is <u>thus</u> stated.

In this example, *thus* means "in that manner."

Most often the conclusion of an argument is put in the form of a statement (as in all the examples we have considered so far). Sometimes, however, the conclusion is given as a command or obligation.

Example:

All things considered, you ought to vote.

Here, the author implies that you are obliged to vote.

Example:

Son, unless you go to college, you will not make a success of yourself. No Carnegie has ever been a failure. So you will go to college.

Here the conclusion is given as an imperative command.

The conclusion can even be put in the form of a question. This rhetorical technique is quite effective in convincing people that a certain position is correct. We are more likely to believe something if we feel that we concluded it on our own, or at least if we feel that we were not told to believe it. A conclusion put in question form can have this result.

Example:

The Nanuuts believe that they should not take from nature anything she cannot replenish during their lifetime. This assures that future generations can enjoy the same riches of nature that they have. At the current rate of destruction, the rain forests will disappear during our lifetime. Do we have an obligation to future generations to prevent this result?

Here the author trusts that the power of her argument will persuade the reader to answer the question affirmatively.

Taking this rhetorical technique one step further, the writer may build up to the conclusion but leave it unstated. This allows the reader to make up his own mind. If the build-up is done skillfully, the reader will be more likely to agree with the author and still not feel manipulated.

Example:

He who is without sin should cast the first stone. There is no one here who does not have a skeleton in his closet.

The unstated but obvious conclusion here is that none of the people has the right to cast the first stone.

D. Quantifiers

When determining the conclusion's scope be careful not to read any more or less into it than the author states. MCAT writers often create wrong answer-choices by slightly overstating or understating the author's claim. Certain words limit the scope of a statement. These words are called quantifiers—pay close attention to them. Following is a list of the most important quantifiers:

Quantifiers

all	except	likely
some	most	many
only	could	no
never	always	everywhere
probably	must	alone

Example:

Whether the world is Euclidean or non-Euclidean is still an open question. However, if a star's position is predicted based on non-Euclidean geometry, then when a telescope is pointed to where the star should be it will be there. Whereas, if the star's position is predicted based on Euclidean geometry, then when a telescope is pointed to where the star should be it won't be there. This strongly indicates that the world is non-Euclidean.

Which one of the following best expresses the main idea of the passage?

A.   The world may or may not be Euclidean.

B.   The world is probably non-Euclidean.

C.   The world is non-Euclidean.

D.   The world is Euclidean.

E.   The world is neither Euclidean nor non-Euclidean.

Choice (A) understates the main idea. Although the opening to the passage states that we don't know whether the world is non-Euclidean, the author goes on to give evidence that it is non-Euclidean. Choice (C) overstates the main idea. The author doesn't say that the world is non-Euclidean, just that evidence strongly indicates that it is. In choice (B), the word "probably" properly limits the scope of the main idea, namely, that the world is probably non-Euclidean, but we can't yet state so definitively. The answer is (B).

Warm-Up Drill I

1. When a man is tired of London, he is tired of life; for there is in London all that life can afford.—Samuel Johnson

2. Some psychiatrists claim that watching violent movies dissipates aggression. Does watching pornography dissipate one's libido?

3. By the age of 10 months, purebred golden retrievers display certain instinctive behaviors. Because this 11-month-old golden retriever does not display these instinctive behaviors, it is not a purebred.

4. Most people would agree that it is immoral to lie. But if a kidnaper accosts you on the street and asks which way his escaped victim went, would it be immoral to point in the opposite direction?

5. Beware, for I am fearless, and therefore, powerful.—Mary Shelley, *Frankenstein*

6. The continuous stream of violent death depicted on television has so jaded society that murder is no longer shocking. It's hardly surprising, then, that violent crime so permeates modern society.

7. Where all other circumstances are equal, wages are generally higher in new than in old trades. When a projector attempts to establish a new manufacture, he must at first entice his workmen from other employments by higher wages than they can either earn in their old trades, or than the nature of his work would otherwise require, and a considerable time must pass away before he can venture to reduce them to the common level.—Adam Smith, *The Wealth of Nations*

8. Existentialists believe that our identity is continually evolving, that we are born into this world without an identity and do not begin to develop one until the act of retrospection. So one's identity is always trailing oneself like the wake of a boat. As one goes through life, the wake becomes wider and wider defining him more and more precisely.

9. In time I began to recognize that all of these smaller complaints about rigidity, emotional suffocation, the tortured logic of the law were part of a more fundamental phenomenon in the law itself. Law is at war with ambiguity, with uncertainty. In the courtroom, the adversary system—plaintiff against defendant—guarantees that someone will always win, someone loses. No matter if justice is evenly with each side, no matter if the issues are indefinite and obscure, the rule of law will be declared.—Scott Turow, *One L*

10. Either God controls all of man's behavior or God does not control any of man's behavior. God must not control man's behavior since there is so much evil in the world.

11. The more deeply I understand the central role of caring in my own life, the more I realize it to be central to the human condition.—Milton Mayeroff, *On Caring*

E. Premises

Once you've found the conclusion, most often everything else in the argument will be either premises or "noise." The premises provide evidence for the conclusion; they form the foundation or infrastructure upon which the conclusion depends. To determine whether a statement is a premise, ask yourself whether it supports the conclusion. If so, it's a premise.

F. Premise Indicators

Earlier we saw that writers use certain words to flag conclusions; likewise writers use certain words to flag premises. Following is a partial list of the most common premise indicators:

PREMISE INDICATORS

because	for
since	is evidence that
if	in that
as	owing to
suppose	inasmuch as
assume	may be derived from

Premise indicators are very helpful. As with conclusion indicators, though, you must use them cautiously because they have other functions. For example, *since* can indicate a premise, or it can merely indicate time.

Example:

Since the incumbent's views are out of step with public opinion, he probably will not be reelected.

Here "since" is used to flag the premise that the incumbent's positions are unpopular. Contrast this use of "since" with the following example.

Example:

Since the incumbent was elected to office, he has spent less and less time with his family.

In this case, "since" merely expresses a temporal relationship. The statement as a whole expresses an observation, rather than an argument.

G. Suppressed Premises

Most arguments depend on one or more unstated premises. Sometimes this indicates a weakness in the argument, an oversight by the writer. More often, however, certain premises are left tacit because they are too numerous, or the writer assumes that his audience is aware of the assumptions, or he wants the audience to fill in the premise themselves and therefore be more likely to believe the conclusion.

Example:

Conclusion: I knew he did it.

Premise: Only a guilty person would accept immunity from prosecution.

The suppressed premise is that he did, in fact, accept immunity. The speaker assumes that his audience is aware of this fact or at least is willing to believe it, so to state it would be redundant and ponderous. If the unstated premise were false (that is, he did not accept immunity), the argument would not technically be a lie; but it would be very deceptive. The unscrupulous writer may use this ploy if he thinks that he can get away with it. That is, his argument has the intended effect and the false premise, though implicit, is hard to find or ambiguous. Politicians are not at all above using this tactic.

Example:

Politician: A hawk should not be elected president because this country has seen too many wars.

The argument has two tacit premises—one obvious, the other subtle. Clearly, the politician has labeled his opponent a hawk, and he hopes the audience will accept that label. Furthermore, although he does not state it explicitly, the argument rests on the assumption that a hawk is likely to start a war. He hopes the audience will fill in that premise, thereby tainting his opponent as a war monger.

A common MCAT question asks you to find the suppressed premise of a passage. Finding the suppressed premise—or assumption—of an argument can be difficult. However, on the MCAT you have an advantage—the suppressed premise is listed as one of the five answer-choices. To test whether an answer-choice is a suppressed premise, ask yourself whether it would make the argument more plausible If so, then it is very likely a suppressed premise.

Example: *(Mini-passage)*

American attitudes tend to be rather insular, but there is much we can learn from other countries. In Japan, for example, workers set aside some time each day to exercise. And many of the corporations provide elaborate exercise facilities for their employees. Few American corporations have such exercise programs. Studies have shown that the Japanese worker is more productive and healthier than the American worker. It must be concluded that the productivity of American workers will lag behind their Japanese counterparts, until mandatory exercise programs are introduced.

The argument presented in the passage depends on the assumption that:

383

A. even if exercise programs do not increase productivity, they will improve the American worker's health.

B. the productivity of all workers can be increased by exercise.

C. exercise is an essential factor in the Japanese worker's superior productivity.

D. American workers can adapt to the longer Japanese workweek.

The unstated essence of the argument is that exercise is an integral part of productivity and that Japanese workers are more productive than American workers because they exercise more. The answer is (C).

Example: *(Mini-passage)*

Kirkland's theory of corporate structure can be represented by a truncated pyramid. There are workers, middle management, and executive management, but no head of the corporation. Instead, all major decisions are made by committee. As a consequence, in Kirkland's structure, risky, cutting-edge technologies cannot be developed.

Implicit in the passage is the assumption that:

A. Cutting-edge technologies are typically developed by entrepreneurs, not by big corporations.

B. Only single individuals make risky decisions.

C. An individual is more likely to take a gamble on his own than in a group.

D. All heads of corporations reached their positions by taking risks.

The link that allows the conclusion to be drawn is the assumption that <u>only</u> individuals make risky decisions. The answer is (B).

Both (A) and (C) are close second-best choices. Both are supported by the passage, but each understates the scope of the suppressed premise. The argument states that in Kirkland's model of corporate structure cutting edge-technologies <u>cannot</u> be developed, not that they are less likely to be developed.

Another common passage-question asks you to either strengthen or weaken an argument. Typically, to answer such questions, you need to show that a suppressed premised is true or that it is false.

Example: *(Mini-passage)*

The petrochemical industry claims that chemical waste dumps pose no threat to people living near them. If this is true, then why do they locate the plants in sparsely populated regions. By not locating the chemical dumps in densely populated areas the petrochemical industry tacitly admits that these chemicals are potentially dangerous to the people living nearby.

Which of the following, if true, would most weaken the author's argument?

A. Funding through the environmental Super Fund to clean up poorly run waste dumps is reserved for rural areas only.

B. Until chemical dumps are proven 100% safe, it would be imprudent to locate them were they could potentially do the most harm.

C. Locating the dumps in sparsely populated areas is less expensive and involves less government red tape.

D. The potential for chemicals to leach into the water table has in the past been underestimated.

The suppressed, *false* premise of the argument is that all things being equal there is no reason to prefer locating the sites in sparsely populated areas. To weaken the argument, we need to show it is <u>not</u> true that all things are equal. In other words, there are advantages other than safety in locating the sites in sparsely populated areas. Choice (C) gives two possible advantages—cost and ease. Hence (C) is the answer.

Warm-Up Drill II

<u>Directions:</u> *For each of the following arguments, identify the suppressed premise and state whether it is a reasonable assumption for the author to make. Answers and solutions are on page 387.*

1. Sacramento is the capital of California; thus it is located northeast of San Francisco.

2. I read it in a book, so it must be true.

3. Any government action that intrudes on the right of privacy is unconstitutional. Therefore, requiring government employees to take a drug test is unconstitutional.

4. After studying assiduously for three months, Sean retook the SAT and increased his score by more than four hundred points. Therefore, the Educational Testing Service canceled his score.

5. When explorers arrived in the Americas in the 1500s A.D., they observed the natives hunting with bronze tipped arrows. Archaeological evidence shows that bronze was not smelted in the Americas until the 1200s A.D. Therefore, native Americans must have begun hunting with arrows sometime between 1200 and 1500 A.D.

6. Fiction is truer than history, because it goes beyond the evidence.—E. M. Forster

7. In Knox's theory of military strategy, all decisions about troop deployment must be made by a committee of generals. If, however, his model of command were in effect during World War II, then daring and successful operations—such as Patton's unilateral decision to land paratroopers behind enemy lines during the Battle of the Bulge—would not have been ordered.

8. In recent years many talented and dedicated teachers have left the public school system for the private sector because the public school system's salary scale is not sufficient for a family to maintain a quality standard of living. To lure these dedicated teachers back to the public schools, we must immediately raise the pay scale to a level comparable to that of the private sector, and thereby save our schools.

Solutions to Warm-Up Drills

Drill I

1. <u>When a man is tired of London, he is tired of life</u>; for there is in London all that life can afford.—Samuel Johnson

2. The conclusion is not stated, but the arguer implies that watching violent movies does *not* dissipate aggression.

3. By the age of 10 months, purebred golden retrievers display certain instinctive behaviors. Because this 11 month-old golden retriever does not display these instinctive behaviors, <u>it is not a purebred.</u>

4. No conclusion is stated. But the author implies that to lie is not always immoral.

5. Beware, for I am fearless, and therefore, <u>powerful</u>.—Mary Shelley, *Frankenstein*

6. The implied conclusion is that violence depicted on television contributes to society's high rate of violence.

7. Where all other circumstances are equal, <u>wages are generally higher in new than in old trades</u>. When a projector attempts to establish a new manufacture, he must at first entice his workmen from other employments by higher wages than they can either earn in their old trades, or than the nature of his work would otherwise require, and a considerable time must pass away before he can venture to reduce them to the common level.—Adam Smith, *The Wealth of Nations*

8. Existentialists believe that our identity is continually evolving, that we are born into this world without an identity and do not begin to develop one until the act of retrospection. So <u>one's identity is always trailing oneself</u> like the wake of a boat. As one goes through life, the wake becomes wider and wider defining him more and more precisely.

9. In time I began to recognize that all of these smaller complaints about rigidity, emotional suffocation, the tortured logic of the law were part of a more fundamental phenomenon in the law itself. <u>Law is at war with ambiguity, with uncertainty</u>. In the courtroom, the adversary system—plaintiff against defendant—guarantees that someone will always win, someone loses. No matter if justice is evenly with each side, no matter if the issues are indefinite and obscure, the rule of law will be declared.—Scott Turow, *One L*

10. Either God controls all of man's behavior or God does not control any of man's behavior. <u>God must not control man's behavior</u> since there is so much evil in the world.

11. The more deeply I understand the central role of caring in my own life, the more I realize <u>it to be central to the human condition</u>.—Milton Mayeroff, *On Caring*

Drill II

1. The suppressed premise is that the capital of California is located northeast of San Francisco. This is a reasonable assumption because it is true!

2. The suppressed premise is that only the truth is published. Clearly this is not a reasonable assumption.

3. The suppressed premise is that being forced to take a drug test is an invasion of privacy. This is a reasonable assumption.

4. ETS's suppressed premise is that extremely high score improvements indicate cheating. This is arguably a reasonable assumption, but it is not consistent with the tradition of assuming one innocent until proven otherwise. (By the way, this is a true story. Sean sued ETS and the courts ordered them to release his score.)

5. The suppressed premise is that hunting with arrows did not begin until the arrows were tipped with bronze. This seems to be a questionable assumption.

6. The suppressed premise is that what goes beyond the evidence is truer that what does not. This is a questionable assumption; arguably just the opposite is the case.

7. The suppressed premise is that only decisions made by a single individual can be daring. This assumption has some truth to it, but it's a bit extreme.

8. The suppressed premise is that comparable pay would be sufficient to entice the teachers to change their careers again. This is probably a reasonable assumption since the teachers were described as dedicated.

Chapter 28
Inductive Arguments

A. Introduction

In this chapter we will classify and study the major types of inductive arguments.

An argument is deductive if its conclusion *necessarily* follows from its premises—otherwise it is inductive. In an inductive argument, the author presents the premises as evidence or reasons for the conclusion. The validity of the conclusion depends on how compelling the premises are. Unlike deductive arguments, the conclusion of an inductive argument is never certain. The *truth* of the conclusion can range from highly likely to highly unlikely. In reasonable arguments, the conclusion is likely. In fallacious arguments, it is improbable. We will study both reasonable and fallacious arguments.

First, we will classify the three major types of inductive reasoning—generalization, analogy, and causal—and their associated fallacies. Next, we will study eight common fallacies.

B. Generalization

Generalization and analogy, which we consider in the next section, are the main tools by which we accumulate knowledge and analyze our world. Many people define *generalization* as "inductive reasoning." In colloquial speech, the phrase "to generalize" carries a negative connotation. To argue by generalization, however, is neither inherently good nor bad. The relative validity of a generalization depends on both the context of the argument and the likelihood that its conclusion is true. Polling organizations make predictions by generalizing information from a small sample of the population, which hopefully represents the general population. The soundness of their predictions (arguments) depends on how representative the sample is and on its size. Clearly, the less comprehensive a conclusion is the more likely it is to be true.

Example:

During the late seventies when Japan was rapidly expanding its share of the American auto market, GM surveyed owners of GM cars and asked them whether they would be more willing to buy a large, powerful car or a small, economical car. Seventy percent of those who responded said that they would prefer a large car. On the basis of this survey, GM decided to continue building large cars. Yet during the '80s, GM lost even more of the market to the Japanese.

Which one of the following, if it were determined to be true, would best explain this discrepancy.

A.   Only 10 percent of those who were polled replied.

B.   Ford which conducted a similar survey with similar results continued to build large cars and also lost more of their market to the Japanese.

C.   The surveyed owners who preferred big cars also preferred big homes.

D.   GM determined that it would be more profitable to make big cars.

E.   Eighty percent of the owners who wanted big cars and only 40 percent of the owners who wanted small cars replied to the survey.

The argument generalizes *from* the survey *to* the general car-buying population, so the reliability of the projection depends on how representative the sample is. At first glance, choice (A) seems rather good, because 10 percent does not seem large enough. However, political opinion polls are typically based on only .001 percent of the population. More importantly, we don't know what percentage of GM car owners received the survey. Choice (B) simply states that Ford made the same mistake that GM did. Choice (C) is irrelevant. Choice (D), rather than explaining the discrepancy, gives even more reason for GM to continue making large cars. Finally, choice (E) points out that part of the survey did not represent the entire public, so (E) is the answer.

C. Analogy

To argue by analogy is to claim that because two things are similar in some respects, they will be similar in others. Medical experimentation on animals is predicated on such reasoning. The argument goes like this: the metabolism of pigs, for example, is similar to that of humans, and high doses of saccharine cause cancer in pigs. Therefore, high doses of saccharine probably cause cancer in humans.

Clearly, the greater the similarity between the two things being compared the stronger the argument will be. Also the less ambitious the conclusion the stronger the argument will be. The argument above would be strengthened by changing "probably" to "may." It can be weakened by pointing out the dissimilarities between pigs and people.

The following words usually indicate that an analogy is being drawn:

ANALOGY INDICATORS

like	**likewise**
similar	**also**
too	**compared to**
as with	**just as . . . so too . . .**

Often, however, a writer will use an analogy without flagging it with any of the above words.

Example:

Just as the fishing line becomes too taut, so too the trials and tribulations of life in the city can become so stressful that one's mind can snap.

Which one of the following most closely parallels the reasoning used in the argument above?

A. Just as the bow may be drawn too taut, so too may one's life be wasted pursuing self-gratification.

B. Just as a gambler's fortunes change unpredictably, so too do one's career opportunities come unexpectedly.

C. Just as a plant can be killed by over watering it, so too can drinking too much water lead to lethargy.

D. Just as the engine may race too quickly, so too may life in the fast lane lead to an early death.

E. Just as an actor may become stressed before a performance, so too may dwelling on the negative cause depression.

The argument compares the tautness in a fishing line to the stress of city life; it then concludes that the mind can snap just as the fishing line can. So we are looking for an answer-choice that compares two things and draws a conclusion based on their similarity. Notice that we are looking for an argument that uses similar reasoning, but not necessarily similar concepts.

As to choice (A), the analogy between a taut bow and self-gratification is weak, if existent. Choice (B) offers a good analogy but no conclusion. Choice (C) offers both a good analogy and a conclusion; however, the conclusion, "leads to lethargy," understates the scope of what the analogy implies. Choice (D) offers a strong analogy and a conclusion with the same scope found in the original: "the engine blows, the person dies"; "the line snaps, the mind snaps." The answer is (D).

D. Causal Reasoning

Of the three types of inductive reasoning we will discuss, causal reasoning is both the weakest and the most prone to fallacy. Nevertheless, it is a useful and common method of thought.

To argue by causation is to claim that one thing causes another. A causal argument can be either weak or strong depending on the context. For example, to claim that you won the lottery because you saw a shooting star the night before is clearly fallacious. However, most people believe that smoking causes cancer because cancer often strikes those with a history of cigarette use. Although the connection between smoking and cancer is virtually certain, as with all inductive arguments it can never be 100 percent certain. Cigarette companies have claimed that there may be a genetic predisposition in some people to both develop cancer and crave nicotine. Although this claim is highly improbable, it is conceivable.

There are two common fallacies associated with causal reasoning:

1. **Confusing <u>Correlation</u> with <u>Causation</u>.**

    To claim that A caused B merely because A occurred immediately before B is clearly questionable. It may be only coincidental that they occurred together, or something else may have caused them to occur together. For example, the fact that insomnia and lack of appetite often occur together does not mean that one necessarily causes the other. They may both be symptoms of an underlying condition.

2. **Confusing Necessary Conditions with Sufficient Conditions.**

    A is necessary for B means "B cannot occur without A." *A is sufficient for B* means "A causes B to occur, but B can still occur without A." For example, a small tax base is sufficient to cause a budget deficit, but excessive spending can cause a deficit even with a large tax base. A common fallacy is to assume that a necessary condition is sufficient to cause a situation. For example, to win a modern war it is necessary to have modern, high-tech equipment, but it is not sufficient, as Iraq discovered in the Persian Gulf War.

Eight Common Fallacies

E. Contradiction

Contradiction is the most glaring type of fallacy. It is committed when two opposing statements are simultaneously asserted. For example, saying "it is raining *and* it is not raining" is a contradiction. If all contradictions were this basic, there would not be much need to study them. Typically, however, the arguer obscures the contradiction to the point that the argument can be quite compelling. Take, for instance, the following argument:

"We cannot know anything, because we intuitively realize that our thoughts are unreliable."

This argument has an air of reasonableness to it. But "intuitively realize" means "to know." Thus the arguer is in essence saying that we *know* that we don't know anything. This is self-contradictory.

Example:

In the game of basketball, scoring a three-point shot is a skill that only those with a soft shooting touch can develop. Wilt Chamberlain, however, was a great player, so even though he did not have a soft shooting touch he would have excelled at scoring three point shots.

Which one of the following contains a flaw that most closely parallels the flaw contained in the passage?

A. Eighty percent of the freshmen at Berkeley go on to get a bachelor's degree. David is a freshman at Berkeley, so he will probably complete his studies and receive a bachelor's degree.

B. If the police don't act immediately to quell the disturbance, it will escalate into a riot. However, since the police are understaffed, there will be a riot.

C. The meek shall inherit the earth. Susie received an inheritance from her grandfather, so she must be meek.

D. During the Vietnam War, the powerful had to serve along with the poor. However, Stevens' father was a federal judge, so Stevens was able to get a draft deferment.

E. All dolphins are mammals and all mammals breathe air. Therefore, all mammals that breathe air are dolphins.

The argument clearly contradicts itself. So look for an answer-choice that contradicts itself in like manner. Choice (A) is not self-contradictory. In fact, it's a fairly sound argument—eliminate it. Choice (B), on the other hand, is not a very sound argument. The police, though understaffed, may realize the seriousness of the situation and rearrange their priorities. Nevertheless, (B) does not contain a contradiction—eliminate it. Choice (C), though questionable, does not contain a contradiction—eliminate it. Choice (D), however, does contain a contradiction. It begins by stating that both the powerful and the poor had to serve in Vietnam and ends by stating that some powerful people—namely, Stevens—did not have to serve. This is a contradiction, so (D) is probably the answer. Choice (E), like the original argument, is invalid but does not contain a contradiction—eliminate it. The answer is (D).

F. Equivocation

Equivocation is the use of a word in more than one sense during an argument. It is often done intentionally.

Example:

Individual rights must be championed by the government. It is right for one to believe in God. So government should promote the belief in God.

In this argument, *right* is used ambiguously. In the phrase "individual rights" it is used in the sense of a privilege, whereas in the second sentence *right* is used to mean correct or moral. The questionable conclusion is possible only if the arguer is allowed to play with the meaning of the critical word *right*.

Example:

Judy: Traditionally, Republican administrations have supported free trade. But the President must veto the North American Free Trade Act because it will drain away American jobs to Mexico and lead to wholesale exploitation of the Mexican workers by international conglomerates.

Tina: I disagree. Exploitation of workers is the essence of any economic system just like the exploitation of natural resources.

Judy and Tina will not be able to settle their argument unless they

A. explain their opinions in more detail

B. ask an expert on international trade to decide who is correct

C. decide whose conclusion is true but irrelevant

D. decide whose conclusion is based on a questionable premise

E. define a critical word

Clearly, Judy and Tina are working with different definitions of the word *exploitation*. Judy is using the meaning that most people attribute to exploitation—abuse. We can't tell the exact meaning Tina intends, but for her exploitation must have a positive, or at least neutral, connotation, otherwise she would be unlikely to defend it as essential. Their argument will be fruitless until they agree on a definition for *exploitation*. Hence the answer is (E).

G. Circular Reasoning

Circular reasoning involves assuming as a premise that which you are trying to prove. Intuitively, it may seem that no one would fall for such an argument. However, the conclusion may appear to state something additional, or the argument may be so long that the reader may forget that the conclusion was stated as a premise.

Example:

The death penalty is appropriate for traitors because it is right to execute those who betray their own country and thereby risk the lives of millions.

This argument is circular because "right" means essentially the same thing as "appropriate." In effect, the writer is saying that the death penalty is appropriate because it is appropriate.

Example:

Democracy is the best form of government yet created. Therefore, we must be vigilant in its defense; that is, we must be prepared to defend the right to freedom. Because this right is fundamental to any progressive form of government, it is clear that democracy is better than any other form of government.

Which one of the following illustrates the same flawed reasoning as found in the passage?

A. I never get a headache when I eat only Chinese food, nor when I drink only wine. But when I eat Chinese food and drink wine, I get a headache. So the combination of the two must be the cause of my headaches.

B. The two times I have gone to that restaurant something bad has happened. The first time the waiter dropped a glass and it shattered all over the table. And after the second time I went there, I got sick. So why should I go there again—something bad will just happen again.

394

C.   I would much rather live a life dedicated to helping my fellow man than one dedicated to gaining material possessions and seeing my fellow man as a competitor. At the end of each day, the satisfaction of having helped people is infinitely greater than the satisfaction of having achieved something material.

D.   I'm obsessed with volleyball; that's why I play it constantly. I train seven days a week, and I enter every tournament. Since I'm always playing it, I must be obsessed with it.

E.   In my academic studies, I have repeatedly changed majors. I decide to major in each new subject that I'm introduced to. Just as a bee lights from one flower to the next, tasting the nectar of each, I jump from one subject to the next getting just a taste of each.

The argument in the passage is circular (and filled with non-sequiturs). It is incumbent on the writer to give evidence or support for the conclusion. In this argument, though, the writer first states that democracy is the best government, the rest is merely "noise," until he restates the conclusion.

Choice (A) is a reasonably valid causation argument—eliminate. (B) argues by generalization. Although it is of questionable validity, it is not circular because the conclusion, "it will happen again," is not stated, nor is it implicit in the premises—eliminate. (C) is not circular because the conclusion is mentioned only once—eliminate. (D) begins by stating, "I'm obsessed with volleyball." It does not, however, provide compelling evidence for that claim: training seven days a week, rather than indicating obsession, may be required for, say, members of the Olympic Volleyball Team. Furthermore, the argument repeats the conclusion at the end. So it is circular in the same manner as the original. Hence (D) is our answer.

H. Shifting the Burden of Proof

As mentioned before, it is incumbent upon the writer to provide evidence or support for her position. To imply that a position is true merely because no one has disproved it is to shift the burden of proof to others.

Example:

Since no one has been able to prove God's existence, there must not be a God.

There are two major weaknesses in this argument. First, the fact that God's existence has yet to be proven does not preclude any future proof of existence. Second, if there is a God, one would expect that his existence is independent of any proof by man.

Reasoning by shifting the burden of proof is not always fallacious. In fact, our legal system is predicated on this method of thought. The defendant is *assumed* innocent until proven guilty. This assumption shifts the onus of proof to the state. Science can also validly use this method of thought to better understand the world—so long as it is not used to claim "truth." Consider the following argument: "The multitude of theories about our world have failed to codify and predict its behavior as well as Einstein's theory of relativity. Therefore, our world is probably Einsteinian." This argument is strong so long as it is qualified with "probably"—otherwise it is fallacious: someone may yet create a better theory of our world.

Example:

Astronomers have created a mathematical model for determining whether life exists outside our solar system. It is based on the assumption that life as we know it can exist only on a planet such as our own, and that our sun, which has nine planets circling it, is the kind of star commonly found throughout the universe. Hence it is projected that there are billions of planets with conditions similar to our own. So astronomers have concluded that it is highly probable, if not virtually certain, that life exists outside our solar system. Yet there has never been detected so much as one planet beyond our solar system. Hence life exists only on planet Earth.

Which one of the following would most weaken the above argument?

A.   Thousands of responsible people, people with reputations in the community to protect, have claimed to have seen UFOs. Statistically, it is virtually impossible for this many people to be mistaken or to be lying.

B.   Recently it has been discovered that Mars has water, and its equatorial region has temperatures in the same range as that of northern Europe. So there may be life on Mars.

C.   Only one percent of the stars in the universe are like our sun.

D.   The technology needed to detect planets outside our solar system has not yet been developed.

E.   Even if all the elements for life as we know it are present, the probability that life would spontaneously generate is infinitesimal.

This argument implies that since no planet has been discovered outside our solar system, none exist and therefore no life exists elsewhere in the universe. Hence the burden of proof is shifted from the arguer to the astronomers.

Although choice (A) weakens the argument, it has a flaw: the UFOs may not be life forms. Choice (B) is irrelevant. Although the argument states that the only life in the universe is on Earth, it is essentially about the possibility of life beyond our solar system. Choice (C) also weakens the argument. However, one percent of billions is still a significant number, and it is not clear whether one percent should be considered "common." Now, the underlying premise of the argument is that since no other planets have been detected, no others exist. Choice (D) attacks this premise directly by stating that no planets outside our solar system have been discovered because we don't yet have the ability to detect them. This is probably the best answer, but we must check all the choices. Choice (E) strengthens the argument by implying that even if there were other planets it would be extremely unlikely that they would contain life. The answer, therefore, is (D).

I. Unwarranted Assumptions

The *fallacy of unwarranted assumption* is committed when the conclusion of an argument is based on a premise (implicit or explicit) that is false or unwarranted. An assumption is unwarranted when it is false—these premises are usually suppressed or vaguely written. An assumption is also unwarranted when it is true but does not apply in the given context—these premises are usually explicit. The varieties of unwarranted assumptions are too numerous to classify, but a few examples should give you the basic idea.

Example: *(False Dichotomy)*

Either restrictions must be placed on freedom of speech or certain subversive elements in society will use it to destroy this country. Since to allow the latter to occur is unconscionable, we must restrict freedom of speech. The conclusion above is unsound because

A.   subversives do not in fact want to destroy the country

B.   the author places too much importance on the freedom of speech

C.   the author fails to consider an accommodation between the two alternatives

D.   the meaning of "freedom of speech" has not been defined

E.   subversives are a true threat to our way of life

The arguer offers two options: either restrict freedom of speech, or lose the country. He hopes the reader will assume that these are the only options available. This is unwarranted. He does not state how the so-called "subversive elements" would destroy the country, nor for that matter why they would want to destroy it. There may be a third option that the author did not mention; namely, that society may be able to tolerate the "subversives"; it may even be improved by the diversity of opinion they offer. The answer is (C).

Example: *(False Dichotomy)*

When workers do not find their assignments challenging, they become bored and so achieve less than their abilities would allow. On the other hand, when workers find their assignments too difficult, they give up and so again achieve less than what they are capable of achieving. It is, therefore, clear that no worker's full potential will ever be realized.

Which one of the following is an error of reasoning contained in the argument?

A.   mistakenly equating what is actual and what is merely possible

B.   assuming without warrant that a situation allows only two possibilities

C.   relying on subjective rather than objective evidence

D.   confusing the coincidence of two events with a causal relation between the two

E.   depending on the ambiguous use of a key term

This argument commits the fallacy of false dichotomy. It assumes that workers have only two reactions to their work—either it's not challenging or it's too challenging. Clearly, there is a wide range of reactions between those two extremes. The answer is (B).

Example:

To score in the ninetieth percentile on the MCAT, one must study hard. If one studies four hours a day for one month, she will score in the ninetieth percentile. Hence, if a person scored in the top ten percent on the MCAT, then she must have studied at least four hours a day for one month.

Which one of the following most accurately describes the weakness in the above argument?

A. The argument fails to take into account that not all test-prep books recommend studying four hours a day for one month.

B. The argument does not consider that excessive studying can be counterproductive.

C. The argument does not consider that some people may be able to score in the ninetieth percentile though they studied less than four hours a day for one month.

D. The argument fails to distinguish between how much people should study and how much they can study.

E. The author fails to realize that the ninetieth percentile and the top ten percent do not mean the same thing.

You may have noticed that this argument uses the converse of the fallacy *"Confusing Necessary Conditions with Sufficient Conditions"* mentioned earlier. In other words, it assumes that something which is sufficient is also necessary. In the given argument, this is fallacious because some people may still score in the ninetieth percentile, though they studied less than four hours a day for one month. Therefore the answer is (C).

Example:

Of course Steve supports government sponsorship of the arts. He's an artist.

Which one of the following uses reasoning that is most similar to the above argument?

A. Of course if a person lies to me, I will never trust that person again.

B. Conservatives in the past have prevented ratification of any nuclear arms limitation treaties with the Soviet Union (or Russia), so they will prevent the ratification of the current treaty.

C. Mr. Sullivan is the police commissioner, so it stands to reason that he would support the NRA's position on gun control.

D. Following her conscience, Congresswoman Martinez voted against the death penalty, in spite of the fact that she knew it would doom her chances for reelection.

E. You're in no position to criticize me for avoiding paying my fair share of taxes. You don't even pay your employees a fair wage.

This argument is fallacious—and unfair—because it assumes that all artists support government sponsorship of the arts. Some artists, however, may have reasons for not supporting government sponsorship of the arts. For example, they may believe that government involvement stifles artistic expression. Or they may reject government involvement on purely philosophical grounds. The argument suggests a person's profession taints his opinion. Choice (C) does the same thing, so it is the answer.

J. True But Irrelevant

This tactic is quite simple: the arguer bases a conclusion on information that is true but not germane to the issue.

Example:

This pain relief product can be bought over the counter or in a stronger form with a prescription. But according to this pamphlet, for the prescription strength product to be effective it must be taken at the immediate onset of pain, it must be taken every four hours thereafter, and it cannot be taken with any dairy products. So it actually doesn't matter whether you use the prescription strength or the over-the-counter strength product.

Which one of the following best identifies the flaw in the above argument?

A.   The fact that many people could not live a full life without the prescription strength product cannot be ignored.

B.   It cannot be concluded that just because the prescription strength product has certain guidelines and restrictions on its use that it is not more effective.

C.   It does not consider that complications may arise from the prescription strength product.

D.   It fails to consider that other products may be more effective in relieving pain.

E.   It is unreasonable to assume that the over-the-counter strength product does not have similar restrictions and guidelines for its use.

It is unreasonable to reject the effectiveness of a product merely because it has modest requirements for use. All medications have directions and restrictions. Hence the answer is (B). Don't make the mistake of choosing (A). Although it is a good rebuttal, it does not address the flaw in the argument. Interestingly, it too is true but irrelevant.

K. Appeal to Authority

To appeal to authority is to cite an expert's opinion as support for one's own opinion. This method of thought is not necessarily fallacious. Clearly, the reasonableness of the argument depends on the "expertise" of the person being cited and whether he or she is an expert in a field relevant to the argument. Appealing to a doctor's authority on a medical issue, for example, would be reasonable; but if the issue is about dermatology and the doctor is an orthopedist, then the argument would be questionable.

Example:

The legalization of drugs is advocated by no less respectable people than William F. Buckley and federal judge Edmund J. Reinholt. These people would not propose a social policy that is likely to be harmful. So there is little risk in experimenting with a one-year legalization of drugs.

In presenting her position the author does which one of the following?

A. Argues from the specific to the general.

B. Attacks the motives of her opponents.

C. Uses the positions of noted social commentators to support her position.

D. Argues in a circular manner.

E. Claims that her position is correct because others cannot disprove it.

The only evidence that the author gives to support her position is that respected people agree with her. She is appealing to the authority of others. Thus, the answer is (C).

L. Personal Attack

In a personal attack (ad hominem), a person's character is challenged instead of her opinions.

Example:

Politician: How can we trust my opponent to be true to the voters? He isn't true to his wife!

This argument is weak because it attacks the opponent's character, not his positions. Some people may consider fidelity a prerequisite for public office. History, however, shows no correlation between fidelity and great political leadership.

Example:

A reporter responded with the following to the charge that he resorted to tabloid journalism when he

rummaged through and reported on the contents of garbage taken from the home of Henry Kissinger.

"Of all the printed commentary . . . only a few editorial writers thought to express the obvious point that when

it comes to invasion of privacy, the man who as National Security Advisor helped to bug the home phones of

his own staff members is one of our nation's leading practitioners."—Washington Monthly, October 1975

In defending his actions, the reporter does which one of the following?

A. Attacks the character of Henry Kissinger.

B. Claims Henry Kissinger caused the reporter to act as he did.

C. Claims that "bugging" is not an invasion of privacy.

D. Appeals to the authority of editorial writers.

E. Claims that his actions were justified because no one was able to show otherwise.

The reporter justifies his actions by claiming that Kissinger is guilty of wrong doing. So, instead of addressing the question, he attacks the character of Henry Kissinger. The answer is (A).

Additional Educational Titles from Nova Press

The MCAT Physics Book presents a thorough analysis of MCAT physics and introduces numerous analytic techniques that will help you immensely, not only on the MCAT but in medical school as well.

Detailed Solutions: We have found that students are frustrated and angered by books in which they cannot get the author's "drift," so all solutions are written in step-by-step detail.

$29.95   Pages 444

The MCAT Biology Book presents a thorough analysis of MCAT biology and introduces numerous analytic techniques that will help you immensely, not only on the MCAT but in medical school as well.

Detailed Solutions: We have found that students are frustrated and angered by books in which they cannot get the author's "drift," so all solutions are written in step-by-step detail.

$29.95   Pages 416

The MCAT Chemistry Book presents a thorough analysis of MCAT chemistry and introduces numerous analytic techniques that will help you immensely, not only on the MCAT but in medical school as well.

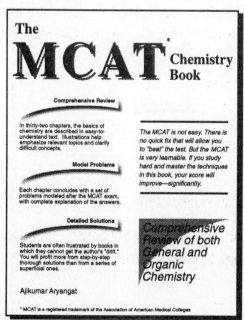

Detailed Solutions: We have found that students are frustrated and angered by books in which they cannot get the author's "drift," so all solutions are written in step-by-step detail.

$29.95   Pages 492

GRE PREP COURSE presents a thorough analysis of the GRE and introduces numerous analytic techniques that will help you immensely, not only on the GRE but in graduate school as well.

Detailed Solutions: We have found that students are frustrated and angered by books in which they cannot get the author's "drift," so all solutions are written in step-by-step detail.

$29.95   Pages 624

Master The LSAT offers the prelaw student a complete and rigorous analysis of the LSAT. In addition, it contains actual LSAT questions, including a complete and official LSAT test.

The LSAT is the most intellectually demanding entrance exam. To prepare for it, students need an equally challenging book. MASTER THE LSAT fills that need.

$29.95   Pages 560

Law School Basics presents a thorough overview of law school, legal reasoning, and legal writing. It was written for those who are considering law school and for those who are about to start law school.

Law School Basics was written with one overriding goal: to enlighten you about everything the author wishes he had known before starting law school.

$14.95   Pages 224

The LSAT is a logic test. Although this makes the test hard, it also makes the test predictable—it is based on fundamental principles of logic. LSAT Prep Course Software analyzes and codifies these basic principles: the contrapositive, the if-then, etc.

You no longer need to worry that the problems you are studying are like those on the LSAT. Now, you can study official LSATs.

$29.95   Windows and Macintosh

Every year students pay $600+ to test prep companies to prepare for the GMAT. Now you can get the same preparation in a book. GMAT PREP COURSE provides the equivalent of a two month, 50 hour course.

Mentor Exercises: These exercises provide hints, insight, and partial solutions to ease your transition from seeing problems solved to solving them on your own.

$29.95   Pages 608

English offers perhaps the richest vocabulary of all languages, in part because its words are culled from so many languages. It is a shame that we do not tap this rich source more often in our daily conversation to express ourselves more clearly and precisely.

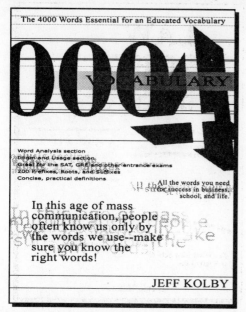
Many vocabulary books lists esoteric words we feel self-conscious using. However, there is a bounty of choice words between the common and the esoteric that often seem be just on the tip of our tongue. Vocabulary 4000 brings these words to the fore.

$9.95   Pages 160

ORDER FORM

Product	Quantity	Price
GRE Prep Course		$29.95
GMAT Prep Course		$29.95
Master The LSAT		$29.95
LSAT Prep Course Software		$29.95
The MCAT Physics Book		$29.95
The MCAT Biology Book		$29.95
The MCAT Chemistry Book		$29.95
SAT Prep Course		$29.95
Law School Basics		$14.95
Vocabulary 4000		$9.95

Name:	
Address:	
City: State: Zip:	
Phone: ( )	

Books are shipped Priority Mail. For delivery, allow 2 to 4 days from the day we receive the order. The shipping charge for ANY size order is $3. There is no tax.

Make check payable and mail to:
NOVA PRESS
11659 Mayfield Ave., Suite 1
Los Angeles, CA 90049

Credit card information

☐ Visa   ☐ MasterCard   ☐ Discovery   ☐ American Express
Name (as printed on card):
Credit card number:
Expiration date:

To Order by Phone, Call
1-800-949-6175

To Order from Our Website, Go to
www.novapress.net

Overnight delivery is available